Takashi Shimura

Takashi Shimura
Chameleon of Japanese Cinema

SCOTT ALLEN NOLLEN
Foreword by Paul M. Jensen

McFarland & Company, Inc., Publishers
Jefferson, North Carolina

ALSO BY SCOTT ALLEN NOLLEN AND FROM MCFARLAND

Abbott and Costello on the Home Front: A Critical Study of the Wartime Films (2009; paperback 2019), *The Making and Influence of* I Am a Fugitive from a Chain Gang (2016), *Three Bad Men: John Ford, John Wayne, Ward Bond* (2013), *Robert Louis Stevenson: Life, Literature and the Silver Screen* (1994; paperback 2012), *Louis Armstrong: The Life, Music and Screen Career* (2004; paperback 2010), *Paul Robeson: Film Pioneer* (2010), *Robin Hood: A Cinematic History of the English Outlaw and His Scottish Counterparts* (1999; paperback 2008), *Boris Karloff: A Critical Account of His Screen, Stage, Radio, Television and Recording Work* (1991; paperback 2008), *Warners Wiseguys: All 112 Films That Robinson, Cagney and Bogart Made for the Studio* (2008), *Sir Arthur Conan Doyle at the Cinema: A Critical Study of the Film Adaptations* (1996; paperback 2005), *Jethro Tull: A History of the Band, 1968–2001* (2002), *The Boys: The Cinematic World of Laurel and Hardy* (1989; paperback 2001)

Frontispiece: Takashi Shimura Dr. Konosuke Fujisaki, in Akira Kurosawa's *Shizukanaru Kettô* [*The Quiet Duel*] (1949).

LIBRARY OF CONGRESS CATALOGUING-IN-PUBLICATION DATA

Names: Nollen, Scott Allen, author. | Jensen, Paul M., writer of foreword.
Title: Takashi Shimura : chameleon of Japanese cinema / Scott Allen Nollen ; foreword by Paul M. Jensen.
Description: Jefferson, North Carolina : McFarland & Company, Inc., Publishers, 2019 | Includes bibliographical references, filmography, and index.
Identifiers: LCCN 2019005638 | ISBN 9781476670133 (paperback : acid free paper) ∞
Subjects: LCSH: Shimura, Takashi, 1905–1982. | Motion picture actors and actresses—Japan—Biography. | Motion pictures—Japan—History—20th century.
Classification: LCC PN2928.S496 N65 2019 | DDC 791.4302/8092 [B] —dc23
LC record available at https://lccn.loc.gov/2019005638

BRITISH LIBRARY CATALOGUING DATA ARE AVAILABLE

ISBN (print) 978-1-4766-7013-3
ISBN (ebook) 978-1-4766-3569-9

© 2019 Scott Allen Nollen. All rights reserved

No part of this book may be reproduced or transmitted in any form or by any means, electronic or mechanical, including photocopying or recording, or by any information storage and retrieval system, without permission in writing from the publisher.

Front cover photograph: Takashi Shimura in 1956; background illustration © 2019 Shutterstock

Printed in the United States of America

McFarland & Company, Inc., Publishers
Box 611, Jefferson, North Carolina 28640
www.mcfarlandpub.com

For my inspirational wife, Yuyun Yuningsih Nollen,
the first person I have known who can *look* like
the subject of my book!

In memory of Takashi Shimura and Akira Kurosawa,
for clarity conveyed to my psyche and
peace imparted to my soul.

Table of Contents

Foreword by Paul M. Jensen	1
Preface	3
1. 島崎捷爾, 1905	9
2. *Toro no o fumu otoko-tachi* (1945)	23
3. *Yoidore tenshi* (1948)	31
4. *Nora inu* (1949)	41
5. *Rashômon* (1950)	50
6. *Ikiru* (1952)	63
7. *Shichinin no Samurai* (1954)	72
8. *Gojira* (1954)	82
9. *Ikimono no Kiroku* (1955)	89
10. More *Kaijû Tokusatsu* and *Jidai-Geki* for Shimura-san	101
11. Akira, Toshirô and Oji-chan	115
12. *Tengoku to jigoku* (1963)	131
13. *Tôjôjinbutsu Senmonka* Supreme	144
Conclusion	162
Appendix A: Takashi Shimura Filmography	165
Appendix B: Takashi Shimura Television Episodes	261
Chapter Notes	265
Bibliography	269
Index	273

Foreword
by Paul M. Jensen

For a number of years, in my Great Films of Great Directors class, I screened both *Ikiru* (1952) and *Seven Samurai* (1954). Naturally, I concentrated on director Akira Kurosawa's narrative choices, visual style and thematic ideas. At the same time, the actor who played the leading role in both films drew substantial attention—for his psychological and emotional insight and for his physical flexibility in expressing that insight. Although diminutive in form, in these two films Takashi Shimura revealed a substantial physical range.

Nicknamed "the mummy" by his colleagues, Shimura's beaten-down clerk in *Ikiru* (*To Live*) is just an empty shell going through the motions of working at his desk. After he learns he is dying of cancer, he makes several self-centered attempts to discover life, none of them successful. Finally, he realizes that the solution is to perform some action that benefits others. It doesn't matter how small the action or how narrow its benefit—and he need not even receive credit for it. All that matters is that it happened.

Shimura depicts this man's transformation from useless passivity to accomplishment without discarding the character's physical fragility and inertia. His assertiveness is quietly passive; he wears down resistance and overcomes disinterest simply by his unwavering presence. He is strong without ever revealing physical strength. His determination could easily be mistaken for tentativeness. As he dies, alone and ignored, he nonetheless emits a glow of satisfaction. It is hard to imagine another actor matching Shimura's achievement in this film.

The range and consistency of his performance in *Ikiru* would be enough to enshrine Shimura in film history, yet two years later, in *Seven Samurai*, he astonishes further. Although still far from physically flamboyant, he conveys a strength and solidity that would forever have eluded his *Ikiru* clerk. As the leader and role model among the film's title characters, he embodies confidence and reveals clarity of thought and action. He is a dauntless, courageous fighter—ingenious in defense and dynamic in attack—but he is no mindlessly aggressive Action Hero. His competence coexists with natural modesty and humility, and he already knows a variation of what the character in *Ikiru* learns: the difference between surviving and winning, the evanescence of true achievement.

Kurosawa clearly appreciated Shimura's talent, for he cast him in quite a few other films, always to good effect. A viewer inevitably wonders about their working relationship and if they had a personal one as well. Surely, despite their frequent collaborations, Shimura could not have been Kurosawa's sole professional property. Indeed, his appearance in the popular monster film *Godzilla* (1954) hints at a more extensive cinematic presence. But just how extensive was it, and was he a leading man or a specialized supporting player?

Although Japanese film aficionados could probably answer those questions, we in the West have long been in the dark. But now, thanks to the curiosity and diligence of Scott Allen Nollen, that darkness is being lifted. Scott is a trained historian and experienced author who combines factual accuracy with perceptive analysis in his many books, including volumes on actor Boris Karloff, singer Frank Sinatra and writer Robert Louis Stevenson. This work on Takashi Shimura can now join that impressive list.

Paul M. Jensen is an author and film scholar, who taught at SUNY Oneonta from 1967 to 2010. He appears in a number of behind the scenes documentaries about the making of classic horror films by Universal Studios, including Frankenstein *and* The Invisible Man.

Preface

At 38,000 feet, bound for Tokyo aboard United Airlines flight 143, this first English-language study of the cinematic career of Takashi Shimura is being polished. Having been a "historian who often writes about films" for the past 40 years, I agree with the late Donald Richie, the original and arguably greatest Western authority on Japanese cinema, that my method is "eclectic ... [not] concerned with any single theory. It follows the mechanics of cause and effect and it believes, along with Alexis de Tocqueville, that 'history is a gallery of pictures in which there are few originals and many copies.'"[1] In his 2001 book, *A Hundred Years of Japanese Film*, Richie explains,

> In Japanese cinema, there was ... no Japanese essence awaiting liberation by a few individual directors. Nor was there a storytelling narrative there from the first. This rose from the needs, often commercial, to regularize production. The storytelling cinema was not so much the result of cinematic discoveries, as that of a consolidation of techniques, many of them old, some of them new, all of them depending upon circumstances. Narrative rose from regularization; style from standardization.
> The enormous if rapidly shrinking weight of the traditional certainly informs Japanese culture, but so does the mass of all its imports. Balancing all this, not succumbing entirely to *volksgeist* theory on one hand, nor, on the other, completely subscribing to the effects of foreign influences, is the task of the historian.[2]

Due primarily to the destruction wrought by World War II and the succeeding Allied occupation, 90 percent of all Japanese films produced before 1945 no longer exist. Therefore, much of what I have written about Takashi Shimura's work prior to his prodigious teaming with Akira Kurosawa in 1943 is based on documents and other written sources (some in English, others in Japanese which I have translated), though I have viewed every film I could find.

Excepting books on important directors like Kurosawa and Yasujirô Ozu, few books have been written in English about individual Japanese filmmakers, and the only actor who has been given lengthy attention is worldwide superstar Toshirô Mifune. Always eager to attempt breaking new ground, I first became interested in writing about Shimura because he was, like Ward

Bond to John Ford, an amazingly frequent face to appear in the work of Kurosawa: 23 of his 33 films (70 percent) as director. The total Shimura-Kurosawa collaborations is 31 when the eight additional titles featuring the director's screenplays are included.

Even more prolific are the acting collaborations between Shimura and Toshirô Mifune: 53 films released during a 31-year span between 1947 and 1978. This on-screen relationship (combined with their close friendship off-screen) tops that of longtime pals Ward Bond and John Wayne, who appeared together in a total of 28 films and television programs, 11 of which were for John Ford (1929–1957).

And, like Bond, one of golden-age Hollywood cinema's most prolific and versatile actors, Shimura's approximately 270 film and television appearances provide a look at a performer whose range was seemingly infinite. However, in the history of world cinema, Shimura's ability to transform himself for each role (with expression and attitude, and not resorting to the more modern tendency of applying heavy makeup and prosthetics) places him on an upper tier to which few actors have risen. In just two of Kurosawa's finest films, Shimura's shift from playing the dying old bureaucrat in the heartbreaking *Ikiru* (1952) to the leader of the rousing, glory-in-defeat *Seven Samurai* (1954) nearly staggers the imagination. The need for an English-language book on this man's art was obvious and essential.

Having spent more than three decades studying and writing about John Ford and his favorite actors, I know that, aside from Shimura bearing some facial resemblance to Bond, any physical similarity ends there; but his versatility as an actor who appears in a vast array of genres is quite similar. Moreover, Shimura excelled, not only as a character actor, but also as a leading man on occasion. (Bond finally demonstrated this ability when cast as the star of the *Wagon Train* television series in 1957.)

Several film historians in the United States have referred to Ford's "influence" on Kurosawa, who did admire the great American director, both as an artist and a man, but the latter also explained that he never consciously tried to imitate the former. Ford liked to project himself as a "man's man," but he also features strong women in many of his films. On the other hand, Kurosawa nearly avoids placing his females outside strictly traditional cultural roles. His often male-dominated films provided the perfect environment for characters played by Mifune and Shimura.

Both Ford and Kurosawa used members of their respective "stock companies" in a great number of their films. Ford's top two actors, Wayne and Bond, share this honor with such fellow artists as Henry Fonda, Victor McLaglen, Francis Ford (John's brother), George O'Brien, Maureen O'Hara, Anna Lee and many others. Among those who supported Kurosawa's formidable team of Mifune and Shimura are Kokuten Kôdô, Minoru Chiaki, Susumu

Fugita, Bokuzen Hidari, Tatsuya Nakadai, Eijirô Tôno, Daisuke Katô, Masayuki Mori (whose chameleonic abilities were on par with those of Shimura), Isuzu Yamada, Kyôko Kagawa, Yoshiko Kuga and Setsuko Hara, ranging from 4 to 13 appearances for Kurosawa and 7 to 28 with Shimura.

Only one major Japanese-language book on Shimura has been published, and very little information on his personal life is available in any English-language sources. This book primarily examines his art and career, while also including as much biographical information as possible.

As any scholar worth his salt should do, I have quoted from earlier, quite insightful works, in this case books on Kurosawa and Mifune by such top historians as Donald Richie, Stephen Prince and Stuart Galbraith IV. Using the acumen of predecessors to support one's own work is the way a proper professional historian is educated; and, rather than paraphrasing (which can lead a less experienced scholar into various quagmires, including unintended plagiarism), 'tis a far better thing to use actual quotes (with proper references included). Moreover, I doff my cap to all the erudite others who have labored to study and write about the Japanese cinema. Without their excellent work, I probably wouldn't have written a book about Takashi Shimura.

The original Japanese-release title of each film, indicated in *italics*, is used. If the film also was released in an official English-subtitled or -dubbed version, that title, *italicized*, is included in [brackets]. In general, Japanese words also are *italicized*, while commonly used terms (also found in the English language) and formal names (of places and people) are not italicized. English translations of Japanese words also are [bracketed].

The book's content focuses on each of the films in which Shimura appears, not only providing a complete chronology of his screen work, but also historical background on the narrative settings and the characters he portrays: proving that watching his films offers the viewer both the entertainment of his prodigious dramatic, emotional and storytelling abilities and his ability to impart, in an indirect way, historical knowledge and even philosophical wisdom.

Four decades ago, I began writing about the history of classic films, when ready access to this media was limited to occasional theatrical bookings (mainly in large cities) and television "late shows," and home video was in its very infancy. The only way to see "golden-age" Japanese films was at a rare art-house festival.

The term "spoilers" did not exist, and my writing usually included at least brief plot synopses. Since most Japanese films (excepting the works of top directors like Kurosawa, Mizoguchi, Ozu, Kobayashi, Keinosuke, Ichikawa and a few others) remain unavailable in the Western world (hence my scouring European distributors), there are some "spoilers," but odds are against your locating many of these titles.

The filmography provides the most complete listing of films featuring Shimura ever published in either printed or electronic form. The date accompanying each title is when the film was first released in Japan. If the film was subsequently released in the United States, that date also is included. Of the nearly 24 books I have written, this volume presented the single biggest challenge, with respect to the filmography. Shimura's verified 270 film and television appearances (the actual number is assumed to be higher) comprise the most massive assemblage of credits for any individual about whom I've written, and preparing it required nearly as much time and effort as the text. Multiple sources have been used in a meticulous research effort, especially to corroborate information and insure as much accuracy as possible. I trust this appendix is thorough and useful.

This unique volume was written over the course of three years, within two hemispheres, in three different countries: United States, Indonesia, and a few paragraphs in Japan. Following a six-month hiatus, ostensibly to travel (limited by my disability and poor health) around the globe and get married, I then returned to the project with renewed energy and enthusiasm.

Images of Takashi Shimura as some of his greatest cinematic characters are *not* included among the photographs; due, not to any oversight on my part, but to strict copyright ownership. Unfortunately, the *reel* Kambei Shimada's mantra, "Such selfishness will not be tolerated!" does not apply in the *real* world.

Completing a substantial part of this book in Southeast Asia, aided by Yuyun Yuningsih Nollen, has infused this work with a level of cultural ambience not even found in my meticulously prepared volumes involving Scottish history. Hopefully this book will help generate more interest in classic Japanese cinema in the Western world. If a single reader begins to be as entertained, interested, educated, fascinated and uplifted as this historian, then the mission will be on the right trek.

I am honored to include a foreword by professor emeritus Paul M. Jensen, a fine film historian whose work had a substantial influence on my early development as a researcher and writer. From the time my first book was published 30 years ago, I have benefited from the contributions of many outstanding individuals: academics, science-fiction "legends," best-selling novelists, popular music icons, Oscar-nominated screenwriter-directors, and the children of top Hollywood actors. Dr. Jensen certainly belongs among this pantheon, and he is the only choice I had for this literary gift that would please Kambei Shimada.

I also would like to acknowledge the excellent and swift assistance of the Japan Information Center, Japanese Consulate, United States; Makiko Kamiya, Assistant Curator of the Non-Film Section, National Film Archive of Japan, Tokyo; Cyril Descans of Japan Eiga for providing me with access to dozens of films featuring Shimura not readily available anywhere else; and my mother, Shirley Ann Nollen, who enjoys classic Japanese films.

Also, an *arigato* goes out to my friend Yosuke Sasaoke, a most-capable United Airlines attendant and fan of Akira Kurosawa, who was very helpful during a 12-hour flight from Tokyo to Houston, Texas. Looking at my Toshirô Mifune t-shirt (which I always wore when passing through Japan), he conspicuously posed for his colleagues on board the Boeing 787; and, calling their attention to the garment, proudly said, "Now that's a *real* Japanese man. I look *just like him*, don't I?"

Never stop dreaming…

1

島崎捷爾, 1905

Takashi Shimura was born 島崎捷爾 (Shoji Shimazaki) in the staff quarters of Ikuno township, Asago district, Hyôgo prefecture, Kansai region, on Honshû, the main island of Japan, on March 12, 1905. To the north of Hyôgo lies the Sea of Japan, to the south the Seto Inland Sea. Most of Hyôgo's people live along the southern coast, while the northern area is sparsely populated, and only small villages are found in the central highlands. The geographical center of the prefecture, the township features an elevation of 984 feet above sea level and rests in a basin surrounded by mountains comprising 90 percent of the area. In the year 807, the discovery of silver in the mountains created Ikuno's first industry, and for nearly a millennium, the mining of silver and copper continued to thrive.

During the Edo period (1603–1867), the mine's wealth helped finance the ruling Tokugawa *shogunate* [samurai government], named after Shogun Tokugawa Ieyasu (1543–1616), a military dictatorship that achieved internal peace, economic growth and political stability for more than two and one-half centuries. When he gained power, Ieyusu reorganized 200 *daimyôs* (feudal lords answerable only to the shogun) into *han*, which were determined by rice production (those that yielded 10,000 *koku*, or 50,000 bushels). Some relatives of the Tokugawa family, the *shinpan*, and *fudai*, those who had been vassals or allies in battle, also were considered *daimyôs*. (Interestingly, a century after Shimura's birth, nearly to the day [on April 1, 2005], the Ikuno township was merged with Asago, Santô and Wadayama to create the modern-day city of Asago.)

Young Shoji was descended from a grandfather of the Tosa clan in the samurai class, warriors in attendance to the nobility, who lived in the capital of Edo (modern-day Tokyo) and castle towns, where many became bureaucrats who helped their *daimyôs* oversee the strict class divisions essential in maintaining the success of the *shogunate*. Eighty percent of the population were farmers stringently regulated to agricultural work supporting their masters. There also were firm religious laws banning Christianity, due to the inroads that Catholic missionaries had made in the country, leading to foreign influence by Spain and Portugal. In 1633, another law was passed, forbidding Japanese subjects to travel abroad or foreigners to enter, save a few Dutch and Chinese merchants allowed to trade at the southern port in Nagasaki.

During the 1830s, the *shogunate*'s attempts at fiscal reforms created a financial strain with which the agricultural class was unable to cope, thus passing on the tension to the samurai, many of whom believed a restoration of the previous Imperial regime was necessary to resolve their problems and reunify the country. Peasant uprisings were bolstered by unrest among samurai displeased with the actions of their *daimyôs*, who also were beginning to welcome Western influence into Japan.

The Boshin War, also known as the Japanese Revolution, was a civil conflict during which Imperial loyalists, mainly *daimyôs* and young samurai, successfully shifted political power from the 264-year-old Tokugawa *shogunate* back to the Imperial Court, or Meiji, on May 3, 1868. Shoji's grandfather took part in the Battle of Toba-Fushimi, which occurred from January 27–30 near the saké-brewing area of Fushimi, Kyoto, between the allied Imperial domain forces of Chôshû and Satsuma, located on the western end of Honshû, and Tosa, on the southwestern coast of Shikoku island (collectively numbering about 5,000), and 15,000 *Shoguni* warriors. Lacking strong leadership and armed with poor weapons, the *Shoguni* were decisively defeated on the final day, when Osaka Castle, much of which had been burned, was surrendered to the loyalists. During the war, approximately 120,000 men participated but only about 3,500 (three percent) were killed. The Imperial victory ultimately barred any political compromise and led to a military settlement. The castle was demolished and then rebuilt during the Meiji Restoration to become part of the Osaka Army Arsenal.

Baby Shoji Shimazaki (1905).

Interestingly, after the victory, the successful Meiji continued to allow Western modernization and recognition of the Unequal Treaty with the West, which had been

1. 島崎捷爾, 1905

Ikuno, Hyôgo, near the mining company's office (c. 1910).

accepted by the late Tokugawa *shogunate*. Saigô Takamori (1828–1877), a major leader of the Imperial victors, also recommended clemency for the Tokugawa forces. In 1869, the *daimyôs* and the *kuge*, the aristocratic class, combined to form a hereditary peerage known as the *kazoku*. However, two years later, the *han* were abolished and prefectures were established. While feudal Japan existed, the samurai class made up only 10 percent of the population but continued to influence national life and particularly the martial arts.

Shoji's father initially was a metallurgical engineer at the Ikuno mine. An older brother, Takao, eventually became President of the Yokohama Rubber company. The family enrolled Shoji, whose discipline had been instilled from an early age by the code of the samurai, in the Ikuno Primary School in 1911. When he was 12 years old, he moved on to the Kobe First Middle School, but missed two years of study due to a mild attack of tuberculosis. When he was well again, he attended the Middle School in Nobeoka, Miyazaki prefecture, located on the eastern coast of the island of Kyûshû, where his father had been transferred by the Mitsubishi Mining Company.

At Nobeoka, Shoji, who was called "Oji-chan" by his friends, was particularly adept at English and wrote poetry for the literary society's magazine. He also was an excellent athlete, becoming one of the top achievers of the rowing club.

In 1923, now 18, Shoji was accepted at Kansai University, a private nonsectarian and coeducational institution in Suita, a suburb of Osaka. Following his father's retirement, however, the family couldn't afford the high tuition, and Shoji had to settle for taking evening classes in English literature, for which he paid with earnings from a job at the Osaka Municipal Waterworks. He benefited greatly from the faculty in the English Literature Department, which included Shakespearean scholar Masayuki Tsubouchi and playwright Sayichirô Toyo-oka.

Encouraged to study drama, Shoji joined the Theatre Studies Society. In 1928, he developed his own amateur dramatic company, the *Shichigatsu-za* ["July Theatre"], and Toyo-oka agreed to serve as director. Unfortunately, his newly discovered passion for the theater led to his arriving late for work and he eventually lost his job. This cataclysmic event convinced Shoji to transform the *Shichigatsu-za* into a professional organization, and they began to tour but soon folded after earning very little money.

Failing to make a living with his own stage company, Shoji returned to Osaka, where he began performing in radio plays, which, in 1930, gained him enough exposure to join the Kindaiza theater, a truly professional company. Following tours of China and Japan for two years, he left Kindaiza and again made his way back to Osaka, where he worked with the Shinseigeki and Shinsenza theatrical troupes. At some point, he married a woman named Masako, who took his family name of Shimazaki.

About three years after motion pictures began to be exhibited in the United States and Europe, the Japanese cinema was founded in 1897. Thomas Edison's Kinetoscope was initially exhibited in the country during November 1896, and Charles Jenkins and Thomas Arnat's Vitascope and the French Lumiere Brothers' Cinematograph followed a few months later. The Lumieres' cameramen were the first to shoot footage in

Shoji Shimazaki as a teenager (c. 1920).

1. 島崎捷爾, 1905

Japan, featuring scenes of Tokyo, and shown in late 1897. Local enthusiasts also began to work on their own short films, primarily focusing on dancing geisha girls.

Japanese audiences viewed the cinema as, not a new photographic development, but an extension of stage productions. The first fictional films, inspired by the traditional kabuki and *bunraku* (puppet) theaters, involved the supernatural. *Bake jizou* [*Jizo the Spook*] and *Shinin no sosei* [*Resurrection of a Corpse*] (both 1898) were shorts produced by Shiro Asano. A scene from a popular kabuki play, *Momijigari*, directed by Tsenikichi Shibata, was released in 1899, when the country's first documentary, *Geisha no teodori*, also appeared.

Benshi, who sat next to the screen, providing narration for silent films, were descended from traditional *kodan* storytellers, who used fans and wooden clappers, and the more stylized and choreographed kabuki performers. They sometimes were accompanied by music, the form of accompaniment favored in Western countries.

In *A Hundred Years of Japanese Film*, Donald Richie succinctly points out:

> [W]hen film was first seen in Japan, a 50-year-old member of this initial movie audience would have been born into a feudal world where the shogun, daimyô and samurai ruled. He could not have left his archipelago or, if he did, he could not have returned upon pain of death. His manner of dress and way of speech were regulated by his status, and his ignorance of the outside world was general. It was still the epoch of the Tokugawa clan ... encompassing what we now know as the Edo period.
>
> During ... the Meiji Era ... this kimono-clad viewer would not only have seen the Meiji Restoration (when the 16-year-old emperor was brought from Kyoto to Edo— now Tokyo—to become the nominal head of the new government), but also the Meiji "Enlightenment."
>
> Here ... he would have seen the abolition of the feudal socioeconomic system ... the adoption of modern (Western) production methods, and universal conscription.... [H]e would have seen the urging of Western clothes and meat eating, the abolition of sword carrying and *chonmage* [topknots], and eventually the disbanding of the samurai themselves.
>
> This hypothetical 50-year-old would have also witnessed the forced adoption of the Western (Gregorian) calendar, the emergence of a nationwide public school system, the inauguration of telephone and postal services, and the construction of railways.[1]

Shôzô Makino (1878–1929), Japan's pioneer director, made his first film, the short *Honnô-ji gassen*, for the Yokota Shokai studio, originally located in Nijo Castle, in 1908. Between 1909 and mid-1916, he directed another 182 shorts and five features, for Yokota Shôkai and then the Nikkatsu (an amalgamation of Nippon Katsudo Shashin, or Japan Motion Pictures) Corporation, which became the country's oldest major film studio, founded in Kyoto when Shôkai merged three other companies, Yoshizawa Shôten, Fukuhôdô and M. Pathe, in 1912. (Originally called the Japanese Cinematograph Company, a division of the Greater Japan Film Machinery Manufacturing Company, Ltd., Nikkatsu was modeled on Edison's monopolistic Motion Picture Patents Company in the United States.)

Makino's favorite actor was Matsonosuke Onoe (1875–1926), originally an itinerant kabuki performer who became Japan's first major movie star, appearing in an incredible 929 shorts and features between 1909 and 1927 (his final two films being released posthumously). Makino and Onoe created the *jidai-geki* genre, historical dramas primarily set during the Edo period.

Japan's first cinema actress was Tokuko Takagi (1891–1919), born in Tokyo but who made her four films for the Thanhouser Company (1911–1914) after moving to the United States with her husband, Chimpei Takagi. In 1915, she returned to Japan to make her stage dance debut with the Imperial Theatre. Tragically, during a tour in 1919, she suddenly died of a cerebral hemorrhage in Fukuoka at the age of only 28.

The first Japanese critical publication, *Katsudô shashinkai* magazine, began an undertaking called the Pure Film Movement, whose reviewers, in such journals as *Kinema Record*, displeased with directors' reliance on traditional theatrical techniques, called for the development of practices indigenous to the camera, including the use of close-ups and shot-reverse shot editing. One major critic and theorist, the engineer Norimasa Kaeriyama (1893–1964), became a pioneering director, making 19 films between 1919 and 1926, including the well-received *Miyama no otome* [*Maid of the Deep Mountains*] (1919) and *Shiragiku monogatari* [*The Tale of the White Chrysanthemum*] (1920).

Actor Masao Inoue (1881–1960) also became a successful director, making the Pure Film *Taii no musume* [*The Captain's Daughter*] (1917), in which he also performed, and then starring in Teinosuke Kinugasa's (1896–1982) experimental success, *Kurutta ippêji* [*A Page of Madness*] (1926), for which he accepted no salary. Pure filmmakers at other studios included Kisaburô ["Thomas"] Kurihara (1885–1926), who directed 24 films from 1920 to 1924 at Taisho Katsuei, Daikatsu and other smaller companies; Eizo Tanaka (1886–1968), who worked steadily at Nikkatsu from 1918 to 1922; and the masterful Kenji Mizoguchi (1898–1956), who began making films there in 1923, completing 58 titles before the end of the decade.

When "talking pictures" slowly became popular in Japan during the early 1930s (in 1932, only 45 of 400 features were released with sound, the others being made as silents resulting from resistance from *benshi* performers), Shoji Shimazaki realized that this medium provided an opportunity for a stage-trained actor. The production company Shinko Kinema, which released its films through Kyoto Studios, hired him, and he made his cinematic debut as Takashi Shimura in a silent, *Ren'ai-gai itchôme* [*Number One, Love Street*]

1. 島崎捷爾, 1905

(1934), as Osachi's Father. After another silent, *Umon torimonochô: Harebare gojûsantsugi–Ranma hen* (1935), as Santa, he made his sound debut in writer-director Mansaku Itami's *Chûji uridasu* (1935). Toho Studios was founded in 1935. Emulating their U.S. precursors, Nikkatsu, Shôchiku and Toho became vertically integrated monopolies controlling all levels of the industry: production, distribution and exhibition. They also specialized in two genres, the *jidai-geki* and the *gendai-geki*, films dealing with contemporary Japanese life. When sound finally took a firm hold, the national cinematic output increased, with 2,500 theaters releasing about 400 films each year. As the Imperial government turned increasingly more militaristic, including the outbreak of the Second Sino-Japanese War on July 7, 1937 (when

Takashi Shimura as a young film actor (mid–1930s).

China's Chiang Kai-shek finally threw his military might against Japan's six-year expansion), cinematic subjects shifted from basic dramas and light entertainment to "tendency films," those of social criticism such as Yasujirô Ozu's *Hitori musuko* [*The Only Son*] (1936) and several major works by Mizoguchi.

Shimura played a significant role, the Inspector, for Mizoguchi in the tendency film *Naniwa Erejî* [*Osaka Elegy*] (1936), which the director considered his first important work (his 72nd film of 101). Like many of Mizoguchi's later works, the film features an oppressed female protagonist, Ayaka Murai (Isuzu Yamada).

Small parts in two more features, *Shura hakkô: Dai-san-pen* and *Chûretsu nikudan sanyûshi*, and a short, *Akagaki Genzô* (all 1936), were followed by a major part, Taranoshin Tsunomata, in director Itami Mansaku's *Akanishi Kakita* [*The Capricious Young Man*] (1936).

The next year, Shimura began working for Nikkatsu, where he appeared in his first studio film, *Mitokomon kaikokuki* (1937), directed by Tomiyasu Ikeda, followed by a good supporting role in the two-part epic, *Seishun gonin*

Naniwa Ereji [Osaka Elegy] (1936; directed by Kenji Mizoguchi): Isuzu Yamada featured on Daiichi Eiga's original Japanese B2 poster. (Takashi Shimura appears in one scene as a police inspector.)

otoko: Zempen and *Seishun gonin otoko: Kôhen* (1937), directed by Masahiro Makino and Hiroshi Seimaru.

Between February 1937 and the end of 1941, Shimura worked steadily in 22 films at Nikkatsu. He acted in *Jiraiya* (1937), for Masahiro Makino, as Gundayû Yao, *Chikemuri Takadanobaba* (1937), co-directed by Hiroshi Inagaki, as Takusan, and *Kurama Tengu* (1938), co-directed by Sadatsugu Matsuda, as Kichinosuke Saigô.

In 1938, he also appeared in a film about Japanese organized crime, *Shamisen yakuza* (1938), directed by Toshizo Kinugasa: the *shamisen* being the Japanese three-stringed, banjo-like musical instrument with a fretless neck and plucked with a large plectrum called a *bachi*; and the yakuza originating during the mid–Edo period from a combination of the *tekiya*, those who sold black-market goods, and the *bakuto*, criminals who ran gambling rackets.

Shoji and Masako Shimazaki (aka Mr. and Mrs. Takashi Shimura; c. late 1930s).

Shimura accepted a small role in Inagaki's *Yami no kageboshi* [*Shadows of Darkness*] (1938), but enjoyed a larger part, as Jôzaemon Sakaya, in Tomiyasu Ikeda's *Akagaki Genzô* (1938). He then went back to work for Makino, in *Yajikita dôchûki* (1938), penned by Hideo Oguni, who went on to become one of Kurosawa's most frequent and powerful screenwriting partners. Alternating between directors, Shimura then appeared in Inagaki's *Shusse taikoki, Mazô, Jigoku no mushi* (1938) and *Zoku mazô–Ibara Ukon* (1939).

Makino cast Shimura in visible roles in *Edo no akutarô* and, as Kyosai Shimura, an umbrella-making *ronin* [master-less samurai], in *Oshidori tagassen* [*Singing Lovebirds*] (both 1939), the latter a popular musical comedy (in which Shimura sings) dealing with an antique addict who purchases a collection of fakes and then considers selling his daughter, Oharu (Haruyo Ichikawa), to pay for them. (This type of story would resonate, though much more dramatically and tragically, through the future of Japanese cinema, particularly in the works of Mizoguchi). Shimura's singing, praised by vocalist Dick Mine, led to several offers from recording companies.

Directed by Ryohei Arai, *Tsubanari ronin* (1939) features Shimura as Sherikov in Yoshitake Hisa's screenplay about mercenary samurai. His next role, Jûbei Tamon, arrived in writer-director Santarô Marune's *Shunjû ittôryû* (1939), before he returned to the team of director Masahiro Makino and screenwriter Hideo Oguni for *Zoku Shimizu minato* (1940).

Inagaki recalled Shimura for *Miyamoto Musashi: Dai-san-bu–Kenshin ichiro* (1940) before he returned to Makino, in the historical drama *Oda Nobunaga* (1940). Again alternating directors, he appeared in Inagaki's drama *Umi wo wataru sairei* (1941) before reporting to the set of Sadatsugu Matsuda for *Sugata naki fukushû* (1941). Inagaki then snared him back for *Edo saigo no hi* (1941).

During this period, Shimura ran afoul of the *Tokubetsu Kôtô Keisatsu* [Special Higher Police] who jailed him for three weeks at the Kyoto Uzumasa station. His earlier associations with leftist theater groups had led to his arrest, but he eventually was released after Masako and fellow actor Ryûnosuke Tsukigata spoke on his behalf.

Outraged by oil, iron and steel embargoes enacted by the United States, Great Britain, Australia and the Netherlands, Japan had begun to plan a war

Oshidori utagassen [*Singing Lovebirds*] (1939; directed by Masahiro Makino): from left, Chiezô Kataoka, Takashi Shimura and supporting cast. Shimura's capable vocals in this popular film led to offers from several recording companies.

1. 島崎捷爾, 1905 19

with the Western powers during the spring of 1941. Following the attack on U.S. forces at Pearl Harbor on December 7, Shimura remained a valuable Japanese asset as a film actor. During the Pacific Theater of World War II (1941–1945), most of the nation's economy was devoured by the military, and the film industry suffered. Interestingly, unlike the complete mobilization of the U.S. motion-picture studios by the Roosevelt administration's Office of War Information (OWI), resulting in nearly every Hollywood feature film containing a war-related plot, and resulting in some outlandish, racist stereotypes (even Sherlock Holmes, Tarzan and the Invisible Man were fighting the Nazis and "Japs"), the Japanese films focused solidly on their nation's industrial and military might.

Like John Ford and Gregg Toland's Academy Award-winning *December 7th* (1943), Kajirô Yamamoto's *Hawai Maree oki kaisen* [*The War at Sea from Hawaii to Malaya*] (1942), featuring Denjirô Ôkôchi, Susumu Fugita and a 21-year-old Setsuko Hara, includes faked combat footage using miniatures, in this case created by Eiji Tsuburaya (1901–1970), Japan's special-effects wizard who later achieved lasting fame by designing the magic behind *Gojira* [*Godzilla*] (1954) and a plethora of "rubber-suit" monster-movie sequels. (Faked footage had been used in war films made as early as the Spanish-American War in 1898.)

Other films had nothing to do with World War II, though they still had to adhere to the government's guidelines. By mid–1942, the Japanese began having difficulties sustaining control of the vast area they had captured, from the Indian Ocean to the Central Pacific. In the 15 films in which Shimura acted during the conflict, his foremost role, Hansuke Murai, came in the powerful judo drama *Sugata Sanshirô* [*Sanshiro Sugata*] (1943), the first film directed by Akira Kurosawa, who also co-wrote the screenplay with novelist Tsuneo Tomita, for Toho. Shimura's good friend, producer Nobuyoshi Morita, knew that he had been impressed by Kurosawa's scripts for three projected projects, and suggested that he audition as Murai for *Sugata*.

Set in 1882, the film presents the efforts of a young man, Sanshiro Sugata (Susumu Fugita), who seeks a *sensei* [master] to train him properly in the skills of martial arts. After witnessing Shogoro Yano (Ôkôchi) level a pack of jujitsu toughs, he is instructed in the new art of judo. His series of matches includes one against Hansuke Marai (Shimura), a very wise, older judo master whom he befriends. He also falls in love with Marai's daughter (Yukiko Todoroki). A portent of Kurosawa films to come, the director carefully builds the events and pacing of the production up to the climactic match, set in a large field racked by high winds as clouds flow through the sky. (In his film debut, Kurosawa already exhibits a John Ford–like visual style.)

Kurosawa and Toshirô Mifune biographer Stuart Galbraith IV writes,

With *Sanshiro*, Kurosawa ... introduces one of his common themes, that of parallel education (i.e., physical or intellectual *and* metaphysical): while learning the art of judo, the protagonist tries to educate himself, spiritually, through the guidance of an older, wiser master. This is what happens to Sanshiro, and this is what would happen to Kurosawa's doctors, his detectives, his samurai. Sanshiro is an ordinary man in search of his self.[2]

Kurosawa had major problems with the military censors before *Sanshiro Sugata* could be released. Although other filmmakers, including Ozu, sat on the board, the censors' objection to the director's Western, specifically "British-American," influences, made Kurosawa, who had to sit in a chair across the room, facing them, think he was "on trial."[3] However, the film was passed and went on to commercial and critical success.

Shimura plays the supporting role of Ryôkichi Ishikawa in Toho's *Himetaru kakugo* (1943), directed by Eisuke Takizawa and costarring Kenzô Asada and Susumu Fugita, who had become a huge star in Japan. Used as a major component of the Imperial government's film propaganda campaign, Fugita plays a Navy officer, another variation on his wartime *gunshin* [military god] character. Stuart Galbraith explains,

> These propaganda films were so powerful that he felt responsible for fanning the flames of a hopeless, brutal conflict which ended in death for so many soldiers who modeled themselves after Fugita's characters. In fact, he very nearly retired after the war because of this overwhelming feeling of culpability.[4]

Next came Tomotaka Tasaka's *Kaigun* (1943), Yasushi Sasaki's *Haha no kinembi* (1943) and Kajirô Yamamoto's *Katô hayabusa sento-tai* [*Colonel Katô's Falcon Squadron*] (1944), another Fugita propaganda war thriller featuring him as real-life, Hokkaido-born Imperial Army Air Force Colonel Tateo Katô (1903–1942), who was not only a flying ace, but also a fair-minded officer highly respected by his men. Fugita convincingly portrays Katô as an outwardly smiling warrior of the skies but one with a conscience that periodically plagues him as his men perish or are wounded in combat.

Katô opens just prior to the attack on Pearl Harbor, of which the colonel is informed on December 8, 1941. As commander of the 64th *Sentai* unit, he sees action against the Flying Tigers on Christmas Day (a yuletide tree is featured in a scene set in the flyers' mess). Shimura appears briefly as an officer at a military hospital, where Katô and a comrade are recuperating from injuries and fatigue. Shortly after, on May 22, 1942, Katô, after flying off in search of his MIA friend, never returns, but is shot down over the Bay of Bengal. His aircraft aflame, he crashes into the sea.

The real-life Katô was posthumously promoted two ranks, to that of Major General. He also was awarded the Order of the Golden Kite (abolished by General Douglas MacArthur following World War II) and declared a "god of war" at a State Shinto ceremony in Tokyo during mid–October 1942.

Katô would not be the only film featuring Shimura with special effects by Eiji Tsuburaya [notably *Gojira* and its descendants]. Tsuburaya's incorporation of model work with actual aerial footage, particularly scenes filmed at night, is exceptional. His future *Gojira* collaborator, Ishirô Honda, served as assistant director on the film.

Shimura returned to collaborate with Akira Kurosawa in the director's second film, *Ichiban utsukushiku* [*The Most Beautiful*] (1944), an unusual, innovative propaganda feature focusing on young women working in a factory producing precision lenses for military implements. Using a nonlinear narrative, Kurosawa presents a series of scenes, set in dormitories where the homesick women live as they attempt to meet exhausting government quotas. Shooting in a semi-documentary style, the director had his performers live in the dorms of an actual Nippon Kogaku factory in Hiratsuka.

Another wartime film featuring only Japanese characters, *The Most Beautiful* emphasizes the humanity of its home-front citizens as they struggle to survive while living under less-than-ideal conditions forced upon them. Stuart Galbraith, who compares the compositions to those of Alexander Dovzhenko and the editing to that of Leni Reifenstahl, points out, "*The Most Beautiful* is alone among Kurosawa's films in that he has unreversed faith in the group. From here on, he reserved his faith for a belief in individuals..."[5]

Top-billed, Shimura appears as Chief Goro Ishida, manager of the factory. His scenes, as well as those of Sôji Kyokawa and Ichirô Sugai, as section leaders Soichi Yoshikawa and Ken Shinda, respectively, primarily were shot on sets at Toho, and their two-dimensional characters rarely interact with the far more developed females, headed by Yôko Yaguchi as Tsuru Watanabe, the "most beautiful" president of the women workers. The near-documentary "truth" of the factory scenes—indeed "the extreme economy and directness of the picture"—Donald Richie claims, may have been due to the very real wartime conditions of "not enough film, not enough lights, not enough sets."[6]

Shimura again appeared with another future Kurosawa star, Isuzu Yamada, in director Mikio Naruse's *Shibaidô*, based on the novel by Kôen Hasegawa and released by Toho on May 11, 1944. He next portrayed Yasukichi Ito alongside Hideko Takamine (later to appear in Keisuke Kinoshita's stunning masterpiece *Nijûshi no hitomi* [*Twenty-Four Eyes*] (1954) and Masaki Kobayashi's pacifist epic *Ningen no jôken* [*The Human Condition*, 1959–61]) in Toho's *San-jaku sagohei* (1944), written by Shintarô Mimura and directed by Tamizo Ishida. Shimura's final film of 1944, the propaganda feature *Nichijô no tatakai*, costarring Susumu Fugita, was written by Hideo Oguni and directed by Yasujirô Shimazu.

Torajirô Saitô directed Shimura in his first 1945 film, Toho's *Tokkan ekichô* [*The Brash Stationmaster*]. He then played Murai's Father in the studio's *Ai to chikai* [*Love and Pledge*] (1945), co-directed by In-kyu Chóe and Tadashi Imai from a screenplay by Ryuichiro Yagi. Shortly after he completed this film, Shimura costarred with Susumu Fugita, Hideko Takamine and Setsuko

Hara in the Film Public Corporation-Toho coproduction *Kita no san-nin* [*Three People of the North*] (1945), written by Yûsaku Yamagata and directed by Kiyoshi Saeki. He again was featured with Fugita and Hara, in writer-director Kajirô Yamamoto's *Koi no fuunji* [*Misfortunes of Love*], which was completed in early September 1945 but delayed due to the presence of the Allied Occupation forces. (Retitled *Kaidanji* [*Energetic Boy*], it was not released until April 4, 1953.)

2

Toro no o fumu otoko-tachi (1945)

Something interesting is interesting, no matter who sees it—
with the exception, of course, of boring people.—Akira Kurosawa, referring to the U.S. Army's General Headquarters'
lifting of the ban on *Toro no o fumu otoko-tachi* [*The Men
Who Tread on the Tiger's Tail*]¹

By the end of the Pacific Theater of World War II, in the wake of two devastating atomic detonations and the incendiary bombings of 66 Japanese cities in which housing had been wiped out and much of the population displaced, Toho's employees were starving but kept producing films at an amazing pace. Sadly, just a few weeks before Japan surrendered, Shimura's elder brother, Takao, was killed in combat.

Akira Kurosawa, at Toho's insistence, had made a sequel to *Sanshiro Sugata*, *Zoku Sugata Sanshirô* [*Sanshiro Sugata—Part Two*] (1945). Now he was in the pre-production phase of "*Dokkoi kono yari*" ["The Lifted Spear"], his first historical epic, but the studio didn't have the resources to complete it. The project required many horses, which were in short supply ("only nags and sickly beasts," writes Kurosawa in his 1982 memoir, *Something Like an Autobiography*).² Kurosawa eventually would make the film as *Kagemusha* in 1980.

In summer 1945, Kurosawa instead turned to *Toro no o fumu otoko-tachi* [*The Men Who Tread on the Tiger's Tail*], a combination of the kabuki play *Kanjincho* [*The Subscription List*] and the Noh drama *Ataka*, both based on an old Japanese legend. (The classical Noh style originated during the 14th century.) Though a period samurai piece, there are no battle scenes. Primarily shot on one studio set, the film, made from a screenplay Kurosawa reportedly wrote in just an evening, sailing it past the censors by using its theme of feudal loyalty, runs only 59 minutes. There are also a few location shots, filmed in the "imperial forest that at that time stretched right to the back gate of the studio."[3]

On August 15, 1945, production on the film was halted when Kurosawa was ordered to appear at Toho's main office to hear a radio address by the Emperor. On his way, he saw his fellow Japanese ready to commit mass *hara kiri*, the "Honorable Death of the Hundred Million," upon hearing news of an imminent Allied invasion. The studio's actresses had been evacuated to work on a film in Tateyama City but, in event of an emergency, would be returned to Tokyo. However, the Emperor told his subjects to sheath their swords. There would be no mass suicide.

Kurosawa was sent back to the *Tiger's Tail* set, to continue just as before, although his cast and crew were tired and hungry. As the Occupation began, visitors observing them work included Captain John Ford, U.S. Naval Reserve, although Kurosawa didn't know one of his favorite directors was there (until he accidentally ran into Ford at London's Savoy Hotel bar in 1957, when "Pappy" shared a bottle of single malt scotch—the universal language—with him). Kurosawa recalled,

> I was up on top of the soundstage setting up an overhead shot when a group of [U.S.] admirals and high-ranking commissioned officers came onto the set. They were remarkably quiet as they observed the shooting and departed, and later I found out that the movie director John Ford had been among them. It was he himself who told me this years later ... and I was amazed. Apparently, he had asked my name at the time and left a message of greeting for me. "Didn't you receive it?" he asked. But I had of course not received it, nor did I have any idea that John Ford had ever visited a movie set of mine until that day I met him in England.[4]

Set during the 12th century, *The Men Who Tread on the Tiger's Tail* tells the story of the general, Lord Yoshitsune (Hanshirô Iwai), and his retainers, who disguise themselves as monks while attempting to cross through an outpost commanded by his brother, Togashi (Susumu Fugita). At turns dramatic and comic, this suspenseful film ends with a monumental saké-drinking contest and one of the retainers (a character added by Kurosawa), the hungover porter-medieval fool Kyoryuku (Ken'ichi ["Enoken"] Enomoto, Toho's popular comic of the previous decade), left behind on the grassy mountainside. (This "Shakespearean" element would drive many of Kurosawa's films, which sometimes were criticized in Japan for being "too Westernized.") The alcohol-fueled climax perhaps has no true parallel in the history of world cinema.

The intense, snarly Denjirô Ôkôchi is top-billed as the chief retainer, Benkei, who makes the decision to move on to the checkpoint, where he convinces Togashi, threatening him with the evil-banishing "Nine-Syllable Mantra," that they really are monks. Susumu Fugita, with his soft, mellifluous voice, gives another standout performance for Kurosawa; and Shimura, with beard and long hair tied in a ponytail, appears in a supporting role as Kataoka, another of the retainers. Along with Masayuki Mori (as Kamei) and Yoshio Kosugi (as Suruga), he manages to imbue his small part with individual depth while maintaining the integrity of their ensemble work. It is Kataoka who first questions Kyoryuku, the "insignificant nobody," about the "intelligence" he possesses of the enemy at the border crossing, thus moving along the major plot.

This comic material (Donald Richie has pointed out that adding Enoken to the original material is "a bit like adding Jerry Lewis to the cast of *Hamlet*"[5]) outraged the Japanese censors, who did not pass on a file to those of the Occupation. Though Kurosawa had been encouraged by Mori Iwao, Toho's executive in charge of production, to "tell them exactly what you think of them," he eventually faced these elite, prideful men, driven out of the Ministry of Interior and "reduced to ... poverty," who railed against him "with an interrogating vengeance."[6]

Deemed by the U.S. Army's General Headquarters as an "illegal, unreported" production, the film was banned, remaining unreleased in Japan until 1952. (Eight more years passed before it was distributed in the United States.) Kurosawa scholar Stephen Prince writes,

[H]e aimed to deconstruct Japan's warrior heritage by providing historically realistic depictions of the flourishing and decline of the samurai class, and in so doing to counter the idealistic and ideological portraits, so prevalent in Japanese culture, that saw samurai as glorious embodiments of virtue, sacrifice and service. These, of course, had been the state's wartime ideals as well, and Kurosawa's explorations of the nation's warrior past were therefore also comments on where it had gone wrong in the present. But he also loved the warrior ideal, and this push-pull of attraction and critique gives the films an uncommon bite and clarity. *The Men Who Tread on the Tiger's Tail* ... is his first portrayal of Japan's medieval warriors, and like his other movies during the war, it shows an artist fully formed, with themes and a narrative that are wholly consistent with his later works.[7]

Of the U.S. military, Kurosawa commented,

Democracy was glorified; freedom of speech was recovered (within the limitations permitted by General MacArthur's military policies). As these things occurred, the film industry came to life again and flourished. For us, of course, the rout of the censors in the Ministry of the Interior was a delight beyond measure.

We who had been able to express nothing of what we were thinking up to that time all began talking at once. Right after the end of the war I wrote a one-act play [that] aroused the interest of the head of the G.H.Q's drama division. He called me in and we spent almost a whole day talking.

I don't know what the American's name was, but he seemed to be a drama specialist ... this was an experience of a strange kind I had never felt during the war. Rather, it wasn't strange at all, but a kind of pleasure that we should always be able to feel. This man did not insist on any one-sided viewpoint but set the desire for mutual

understanding as a pre-condition for our talk. My meeting with this American censor is a heart-warming memory. Having lived through an age that had no respect for creation, I recognized for the first time that freedom of creation can exist...
Of course, I am not saying that all the American censors were like him. But they all behaved toward us in a gentlemanly fashion. Not a single one among them treated us as criminals, the way the Japanese censors had.[8]

Kurosawa and cinematographer Takeo Itô's brilliant use of compositions and camera movement often hides the fact that the film was shot mostly on limited studio sets. Sometimes the visual flow, created by combining the leftward movement of the characters with the steady rightward pan of the camera, creates an effect seldom seem in the cinema. Every pan, track and edit (sometimes in fast montage sequences, showing close-ups of the various characters, each of whom has his own distinctive appearance) is there, as John Ford often stressed, for a reason. Writing in 2001, Stuart Galbraith noted,

[The] cameras ... effect becomes invisible. This is the very opposite of most of today's Hollywood movies, where often elegant cinematography is ruined by showy, self-conscious dollying, awkward if striking compositions, and trite slow-motion effects. *Tiger's Tail* opens with angles subtly favoring Enoken, but as the motives and bravery of the retainers, especially Benkei, become clear, the camera is placed in not-quite subjective positions from their point of view. This works to involve the audience with the extreme tension felt by the retainers as they risk their and their lord's lives. Again ... one is almost never aware of the camera.[9]

The thematic ambiguity that angered the Japanese and irritated the occupation censors is supported by the film's visual strategy. *The Men Who Tread on the Tiger's Tail*, highlighted by Kurosawa's refusal to champion a single viewpoint, refutes those who have accused the director of depicting morally simplistic characters in his films prior to *Yoidore Tenshi* [*Drunken Angel*] (1948), and lends his first samurai film a timeless element.

Shimura began 1946 with another supporting role opposite Susumu Fugita, in *Minshu no teki* [*An Enemy of the People*] for director Tadashi Imai. He then played the theater manager in *Asu o tsukuru hitobito* [*Those Who Make Tomorrow*] (1946), an obscure Toho feature directed by Kurosawa, Hideo Sekigawa and Kajirô Yamamoto that has not been shown in Japan since its first release (and never seen in the U.S.). Kurosawa loathed this film, costarring Susumu Fugita, Hideko Takemine (playing themselves) and Masayuki Mori, made during labor problems at the studio, and he completely left any mention of it out of his memoir.

During the early days of the Occupation, just before the Cold War began, the U.S. forces encouraged the pro-labor atmosphere reflected in the film, particularly in its depiction of picketing at a film studio (obviously Toho). Shimura's unpleasant characterization of the theater boss clearly represented the opposition.

Waga seishun ni kuinashi [No Regrets for Our Youth] (1946)

Toho's *Juichinin no jogakusei* [*Eleven Girl Students*] (1946), directed by Motoyoshi Oda and including Shimura in a supporting role, was followed by Kurosawa's first solo postwar project, *No Regrets for Our Youth* (1946), a narrative of antinationalist revolt in modern Japan (covering 1933–1945) featuring Shimura as the colorfully named character, Police Commissioner "Poison Strawberry" Dokuichigo. Shot in Kyoto between two union strikes that occurred at Toho in February and October 1946, the film was rewritten by producer Keiji Matsuzaki at the insistence of the Communist-influenced Scenario Review Committee (who claimed a similar project was being made), despite Kurosawa's pleas that they allow him to shoot Eijirô Hisaita's original screenplay. Hisaita had based his work on the persecution of Yukitoki Takigawa, a liberal Kyoto Imperial University professor, and the 1944 wrongful execution (for treason) of Hotsumi Ozaki, an expelled student.

The director later wrote that, with so much of the shooting script distorted from the first draft, he took care in crafting the final 20 minutes of the 110-minute film. He recalled, "When the two films were completed, members of the Review Committee said to me, 'You were right. If we had known they would turn out like this, we would have let you shoot from your first script.' This was the height of irresponsibility."[10]

Japanese critics and colleagues thought little of *No Regrets for Our Youth*, the only Kurosawa film, other than *The Most Beautiful*, to feature a female protagonist, Yukie Hagihara (Setsuko Hara). Born Masae Aida in Yokohama in 1920, the stunning Hara made her film debut at age 15 in director Tetsu Taguchi's *Tamerau nakare wakodo yo* [*Don't Hesitate, Young Folks*] (1935) and went on to become one of Japan's major stars. Dominating *No Regrets for Our Youth*, her 53rd film, with her unique, quietly expressive yet often dynamic style and impressive range, she later played a variety of female leads in six major films of Yasujirô Ozu, including *Banshun* [*Late Spring*] (1949) and *Tokyo monogatari* [*Tokyo Story*] (1953), as well as five films for Mikio Naruse, including *Meshi* [*Repast*] (1951) and *Yama no oto* [*Sound of the Mountain*] (1954).

American censors were impressed by the film, but a planned party and overseas release were quashed by the second strike, which ended with "The Flag of Ten," the studio's more opposed, rightward stars, and 400 technicians leaving to form a second company, Shintoho, where they remained for the next decade. (The film remained unreleased in the U.S. until 1980, when it received praise from major reviewers nationwide.)

Viewed in retrospect, the highly underrated *No Regrets for Our Youth* supports the views of the 1980 U.S. critics. The entire dynamic production is impressive, featuring solid performances all around. Shimura appears in only one sequence, but is memorable as the nasty, sweating, constantly pacing, nightstick swinging, matchstick chewing, cigarette smoking police commissioner who relentlessly grills Yukie about her relationship with the arrested outspoken liberal student Ruykichi Noge (Susumu Fugita, not miscast, as some have claimed), who just happens to "die in his cell" shortly afterward. Shimura recalled that he based "Poison Strawberry" Dokuichigo on memories of the police officers who had detained him at the Kyoto Uzumasa station a few years earlier.

Kurosawa's camerawork (executed by cinematographer Asakazu Nakai) again is stunning, with his trademark use of lush outdoor foliage highlighted by smooth panning and quick tracking movements. The final 20 minutes, consisting of Soviet-like montages (edited by Kurosawa) of the mud-caked Yukie and her mother-in-law, Madame Noge (Haruko Sugimura), also branded a "spy" by the populace, as they endlessly toil (first by the light of the moon, and then during the day after Yukie decides to face down the "spy" label) to plow and plant their large rice paddies (which then are partially trampled by local farmers who support the military), are entirely visualized with the camera, sans dialogue.

Though the ending of the film, with Kurosawa's female protagonist returning with her in-laws, has been criticized as "non-feminist," it fits into its contemporary culture. It also makes thematic sense, as Yukie, reminded that Noge had told her, "No regrets in my life," goes back to perform a noble service for the people of the village (especially the women) with the new rural cultural movement where Mr. (Kokuten Kôdô) and Madame Noge live.

Kurosawa concluded,

> Under wartime conditions we had not been able to portray the fullness of youth in the movies. As the censors viewed things, love was indecent and the fresh, keen sensibilities of youth were a psychological state of "British-American" weakness. Being youth in those times consisted of suppressing the sound of one's breathing in the jail cell that was called the "home front."[11]

Without a big-name star left to put in their films, Toho's remaining contract producers, directors and screenwriters convened at a hot-spring inn on the Izu Peninsula south of Tokyo, "a most pompous affair, the result of which was a schedule of new releases to be publicized with the directors' names."[12]

The loyal, pro-labor Shimura (along with Hideko Takamine, Susumu Fugita, Denjirô Ôkôchi and Isuzu Yamada) remained at Toho, appearing in Teinosuke Kinugasa's *Aru yo no tonosama* [*Lord for a Night*] (1946), the first episode of *Yottsu no koi no monogatari* [*Four Love Stories*] (1947), on which Kurosawa and Hideo Oguni served as writers, and Tadashi Imai, Kiyoshi Kusuda and Hideo Sekigawa's *Chikagai nijuyojikan* [*24 Hours of a Secret Life*] (1947).

2. Toro no o fumu otoko-tachi *(1945)*

In *Ginrei no hate* [originally *To the End of the Silver Mountains*, but changed to *Snow Trail*] (1947), written by Kurosawa, working from "an insane schedule,"[13] in three weeks, and directed by Senkichi Taniguchi, Shimura is second-billed as Nojiro, behind Toshirô Mifune (in his film debut, as Eijima), as two of three bank robbers (the third, Takasugi, is played by Yoshio Kosugi) who flee into the Japanese alps. After Takasugi dies in an avalanche, the remaining pair lodge at an old inn also housing Honda (Akitake Kôno), a mountaineer, Haruko (Setsuko Wakayama), a young woman, and her grandfather (Kokuten Kôdô). Eijima eventually threatens Honda, who leads them through the mountains. When the irritated Eijima slips and falls off a ledge after wrestling with Nojiro, Honda breaks his arm while pulling them up. Finally, Nojiro is fed up with Eijima after the latter chooses to leave the injured Honda behind while also depriving his boss of most of the remaining stolen yen. Another struggle ensues, Eijima shoots Honda in the leg before plummeting (off camera) to a horrible death, and Nojiro backbreakingly carries the still-breathing hero back to the inn, where he gives himself up to the authorities.

Mifune, who wanted to be a cameraman at Toho, initially turned down *Snow Trail*, but Taniguchi, noticing that the future star wore the same suit day after day, offered to buy him new clothes if he would accept the starring role. The location shooting, beginning in January 1947, on Mt. Habuka in Hokkaido was treacherous, and Mifune, who had to be coached constantly by the mountain-climbing Taniguchi, believed that he was really given the part because of the strike and that he was "an unknown actor [who] was more expendable."[14] The cinematography by Junichi Segawa, especially during the mountain-climbing scenes, is awe-inspiring, convincingly showing how dangerous it was making this often harrowing film.

The cast and crew all slept in their own sleeping bags, out in freezing conditions in a government-built shed. Mifune, who was only 26, carried over 100 pounds of equipment into the mountains, as well as helping the 41-year-old Shimura up and down each day. Working so closely together made the two even better friends, an association that also would continue on-screen until 1965.

Kurosawa, though making *Sabarashiki nichiyôbi* [*One Wonderful Sunday*] (1947), a look at postwar Tokyo through the eyes of a young couple (Isao Numasaki and Chieko Nakakita), kept a close eye on Taniguchi's work, watching the dailies and sending telegrams about which scenes needed to be reshot. After Taniguchi, directing his second film, ignored the advice, Kurosawa coedited the final cut of *Snow Trail*.

Mifune, Toho's "new star," received top billing, and does the role more than justice, but Shimura is the most impressive actor in the film. He is introduced mysteriously in a nearly nude scene when he takes a bath in a hot spring at the first inn at which the bank robbers stop in the mountains. (The only thing covered in his left hand, which is missing some fingers, with a cloth as he relaxes in the steaming water.) His Nojiro initially appears sinister, wearing dark glasses, unshaven and unkempt with a shock of slightly graying hair, but later glares contemptuously at the selfish and uncaring remarks and behavior of Mifune's Eijima.

After reaching the remote ski lodge, Nojiro is deeply moved by Haruko and her love for Stephen Foster's 1852 anti-slavery ballad "My Old Kentucky Home," the origin and meaning of which she and Honda attempt to explain to him. The girl also kindly gives him a glass of "Lily of the Valley" honey, which reminds him of springtime, thus also bringing back memories of his own daughter. In return, the hateful Eijima declares his feelings to be complete nonsense.

The "My Old Kentucky Home" record is played once more as Haruko watches and waves farewell as Nojiro leaves with the police. Never becoming sentimental, the music (like Foster's 1848 minstrel song "Oh, Susanna" in an earlier scene) is balanced perfectly with the convincing emotional bonding, and quite reminiscent of John Ford's use of "Red River Valley" in *The Grapes of Wrath* (1940), during the famous sequence in which Ma Joad (Jane Darwell) sadly says goodbye to her son, Tom (Henry Fonda), who accidentally has killed a man. (Ford frequently made use of traditional songs and similar endings, such as when Clementine Carter [Cathy Downs] watches as Wyatt Earp [also Henry Fonda] rides away at the close of *My Darling Clementine* [1946]).

Though *Snow Trail* was a critical and commercial success in Japan during the summer of 1947, it unfortunately has never been officially released in the United States. Shimura's role, written for him by Kurosawa, is essential viewing for an understanding of the finest period in his career.

Shimura moved on to costar (fourth-billed, as the sensitive Dr. Kenzô Ogura) with lovely 16-year-old actress Yoshiko Kuga (who later would appear in Kurosawa's *Drunken Angel* and *Hakuchi* [*The Idiot*] [1951], and Ozu's *Equinox Flower* [1958] and *Good Morning* [1959]) in *Haru no mezame* [*Spring Awakens*] (1947), directed by Mikio Naruse. This Ozu–like adolescent coming-of-age story involving the curious children of two couples concludes with Dr. Ogura's suggestion that parents allow their offspring to develop naturally, unhampered by outmoded, negative notions and instead helped by positive advice. Shimura gives a solid, calm performance as the supportive Naruse father and physician. Another second-billed role followed, in Hideo Sekigawa's *Daini no jinsei* (1948), in which Sô Yamamura plays the lead.

3

Yoidore tenshi (1948)

> I am not a special person. I am not especially strong; I am not especially gifted. I simply do not like to show my weakness, and I hate to lose, so I am a person who tries hard. That's all there is to me.—Akira Kurosawa, *Something Like an Autobiography*[1]
>
> [T]he film is about two men wrestling with their angels; each is the adversarial angel of the other.—Professor Ian Burumu, on Kurosawa's *Yoidore tenshi* [*Drunken Angel*][2]

Akira Kurosawa developed the idea for *Yoidore tenshi* [*Drunken Angel*] (1948) with cowriter Keinosuke Uekusa while staying at the seaside hot-spring resort of Atami. Through their window, Kurosawa gazed at a sunken Japanese concrete war freighter and the children diving from it into the water. He saw this "depressing image" as a "kind of a parody of defeated Japan."[3]

Back at Toho, they were further inspired by the existing set of a postwar shopping street with a black-market area built for director Kajirô Yamamoto's two-part *Shin baka jidai* [*These Foolish Times*, aka *The New Age of Fools*] (1947), in which Toshirô Mifune plays an aspiring but very ill gang boss. For their new film, Uekusa met regularly with a member of the yakuza, and began to develop a sympathy toward the gangster life, which troubled Kurosawa, and the two argued while writing the screenplay. The sump area in the middle of the set, sprinkled with the local inhabitant's trash (a humid, mosquito-infested area that could be found in any bombed-out postwar Japanese city) was a true background for the development of the characters. Kurosawa later recalled how they decided upon the hypocritical, medicinal alcohol-swilling character to be portrayed by Shimura:

> In a slum in the port city of Yokohama we had come across an alcoholic doctor. The man fascinated us with his arrogant manner, and we took him with us to three or four bars to listen to his stories while we drank. It seems he operated without a physician's license, and his patients were the streetwalkers of the slums. His talk about his illegal

gynecology practice was so vulgar it nearly made us sick, but every so often he said something so bitterly sarcastic about human nature that gleamed with aptness. He also interspersed his talk with peals of loud laughter, and in that raucous wide-open mouth there was a strange feeling of raw humanity. He was probably a rebellious young man ending his days in cynicism, but Uekusa and I remembered, looked at each other and simultaneously felt, "This is it!" ...At last the "Drunken Angel" came on stage. The character immediately took on life and breath and began to move. He was a man past his mid-fifties, an alcoholic doctor with his own clinic. Turning his back on fame and fortune, he settled among the common people.[4]

They situated the doctor's clinic on the far side of the swamp, opposite the black market operated by the yakuza, and then developed an idea that would connect Dr. Sanada (Shimura, top-billed this time) with Matsunaga (Mifune): The gangster is wounded in the hand during a shootout and, while the illegally operating physician is removing the bullet, refusing to administer anesthetic, he also diagnoses tuberculosis, the disease that continually would bring them together and create conflict. Kurosawa claimed that, once he and Uekusa hit upon this plot, they wrote the remainder of the script in a single sitting.[5] Although Kurosawa claimed he was influenced by Fyodor Dostoevsky when working on the script, he actually brought his own postwar, anti-feudal message into the film.

Of the gangsters, Kurosawa explained,

Uekusa ... began to object to my attitude of opposition to the yakuza system.
Uekusa's dissatisfactions hinged on the argument that the failures and perversions in the yakuza personality were not the sole responsibility of the individual. This may well be true. But even if the society that gave birth to them must assume a part, or even the greater share, of the responsibility for the existence of yakuza, I still can't approve of their behavior. In the very same society that gave birth to such evil, there are also good people who are living honest, decent lives. I can't excuse those who make their living by threatening and destroying the lives of these good people....
Granting that there is some truth to the theory that defects in society give rise to the emergence of criminals, I still maintain that those who use this theory as a defense of criminality are overlooking the fact that there are many people in this defective society who survive without resorting to crime.[6]

Though Kurosawa doesn't specifically mention them, many of the criminals who became yakuza had just taken off their *kamikaze* uniforms, in which they had sworn to die for Imperial Japan, after their flight missions were aborted in the wake of defeat. In his essay "The Spoils of War," Bard college professor Ian Burumu notes, "But some, in a perverse way, transformed their military code of honor into a gangland code that was just as deadly."[7] Burumu also explains,

Although *Drunken Angel* is about postwar Japan, the historical echoes are strong.... In contrast to Germany, blame for the Japanese war could not be pinned on the Nazi Party or a murderous dictator. The war was fought in the name of the Japanese emperor, but Hirohito was no Hitler. Instead the war was blamed on the "militarists," but also something usually described as "feudalism," the warrior tradition, the culture of male domination, of self-sacrifice for the sake of samurai honor. This was the culture that Japanese liberals and Americans working for the Allied occupation of Japan sought to eradicate from the Japanese psyche. Democracy, equality between men and women, and an end to "feudal" warrior ethics were the stated goals of postwar education. Sword-fight movies, and even some kabuki plays that extolled samurai virtues were banned for a time.[8]

Burumu also is spot-on when he points out that, in his films, "relationships interested Kurosawa more than political messages."[9] *Drunken Angel* deals with the larger issues of postwar devastation and the possibility of recovery, but it is the complex relationship between Sanada and Matsunaga, against the purely evil character of the yakuza boss Okada, that makes this outstanding film so universally understood and enjoyed. Sanada is a character type Kurosawa often would portray, perhaps most notably (by Mifune) in *Red Beard*.

The initial script of *Drunken Angel*, dated October 15, 1947, was rejected by the Allied Occupation's official censorship board, the Civil Information and Education Administration Section (CIE), as "a bit gruesome," so Kurosawa and Uekusa wrote a more acceptable draft. Production began in mid-November 1947 and wrapped on March 10, 1948. Kurosawa praised Mifune's innate, intense performance abilities:

> Mifune had a kind of talent I had never encountered before in the Japanese film world. It was, above all, the speed with which he expressed himself that was so astounding. The ordinary Japanese actor might need 10 feet of film to get across an impression. Mifune needed only three feet. The speed of his movements was such that he said in a single action what took ordinary actors three separate movements to express. He put forth everything directly and boldly, and his sense of timing was the keenest I had ever seen in a Japanese actor. And yet with all his quickness he also had surprisingly fine sensibilities.[10]

In fact, Mifune's attractiveness was so powerful that it created a dilemma for Kurosawa, who had intended the focus of *Drunken Angel* to be on the title character, Dr. Sanada, whom Shimura based loosely on Thomas Mitchell's Oscar-winning portrayal of "Doc Boone" in John Ford's *Stagecoach* (1939).[11] The director recalled, "The drunken-doctor performance Shimura gave was a superb 90 percent, but because his adversary, Mifune, turned in 120 percent, I had to feel a little sorry for him."[12]

For the first time, Kurosawa sought out composer Fumio Hayasaka, who scored the director's subsequent films until his premature death of, ironically, tuberculosis at age 41 in 1955. Fortunately, the ethereal work of Hayasaka also can be heard to superb effect in three of Mizoguchi's late masterpieces, *Ugetsu monogatari* [*Ugetsu*] (1953), which reteamed Masayuki Mori with Machiko Kyô, *Sanshô dayû* [*Sansho the Bailiff*] (1954) and *Chikamatsu monogatari* [*Crucified Lovers*] (1954).

Drunken Angel opens with a guitarist (Sachio Sakai) playing a sort of "swamp blues" on the black-market side of the bubbling morass. He can be heard creating a haunting, melancholy mood during many transitions in which the disease-ridden bog is featured.

Kurosawa may have been exaggerating when comparing Shimura's "90 percent" to Mifune's "120." Mifune's animalistic intensity is well to the fore, but Shimura's Sanada, with his wild, graying hair and beard, gives him a unique appearance in the film. He often is thunderous in his condemnation of patients who care little for their well-being, while he risks his own health by drinking the medicinal alcohol from his stash of clinical supplies.

When Matsunaga attacks Sanada physically on several occasions, the doctor fights him off, then still treats him, feeling sorry for a man who swaggers around, projecting a front as a young thug who wants to become a yakuza boss. Advised to leave alcohol and women alone, Matsunaga soon runs into his boss, Okada (Reizaburô Yamamoto), just released from a stretch in prison, and married to Miyo (Chieko Nakakita), Sanada's nurse, one of the doctor's charity cases, who expectedly feared the yakuza's return. Following "just one drink" with the insistent Okada, Matsunaga is carried by two prostitutes out of the yakuza dive to a nightclub, where he and the boss dance with them to a Cab Calloway–style Western jazz number ("Jungle Boogie," with lyrics by Kurosawa and music by Ryoichi Hattori). Shizuko Kasagi, a very popular Japanese singer at the time, appears in the scene.

The next morning, Sanada, claiming he's "not a veterinarian," shouts and slaps the alcohol-reeking Matsunaga. The young yakuza, however, continues his path of boozing and smoking, having referred to the hole in his lung as "ventilation."

In his attempts to learn something about the gangster's past and references to altering physical behavior and moral codes as well, Sanada voices a very postwar attitude about the potential for change. Roused in the middle of the night by two of Okada's men bringing Matsunaga, who is now coughing up blood, Sanada at first refuses to help but capitulates. In a touching sequence, Sanada sits at Matsunaga's bedside, advises him not to speak, and tells him to dream of his childhood. This moment may be the only one during which anyone has shown genuine concern for the gangster. Later, when Sanada is visited and threatened by Okada and his men, Matsunaga rises from his sickbed, admitting, "I owe this doctor everything.... I'll stake my life on this man"

"Yakuza power is a myth," says Sanada. "They're just good at scaring people."

When he leaves the clinic for the day, the doctor warns Miyo not to return to Okada, and Matsunaga not to get up from his bed. Afraid Sanada will "go to the cops," he forces his way past Miyo. Meanwhile, the "big boss"

3. Yoidore tenshi *(1948)* 35

(Masao Shimizu) plans to use him as a sacrifice in a war with a rival outfit, a plan the tubercular yakuza overhears.

In an extreme long shot showing an expressionistically lit hallway, Matsunaga enters the room of Okada, who is playing the instrument he stole from the guitar player. Instantly, the music stops. Now with nothing to lose, Matsunaga pulls his knife. Kurosawa cuts from a close-up of the knife to a shot of the terrified Okada, and then an image of a triple mirror (paralleling an earlier shot of Sanada in a similar mirror in his quarters).

Titled medium close-ups of the combatants lead to Matsunaga coughing and a close-up of blood spattering the floor, temporarily giving Okada the upper hand. Now threatened with his own knife, Matsunaga is backed into a corner. Here, Kurosawa crosscuts between the fight and Sanada buying eggs for his patient at a nearby open market.

The duel dramatically continues, as Matsunaga crawls out into the long hallway, tossing and spilling cans of paint as he goes. Originally, Kurosawa considered the hallway too wide, so the ladders topped with paint cans were placed in a fashion that narrowed the space in which the two men would fight. The slippery paint not only hampers their duel but also acts as a symbol for the blood Matsunaga coughs up as they continue to wrestle on the floor, covering themselves with the pigment. Ultimately stabbed in the lower right abdomen by Okada, Matsunaga makes his way out onto a balcony, where he expires under a line of hanging laundry (perhaps Kurosawa's dark tip of the hat to the clothesline-favoring Yasujirô Ozu).

Sanada returns home with the eggs. Now staring at the swamp, Sanada and Miyo discuss Matsunaga's violent end. When the doctor says that she was in love with him, she denies it. But she has paid for his funeral ("a little over 6,000 yen") and has his ashes with her. "I just felt so sorry for him," she admits. The yakuza wouldn't raise money for his arrangements, "because he wasn't loyal enough," but the big boss saw to it that Okada would have plenty after he again is released from prison. Miyo has decided to return to her home in the country, where she will bury Matsunaga's ashes, something they had discussed right before his death. She then admits her love for him, whom she was convinced could change, including leaving the yakuza.

Perhaps Kurosawa's personal thoughts about the yakuza are best represented in a tight close-up of an intense Shimura as Sanada says, "But yakuza will always do the wrong thing in the end. That's why they're so pointless. And so senseless.... That's why I can't forgive him." The film ends with a ray of hope as a 17-year-old girl (Yoshiko Kuga), whose tuberculosis he has cured, runs to him from the other side of the sump hole with her high school diploma.

"Doctor, you owe me a sweet," she reminds him. Miyo declines to accompany them; and both wishing her goodbye, they head for the sweetshop. Taking Sanada's arm, the girl tells him, "If you approach it rationally, TB's no big deal."

"It's not just TB," replies the doctor sternly as ever. "A rational approach is the best medicine for life." Sanada laughs, and off they walk onto the crowded sidewalk.

Of Sanada, Stephen Prince points out,

> [Kurosawa's] hero ... has been defeated, and Matsunaga ... has been linked to the sump for a last time.... Unable to find a way out of this dilemma, Kurosawa wishes his way through ... proclaiming once more that willpower can cure all human ailments.... Yet one feels it is the sump that has had the last word.[13]

Shimura is at turns restrained and roaring in *Drunken Angel*, displaying the full range of his talent, creating a character remarkably different from others he would craft in later films for Kurosawa and other Japanese filmmakers. Early on in his work for Kurosawa, it is one of his top performances. As Kurosawa wrote, Mifune also does accomplish an impressive dramatic feat. But Stephen Prince, commenting on the director's subsequent pairings of Shimura with Mifune, contradicts the idea that the latter actor steals the film:

> [In *Drunken Angel*], Shimura's doctor is an equally memorable character and just as powerful [as Mifune's]. More important, Kurosawa would continue to pair the two actors together ... often with Shimura in the role of the master and teacher. Throughout the first half of Kurosawa's career, Shimura's performances very often provide the moral center of the films until he is eclipsed by Mifune.... The gentleness and compassion that Shimura projects are central to the moral dialogue of these films...[14]

Kurosawa's visual style is kinetic in *Drunken Angel*. He and cinematographer Takeo Itô use moving camera with a distinct rationale, and their compositions always capture the characters in juxtapositions that accentuate their dramatic relationships. A very effective, unnerving dream sequence, triggered by Matsunaga's staring at a doll floating in the swamp, "like his lungs," depicts him chopping open his coffin on the seashore and then being chased by his reanimated corpse.

Even though the characters use fans and wipe their faces with handkerchiefs, the summer setting in the film is belied by the constant sight of their breaths emanating from their mouths, a telltale sign that the film was shot during the winter. A crew member humorously recalled,

> We were going to shoot an actress eating a popsicle in front of dance hall no. 1. We were filming in the winter, and they didn't sell popsicles in winter back then, so we had some made. It rained the morning of the shoot, so we thought it was canceled. The guy who had the key to the freezer took off. Then Kobayashi [the assistant director] came and said, "We're going to shoot. Get ready." We were in trouble. The guy with the key was gone. The rain was clearing up, and we were told to get ready. So I discussed it with Yamamoto, and we made a fake popsicle using Japanese radish and a chopstick. I warned the actress not to lick it, because it was fiery hot. Kurosawa never suspected.[15]

Sanada eats a popsicle in a scene also featuring Matsunaga, but Shimura had been able to procure one of the real frozen treats.

After being approved (even with several elements that should have offended the CIE) by the Civil Censorship Detachment (CCD), the organization that scrutinized completed films, *Drunken Angel* proved to be Kurosawa's "breakthrough film" in Japan, where it opened to smash reviews on April 27, 1948. Ian Burumu sums it up well: "Sanada ... an alcoholic doctor who boozes from his own medical supplies, is redeemable by his desire to cure even the most unredeemable patients; Matsunaga is a violent hoodlum humanized by his fear of death, which lies just underneath the swaggering surface."[16]

Shortly after Kurosawa completed the *Drunken Angel* shoot, another labor strike in December 1948 shut down Toho, which now was under the management of president Tetsuzo Watanabe, a virulent anti–Communist, who knew nothing about producing films, claiming that the last one he'd seen, *Zigomar*, a French detective drama, was released in Japan in 1911! However, proposed projects by union members were dropped, 1,200 employees were fired, and section chiefs were restored to the system. In protest, unionists camped out on the grounds and stopped all production for 134 days. They used fire hoses, wind machines and threats of a blinding with cayenne pepper against police, U.S. military tanks and anti–Communists.

To remain afloat, Kurosawa, taking Shimura and Mifune along, adapted *Drunken Angel* for the stage, as a two-act, seven-scene play. The tour included performances in Shizuoka, Kyoto, Osaka and Awajishima, remaining in each city from 10 to 20 days. Audiences at every venue responded enthusiastically. Then the three proceeded to other studios to make more innovative films.

Decades after making *Drunken Angel*, Kurosawa revealed,

> When I start on a film project.... I first imagine how I would shoot it if it were a silent film. Films nowadays are full of dialogue, but it shouldn't be explanatory. So I begin by imagining how to express the story as a silent film. The viewer should engage their imagination as they watch a film with the filmmaker's imagination. But with all the colors and sounds in a film, everything tends to get overly explained. The worst offense is when dialogue becomes explanatory, although that may make a film easier to understand. Rather than expressing, film has evolved towards describing.[17]

Shizukanaru kettô [*The Quiet Duel*] (1949)

Under the direction of Fumio Kamei, Shimura joined Tomotsu Kawasaki for *Onna no issho*, released by Toho on January 25, 1949. He then reteamed with Kurosawa and Mifune for *The Quiet Duel* (1949), a collaboration between Eiga geijutsu kyokai (Film Art Association), founded by Kurosawa, Senkichi Taniguchi, Kajirô Yamamoto, Mikio Naruse and producer Sôjirô Motoki, and

Daiei Studios, the first company outside Toho (and located in Chofu City on the outskirts of Tokyo) to offer the director an opportunity to helm his own project. Since Mifune had portrayed only gangsters to date, Kurosawa, in a move that troubled executives at Daiei, cast him in the lead role of Kyoji Fujisaki, a physician who becomes infected with syphilis after cutting himself while performing surgery on a diseased soldier during World War II.

In his autobiography, though referring to Mifune, Kurosawa also could be describing the varied roles he gave to Shimura, who plays Dr. Konosuke Fujisake (Mifune's father) in the film:

> A sad truth in the film business is that when an actor succeeds in a particular role there is a tendency to keep casting him in similar roles. This stems, of course, from the convenience and advantage of those who use him, but for the actor himself there is no greater misfortune. Repeating the same role over and over, like a machine-stamped image, is unbearable. An actor who is not constantly given new roles and new subjects to tackle dries out and withers like a tree you plant in the garden and then fail to water.[18]

One of the film's most interesting acting elements is Kurosawa's choice of having Shimura use the back of his body to suggest his character's feelings. Stuart Galbraith notes,

> After the war, when Konosuke overhears his son discussing his affliction, Kurosawa does not show Takashi Shimura's face. Rather than the camera conventionally focusing in on him in a tight shot, we see only his back, his hands clasped behind him. When he hears the news, his hands come apart, and slumping slightly, he walks away. This invites the viewer to infer Shimura's reaction and is rather clever.[19]

Konosuke initially is appalled by the realization that his son has contracted syphilis. But after Kyoji manages to explain the accidental nature of the incident, the elder doctor asks for forgiveness. Mifune and Shimura both play this scene beautifully. Kurosawa uses a long-take two-shot for much of this sequence, and then follows it with a rapid montage of Kyoji's patients celebrating a young boy's gas-passing recovery from an appendectomy. As they continue to laugh while one of the other boys plays a large harmonica, Kurosawa adds additional visual counterpoint with a closing shot of the two doctors sitting with their heads bowed in shared grief.

The subject of syphilis, set in a 1945 Tokyo clinic, caused trouble between Kurosawa and the occupation GHQ, whose censors insisted that the original ending be altered. It was feared that showing Kyoji go insane from the disease would frighten filmgoers from seeking treatment at actual clinics. In the finished film, the young doctor staves off the effects of the disease with systematic injections and, with the support of his father and Rui Minegishi (Noriko Sengoku), a nurse whose life he has helped turn around, continues to be a successful and caring healer.

However, the still-daring depiction and occasional use of profane language in the film sets *The Quiet Duel* apart from anything made in Hollywood for another two decades. Though the subject of treatment for syphilis had been dramatized in Warner Bros.' fact-based *Dr. Ehrlich's Magic Bullet* (1940), starring Edward G. Robinson in his favorite role, that production was carefully censored by the Production Code Administration (PCA).

The Quiet Duel's plot of the young doctor's self-repression, secretly refusing to marry Misao Matsumoto (Miki Sanjô), his former fiancée, after asking her to wait six long years, stretches the bounds of believability, but Mifune's performance does not. As Kurosawa had predicted, the actor who previously only had played gangsters is completely convincing, and Kyoji's sudden wrenching confession to Rui of his long-sublimated desires (a scene which rattled the director

Shizukanaru kettô [*The Quiet Duel*] (1949; directed by Akira Kurosawa): Toshirô Mifune, Kenjirô Uemura, Miki Sanjô, Takashi Shimura and Noriko Sengoku featured on Daiei's original Japanese B2 poster.

during shooting) provides the most powerful moments in the film. Shimura may have had 15 years' acting experience at this point in his career, but here Mifune was making himself into a star.

Shimura does enjoy his own effective scene near the end, when Konosuke, holding Rui's baby (which the nurse originally wanted to abort), speaks to Nosaka (Isamu Yamaguchi), the police officer who earlier had asked Kyoji to attend to Susumu Nakada (Kenjurô Uemura), the syphilitic soldier from the field hospital. Though Kyoji had warned him not to risk spreading the disease, he had uncaringly infected his wife (Chieko Nakakita) and caused the death of their fetus, an event that caused him finally to lose his mind. After Nosaka calls Kyoji "a saint," Konosuke replies that if his son "had been happy, he might have been a snob."

Though Kurosawa ultimately was disappointed with *The Quiet Duel*, the film did well critically and commercially in Japan. When it finally was released 30 years later in the U.S., though dated, it still was well received, with Vincent Canby, in a November 25, 1983, *New York Times* review, mentioning "the late, great Takashi Shimura."[20]

Following *The Quiet Duel*, Shimura played the Chief of Police in *Jigoku no kifukin* [*Lady from Hell*] (1949), for which Kurosawa collaborated on the screenplay with Eitarô Ozawa and Ichirô Ryûzaki. Next, he appeared with Susumu Fugita and Ozu-favorite Chishû Ryû in director Kôzaburô Yoshimura's *Mori no Ishimatsu* [*Ishimatsu of the Forest*] (1949).

#　4

Nora inu (1949)

> Shimura is quite good...—Akira Kurosawa, on Shimura's
> award-winning performance in *Nora inu* [*Stray Dog*][1]

Akira Kurosawa, over the course of six weeks, initially wrote *Nora inu* [*Stray Dog*] (1949), a police thriller based on an actual detective who lost his pistol, as a Georges Simenon-influenced novel. Then, with his new co-writer Ryûzô Kikushima, painstakingly spent the next two months transforming it into a screenplay for Toho. Securing the participation of the Film Art Association and Shintoho, he again was able to collaborate with crew members from whom he'd been separated by the Toho strike. Asakazu Nakai signed on as director of photography, Ishirô Honda as assistant director, and Fumio Hayasaka as composer. To avoid any resentment lingering from the strike, Kurosawa moved his cast, including Mifune and Shimura, and crew to the old, quiet Oizumi studio, which included a building they all used as a dormitory, in Tokyo's Ikebukuro district.

Kurosawa later wrote, "The leads in this film were once again Mifune and Takashi Shimura, and most of the rest of the cast, too, were old friends, so the work proceeded in an almost familial atmosphere."[2] Having assigned his second-unit work to Honda, he also admitted,

> There are as few men as honest or reliable as Honda. He faithfully brought back exactly the footage I requested, so almost everything he shot was used in the final cut of the film. I'm often told that I captured the atmosphere of postwar Japan in *Stray Dog*, and, if so, I owe a great deal of that success to Honda.[3]

Honda not only fulfilled his many duties as chief assistant director, he also doubled for Toshirô Mifune and played a criminal fleeing from the police.

Singled out by many reviewers for his performance, Shimura especially liked his character in *Stray Dog*:

> When you learn [Sato] is a skilled detective, you imagine that his personality must be intimidating. Quite the contrary. The character I played had a calm demeanor and

ate ice cream with the woman he was questioning. I was impressed with Mr. Kurosawa's skillful direction. I guess it was the first Japanese film about an ordinary detective searching for clues to find a criminal.[4]

While the old-fashioned Sato believes that criminals are truly evil, Murakami, a younger man with recent war experiences, sees criminality as having some environmental causes. Stephen Prince writes,

> Yusa is Murakami's evil double, a doppelganger who must be symbolically apprehended. The ethical component advanced by this portrayal is the insistence that people are not determined by their social conditions but retain a power of will and action independently of their circumstances, as Murakami demonstrated when he decided to become a cop. To this degree, then, *Stray Dog* is a film about the danger of feeling and about the need to renounce compassion. All Sato's warnings to Murakami are admonitions about the essential evil of criminals. They are evil because they lack the will to do differently and must be condemned and exorcised from the social fabric. Sato says that the police guard society, and Kurosawa cuts to shots of Sato's children sleeping peacefully, showing the prize and tranquility that Sato protects. From the sleeping children Kurosawa then cuts to an abandoned child's toy at the home of a woman Yusa has just murdered, clearly demonstrating that Yusa's essential sin is the breach in social sanctity.... Yusa's violation is unforgivable because it threatens the sleeping children of the next generation, those who will emerge from the ashes of war and inhabit a new Japan.[5]

However, Kurosawa's ending of *Stray Dog*, with Yusa finally apprehended and handcuffed in a field by Murakami, is ambiguous. Prince continues,

> The dynamic between the older and the younger detective is the struggle for an emergent and a coherent social program that takes as a central problem the place and role of the compassionate response in an oppressive world. The difference in the models offered by Sato and Murakami are left in tension, their irresolution haunting the film.[6]

Kurosawa's 10-minute montage sequence of Murakami searching Tokyo's Asakusa and Ueno districts for his pickpocketed piece drives home both his growing frustration and increasing determination to track it down. Finally, the sweat-soaked, exhausted young detective lies down on the edge of a village fountain to rest, only to be approached by a young black-market criminal dealing in stolen weapons.

The most touching scenes involve Murakami's growing personal relationship with Sato, who shows his compassionate side when introducing his younger colleague to his family, including his wife (Kazuko Ihonbashi). Then, when Sato is wounded and may die while in surgery, Murakami (Mifune, in another standout performance), breaks down outside the door of the operating room.

Production on *Stray Dog*, the first police procedural ever made in Japan, wrapped during September 1949 and was released to considerable acclaim on October 17. Shimura received a Best Actor Award from Mainichi Film Concurs, sponsored by the *Mainichi Shimbun* newspapers, who also presented wins to Asakazu Nakai (cinematography), Fumio Hayasaka (score) and Takashi Matsuyama (art direction).

The film was not released in the United States until August 31, 1963, when *BoxOffice* reported,

> Kurosawa takes one ... into the slums of Tokyo and with the superb acting of the seasoned Takashi Shimura as Sato, Keiko Awaji as Harumi, and Reizaburô Yamamoto as Honda, presents a survey of criminal motivations, procedures used by police to bring them to justice, and a reason for criminal actions. America's half-million police officers, correction and juvenile authorities, all will enjoy Kurosawa's sympathetic handling of a peace officer as a human being.[7]

Pen itsuwarazu boryoku no machi [*Streets of Violence—The Pen Never Lies*] (1950; directed by Satsuo Yamamoto): Takashi Shimura as Sagawa, editor of the *Tochio Daily*, in this ambitious, documentary-style political exposé released by Daiei Studios.

On January 5, 1950, 29-year-old Toshirô Mifune married 21-year-old Sochiko Yoshimine in a Christian ceremony. Mifune had met Sochiko during Toho's search for New Faces in 1946, but her father had prevented her from accepting film offers and objected to having an actor in the family. For a while, Mifune roomed with *Snow Trail* assistant director Kihachi Okamoto near Toho and, during that time, was able to see Sochiko. Kurosawa and *Snow Trail* director Senkichi Taniguchi visited Sochiko's father, a successful dentist, and made a good case for Mifune.

Soon, Mifune was living just down the street from Takashi and Masako Shimura, also near Toho. The RSVP envelopes had been mailed back to Mifune and his fiancée via the Shimuras, who had become surrogate parents for the younger actor. Mifune's son, Shirô, born a little less than 11 months after his parents' wedding, later said,

> When I was a child, Mr. Shimura was a kind of father figure for him.... The first place my mother and father lived had no bath, and they used to take baths in [the Shimura's] home [nearby]. I used to call them Grandma and Grandpa. I thought [my grandfather] was Mr. Shimura.[8]

Mifune's wedding was followed by an abundant reception. His personal guests included Nenji Oyama, the cameraman who introduced him at Toho, and fellow New Face members Ryô Ikebe and Masumi Okada. Kajirô Yamamoto, Akira and Yôko Kurosawa and, of course, Takashi and Masako Shimura, celebrated the nuptials of their good colleagues and friends.

In the atmosphere of occupied Tokyo, Mifune, a formidable natural talent with no formal training, stood out from the other Toho New Faces. This dichotomy made him feel quite uncomfortable, and the constant attention from the public, fan magazines and the studio's publicity machine led him to begin drinking heavily. Nearly every evening, he imbibed an entire bottle of saké, brandy or whiskey to take off the edge. He continued this for the rest of his career, always teetering on the brink of alcoholism. Often, he joined Kurosawa in his own after-work saké and whiskey celebrations. Though a heavy smoker, Shimura did not join in these parties, and spent most of his free time with Masako.

Shimura's first performance of 1950 came in director Minoru Shibuya's *Tenya Wanya* [*Crazy Uproar*]. He then worked for Hiroshi Inagaki in *Ore wa jojinbo* [*I'm the Bodyguard*], Senkichi Taniguchi in *Ma no ogon*, and Satsuo Yamamoto in *Pen itsuwarazu boryoku no machi* [*Streets of Violence: The Pen Never Lies*] (all 1950).

Streets of Violence, released by Daiei, is an ambitious, documentary-style political exposé starring Shimura as *Tochio Daily* newspaper editor Sagawa, who joins with threatened members of youth, student and women's groups to fight gangsters, black marketeers and corruption in a major Japanese city. Including voice-over narration and such ethical statements as "The mass media must adhere faithfully to the truth" and "Despite massive interference, we finally made this film," this epic of one young journalist's crusade blossoming into a public outcry for justice is a postwar document about Japan's move away from its feudalistic past and toward democracy.

Yamamoto often uses Hollywood-style newspaper montages to move his 111-minute narrative along. At one point, Sagawa, referring to the first citizens who join their press movement, speaks the classic line, "Build a field and they will come." The role is ideal for Shimura, who brings all his naturalism and immense integrity to the devoted journalist.

Shûbun, aka *Skandaru* [*Scandal*] (1950)

In his autobiography, Akira Kurosawa writes, "After the Pacific War a great deal of noise began to be made about freedom of speech, and almost immediately abuses and loss of self-control ensued."[9] Specifically the director refers to the type of "yellow journalism" that permeated magazines devoted to sensationalizing the lives of popular Japanese entertainers in the newly

Shûbun, aka *Skandaru* [*Scandal*] (1950; directed by Akira Kurosawa): Toshirô Mifune, Noriko Sengoku, Yoshiko [Shirley] Yamaguchi and Takashi Shimura featured on Shochiku's original Japanese B2 poster.

flourishing, celebrity-possessed culture sparked by postwar Western influence. Released just five months after Yamamoto's *Streets of Violence*, Kurosawa's new film would show the flip side of the contemporary Japanese press.

Previously Kurosawa had made films about postwar gangsters, disease and individual criminals. Now he went after those who used the press to attack the innocent. He didn't name the artist toward whom the slander was aimed, but he explained,

> I did not know X personally. I only knew her name and profession, but when I saw the sensationalistic way this headline article was presented, I couldn't help thinking about how helpless she must feel. Outraged, I reacted as if the thing had been written about me, and I couldn't remain silent. Such slander cannot be permitted. This was not freedom of expression, I felt, it was violence against a person on the part of those who possess the weapon of publicity. I felt that this new tendency had to be stamped out before it could spread. Someone had to come out and fight back against this violence, I felt; there was no time for crying oneself to sleep.[10]

The result was the screenplay *Scandal* (1950), co-written by Kurosawa and Ryûzô Kikushima, directed for Shochiku and starring Mifune, the beautiful Yoshiko [Shirley] Yamaguchi, Yôko Katsuragi, Noriko Sengoku, Eitarô Ozawa and Shimura, who creates another distinct, brilliant characterization, as Otokichi Hiruta, an attorney who, while playing both sides of the legal fence during a civil trial, reveals deep flaws in his unscrupulous, ultimately pitiful and sympathetic personality.

Mifune plays Ichirô Ayoe, a motorcycle-riding painter, who, after politely giving a ride to the famous singer Miyako Saijo (Yamaguchi) and visiting her on a balcony outside her room in the hotel where they both are staying, becomes embroiled in a scandal perpetrated by *Amour* magazine, whose photographer has snapped an image of them together. The initial feature article, "Love on a Motorcycle," greatly bothers Miyako and her mother (Fumiko Okamura), and Aoye decides to sue following an altercation with Asai (Shin'ichi Himori), the editor of *Amour*. He then hires Hiruta, who is plied with alcohol and bribed to torpedo the litigation. Following a drunken night on the town with Aoye and the death of his young daughter, Yasu (Tanie Kitabayashi), from tuberculosis, Hiruta finally takes the stand to tell the truth, and Asai's criminality is exposed.

Kurosawa admitted, "*Scandal* proved to be as ineffectual a weapon as a praying mantis against a hatchet. But I have not given up. I am still waiting for the day when someone emerges who is willing to take on this verbal gangsterism for a fight to the finish."[11] Perhaps due in part to Shimura's powerful performance dominating the film, Kurosawa explained,

> [A]n entirely unexpected character began to take on more life than the main characters, and I ended up being led around by the nose by him. This fellow was the corrupt lawyer Hiruta ("Leech Field"). He comes to the defendants to sell out his client, the

4. Nora inu (1949)

plaintiff, who is sincerely attempting to battle the verbal gangsters in court. From this point on, the film went in a direction I had not intended and turned into something quite different.... From the moment this Hiruta appeared, the pen I was using to write the screenplay seemed almost bewitched. It wrote on, detailing Hiruta's actions and words as if of its own accord.... I didn't think about the circumstances in which Hiruta lived; the pen just glided on and described his poverty and shame. As this happened, the character of Hiruta quite naturally took over the film and nudged the hero aside.[12]

About six months after making *Scandal*, Kurosawa, during a train trip home from seeing a film in Shibuya, saw a man whom he'd encountered before, realizing that it was the real-life Hiruta, an attorney who remained in his subconscious and secretly had driven his co-writing of the screenplay.

Stuart Galbraith notes,

> *Scandal*, far more than any other film Kurosawa made, is directly influenced by the Hollywood pictures Kurosawa and the rest of postwar Japan were now able to see...
> The second part of Kurosawa's film rather obviously apes Capra in general and *It's a Wonderful Life* (1946) in particular. There are close-ups of ornaments on trees, Shimura goes around yelling, "Merry Kurisumaas! Merry Kurisumaas!" at no one in particular, and his courtroom scenes recall both Lionel Barrymore in Clarence Brown's *A Free Soul* (1931) and Claude Rains in *Mr. Smith Goes to Washington* (1939). Finally, in a run-down bar adorned with the tiniest bit of tinsel, Shimura drunkenly leads everyone in a Japanese rendition of "Auld Lang Syne."[13]

A moving scene involving "Silent Night" sung by Aoye and Miyako to the ailing Yasu leads to Hiruta's inebriated rampage, briefly quelled by Aoye, who takes him to the tavern where a local drunk (Bokuzen Hidari) is joined by the depressed attorney to spark the band into playing Scottish bard Robert Burns' song of universal brotherhood. A booze-soaked homage to *It's a Wonderful Life* indeed flavors Ayoe's leading Hiruta home: The painter, wearing a high paper crown, suggests that the stars have fallen from the sky into the filthy pool between the houses, and the attorney (giving Shimura a chance to speak a little English) shouts, "Merry Christmas—everybody" just before he passes out, falling flat on his back into the mud.

Shûbun, aka *Skandaru* [*Scandal*] (1950; directed by Akira Kurosawa): Another of Akira Kurosawa's favorite actors, Bokuzen Hidari (left, as the "Drunk"), and Takashi Shimura (as unscrupulous attorney Otokichi Hiiruta) in the director's exposé on post–World War II yellow journalism.

Kurosawa recalled, "People who don't drink are usually the best at portraying drunks. Shimura was ... so good. I guess he was watching when others got drunk."[14]

The pinnacle of Shimura's film-stealing performance arguably arrives in the scene in which the drunken, ashamed Hiruta, having just taken the bribe from Asai, comes home with a large stuffed rabbit and other gifts for Yasu, who cries and then encourages him to reveal his true feelings—something his wife prefers to ignore. "If a person doesn't let out what's deep in his heart," he tells his daughter, "he'll end up choking to death on it."

Earlier, Aoye suggests to Miyako, "The father of a girl like that can't be all bad." Following the trial, Ayoe tells the press that Hiruta's redemption, which he describes as "becoming a star," is more important than their own vindication. The film ends with the disheveled attorney all alone, walking the windblown streets.

During the years after *Scandal* was released, Kurosawa and Mifune also were the subjects of typically scurrilous and slanderous press attacks, just the kind the film failed to effect in any tangible way. Kurosawa even considered making another film tougher on the tabloids, but never did so.

When the film was released in the U.S. on July 17, 1964, it was paired with Ozu's *An Autumn Afternoon* (1962), the "family" master's final film and starring his favorite actor, Chishû Ryû. The *Los Angeles Times*' Kevin Thomas wrote that the double bill

> provides a unique opportunity to compare the completely different styles of two of the greatest directors of all time. The presentation of a Kurosawa picture new to American audiences is in itself an important occasion, but the premiere of a film by Ozu, the least known of the Japanese directors ... makes this double feature ... a major event for anyone who enjoys good films protesting the moral chaos of postwar Japan.... The scenes between [Shimura] and his daughter are straight out of *The Old Curiosity Shop*.[15]

In his 2012 British Film Institute essay, Alex Cox notes,

> From the moment he appears, Shimura dominates the film, and indeed Hiruta is its only interesting character: by turns wheedling, aggressive, cowardly and confused, he is redeemed by his sincere love for his sick daughter, and his breakdown in the long courtroom scene is marvelously performed. Mifune, as the painter Aoye, is out-acted for a change.[16]

Shimura again was directed by Mikio Naruse, in the small supporting role of Kimiko Miyabe's Father, a prosperous butcher, in *Ikari no machi* [*The Angry Street*] (1950). The film features an excellent cast including Ichirô Sugai, Yoshiko Kuga (now 19 years old) and the gorgeous Mayuri Mokushô (as Kimiko), but Naruse and Motosada Nishiki's screenplay, adapted from the novel by Fumio Niwa, and dealing with a bunco racket waged by two university students (Jûkichi Uno and Yasumi Hara) against naïve females, includes too many underdeveloped characters and enough loose ends to fill another 105 minutes. Though billed seventh, Shimura is given little to do as Kimiko becomes a victim of Shigetaka Sudô (Hara), the small-time racketeer whose plans are stifled when he attempts to encroach upon true gangsters' turf. The often subtle, fluid camerawork by Masao Tamai is impressive, but *The Angry Street* understandably is not considered one of Naruse's major works.

5

Rashômon (1950)

> I don't tell lies. I saw it with my own eyes.—The Woodcutter
> (Takashi Shimura), in *Rashômon*

Using the three-part story *Yabu no naka* ("In a Grove") by Ryûnosuke Akutagawa (a suicide at age 35 in 1927) as source material, Akira Kurosawa collaborated with Shinobu Hashimoto on the screenplay for *Rashômon*, the director's first major samurai epic, this one involving a rape and murder during the 11th century. To expand a draft by Hashimoto to feature length, Kurosawa added one more tale, and the actual plot for the film, featuring various characters' supposedly "eyewitness" recollections of the same event, began to brew in his imagination.

The title of the film was derived from the original *Rajômon* gate leading to the outer grounds of the castle in the ancient Japanese capital of Kyôto (called *Heian-Kyô* during the 11th century). The name later was altered to *Rashômon* by Noh playwright Nobumitsu Kanze. Kurosawa wanted to build a set for the gate that would closely recreate its original size, "as big as the main two-story gates of the Ninnaji and Tôdaiji temples in Nara."[1]

Kurosawa revealed, "The Daiei management was not very happy with the project. They said the content was difficult and the title had no appeal. They were reluctant to let the shooting begin."[2] (Two companies, Toyoko and Toho, already had passed on the project.) Nonetheless, the director, production designer Takashi Matsuyama and set decorator H. Motsumoto were able to construct a reasonable facsimile of the original gate, using the ravages of time as artistic license, as well as cutouts to substitute for the lack of proper distance, on the studio backlot. The final cost of the film reached $140,000 (about twice that of a usual budget), with half paying for the gate set.

Kurosawa explained the complexity of the characters in *Rashômon*:

> Human beings are unable to be honest with themselves about themselves. They cannot talk about themselves without embellishing. This script portrays such human beings—the kind who cannot survive without lies to make them feel they are better

5. Rashômon (1950)   51

people than they really are. It even shows this sinful need for flattering falsehood going beyond the grave—even the character who dies cannot give up his lies when he speaks to the living though a medium. Egoism is a sin the human being carries with him from birth; it is the most difficult to redeem. This film is like a strange picture scroll that is unrolled and displayed by the ego.[3]

Kurosawa remembered his cast as "all actors whose temperaments I knew, and I could not have wished for a better lineup."[4] During production, Shimura, Mifune, Machiko Kyô and their fellow actors ate a dish called *Sanyoku-yaki* ("Mountain Bandit Broil"), made of beef strips sautéed in oil, dipped in curry powder and butter, and eaten off a raw onion, a practice Kurosawa called "thoroughly barbaric."[5] He wanted them to hark back to silent acting style as a basis for their performances.

While shooting in the virgin forest at Kana, the crew kept a tub of salt at the entrance to the inn, where everyone could cover themselves before shooting each day. Large mountain leeches dropped from the cryptomeria and cypress trees and crawled up from the ground to gorge themselves on the blood of the cast and crew. The company then moved to the Kômyôji temple forest at Kyôto, where some crew members suffered heat stroke as Kurosawa pushed them hard all day. When each day's shooting was wrapped, they all would retire to quaff about a gallon of beer at a tavern in the city's Shijô-Kawara-machi district. Following dinner, according to Kurosawa, they would "gather again and pour whiskey down our throats with a vengeance."[6] Major shooting was completed in just a few weeks, due to all of Kurosawa's meticulous preproduction work.

Kurosawa did not, as some Western critics have assumed, emphasize traditional Japanese theatrical style in the development of the characters for *Rashômon*. Instead, he suggested that Mifune, Kyô, Mori and Shimura focus on the methods of *Shingeki* (or 20th-century "New Drama") and also watch a "jungle picture" which he recently had seen. The four actors, particularly Mifune, observed the amorality of the big jungle cats in the film, took extensive notes and used them to good effect, particularly via the strong emotions displayed by their characters in the many tense situations that dominate *Rashômon*.

A cinematographic first was Kurosawa's decision to include subjective, impressionistic compositions, some shot directly into the sun, which lead the viewer (from the point of view of the woodcutter [Shimura]) into the heart of the forest, a scene later praised at the Venice Film Festival. Very pleased with this daring decision, the director realized he'd forgotten to pass on the praise to director of photography Kazuo Miyagawa (after Shimura informed him of this oversight, something which immediately was corrected).

To cast atmospheric shadows on Shimura during his trek, and Mifune's bandit, Tajômaru, as he first sees the samurai's wife, Masako Kanazawa (Kyô), riding sidesaddle through the forest, wire webbing was strung through the bamboo trees, with leaves scattered across it, and mirrors were used strategically to reflect the sun at various points.

On cloudy days, Kurosawa and Miyagawa shot the rain-soaked scenes at the gate, adding pitch-black ink to the water blasted from fire hoses so it would register on the black-and-white film. As the three men sitting at the entrance, Shimura, Minoru Chiaki (a priest) and Kichijirô Ueda (a commoner, a character added by Kurosawa to the original story, who asks probing questions about the others' recollections), attempt to avoid being drenched as the woodcutter relates his version of the story involving the bandit and the samurai's wife.

Miyagawa also laid a rail at one spot in the forest to achieve a bold camera movement, appearing to track completely around Shimura at one point. This was achieved by having Shimura cross the rail as the cinematographer continued to move the camera along the track while also pivoting his own

Rashômon (1950; directed by Akira Kurosawa): Another Kurosawa favorite, Minoru Chiaki (left, as the Priest), Kichijirô Ueda (as the Commoner) and Takashi Shimura (right, as the Woodcutter) in one of the transcendent masterpieces of World Cinema.

body (later claiming that he "twisted his intestines" while performing the maneuver!).[7] Kurosawa said, "The camera has a starring role compared to other films."[8] (As in so many other of the director's films, so does the *rain*.) Kurosawa and Miyagawa's camera movements are fine examples of stylistic choices being used for a reason. (Among Miyagawa's other peerless achievements are his cinematography for Mizoguchi's *Ugetsu* and *Sansho the Bailiff*, for which he created some of the most exquisite compositions and complex, shimmering shades of gray in cinema history.)

Toward the film's end, the flashback scene recalled from the woodcutter's perspective is rendered as *pure cinema*, almost like a silent film, a visual feast including only ambient sound and devoid of a musical score, dialogue and sound effects. The few audible sword clashes between the bandit and the samurai, Takehiro Kanazawa (Masayuki Mori), are real, not overdubbed with the ridiculous "clanging" sounds that have hampered adventure films for decades. The spare, tight editing in this scene, as in the rest of the film, was also personally accomplished by Kurosawa.

Shimura plays a crucial role (his woodcutter being the only actual eyewitness, but who also may be lying) in this arguably perfect, totally innovative film. At the conclusion (another element added by Kurosawa), when the three men discover an abandoned infant at the gate, the immoral commoner steals its clothes, but Shimura's woodcutter restores the priest's faith in humanity when he (perhaps atoning for his lies) walks off with the baby. "I have six children of my own," movingly reveals the woodcutter. "One more won't make it any more difficult." The rain finally stops, the sky clears, and the film ends.

To some viewers and film executives, *Rashômon*, a complex, nonlinear narrative, seemed baffling, but its success made it not only aesthetically but historically significant and, like Kurosawa's later samurai films, was liberally plundered by other filmmakers all over the world. Donald Richie possibly explains it best:

> Five people interpret an action and each interpretation is different because, in the telling and retelling, the people reveal not the action but themselves. This is why Kurosawa could leave the plot, insofar as there is one, dangling and unresolved. The fact that it is unresolved *is* itself one of the meanings of the film.[9]

Eleven years later, while attending the 11th Berlin Film Festival with his wife and Mr. and Mrs. Toshirô Mifune, Shimura was interviewed at the Kapinski Hotel by journalist Gideon Bachmann, with Donald Richie serving as interpreter. Shimura revealed the "community effort" that took place while rehearsing for Kurosawa's films: The first run-through corrected weaknesses in the dialogue; the second was used to work out the actors' actual movements; and a third, in full makeup, was done for the benefit of the cinematographer and lighting crew. Though Kurosawa had been called an "emperor," said

Shimura, this label was unfair, since the director "allowed the actors to improve," giving them plenty of "artistic freedom" to create their own characterizations.[10]

In general, Shimura added that "being with Mr. Kurosawa allowed him to realize his own potentialities." He never grew weary of working on his films, because "each one is different—the self-realization is different on both sides." Nothing excited him more than a Kurosawa film, because he did "not have the experience with any other director."[11]

Shimura's ability to act solely with his expressive eyes is evident from the first shot of him in *Rashômon*. His woodcutter is focused and intense while listening to the comments of the priest and the commoner, who, at one point, remarks, "Maybe goodness is just make believe." The flashback to the testimony of the dead samurai speaking through a medium (Noriko Honma) prompts the woodcutter to exclaim, "Lies!"

As a counterpoint to the woodcutter's intensity while listening to the comments and his own recollections at the gate, he appears almost disinterested while seen in the background at the "trial," often blinking his eyes while hearing the "official" testimony of the others. When he finally decides to tell

Rashômon (1950; directed by Akira Kurosawa): (left to right) The Commoner (Kichijirô Ueda), the Woodcutter (Takashi Shimura) and the Priest (Minoru Chiaki), waiting out the rain at Rashômon Gate, discuss the human tendency to alter the truth.

the commoner that he "didn't want to get involved" with the police, but then recalls his full "eyewitness account," be becomes quite emotional and then tearful before walking off, coddling his "seventh child."

While Mifune, Kyô and Honma play their parts in an exaggerated, "animalistic" style, Shimura (and his frequent on-screen colleague Minoru Chiaki) are more realistic. (Prior to his role in *Ikiru*, the woodcutter may be his finest film performance.)

Following small roles in Yasuki Chiba's *Yoru no hibotan* (1950) and Kon Ichikawa's *Ginza Sanshiro* [*A Ginza Veteran*] (1950), Shimura was secondbilled (above Toshirô Mifune) in *Datsugoku* [*Escape from Prison*] (1950), directed by Kajirô Yamamoto and costarring Mieko Takamine. Mifune and Shimura then appeared in the Film Art Association-Toho production *Ai to nikushimi no kanata e* [*Beyond Love and Hate*] (1951), directed by Senkichi Taniguchi and adapted by Kurosawa and Kotaro Samukawa from the story "The Fugitive." Somewhat similar to *Snow Trail*, the film focuses on a convict who, seeking the truth about his wife's possible affair, escapes from prison, only to be chased into the mountains.

Shimura and Mifune again joined for *Aika* [*Elegy*] (1951), another Film Art-Toho film, directed by Kajirô Yamamoto and adapted by Hideo Oguni and Yamamoto from Oguni's short story "Saint Woman." Ken Uehara and Mieko Takamine received the lead roles.

Hakuchi [*The Idiot*] (1951)

Always glad to be back working with Kurosawa, Shimura received fifth billing in an impressive cast including Setsuko Hara, Masayuki Mori, Toshirô Mifune, Minoru Chiaki and Yoshiko Kuga, for *The Idiot*, Kurosawa and Eijirô Hisaita's adaptation of Fyodor Dostoevsky's novel Идіотъ [*The Idiot*]. Kurosawa's longtime admiration (instilled in him by his late brother, Heigo, who had committed suicide) for Dostoevsky's "power of compassion ... suffer[ing] with the victim ... [and being] more God than human"[12] led him to write a screenplay, though set in postwar Hokkaido, so faithful to its text that the film often became more literary than cinematic. Kurosawa and Hisaita previously had collaborated on *No Regrets for Our Youth*.

Kurosawa's original cut, intended to be shown in two parts, ran four hours and 25 minutes, but Shochiku would have none of it, nor would the studio approve a shorter three-hour version premiered at Tokyo's Togeki Theater in May 1951. A cut running two hours and 46 minutes finally was passed by the studio suits. Kurosawa, totally furious, suggested they go ahead and cut the film lengthwise, from beginning to end.[13]

Hisaita, recalling that the film did not do well in their home country,

Hakuchi [*The Idiot*] (1951; directed by Akira Kurosawa): From left: Toshirô Mifune, Masayuki Mori and Setsuko Hara featured on Shochiku's original Japanese B2 poster. (Takashi Shimura portrays Ono, the father of Ayako [Yoshiko Kuga].)

said that Kurosawa "fell in love with the book and wanted to make the film with a Japanese cast, in Japan. I know it wasn't natural, but filming with Japanese actors in Japan meant so much to Mr. Kurosawa and me."[14] As Stuart Galbraith has suggested, of all the Dostoevsky novels, *The Idiot* is the most un-filmable, do its reliance on internal psychological elements. The result of Kurosawa's work, especially having Japanese actors displaying Russian characteristics (though Hokkaido, a northern island of Japan, had the most contact with Russia), is problematic, regardless of Shochiku's considerable butchering, which caused many continuity and narrative problems.[15]

While Setsuko Hara, gorgeous, at the apex of her stardom and intended to insure box-office success, is precariously cast, and Yoshiko Kuga (who plays the young tubercular girl in *Drunken Angel* and later would give a superb performance in Mizoguchi's *Sansho the Bailiff*) was treated harshly by the director, Shimura and Minoru Chiaki make the most out of underdeveloped supporting characters. The visual style is hampered considerably by small sets in which too many actors are required to perform, often resulting in a stagey and stilted atmosphere. As Donald Richie notes, "Kurosawa's refusal to tamper with Dostoevsky gave him endless problems.... This desire to 'preserve' Dostoevsky weakens the film at every turn..."[16]

Returning from World War II, Kinji Kameda (Mori) is an innocent man condemned to death but given a reprieve due to his "epileptic dementia" and classification as an "idiot." (Actually, he is the ultimate nonconformist, a gentle soul totally different from everyone surrounding him.)

Part one of the film was edited considerably, making little sense at times, even with the inclusion of explanatory intertitles. The uncomfortable fusion of Japanese culture with strong elements from the novel's Russian origin, and the operatic style and pacing is unsuccessful during Part One; but Part Two, perhaps left more intact by the studio, becomes quite engrossing, due in large part to Mifune's intense and often frightening performance. (Kurosawa makes him appear positively Satanic at times.)

Hakuchi [*The Idiot*] (1951; directed by Akira Kurosawa): Takashi Shimura as Ono, Ayako's father, in Kurosawa's Japanese transformation of Fyodor Dostoyevsky's classic Russian novel.

The overall dark and depressing Dostoevsky atmosphere and visual style suggests the influence of many Hollywood films, made by such directors as diverse as John Ford, James Whale, and the great German Expressionst émigrés Fritz Lang and Joseph von Sternberg. Specifically, Kurosawa's direction of Mifune, and the editing of successfully closer shots of his face during one scene suggests Whale's introduction of the Monster (Boris Karloff) in *Frankenstein* (1931). Even more obvious is his direction of the eminently versatile Masayuki Mori, who apes the performance style of Peter Lorre in von Sternberg's adaptation of *Crime and Punishment* (1935). Throughout the film, Mori rarely deviates from using his eyes in a bold manner, and constantly places his hands at the base of his neck, in the trademark Lorre style (first seen in Lang's *M* [1930]). The influence of German Expressionism infuses all of Part Two, from the dark rooms and hallways of the gloomy home of Denkichi Ayama (Mifune), to constant distorted images formed by the unending mountains of snow heavily covering every home.

The ending is what is expected from the adaptation of a Dostoevsky novel, with Ayama's final solution to the pervasive, tragic unhappiness of Taeko Nasu (Hara, at times sensitive, and at others uncharacteristically over-the-top while wearing a very Russian long cape and cowl), and his and Kameda's own dramatic ends. Perhaps due to the studio's cutting of 98 minutes from the original version, the supporting roles of Mr. Ono (Shimura), the father of Ayako (Kuga), and Matsuo Kayama (Chiaki), performed with the actors' usual individualism (and not based on, perhaps, 1930s Boris Karloff and, obviously, Peter Lorre) leave the viewer wanting more of them.

Shimura was pleased to accept the lead role in director Tatsuyasu Osone's *Kedamono no yado* [*The Den of Beasts*] (1951), adapted from the short story "*Mizumi Nobara*" by its author, Shinya Fujiwara, and that ubiquitous co-writer, Akira Kurosawa. Toho's *Aoi Shinju* [*The Blue Pearl*] (1951), written and directed by Kurosawa's former assistant, Ishirô Honda, gave Shimura another character part, before Daiei came calling to cast him as the male lead, Horie, alongside his *Rashômon* costar Machiko Kyô, as Emmy, in *Mesu Inu* [*Bitch*] (1951). The excellent cast also includes Yoshiko Kuga (Yukiko) and Kamatari Fugiwara (Matsuda), directed by Keigo Kimura, who co-wrote the screenplay with Masashige Narusawa. Shimura then returned to Toho with Kajirô Yamamoto, who directed and co-wrote, with Toshirô Ide, *Hopu-san: sarariman no maki* (1951). In a good character part, he supported Keiji Kobayashi, Eiko Miyoshi, and Eijirô Tôno.

Bakurô ichidai [*The Life of a Horse-Trader*] (1951)

Back at Daiei, director Keigo Kimura reunited three *Rashômon* costars, Mifune and Machiko Kyô in the leads, and Shimura in the main supporting role, for the excellent *The Life of a Horse-Trader*, adapted by Masao Nakayama, from his novel, with the aid of Masashige Nurusawa and Kimura. Another atmospheric drama set on the northern Japanese island of Hokkaido after the fall of the Tokugawa shogunate, this moving story about Yonetaro ("The Shark") Katayama (Mifune), a proud, stubborn horse-trader, who gives up his gambling and hell-raising lifestyle to care for his young son, Daihei, following the premature death of his wife, features the star at his most skillfully powerful.

Mifune benefits from the strong work of Kyô as Yuki, a woman who offers herself as collateral to loan shark and local assemblyman Rokutaro Kosaka (Shimura) to provide funds to send Yonetaro's son to middle school. But the proud Yone-san will have none of it, instead nursing his racehorse, Fushimi, back to health to run head-to-head against Roku-san's swift animal in the Hokkaido Derby. The conclusion highlights Mifune at his most genuinely poignant, as Yone-san rides his neighbor's horse after the train carrying young Daihei off to school paid for with the Derby purse.

Roku-san is one of Shimura's best non–Kurosawa characters. Crafty, selfish, though honest in his own way, he never offers "money with no return," but finally does at the film's end by becoming matchmaker for Yone and Yuki. His delight while watching Yone engage in a series of three sumo wrestling contests (Mifune nearly nude three years prior to his several buff scenes in *Seven Samurai*) is a true high point. This little-known gem from all concerned deserves a much wider audience. Actor Yoshio Tsuchiya recalled,

> Mr. Shimura was a very fine actor and just like an uncle. In fact, I always called him "Uncle" and never Shimura-san. For me, he was the epitome of an actor ... in my opinion, his finest work on film was.... *The Life of a Horse-Trader*. Shimura's character was a kind of good/bad guy—a very twisted characterization. And every time I saw Mr. Shimura I'd say, "Hey, Uncle! Act like you did in *The Life of a Horse-Trader!*" He loved it every time I mentioned that film.[17]

At Shintoho, Shimura played the major supporting part in *Nusumareta koi* [*Stolen Love*] (1951), directed and adapted from Kyotaro Namiki's story by Kon Ichikawa., before the constantly busy actor's first release of the new year, *Araki Mataemon: Kettô kagiya no tsuji* [*Vendetta of Samurai*] (1952), had him following Kazuo Mori's direction from an original Kurosawa screenplay. Mifune was the top-billed star once more (as Mataemon, a great swordsman who helps a younger man exact revenge), followed by Yuriko Hamada and character actors who became Kurosawa regulars: Shimura, Minoru Chiaki, Daisuke Katô and Bokuzen Hidari. Produced at Daiei and distributed by Toho, *Vendetta of Samurai* was intended to keep Mifune busy while Shimura prepared for Kurosawa's next directorial project, *Ikiru*, but both actors worked together extensively in this film and two more before the busy character specialist tackled the most difficult role of his career.

Bakurô ichidai [*The Life of a Horse Trader*] (1951; directed by Keigo Kimura): Toshirô Mifune and Machiko Kyô featured on Daiei's original Japanese B2 poster.

5. Rashômon *(1950)* 61

Vendetta is exactly what the Kurosawa-Mori collaboration became, with the film's entire 82-minute running time devoted to the revenge story, which opens (rather heavy-handedly) in John Ford style, as a narrator relates the exaggerated legend of Mataemon (shot in the ballet-like manner of a Japanese silent) before shifting to the more believable, "true" tale set in 1634. Though Mataemon personally likes Jinzaemon "Jinza" Kawai (Shimura, with his hair dyed black and shaved back to the *chonmage*), his code demands that he kill him in the end. "Being samurai is an unfortunate business," Jinza tells him as they share saké and a turn at archery, a comment that haunts him during the denouement, just before he walks off to turn himself over to the lord of the Todo Clan.

Vendetta, shot almost entirely in medium close-ups by Mori and cinematographer Kazuo Yamazaki, suffers from the lack of a stronger directorial hand; and though well-acted, the mediocre screenplay, dashed off by Kurosawa between bona fide masterpieces, did little more than put some food on the table for its makers.

Newly creative writer-director Ishirô Honda cast Shimura in the top supporting role, billed just below leads Hajimi Izu and Yôko Fugita, in Toho's

Bakurô ichidai [*The Life of a Horse-Trader*] (1951; directed by Keigo Kimura): In this atmospheric drama set on the northern Japanese island of Hokkaido, Rokutaro Kosaka (Takashi Shimura) bets against the proud Yonetaro Katayama in a sumo wrestling match.

Nangoku no hada [*The Skin of the South*] (1952), before Shimura reteamed with Mifune (and billed behind Yoshiko [Shirley] Yamaguchi) in *Muteki* [*Foghorn*] (1952), adapted from the Jirô Osaragi novel by the author, director Sengichi Taniguchi and Toshio Yasumi.

Shimura is credited (by several references) as playing an "Old Man" in Kenji Mizoguchi's stunning masterpiece *Saikaku ichidai onna* [*The Life of Oharu*] (1952), the heartbreaking story of an imperial court lady-in-waiting (Tinoyu Tanaka) whose taboo dalliance with a man of lower station (Toshirô Mifune) leads her down a path ending in prostitution, but he does not conspicuously appear in the finished film. At the Venice Film Festival that year, Mizoguchi won the International Award for this powerful and elegantly shot film (with a great deal of fluid and subjective camera by Yoshimi Hirano). If Shimura did work in this film for Mizoguchi, 16 years after being included in the director's *Osaka Elegy*, his scenes were cut.

Action master Hiroshi Inagaki cast Toshirô Mifune in the lead role of soldier and spy Sasa Hayatenosuke in *Sengoku burai* [*Sword for Hire*] (1952), again teaming him with Yoshiko [Shirley] Yamaguchi and Shimura in top supporting parts. Adapted from the novel by its author, Yasushi Inoue, Inagaki and Kurosawa, the film marked the third foray into the historical genre for the latter.

Shimura appears in a rather minor supporting role in another *jidai-geki* film, Daiei's *Bijo to touzoku* [*Beauty and the Thieves*] (1952), costarring the impressive cast of Machiko Kyô, Masayuki Mori, Rentarô Mikuni and Minoru Chiaki. Directed by Keigo Kimura, the film benefits from a tight screenplay co-written by Ryûnosuke Akutagawa (based on his novel) and Kimura.

6

Ikiru (1952)

> Watanabe's example is a tiny ray of enlightenment in an otherwise forbidding world. *Ikiru* is one of the supreme statements of Kurosawa's heroic cinema.—Stephen Prince, *The Warrior's Camera: The Cinema of Akira Kurosawa*[1]
>
> Shimura always says that he is no good. That is certainly not the truth. He grows with every film. If he did *Drunken Angel* with the power he has now something very different would have happened. Shimura is the kind of man who is always making things difficult for himself and he strains too much.—Akira Kurosawa[2]

When Akira Kurosawa accepted the Golden Lion for *Rashômon* at the Venice Film Festival, he said, "Everyone likes to receive prizes and so I'm happy ... but I'd be even happier if I were getting it for having shown something of contemporary Japan."[3] On another occasion, he admitted, "Sometimes I think of my own death. I think of ceasing to be ... and it is from these thoughts that *Ikiru* came."[4]

The concept for *Ikiru* [which translates as "To Live"] (1952) was an original one by Kurosawa and Shinobu Hashimoto, both of whom wrote the screenplay with Hideo Oguni, a master of story construction and character development. Oguni later recalled that Kurosawa envisioned Leo Tolstoy's 1886 novella *The Death of Ivan Ilyich* as inspiration. Hashimoto wrote the first draft of the script, in which government official Kanji Watanabe (Shimura) dies of terminal stomach cancer at the end. Oguni, who didn't care for it, altered the structure, adding the brilliant idea of having the character pass away at midpoint: an idea that endeared the elder writer to Kurosawa, who worked with him all the way through *Ran* (1985), after which Oguni died at age 92. Hashimoto explained,

> Kurosawa ... never compromised. Most importantly, he concentrated on writing good scripts. He directed actors, of course, but he also directed the writers, and that

was the hardest thing for him, because they're stubborn, difficult people to direct. For him, the script was the foundation of a film.[5]

The initial title of the screenplay, "The Life of Kanji Watanabe," was changed by Kurosawa to *Ikiru*, although Hashimoto considered this pretentious.[6]

Preproduction, including rehearsals, for *Ikiru* began in mid-January 1952, with Shimura supported by the ubiquitous Minoru Chiaki, Bokuzen Hidari and young Miki Odagiri (as Toyo, the girl who befriends Watanabe). Shooting started on March 14, with a break for summer vacation in early June, but everyone was back at work by the 17th of the month. Kurosawa wrapped the six-month shoot in mid-September.

Odagiri (1930–2006), then a first-year student at the Tokyo theater company Haiyu-za, had already acted in films as a child. She had accompanied a friend to the *Ikiru* audition, but Kurosawa awarded her the role after seeing more than 200 women. The director ordered her never to observe the other actors playing their scenes prior to acting with them. She remembered,

> In the scene where I told Mr. Shimura, "It would be great if you were to do such a thing," I was able to act well because his performance was incredible. When he said, "Teach me! How can I be like you?" I was really frightened by his powerful playing.
>
> When the film opened, I went to a theater in Hibuya to see it. There I saw the completed *Ikiru* for the first time. The surprise and impression it made upon me was indescribable.... *Ikiru* is my life's treasure.[7]

Odagiri's Toyo, young and vibrant, infuses some life into Watanabe after she quits her city hall job to work at a toy shop. While out on the town one evening, she reveals the nicknames she has awarded to each of her bureaucratic coworkers. When pressed, she tells Watanabe he is "The Mummy." (One wonders if Kurosawa had seen Universal's 1932 fantasy classic starring Boris Karloff and directed by expressionist cinematographer extraordinaire Karl Freund.)

Late in life, Kurosawa said,

> Even in tragic stories, there should be some happy parts, so that the audience will have a certain emotional experience. That's what a movie should do. The world of a movie transcends reality. There are some filmmakers who show dreary or ugly things just as they are. I think that's wrong. If you express these things in a cinematic way— it's fine if you show them as elements of cinematic beauty. But actually killing a horse in a movie for the sake of being realistic isn't going to move people. But currently there's a trend in that direction. If a scene calls for a person to die, do they really have to be killed? That's what I often say to people.[8]

Initially, Masako Shimura was concerned about whether her husband could draw large enough audiences when cast in a title role. But his brilliant, arguably unequalled, multifaceted performance was achieved in part because he was *living* the part. Shimura explained,

6. Ikiru (1952)

Prior to shooting, I was having trouble with my cecum [the pouch at the beginning of the large intestine]. I told Mr. Kurosawa about it, and he said, "Why don't you have surgery to correct it?" He didn't want me to be hospitalized during shooting. I had surgery and lost weight.... He told me not to gain the weight back, but the more I was told, the more weight I gained. I took steam baths to try and keep the weight off. I was playing a man who had cancer over a six-month period, and my own stomach wasn't feeling well, either. After we finished shooting, I went to see a doctor. He said I was suffering from an inflammation and had to take medicine for quite a while....

There's a scene in a coffee shop, where I tell [Toyo] that I didn't have long to live. She suggested that I do what I want to do, and I said, "It is too late." I spent a week thinking about that one line...

I knew of "Song of the Gondola" because it had been popular when I was young but didn't learn it until I met with Mr. Fumio Hayasaka and one of his musicians. Mr. Kurosawa instructed me, "Sing the song as if you are a stranger in a world where no one believes you exist." Of course, I hadn't a clue how to sing like that. I thought it a rather difficult request. I made three kinds of recordings and had him listen to them. He picked one out of those three."[9]

Shimura also remembered, "Before the shoot began, Kurosawa-san brought this—I think it was a magazine or something. Anyway, he showed me a picture of a monkey and said, 'This is him.'"[10] At the end of the shoot, Shimura's stomach difficulties, complicated by his unswerving dedication to the role, had transformed into an actual ulcer. (Others who worked on the film recalled his operation as being for appendicitis.)

Again, Kurosawa recalled that Shimura, who didn't usually imbibe alcohol in his private life, was always very effective at playing a drunk on-screen. Odagiri added,

> Mr. Kurosawa helped me, of course, but it was Mr. Shimura's acting, what he brought to our scenes, that helped me a lot. It felt so real that it didn't seem like he was acting. The way Mr. Shimura's face changed expression was making me uncomfortable, so I actually wanted to get away from there, just as my character felt in the scene.
> Mr. Shimura's dedication to his work just astonished me. I thought, "That's what a real actor is."[11]

Script supervisor Teruyo Nogami said that Shimura

> put a lot of effort into experimenting with his voice. That's why his character has this weak voice. In the strip-joint scene, he uses a strange voice. He came up with it out of the blue. He worked very hard to bring different textures to his voice. Mr. Shimura was striving hard to find the right quality for his character's voice.[12]

In fact, Shimura studied an actual cancer patient's voice to obtain the raspy falsetto that he used. For the "Gondola Song" sequence, Kurosawa requested that he appropriate an "otherworldly" sound. When Watanabe is drunk, at the strip joint and in the street afterward, Shimura recalls Kurosawa's photo of the monkey by using a simian-like voice.

Shimura added,

> As you know, working in one of Mr. Kurosawa's films means you can't be sloppy. He is a perfectionist. There were times when I gave my all, squeezed out all I could, until I had given everything and had nothing left to give. Then, finally, Mr. Kurosawa would be satisfied.
> I think underlying Mr. Kurosawa's films there was always a sense of humanism. All of his films had this sense of humanism as their foundation, and the films and stories developed out of that.[13]

At the premiere, when his name first appeared on-screen, Masako Shimura could not stop crying.

Stuart Galbraith provides a fine summation of the film:

> The effect *Ikiru* can have on audiences is almost religious. Is it possible to watch *Ikiru* and not have it change you? Or is its effect much the same as Watanabe's impact on his co-workers? What does it mean to truly be alive? The film, ultimately, is about Watanabe's search for some kind of affirmation in his last months. He regains his self by finally taking responsibility for the needs of others.
> From the very beginning of the picture, Kurosawa explores the difference between existing and living. In short, [Watanabe] exists, but little else. He has forgotten how to live, how precious it is to be alive, and how existence is meaningless unless one uses it for something better than himself...
> *Ikiru* is really two films: one about a man in search of validation and the other a biting indictment of the impersonal bureaucracy that serves as its background...
> Thematically, these two halves come together in the final 30 minutes of the picture, during Watanabe's wake, where we see the illusion, and in flashbacks the reality. By having Watanabe die in the middle of the film, rather than at its end, both serve each other. Through the irony of the politicians and bureaucrats taking credit for Watanabe's work, Kurosawa exposes what is true and what is false. As in so much of his other work, Kurosawa is exploring the differences between perception and reality.[14]

Of the actor's work, Galbraith adds, "Shimura's performance is in turn empathetic, endearing, heartbreaking, inspiring. Never before or since has an actor so eloquently expressed the terrible dread and loneliness that accompany terminal illness."[15] Indeed, Shimura's nonverbal prowess, always remaining in character while acting with, not only his infinitely expressive face, but his entire body, including only his back in many scenes, is staggering. His habit of taking steam baths obviously affected his appearance, as Watanabe noticeably becomes thinner over the course of the flashback scenes.

No coverage of *Ikiru* would be complete without comments from arguably the greatest of all Japanese film historians, Donald Richie:

> Kurosawa's classic statement on personal responsibility and the ills of the world is found in *Ikiru*, a film about the largest possible social issue—death. A petty official (Takashi Shimura) learns he is dying. For the first time he realizes that he has accomplished nothing, has never enjoyed anything. He spends his savings on a spree, but this brings him only grief, as he indicates in the celebrated scene where he sings a song of his youth.

6. Ikiru (1952)

Life is so short,
Fall in love dear maiden,
While your hair is still black,
Before your heart stops—
For there will be no more tomorrows.
The dying man returns to the office and uses all of his strength to bring to realization a petition (for months on his desk and on the desks of others), a request for a children's park. In the face of official antagonism he pushes the project through...

Despite Kurosawa's criticisms—and the film, in part, is as sweeping an indictment of bureaucracy as has been filmed—*Ikiru* is not an angry movie. We are not so concerned with a bad society as we are with a good man, and Kurosawa makes us realize this by framing the latter half of the film with his wake. The tone is frankly elegiac, but there is little *mono no aware*. Instead, there is the statement that we are what we do. Others may be in states of self-delusion but the dead man has escaped. He created himself.

The way in which he is seen to do so is through a cinematic style which is as controlled as it is inventive, as incisive as it is subjective. All directors create their films in just this way—showing what they have learned both from life and from other pictures—but Kurosawa displays this with extraordinary panache. It is this genius for amalgamation which one may find typical of Kurosawa and very Japanese of him.[16]

Richie describes the flashback sequence involving Watanabe and his son, Mitsuo (Nobuo Kaneko), who is going off to war, as "magnificent ... one of the most compelling in modern cinema."[17] He calls Watanabe's night on the town

a tour de force of cinema which brings the immediate immediately before us....
Enormous use is made of mirrors, reflecting surfaces, the shiny tops of automobiles, prisms—all those things which reflect (distort) reality.... There is also constant motion: flash-pans, elevators, elaborate dollies, all enforcing the idea of the living, the actual. There is even a literary reference: at the beginning, the writer fancifully refers to himself as Mephistopheles ("but a good one, who won't ask to be paid") and then notices at his feet a black dog—familiar to the devil himself—thus enforcing the Faustian element that others have noticed in this film. And indeed it would be possible to build a like morality around the night-town scenes, each as one of the deadly sins ... each as one of the stations of the cross along Watanabe's way.... All are welded into a sequence of the most superb brilliance, filled with visual irony, and musical ridicule.[18]

Ikiru was an enormous critical and commercial smash in Japan, winning the 1953 Best Picture award from *Kinema Junpô*, 1953 Best Picture, Best Screenplay and Best Sound Recording honors from the Mainichi Film Concours, and a special Minister of Education Award, but this success was devastated for Kurosawa by the death of his beloved mother, Shima, aged 82, less than a month after the premiere. On June 19, 1954, about 20 months after it was released in Japan, the film won the Silver Bear prize at the fourth Berlin International Film Festival.

In May 1956, the film finally was screened in the U.S., under the unfortunate title *Doomed*, at UCLA, where the Royce Hall was standing-room only for a Sunday night showing. It took another four years before *Ikiru* received an official U.S. release, when most journalists, including popular reviewer Bosley Crowther of *The New York Times* (in the words of Stuart Galbraith) "simply didn't get it."[19] Crowther, however, did note that Shimura "measures up ... with the top film actors anywhere."[20]

Some reviewers thought the wake sequence, which includes several flashbacks of Watanabe's refusal to give up on his last-ditch effort to build the children's playground, overlong; but, in fact, its length is necessary. Kurosawa's tracking shot of Shimura, singing on the swing as the snow slowly falls, would have made an indelibly powerful final image, but at that point, there is still a little story to be told. The city hall bureaucrats (including Minoru Chiaki in another superb performance for Kurosawa), initially unwilling to speak up about the deputy mayor's cover-up of Watanabe's responsibility for pushing through the park proposal, and then, under the influence of saké, pretending they would perform similar, nearly impossible feats of individual endeavor, need to be seen crawling back into their institutional holes. Only one of Watanabe's coworkers, who consistently supports him throughout the wake, cares enough to show his contempt at the others' subsequent apathy and then visit the playground teaming with happy children. (One unforgettable flashback involves Watanabe, now with nothing to lose, standing up to a yakuza boss who wants to build a red-light district in the area proposed for the park.)

The film's reputation did eventually grow in the U.S. In February 1960, Arthur Knight, in *The Saturday Review*, wrote that *Ikiru*

> is to this viewer Kurosawa's most notable achievement in a long line of masterpieces.... Inevitably today Kurosawa must be compared to Ingmar Bergman. Not that there is any particular spiritual affinity between the mystic Swede and the hyperrealistic Japanese. (Indeed, as far as film *style* goes, Kurosawa rather strikingly resembles our own John Huston.) But Bergman has emerged as the symbol of the individualist director, the complete filmmaker who originates a story that is meaningful to him and illuminates it through his own special handling of the camera and soundtrack. Kurosawa is no less personal, even to the extent of building, like Bergman, his own stock company of actors—notably Takashi Shimura and Toshirô Mifune.... Kurosawa, Bergman, India's Satyajit Ray, de Sica, Fellini—the list is not a long one, of these men who create films to their own vision of life and art.[21]

The February 27, 1960, issue of *Harrison's Reports* (with an obvious tinge of intolerance) reported,

> Detracting from its general acceptance at America's box offices are its seriousness, its hard-on-the-ears Japanese dialogue, especially the voice of the protagonist; and its subject: cancer. Sophisticated filmgoers will flock to see this one, however. Takashi Shimura is ideal as the afflicted official and Miki Odagiri is excellent as the young

6. Ikiru (1952)

woman who quits her desk job to stuff toys. The photography is exceptional. Especially outstanding are the scenes of the bureaucrat's night on the town...[22]

Time magazine, which originally published a negative review in February 1960, changed its tune on September 21, 1962, praising *Ikiru* as "one of the cinema's great rare works of art ... a rugged realism, an exquisite humanity, a sense of what is sublime in being human."[23]

In England, Shimura received a Best Foreign Actor nomination from the British Film and Television Awards (BAFTA) when the film was released there in 1960. This individual award was only part of the BAFTA from 1952 to 1967. Pitted against Zbigniew Cybulski (*Ashes and Diamonds* [1958], Andrzej Wadja; Poland), Jean Desailly (*Maigret Sets a Trap* [1958], Jean Delannoy; France), Jean Gabin (*Maigret Sets a Trap*), Jack Lemmon (*Some Like It Hot* [1959], Billy Wilder; U.S.) and James Stewart (*Anatomy of a Murder* [1959]; Otto Preminger, U.S.), Shimura lost out to the very popular Lemmon in Wilder's wildly comic drag-fest also starring Marilyn Monroe and Tony Curtis.

Some Like It Hot also won the BAFTA for "Best Film from Any Source," three U.S. Golden Globes (Best Motion Picture—Comedy, Best Actor [Lemmon] and Best Actress [Monroe]) and one U.S. Academy Award (Best Costume Design, Black and White [Orry-Kelly]). There were also five more Oscar nominations for *Some Like It Hot*, with a recent release and publicity campaign that made a win against Lemmon for Shimura (in a downbeat role from eight years earlier) obviously impossible.

During his last years, teacher and popular film critic Roger Ebert referred to *Ikiru* as Kurosawa's best film. And in 2015, fellow Chicago author and film scholar Raymond Benson, when reviewing the Criterion Collection's Blu-ray edition of the film, called Shimura "Japan's greatest unsung thespian," superior to Toshirô Mifune, with "a longer, deeper and more varied career ... a genius."[24] In his 2015 review, professor Jeremy Carr praises Shimura's "astonishing range over the course of 200-plus films" and, in *Ikiru*, "Every emotion and every thought ... transparently written on his aged and weary face."[25]

In 2012, the British Film Institute's Alex Cox, in an essay praising Shimura's "embodi[ment of] all the traditional virtues of restraint in Japanese cinema," wrote,

> Watanabe is the most complex of Kurosawa's triumphant individualists—the only bureaucrat in his division ever to have stepped out of line or achieved anything—and it's hard to imagine any [other] actor giving a more restrained or sympathetic performance.[26]

And in the foreword of this book, Dr. Paul M. Jensen points out, "It is hard to imagine another actor matching Shimura's achievement in this film. The range and consistency of his performance in *Ikiru* would be enough to enshrine Shimura in film history."

In the final analysis, Donald Richie's selection of the words of Richard Brown is superlative:

> *Ikiru* is a cinematic expression of modern existentialist thought. It consists of a restrained affirmation within the context of a giant negation. What is says in starkly lucid terms is that "life" is meaningless when everything is said and done; at the same time one man's life can acquire meaning when he undertakes to perform some task which to *him* is meaningful. What everyone else thinks about that man's life is utterly beside the point, even ludicrous. The meaning of his life is what he commits the meaning of his life to be. There is nothing else.[27]

Perhaps the best line in the screenplay given to Shimura occurs when, in one of the flashbacks, Watanabe tells his assistant helping him to push through the park proposal, "I can't afford to hate people. I haven't got the time."

More character roles were in store for Shimura following his difficult and taxing star performance in *Ikiru*. In director Yasuki Chiba's *Oka wa hanazakari* (1952), scripted from the novel by its author, Yojirô Ishizaka, and Toshirô Ide, he played Kenkichi Kimura, backing up Michiyo Kogure, Ryô Ikebe, Yôko Sugi, Sô Yamamura and Ken Uehara.

In *Minato e kita otoko* [*The Man Who Came to Port*] (1952), another Ishirô Honda directorial project, though he shared the script duties, based on the story "Dance of the Stormy Waves," with Shinzo Kajino and Masashiga Narasawa this time, Mifune and Shimura again enjoyed the top costarring roles, respectively. Eiji Tsuburaya, the man with whom Honda would soon make science-fiction film history, served as special effects supervisor on the film.

For *Fuun senryobune*, Shimura's final film of 1952, he again worked with Hiroshi Inagaki, who directed and co-wrote the screenplay with Shintaro Mimura. Yoshiko [Shirley] Yamaguchi also appears in a major supporting role.

Yamaguchi and Mifune play the leads in *Hoyo* [*The Last Embrace*] (1953), directed by Masahiro Makino and scripted

Takashi Shimura (early 1950s).

by Motosada Nishiki, Haruo Umeda and Toshio Yasumi for Toho. In this contrived doppelgänger story in which Mifune plays two roles (forester Shinkichi and near-lookalike gangster Hayakawa), Shimura receives third billing as Watanabe (alias Nabesan), one of the patrons in a bar where Yamaguchi as the heroine, Yukiko Nogami, seeks refuge during a mountain blizzard.

Senkichi Taniguchi again directed Shimura in *Yoru no awari* (1953), scripted by Ryûzô Kikushima and photographed by Kazuo Yamada. Costars Ryô Ikebe (as Shinji Kizaki) and Mariko Okada (as Miyo) are well-supported by Shimura (billed third as Yoshikawa) and another Kurosawa favorite, Kamatari Fujiwara.

Shimura, billed seventh, portrays an Imperial Japanese Army colonel in the Ishirô Honda (director) and Eiji Tsuburaya (director of special effects) collaboration *Taiheiyo no washi* [*Eagle of the Pacific*] (1953), focusing on Admiral Isoroku Yamamato (Denjirô Ôkôchi) and his initial misgivings about going to war against the United States, where he previously had attended Harvard University (1919–21) and served as a Naval attaché in Washington, D.C. He became fluent in English, traveled throughout the nation, studying U.S. culture and business, and greatly enjoyed touring the Naval War College in Newport, Rhode Island. The film, with a screenplay by Shinobu Hashimoto, was Toho's revival of the war genre following the U.S. Occupation, and includes a dramatization of Yamamoto's objection to the attack on Pearl Harbor (he also had opposed the invasion of China) and his overruling by Emperor Hirohito.

On April 18, 1943, during an inspection tour through the South Pacific, the admiral died when his plane was shot down by U.S. aircraft over the island of Bougainville. The supporting cast of *Eagle of the Pacific* also includes Ichirô Sugai (as Admiral Koshiro Oikawa), Takamaru Sasaki (as the Combined Fleet Chief of Staff) and Toshirô Mifune (billed 13th as First Lieutenant Tomanaga). Shimura and Mifune's appearances are brief, and the overall unrealistic atmosphere created by Honda is not alleviated by producer Tomoyuki Tanaka's tightfisted use of wartime stock footage during the battle sequences.

7

Shichinin no Samurai (1954)

> By protecting others, you save yourself. There is nothing
> heroic selfishly grabbing for glory.—Kambei Shimada (Takashi
> Shimura) in Shichinin no Samurai [Seven Samurai]

In 1954, Japan, possessing 7,000 theaters, produced more feature films than any other nation on the globe. The innovative idea of 16th-century farmers hiring samurai to protect their village from savage bandits was conceived by the same trio that crafted *Ikiru*, Akira Kurosawa, Shinobu Hashimoto and Hideo Oguni, while intentionally sequestered at the Minaguchi-en in Atami, forbidding phone calls and (excepting Toshirô Mifune) visitors, for 45 days. Prior to the initiation of this project, *chanbara* depictions of samurai, set during the Tokugawa period, had been highly stylized and romanticized, featuring kabuki-influenced, choreographed fight scenes.

As he had done for *Ikiru*, Oguni criticized and shaped the storyline, while Kurosawa and Hashimoto wrote the screenplay for *Shichinin no Samurai [Seven Samurai]*. Earlier script ideas by Kurosawa, focusing on a day in the life of a lone samurai, and then five great swordsmen's battles, had been rejected by Hashimoto. Searching amid all the research material gathered by Hashimoto, producer Sôjirô Motoki and assistant producer Hiroshi Nezu, Kurosawa ultimately discovered a short historical account of an incident in which farmers hired a samurai to defend them.

The *Sengoku Jidai* (1467–1568) proved a perfect period for the new film: The early 1500s were a time of rampant civil war, succeeded by a time when bandits roamed the countryside, preying on peasants. Many of these criminals were *ronin*, forced to become bandits because the samurai code forbade them from performing menial labor. The *Sengoku* period finally ended when the warlord Oda Nobunaga began the reunification of Japan, which eventually developed into the rigid Tokugawa shogunate. In time, "many samurai became teachers or doctors, a fact reflected in Kurosawa's own family."[1]

Seven Samurai, unlike most *jidai-geki*, which merely use period as a back-

7. Shichinin no Samurai (1954)   73

drop for the actions of familiar two-dimensional characters, is a richly detailed film deeply rooted in history. Donald Richie points out,

> One can ... trace the development of the "real" Japanese period films from the early pictures of Daisuke Ito and Mansaka Itami, through Sadao Yamanaka and Kenji Mizoguchi, to Masaki Kobayashi, and Kurosawa himself. These latter are "real" because they do not stop at simple historical reconstruction, inhabited by stock figures (which is true of costume pictures all over the world), but insist upon the validity of the past, and the continuing meaning of the historical.... The ordinary *jidai-geki* has no more vital connection to the past than does any Steve Reeves epic.[2]

The completed *Seven Samurai* screenplay opens with bandits thundering up to a village, and then deciding to reserve their attack for when the barley is harvested. The farmers, conferring with Old Man Gisaku (Kokuten Kôdô), the village elder, decide to hire samurai to defend their homes and fields. This is no easy proposition, but their spirits are lifted when they observe the mysterious Kambei Shimada (Shimura), based on real-life samurai Isanomukami Koizumi, have his head shaved and dress like a Buddhist monk so he can save a baby from the clutches of a murderous thief and kidnapper. (Here Kurosawa, in a rare use of slow motion, masterfully controls time as the would-be child killer springs from the hut to his death in the mud, from the point of view of the startled crowd.)

The removal of Kambei's *chonmage* is proof of his true priority: aiding others rather than maintaining this symbol of samurai prestige. Stephen Prince notes, "Kambei becomes heroic, it would seem, only through the dissolution of his class identity." By accepting the farmers' offer of rice for his protection, "Kambei's decision is an exceptional act of conscience far beyond the capability of the ordinary samurai."[3]

Each of the seven samurai has his own distinct personality. Prior to working with Hashimoto, Kurosawa had prepared detailed notes on the characters' physical and psychological traits, some of which came to be used as actual dialogue in the completed script. This complexity added a new layer to a depiction of samurai individuals while remaining true to the historical period in which they lived. Ultimately, the superb, high classical score by longtime Kurosawa associate Fumio Hayasaka, who labored from his sickbed under harsh requirements from the director, would include themes for the samurai, the bandits, the peasants, and seven separate character motifs underlining the images characteristically featuring the perfect amount of dialogue.

Pre-production on the project lasted three months. By the time the film was finished, it ran 207 minutes, but the dynamic storytelling rings true to *Los Angeles Times* film critic Kenneth Turan's statement that "more than any other kind of cinema, long films done right have the potential to envelop you completely in character and experience."[4] Writing in 2010, Turan eloquently continues,

> Unlike the often self-indulgent long films of today's Hollywood auteurs, *Seven Samurai* uses its length creatively, not merely to burnish egos. Confident of his powers and not in any kind of rush, Kurosawa proceeds like a master chef…. And this particular story … seems to demand just that kind of treatment.
>
> *Seven Samurai* unrolls naturally and pleasurably, like a beautiful scroll … luxuriating in its elongation—it takes an entire hour just for the basic task of choosing the titular seven. Rather than try to ignore time, the film emphasizes its passage, underlining key scenes with a quiet but insistent drumbeat that could almost be a clock ticking off the inexorable seconds.[5]

In the top-billed role, Mifune is Kikuchiyo, "the Would-be Samurai," fashioned by Kurosawa as a "buffoon who serves as a bridge between the farmers and the samurai."[6] Mifune, allowed great scope to craft the character's behavior, recalled the strenuous physical challenges required:

> I didn't learn to ride for this film—I'd started picking it up earlier, just outside of a place called Seijo where there was a stable. I talked Shimura, Chiaki, and some others into coming along with me. Shimura kept saying that he was too old for horseback riding and wanted to quit, but I tricked him into thinking that it was good for his health. In the end, we all became pretty good horsemen.[7]

For the "most important role," Shimura had been cast from the outset.[8] His abilities as a chameleonic performer are never more evident in the differences between his characterizations in *Ikiru* and *Seven Samurai*. His clearly enunciated yet natural voice for Kambei is completely unlike that of the dying, muttering Kanji Watanabe. Where he uses his humped-over, simian-like body language to connote debility in *Ikiru*, his Kambei is middle-aged yet virile, speeding toward the enemy in a threatening posture with his samurai sword, chasing the enemy away from his even more formidable comrades.

The influence of Sergei Eisenstein, especially the Soviet film pioneer's *Bronenosets Potemkin [Battleship Potemkin]* (1925), is apparent in Kurosawa's mighty use of montage in *Seven Samurai* and many of his other films. In her analysis of the 1954 epic, Joan Mellen writes,

"*Seven Samurai* embodies Eisenstein's classic formulation of montage…. Kurosawa accomplishes for his society what Eisenstein achieved for his own."[9] She adds, "Nowhere does any later director better fulfil the promise of Eisenstein's innovations in montage than Kurosawa does in this film."[10]

During the shoot, which ran from May 27, 1953, to March 18, 1954, Kurosawa's tendency to feature nature's elements often backfired on cast and crew, as fire, earth and water all seemingly conspired against them. Spread over nearly 10 months, 148 days were required to film, and the Toho executives wrangled in their seats as Kurosawa multiplied the schedule by four. At one point, production funding ran out, and the director was threatened with the possibility of being replaced by Toho "hack" Kunio Watanabe.

Kurosawa's meticulous notes extended to all 101 performers (including

7. Shichinin no Samurai (1954) 75

many non-actors) who played the villagers, providing each of them with enough character background so that "anyone could be central in a particular shot."[11] This detail gives the film a unique continuity, with even minor characters having individual identities as they engage in everyday activities, creating a realistic milieu connecting every shot as the major players command attention. During an early sequence in which the farmers begin to search for samurai who may be persuaded to help them, one of the passing warriors is played by Tatsuya Nakadai in his first screen appearance.

Burning down a mill and fortress proved extremely problematic, and the famous six-minute sequence of a ferocious battle in the rain also proved dangerous. During the night before the battle began to be filmed, a heavy snow fell. This all had to be melted, and a vast bog of mud throughout the village set was the result. For two months, January and February 1954 (Japan's coldest part of the year), Kurosawa proved "the world's toughest taskmaster" as he mercilessly drove the cast and crew, all of whom risked contracting frostbite.[12]

Kurosawa used a groundbreaking three-camera set-up to capture action takes that could not be reshot. The performers and crew would first do several rehearsal test shots before an actual take was attempted. The mud kept freezing, but everyone was forced to soldier on nonetheless. Mellen notes, "That special effects were not available to him accentuates the power of his filmmaking."[13] Kurosawa's catalog of visual techniques that potently manipulate space also include cross-cutting (affirming the influence of Eisenstein) and a frequent use of deep focus (by means of the telephoto lens). Stephen Prince explains,

> The cinematic energy of the film, energy and movement, communicate the social ties among characters, denying their isolation. In this respect, *Seven Samurai* is a reversal and refutation of the example of *Ikiru*, arguing against the possibility of solitary, existential heroics. There is simply no space in this film where a hero can stand as an individual. That space is constantly being transformed into social terms where isolation and individualism are regardless as pathologies.[14]

Mellen also precisely assesses the role played by Shimura:

> Kambei embodies samurai modesty, expressed not in words but in gesture. He rubs his shaved head throughout the film at moments when praise would embarrass.... Self-effacement is a redeeming and vanishing trait, evocative of samurai integrity for Kurosawa. Kambei expresses it in full measure.[15]

Introducing the dynamic samurai film to the Western world, *Seven Samurai*, then the longest and most expensive feature made in Japan, was not only an enormous hit in its home country (where, as the third-ranked domestic release, it reestablished the genre) but across the globe. Released two years after the end of the U.S. Occupation, and not subjected to previous postwar censorship, it depicts decent men of honor, bravery, loyalty and a high moral code supporting the Japanese need for a reidentification with their own unique culture. (Unfortunately, the film was cut by 50 minutes for its initial release in the U.S., where it wasn't shown uncut until 1983.)

Kurosawa also includes good doses of social criticism, aimed not only at the farmers and bandits, but also the samurai, particularly when their faults are pointed out by Kikuchiyo. Since many *ronin* turned to banditry, farmers often made little distinction between samurai and outlaws. When the samurai first arrive at the village, no one comes out to greet them. Though the farmers want to be saved from the bandits, they also are concerned that their women are in danger from their protectors. "All they know is fear," announces Kambei.

Finally, Kikuchiyo officially becomes one of the seven by using a ruse (hammering the village alarm) to bring the farmers out of hiding. Hearing Shimura raise his voice as Kambei calms them down is a startling moment. After Kikuchiyo points out the faults of the farmers *and* the samurai, Kambei realizes that he really is a farmer's son. A moment of humor is interjected when the line "Why the hell are you always screaming?" is offered by Heihachi, "the Cheerful Samurai" (Minoru Chiaki, in another excellent performance for Kurosawa), unfortunately the first of the seven to die.

Historian and film critic Philip Kemp notes,

> Kurosawa ... makes no bones about this dark side of the samurai tradition. And there's an implicit side-glance at more recent history, the period preceding and during the Second World War, when Japan's militaristic government perpetrated a still crueler distortion of the samurai code of Bushido.... But as a counterbalance, Kurosawa offers the selfless and altruistic figure of Kambei ... who personifies the Bushido code at its purest and most Zen-based.[16]

"There's a tough battle ahead," Kambei admits as he recruits his fellow samurai, "leading to neither money nor rank. Will you join us?" His depth of character is well represented in many scenes: one in which he demonstrates his fatherly qualities while enjoying holding a small child with a runny nose; and another when he awakens the sleeping Kikuchiyo, who is slacking while on guard duty. Grasping the huge sword of the slumbering farmer-turned-samurai, Kambei and his friend, Gorobei Katayama, "the Wise Warrior" (Yoshio Inaba), kick him awake. "You're lucky it was us," he declares. "If we were bandits, you'd be headless right now."

At another point, Kambei informs, "When you think you're safe is precisely when you're most vulnerable." As the first half of the film ends, Kambei is forced to deal with a small group of rebellious farmers led by Mosuke (Yoshio Kosugi), concerned about three outlying houses intended to be sacrificed to save the other 20. Stephen Prince notes,

> The samurai tell the villagers they must move in pairs, not as individuals, for safety. Mosuke ... breaks this circular movement with a tangential flight. After forcing him back in line, Kambei tells the others that everyone must act together as a group and

7. Shichinin no Samurai (1954)

that those who think only of themselves will destroy themselves and all others. Kambei's words are extraordinary, given the ethical context established by Kurosawa's contemporary-life films, where the hero is expected, as a matter of course, to define an individual path. But here the material of the past discloses no spaces in which the individual can move, no spaces not already inhabited by groups and their demands. The self must be an interactionist self or cease to exist.[17]

After Kambei orders the chastened "rebels" not to place their own desires above the welfare of the group, he warns, "Anyone caught doing that..." Shimura adds a powerful grace note to the scene by nimbly sliding the entire length of his katana blade between his fingers, illustrating Kurosawa's axiom of not using dialogue where purely visual cinema will suffice.

One of the film's most moving, hair-raising shots involves the planting by Kukichiyo of the deceased Heihachi's flag, representing the seven members of the group and the village, at the top of one of the farmers' shacks. Another poignant scene, involving the burning of the Old Man in his beloved mill, features Kikuchiyo rescuing an infant, breaking down in tears, admitting, "This baby is me! This is exactly what happened to me." Kambei then demonstrates his physicality by picking up the baby's speared mother and carrying her over his right shoulder.

Kambei's prowess as a military commander is demonstrated throughout, as he prepares a map of the village, the fortifications they build, and circles that represent each of the 40 bandits. This mathematical precision is epitomized during the battles, as he paints an "X" over each of circles until all the bandits are killed. He also proves his ability with a bow and arrow when he effortlessly dispatches two of the mounted marauders. (Shigeru Endo and Ienori Kaneko served as advisors for Shimura, who is an impressive, flawless archer, and Inaba.) Joan Mellen adds,

> As he trains the villagers, Kambei expresses what Kurosawa defines as the most important of samurai ideals: that of selflessness. For the village to survive, three of the houses must be sacrificed, flooded to deprive the bandits of egress through the open fields. At dead center of the film is the culminating scene in which Kambei (and Kurosawa, for whom he stands) offers the essential wisdom of the film. That Kambei speaks for Kurosawa, that his character offers facets of the director's own, becomes apparent...
> In Kambei, in his modesty, the concealment of his own doubts and the fortitude with which he refuses to admit the possibility of the bandits emerging victorious, is a figure remarkably similar to the man Kurosawa has described as himself: "I am not a special person. I am not especially strong. I am not especially gifted. I simply do not like to show my weakness, and I hate to lose, so I am a person who tried hard. That's all there is to me."[18]

Kurosawa's attention to strict detail can be witnessed in his obvious shooting of Shimura's scenes in sequence, as Kambei's hair can be seen growing back as the film progresses. Kambei can be viewed as the ultimate samurai who has never won. At the film's end, before the camera tilts up to the sword-graced graves of his four fallen comrades (a more stunning echo of a shot involving Victor McLaglen at the close of John Ford's *The Lost Patrol* [1934]), he states to Shichirôji, "Kambei's Old Friend" (Daisuke Katô), "In the end, we've lost this battle, too. The victory belongs to those peasants—not to us."

Kurosawa's trademark use of rain to create an environment of crisis begins immediately following a romantic scene involving Katsushirô Okamoto, "Kambei's Young Disciple" (Isao Kimura) and Shino (Keiko Tsushima), who has been masquerading as a boy at the insistence of her abusive father, Manzô (Kamatari Fujiwara). The scenes featuring young Katsushirô, who has yearned to be a samurai, among a field of Chrysanthemums lend a stunning texture to Asakazu Nakai's magnificent black-and-white cinematography. These images prove quite a contrast to the filthy battle in the mud, concluding with the sad deaths of the intrepid, humble Kyûzo, "the Master Swordsman" (Seiji Miyaguchi) and Kukichiyo, the final shot showing the latter's bare buttocks as he lies face down in the filth. (This position was suggested to Kurosawa by Mifune, who also struts around bare-assed in several other scenes; Kurosawa refined it so Kukichiyo dies in a pose like that of the kidnapper he earlier watches die at the hands of Kambei.)

All four *ronin* who die are felled by musket fire, a sign of the changing military technology and strategy that would supplant the samurai. The rain represents Kurosawa's attitude that "Everybody had to fight for himself. They all melted into the same class."[19]

In the U.S., *Seven Samurai* attracted many filmgoers who identified with the parallels between the Japanese *jidai-geki* genre and their own long history of reading Western stories and seeing them depicted on-screen for more than a half-century. Here, the influence of John Ford (who, like Kurosawa, studied painting) also can be seen, particularly in the depiction of action consistently rendered in superb compositions, while not being overly stylized, as well as the emphasis on male bonding. His use of violence is not gratuitous nor glorified, but necessary to the story and quite nasty, dirty and realistic. Kurosawa's use of the moving camera *for a reason*, to create kinetic action is also quite "Fordian." The first battle scene doesn't occur until nearly halfway through the film, but its 207-minute running time seems to end *sooner*, due to the mesmeric world created by Kurosawa and his associates.

Keisuke Kinoshita's masterpiece *Nijûshi no hitomi* [*Twenty-Four Eyes*] also was released in 1954, winning best picture prizes from *Kinema Junpô*, the Blue Ribbon Awards and the Mainichi Film Concours. Teinosuke Kinugasa's *Jigokumon* [*Gate of Hell*] (1953) shot in Eastmancolor, won the top honor at Cannes and two U.S. Academy Awards in 1954.

In 1980, when asked his opinion of John Sturges' popular, more simplistic Hollywood remake of *Seven Samurai*, *The Magnificent Seven* (1960), starring

7. Shichinin no Samurai (1954) 79

Yul Brynner and Steve McQueen, Kurosawa replied, "Gunslingers are not samurai."[20] Stephen Prince explains,

[T]he Americanization of Kurosawa's film entailed a domestication of style, the substitution of dialogue and pedestrian camerawork for its essentially visual qualities, the vitality of its cutting and imagery. What is always impressive about *Seven Samurai* is its boundless energy, the speed of its tracking shots, the aggressiveness of its wipe-linked transitions, and the dazzling use of multicamera perspective. The film is an exercise in kinesis, in the realization of a cinema defined as pure motion.[21]

Joan Mellen concludes,

Seven Samurai is a classic epic transcending even the limitations of that genre. On the surface an action drama of men in conflict, it rises to the level of tragedy. The heroism and debilitating flaws of a class are dramatized through the emotions of seven individuals. The apotheosis of its conclusion, as in all tragic works, comes complete with a final, cleansing catharsis.[22]

Stuart Galbraith notes,

On the surface, the film may appear just a great adventure, but the questions *Seven Samurai* poses its audience are far more complex than its simple premise suggests. It is a subtler and more mature work than the more overtly intellectual *Rashômon*.

Most important, *Seven Samurai* is universal. Like Mizoguchi did in his period films, Kurosawa creates a world so believably real and lived in that it becomes contemporary, one so emotionally true that its time and place become our time, our place. Using everything that he has learned as a filmmaker, Kurosawa's greatest success with the film is that he puts us in the thick of it.... [He] has ... so carefully defined and established the characters that once the bandits arrive, the audience never forgets the function of the various samurai and farmers, nor does it have difficulty distinguishing one from another, their relationship to one another, or their psychological state at any given moment. Compare *Seven Samurai* to the average Hollywood war movie, where it is often impossible to know where characters are, or even at times to tell one soldier from the next.[23]

For the documentary *Akira Kurosawa: It Is Wonderful to Create*, Hashimoto later commented,

I feel like the first era in cinema has ended, and I think it ended with Kurosawa's death. Now as the second era begins, it seems to me that it'll be some time before it begins to blossom. I am talking about quality movies—not only in Japan but all over the world. Kurosawa's death may have had that great an impact. Although 100 years have passed since the birth of cinema, there was no one like Kurosawa before him, and there's no one that comes close to Kurosawa after him, either.[24]

Like Kanji Watanabe in *Ikiru*, Kambei Shimada would remain one of Shimura's greatest achievements as an actor. As always, he accepted a steady flow of supporting roles following a major starring performance in a Kurosawa masterpiece. In Masahiro Makino's *Jirochô sangokushi: kaitô-ichi no abarenbô* [*Jetocho Sangokushi VIII: The Toughest Guy on the Seaside Street*]

Miniature action figure of Takashi Shimura's Kambei Shimada, the intrepid, selfless leader, in Akira Kurosawa's *Seven Samurai* (1954).

(1954), released by Toho, he joined Seizaburô Kawazu, Kyôko Aoyama and Hiroshi Koizumi. Back with Daiei leading lady Machiko Kyô (as Setsuko Takashima), he played Komazo in director Koji Shima's romantic drama *Asakusa no yoru* (1954), co-scripted by Shima and Matsutarô Kawaguchi (from his novel). In the drama *Kimi shinitamo koto nakare* (1954), directed

7. Shichinin no Samurai (1954)

by Seiji Maruyama, who also co-wrote the screenplay with Shin'ichiro Nakamura, he again aptly plays third fiddle, to leads Ryô Ikebe and Yôko Sugi.

At Toho, Shimura supported Keiko Kishi, Kyôko Kagawa, Ken Uehara and Kuniko Miyake in Noriyuki Yata's dramatic screenplay, *Haha no hatsukoi* [*Mother's First Love*] (1954), directed by Seiji Hisamatsu. The studio then billed him third in the action adventure *Shin kurama tengu daiichi wa: Tengu shutsugen* (1954), directed by Nobuo Aoyagi from a screenplay by Takeo Matsuura. Backing leads Akio Kobori and Mariko Okada, he again appeared with fellow Kurosawa "stock company member" Kamatari Fugiwara, so memorable as Farmer Manzô in *Seven Samurai*.

8

Gojira (1954)

Born just nine years after the A-bomb was dropped on Hiroshima and Nagasaki, and made by a director who had witnessed the destruction firsthand, Godzilla wasn't just Japan's answer to *King Kong* but a grave warning about the dangers of the nuclear arms race, and a sobering reflection on the devastation of Hiroshima and Nagasaki. It took 50 years, but *Gojira* can now be recognized not as a vintage science fiction movie, but an epic postwar tragedy.—Steve Ryfle, "Godzilla's Footprint"[1]

Toho's producer Tomoyuki Tanaka was quickly rising in the ranks. At the outset of making *Gojira*, he revealed, "The theme of the film, from the beginning, was the terror of the bomb. Mankind had created the bomb, and now nature was going to take revenge on mankind."[2]

Following a disastrous political experience in Jakarta, Tanaka was returning to Tokyo, empty-handed. The proposed Toho film "*Eiko-no Kagi-ni*" ["In the Shadow of Glory"], which had been cancelled, was intended to depict the aftermath of the Japanese occupation of Indonesia (March 1942–September 1945), then the Dutch East Indies (which resulted in great hardship for the native people, particularly on Java and Sumatra, but also set the stage for their subsequent independence from the Netherlands).

Now the producer glanced out the train window at the sea, a view that sparked an idea for a giant monster movie. When he pitched it to Toho production head Iwao Mori, Tanaka was aware of the Cold War science-fiction genre in the United States, which had and would include giant beasts, both from nature and humanity, created by radiation.

Although Tanaka had no real story concept at this point, he knew that his film would be quite different and innovative. Steve Ryfle writes so aptly, "On the surface, *Gojira* might look like just another Cold War–era monster film, but its haunting mood and imagery, evoking memories of the atomic bombings and the Tokyo fire raids that killed hundreds of thousands, place this film in a category all by itself."[3]

Recent radioactive and political fallout had resulted from a powerful U.S. H-bomb test in the Marshall Islands (located 2,391 miles, as the crow flies, south of Japan, but 6,228 miles from the U.S. West Coast). This fallout had exposed more than 800 fishing vessels (most notably the *Fukuryu Maru* [*Fortunate Dragon*]) and displaced hundreds of people, a fact that fueled the film project, first titled *"Kaitei Niman-ri Karakita Daikaiju"* ["The Giant Monster from 20,000 Leagues Under the Sea"].

Tanaka's choice to direct *Gojira* (the origin of the name has never been verified) was former cinematographer and assistant to Kurosawa, Ishirô Honda, a close lifelong friend of the master filmmaker. The son of a Buddhist priest, Honda had begun working in the Japanese film industry during the early 1930s, but his career became sidetracked by the Imperial Army when he was drafted in 1936, and he spent the next eight years as an infantryman in occupied China. Following the Japanese surrender, he had to forage through cremated Hiroshima, and the images troubled him thereafter. His idea was, not to use "Godzilla" as a metaphor for the atomic bomb, but an actual physical version of it. He said, "If Godzilla had been a dinosaur or some other animal, he would have been killed by just one cannonball. But if he were equal to an atomic bomb, we wouldn't know what to do. So, I took the characteristics of an atomic bomb and applied them to Godzilla."[4]

To create the special effects, particularly the gigantic behemoth himself, Tanaka and Honda relied on the very imaginative cinematographer Eiji Tsuburaya, who was allowed a budget and shooting schedule amounting to tiny fractions of what his Hollywood contemporaries were given for their monster movies. The kind of stop-motion animation developed by Willis O'Brien for *The Lost World* (1925) and *King Kong* (1933), and further perfected by his apprentice, Ray Harryhausen, whose recent work on *The Beast from 20,000 Fathoms* (1953), based on a story by Ray Bradbury, proved an incredible smash, were absolutely forbidden at Toho, so Tsuburaya had to devise his own innovative method of creating convincing miniature sets (in $1/25$- and $1/33$-scale) as well as a monster suit that could be worn by an actor, thus creating what came to be known as "suit-mation." The entire process would be planned and controlled by a meticulous storyboarding technique.

Several concepts and drawings, including that of a giant octopus pitched by original treatment writer Shigeru Kayama, came and went, but Tsuburaya eventually decided that Godzilla should be a dinosaur-type animal combining the features of a Tyrannosaurus Rex (Cretaceous carnivore, 66–68 million years ago), Iguanodon (Cretaceous herbivore, 125–126 million years ago) and Stegosaurus (Jurassic herbivore, 150–155 million years ago) with the skin texture of an alligator (Oligocene carnivore, originating 37 million years ago). Obviously the nearly indestructible Godzilla would have earned his superiority from quite an amalgam of reptilian ancestry spanning more than 125 million years.

The first suit, constructed of a bamboo-and-wire frame coated with latex, weighed over 200 pounds and featured tiny holes in the neck for the two stunt actors to "see and breathe," but this immovable tomb nearly killed the poor devils. Actor Haruo Nakajima remembered, "I and Katsumi Tezuka tried on the suit in front of Mr. Honda, Mr. Tsuburaya, Mr. Tanaka and members of the staff, but the suit was so heavy, so stiff. I thought, 'This is going to be impossible.'"[5]

A second suit, coated with plastic, still weighed 220 pounds, but was a bit more flexible, due to wires attached to various areas, especially the tail, and was deemed film-worthy. However, the actors still suffered from heat exhaustion, blackouts, various injuries and considerable weight loss.

Steve Ryfle notes,

With even just a glimmer of understanding about the filmmakers' intentions and the political climate of the time, *Gojira* emerges as one of the great antinuclear films, comparable in its power and pacifism (if not in its approach to the subject) as Stanley Kubrick's *Dr. Strangelove* (1964) or Stanley Kramer's *On the Beach* (1959). This is not an angry film and not, as some have suggested, a simplistic indictment of the United States for the events of August 1945. It is a powerful condemnation of the atomic age and a plea for nuclear powers to end the march toward oblivion.[6]

All the experimentation with creating a believable monster suit and the other special effects racked up a final cost of 100-million yen ($1.5 million U.S.), roughly three times the amount of most Japanese feature films. Incredibly, *Gojira*, completed in 62 days, cost Toho even more than *Seven Samurai* to become the most expensive film ever made in Japan, but it also topped the great box-office success of Kurosawa's epic. These two films, along with Teinosuke Kinugasa's *Gate of Hell*, starring Machiko Kyô, earned the studio great profits and international respect that year.

Playing the specially billed role of the expert paleontologist Dr. Kyohei Yamane-hakase with complete earnestness, Shimura brings a degree of melancholia to the film not unlike the quality he demonstrates in *Ikiru*. Yamane, who first identifies the giant beast's radioactive footprint, is also the first to see him as the Stegosaurus-like spines appear over the ridge of a mountain. When Godzilla's head comes into view, he is fascinated as the others run in terror down the hillside. Yamane immediately identifies the monster as emanating from the Jurassic Period.

Soon the conflict between a political cover up and revealing the scientific truth emerges. After Yamane (who originally was scripted as a more sinister character) explains the facts during a televised press conference, he is shown at home with his daughter, Emiko (Momoko Kochi) and her boyfriend, Hideto Ogata (Akira Takarada), who sides with those who want to destroy Godzilla. Yamane sits in his study, very despondent over the situation, with Shimura bringing just the right touch of subtle emotion to the film. (Later, during Godzilla's nuclear rampage through Tokyo, Honda includes a brief, very moving scene from another point of view: that of a mother cradling her two children as they hide in an outdoor corner of a partially destroyed building.)

Honda's direction is impressive throughout. *Gojira*, the first Japanese film to be made from storyboards, features the expert moving camera of director of photography Masao Tamai (who shot 16 films for Mikio Naruse, including three featuring Shimura), often fluid tracking shots emphasizing key dramatic moments, and the lighting in the black-and-white format greatly enhances the remarkable realism created by the miniatures and suit created by Tsuburaya and crew. A flashback scene, involving Daisuke Serizawa-hakase (Akihiko Hirata) and the invention of his doomsday weapon, the "oxygen destroyer," is also a highlight. The pace of the film is exciting, made even more stirring by Akira Ifukube's musical score.

At the film's end, Yamane stands on the boat that had lowered the suicidal Serizawa into the depths of the sea to kill Godzilla with the oxygen destroyer, the *only* way to accomplish the feat. While summing up the potential effects of nuclear testing creating another such creature, this remarkable humanitarian film includes Yamane rather sadly concluding, "I can't believe Godzilla is the only survivor of its species." Soon Toho would prove that the monster was not; and on April 25, 1955, the quickly cranked-out *Gojira no gyakushû* [*Godzilla Raids Again*] was released in Japan.

Godzilla, King of the Monsters! (Embassy Pictures, 1956)

Released on April 27, 1956, the U.S. version of *Godzilla, King of the Monsters!* became just another giant monster movie, with 18 minutes shorn from the Japanese original. Most of the scenes from *Gojira* are edited into a completely different order with new sequences shot in just five days by veteran editor and B-film director Terry Morse (who spent a majority of his career at Warner Bros.), told in flashback and held together by the voiceover narration of Raymond Burr, who had spent much of his previous career very effectively playing heavies. Now Burr was just one year from smash television stardom as a heroic attorney on the long-running *Perry Mason* series, inspired by the stories of Erle Stanley Gardner, some of which had been filmed during the 1930s by Warner Bros. with Warren William in the lead role.

Totally emasculated of its nuclear weapons and testing material (save for one brief mention of "the H-bomb" by Dr. Yamane in a severely truncated version of the conference scene), *Godzilla* depicts the enormous dinosaur, not as an atomic juggernaut, but as the return of a monster the Odo Islanders have previously seen and to whom they have offered female sacrifices. Burr's substantial screen time, a portion of which features him interacting with Japanese actors, some speaking their native language (requiring an interpreter) and others English, gives the film some degree of realism; but other sequences feature unconvincing editing proving that Burr's character, Steve Martin, foreign correspondent for United World News, is not there at all. His *film noir*-like narration does substitute for the unconvincing dubbing (the first time this was done for a U.S. version of a non–English-language film), but it also renders Shimura's character a mere cinematic cipher. In some scenes, Shimura speaks Japanese; in others, he is dubbed by voice actor Sammee Tong. (Without seeing any of the footage, a total of three performers, including the American, ethnically Chinese character actor James Hong, did all the dubbing work.)

The climactic scene is very disappointing compared to the Japanese original, with only a close-up of Yamane substituted for his speech about nuclear testing and the fact that humankind probably has not seen the last Godzilla. The close-up shots of Burr are so badly inserted into this scene on the ship that viewers should instantly know they were shot on a Hollywood soundstage and then awkwardly inserted into the sequence. *Godzilla, King of the Monsters!* (1956) is not a bad horror/science-fiction film, much like its 1950s U.S. brethren, such as *The Beast from 20,000 Fathoms* and *Them!* (1954), but a truly sad travesty of *Gojira* with all the sociopolitical content removed.

Again, Steve Ryfle makes a salient point:

> Perhaps director Ishirô Honda was a bit naïve. In 1991, two years before his death, Honda said that he had always hoped that Godzilla could help bring an end to nuclear testing and arms proliferation and lamented that he had failed. Indeed, the situation has grown ever more dangerous since Godzilla's first rampage. More and more countries are going nuclear, and terrorists covet the bomb. A monster movie can't change the world, but Godzilla is a lasting reminder of the Pandora's Box opened in August 1945. Born in the hellfire of a mushroom cloud, the King of the Monsters warned man to shut that box and extinguish the fire. If we can't look beyond the rubber suits and the flaming Tokyos and stare the monster in the eye before it's too late, perhaps we're all a bit naïve.[7]

Despite its artistic shortcomings, *Godzilla, King of the Monsters!* was approved by Toho. An enormous hit in the U.S., the film continued to rack up box-office receipts throughout the world, leading to a continuing series of English-dubbed Japanese *kaijû tokusatsu eiga* [giant monster special-effects films] that became subjected to more rushed hatchet jobs over the years.

8. Gojira *(1954)* 87

Following *Gojira*, Toho released *Shin kurama yengu daini wa: Azumadera no ketto* (1954), the second installment in director Nubuo Aoyagi's continuing action-adventure epic, featuring Shimura in the lead supporting role. Back at Daiei, he again supported Machiko Kyô in *Bazoku geisha* (1954), adapted by Kôji Shima from the Shohei Hino novel.

Masahiro Makino again directed him, in the independent film *Mekura neko* (1955), made and distributed by producer Kazuo Takimura's own company, in which he was billed behind leads Hiroshi Koizumi and Jun Tazaki.

Gojira no gyakushû [*Godzilla Raids Again*] (1955)

On April 24, 1955, Toho released *Godzilla Raids Again* (aka *Counterattack of Godzilla*), a follow-up film to *Gojira*, that opens with two sea flyers, Shoichi Tsukioka (Hiroshi Koizumi) and Koji Kobayashi (Minoru Chiaki), scouting tuna for an Osaka cannery. After Kobayashi is forced to crash land on the uninhabited island of Iwato, Tsukioka locates him. During the rescue, the men see the head of Godzilla appear behind a rock formation. Soon there is not only one monster, but two!

Shimura reprises his role of Dr. Kyohei Yamane-hakase, but in only a single scene, as he describes the newly discovered creature, a spiny-backed ankylosaur called "Anguirus," explaining that, like its predecessor, this "second" Godzilla cannot be destroyed, because of the loss of the "oxygen destroyer" and death of Dr. Serizawa. Shimura, even in a cameo appearance, brings his trademark hangdog mood to this very dark, black-and-white film that at times resembles a Hollywood *film noir*. His Yamane again is believable, a man to be trusted.

By contrast, Shimura's frequent colleague Minoru Chiaki portrays a major supporting character involved in a bittersweet romantic subplot. Continually seeking, but never finding, "his bride," Kobayashi finally lets his emotions get the best of him: During a reconnaissance flight to locate Godzilla, who has destroyed most of Osaka while killing Anguirus (called "The Battle of the Century," during which Osaka Castle is leveled), he angrily decides to dive bomb the monster, crashing into an ice-covered mountain. He dies when the airplane explodes, but also gives his fellow flyers, actual bombers including Tsukioka, the idea to wage a full-scale assault on the ice mountains, which then cause an avalanche that suffocates the beast.

Directed by Motoyoshi Oda, *Godzilla Raids Again* is a fine companion to the first *Gojira* film, with Eiji Tsubaraya's special effects again blending well with on-location footage during the numerous montage sequences. Seiichi Endo's fluid camerawork and Kazuji Taira's sharp editing help create a flowing pace during all 81 minutes.

The film wasn't released in the U.S. until 1959, and then in a dubbed version combining only the special effects footage from *Godzilla Raids Again* with new live-action sequences directed by Hugo Grimaldi and a spate of painfully obvious stock footage from various sources. Retitled *Gigantis, the Fire Monster*, it was booked on a double feature with the ridiculous Hollywood Z-feature *Teenagers from Outer Space*! In 1989, at the insistence of Toho, the English version was released on home video under the original title. In 2007, as the company had done with *Gojira* the previous year, Sony BMG Entertainment released an officially licensed Toho double feature DVD package, including both the Japanese and English-dubbed editions of *Godzilla Raids Again* in the original widescreen aspect ratio.

Following his reprise of Dr. Yamane, Shimura's Toho character roles continued, as he worked for writer-director Shirô Toyoda in *Love Never Fails* [aka *The Grass Whistle*] (1955), but he was cast in the lead role of baseball coach Tatsuro Shimamura in *Otoko arite* [*No Time for Tears*] (1955), in which the second-billed Toshirô Mifune portrays Mitsuo Yano, the only real star player on their struggling team, the Sparrows. When a new pitcher, Hiroshi Onishi (Yû Fujiki), is hired, trouble brews when he becomes romantically involved with Shimamura's daughter, Michiko (Mariko Okada). After tragedy strikes the Shimamura family, Tatsuro attempts to mask his agony by pitching a winning game himself. Directed by Seiji Maruyama from a script by Kurosawa's frequent collaborator Ryûzô Kikushima, who won the Best Screenplay prize at the 1956 Blue Ribbon Awards, *No Time for Tears* is less a sports action picture than a very effective, powerful family drama featuring another standout performance by Shimura.

9

Ikimono no Kiroku (1955)

This film is again about a social problem. And one of the reasons that I like social problems is simply that by using them I can make a question better understandable to my audience. Indeed, there is something topical about films. If they don't have topicality, they are not meaningful. Films are not for museums.—Akira Kurosawa, on *Ikimono no Kiroku* [*Record of a Living Being*] (1955)[1]

Shimura spent 1955 playing a host of character roles for a lineup of excellent directors: Senkichi Taniguchi, in *Sanjusan go sha otonashi* [*No Response from Car 33*]; Toshio Sugie, in *Shin kurama tengu daisanbu*; Kajirô Yamamoto, in *Muttsuri Umon torimonocho*; Nobuo Aoyagi, in *Geisha Konatsu: Hitori neru yo no Konatsu* [*The Tears of Geisha Konatsu*]; and Shigeaki Hidaka, in *Sugata naki mokugekisha*. Inevitably, Akira Kurosawa again came calling for his favorite actor.

Ikimono no Kiroku [Record of a Living Being, aka I Live in Fear] (1955)

A decade after the end of World War II, at the height of the Cold War, the possibility of total nuclear annihilation was very real. Especially fearful were the Japanese, whose nation was the only one ever to be blasted by atomic bombs, killing 300,000 people. Kurosawa, not about to let this subject go unaddressed, again collaborated with Shinobu Hashimoto and Hideo Oguni, on the screenplay for *Record of a Living Being*.

Inspired by the previous year's incident involving fishermen contaminated by radioactive fallout from U.S. hydrogen bomb tests in the Marshall Islands (the last of which was 2,400 times more powerful than the Hiroshima detonation), the fact that Great Britain and the U.S.S.R. also were exploding similar devices in the Pacific Ocean, and the resulting peace and anti-nuclear movements in Japan, *Record of a Living Being* depicts the increasing paranoia of elderly businessman Kiichi Nakajima (Toshirô Mifune, only 35), whose terror of an atomic attack becomes so severe that he considers moving his entire family, including mistresses and several children, to a farm in Brazil. His apathetic family attempts to have him committed as mentally deficient, and after he burns down his own factory, he goes insane, believing to be living on another planet. Kurosawa's "usual suspects" in the cast include Shimura (billed second as Dr. Harada, a dentist nominated by his professional association to the Domestic Relations Department of the Tokyo Family Center), Minoru Chiaki (in another memorable performance, as Nakajima's selfish son, Jirô) and the ubiquitous Bokuzen Hidari (as a landowner).

After the Occupation forces left Japan in 1952, several films about "the bomb" were produced. *Genbauku no ko* [*Children of Hiroshima*] (1952), directed by Kaneto Shindô, and *Hiroshima* (1952), directed by Hideo Sekigawa, were followed by Toho's *Gojira*, which indirectly depicts the *Fukuryu Maru* fishing boat incident, as well as the rampaging prehistoric monster unleashed by a nuclear explosion.

Kurosawa began production on *Record of a Living Being* on May 19, 1955. Following the grueling experience of making *Seven Samurai*, he had waited 11 months to undertake another project. Rehearsals, primarily with small groups interacting with Mifune, began on June 20, but were suspended when Kurosawa was hospitalized in early July. Shooting commenced in Harada's dental office on August 1, 1955, when Shimura became the first major actor to step before the cameras. (As soon as he appears, very fit and trim, his weight loss between Kurosawa projects is apparent.)

As in *Seven Samurai*, Kurosawa used a three-camera setup to shoot certain scenes. When he was accused by Toho executives of "wasting raw footage," he replied,

> I didn't start using a number of cameras at once merely to become more efficient myself ... just because we get results this way doesn't mean we're going to shoot every scene this way. Actually, I'd like never again to use more than one camera. I get exhausted. Even if we only do a single shot a day, we get so tired doing it we can hardly go on.
>
> To say that three cameras wastes three times the amount of raw film is amateur talk. Actually—and this surprised even me—there is no waste at all ... the amount of retakes necessarily drops tremendously. If we had shot *Record* in the standard way, I think we'd have used another 30- or 40-thousand feet. Actually, we did not exceed our allowance very much.[2]

The production went smoothly, with all the shooting nearly wrapped in six weeks, until the great, long-suffering Fumio Hayasaka, just 41, died of tuberculosis on October 15. Like John Ford, who dearly loved the members of his "stock company," Kurosawa received this news with a heavy heart, and the composer's death likewise affected every member of the cast and crew. In fact, the idea for *Record of a Living Being* had been suggested by Hayasaka during one of Kurosawa's visits. The composer's assistant, Masaru Satô, then was chosen to score the film, and thereafter worked steadily with Kurosawa. Mike Inoue, the director's nephew, commenting on Hayasaka, recalled, "After his death, we were forbidden to mention his name around Kurosawa."[3]

Kurosawa said of his work with Hashimoto and Oguni, "After it was all over and the last judgment was upon us, we could stand up and account for our past lives by saying proudly, 'We made *Ikimonu no Kiroku*.'"[4]

Kurosawa opens *Record of a Living Being* with powerful moving-camera shots of Tokyo residents amidst the blazing summer, before Shimura appears as Dr. Harada in his dental clinic. Donald Richie notes, "the endless brilliance of the sun, the windless confines of a sweat-drenched city, suggests fear and the apocalypse."[5]

Shimura, again playing an earnest, intelligent, soft-spoken character, gives his thoughtful and sympathetic view of Nakajima's apparently extreme desire to escape from possible nuclear devastation:

> I agree that he has gone too far but, after all, we're as worried as he is ... only we don't build underground shelters nor try to go to Brazil. But that doesn't mean that we can fail to understand how he feels. It is, after all, a feeling that all of us Japanese know all too well. He has gone too far, perhaps, but we cannot for that reason take his fears any the less seriously.

Later his Dr. Harada reads the book *Ashes of Death* and tells his glib son, who asks if he, too, wants to head for Brazil, "Well, here. Read it. If birds and animals could read, they would get out of Japan as fast as they could."

Nakajima, attempting to drive his family to Brazil, burns down his factory, puts his employees out of work, and is sent to a mental hospital. Harada pays a visit, admitting (in Shimura's masterful cadence), "You see, I feel ... well, a sort of guilt. I feel that perhaps the court gave the wrong decision."

Nakajima's psychiatrist replies, "This patient, I must admit, does disturb me. It is the first time this has happened—he is the first one to make me feel that maybe we are not sane. And so I wonder, who is mad: he or me?"

Speaking to Harada, Nakajima, now thinking he is on a different planet, looks at the sun and says, "Oh, my god. It is burning. The earth is burning. Burning. At last, finally, it is burning."

Harada is then seen walking down a ramp and out of the hospital, allowing Shimura to "bookend" the film. Nakajima's young mistress also is seen, walking up the ramp, the only member of the family arriving to visit her father. Stephen Prince has analyzed the importance of Shimura's characterization in the film:

Harada is a character who formalizes the query of the narrative and who acts as a foil for Nakajima, prompting his self-revelation...[T]he narrative focus, and the problem that fascinates Harada, will be on learning the causes of Nakajima's extraordinary fear, which neither his family nor anyone else can grasp.... Harada thus articulates the enigmatic code of the narrative, and the political analysis of the film will turn on a credible account of Nakajima's "illness."[6]

Of Nakajima, Prince concludes,

> Record of a Living Being is a meditation on what sustains the Kurosawa hero and on the consequences of its withdrawal. Blocked from physical action, Nakajima retreats into the insanity of which his family has long accused him.... Immobilized forever by the power of the state, from which he had attempted to escape, Nakajima in despair resorts to the only kind of movement left him, psychic movement. In his mind, he travels to a secure place on some other planet, where he hallucinates the burning of the Earth, which Kurosawa simulates by filming directly into the sun. As in many of his other films, dreams become a substitute for the lost possibilities of real political action.[7]

Japanese audiences, not wanting to see a film directly addressing the atomic bomb, primarily stayed away when *Record of a Living Being* was released on November 22, 1955. At the box office, it lost more money than any other Kurosawa picture. In 1956, it was exhibited outside Japan at Cannes, where Kurosawa was nominated for the *Palme d'or*, and at the 1961 Berlin Film Festival. Following a 1963 screening in the United States, Brandon Films withheld its release as *I Live in Fear* until January 25, 1967. In Japan, the film received good notices, placing fourth on *Kinema Junpô*'s Ten-Best List, and highly impressing director Nagisa Oshima.

In the U.S., where audiences were seeing a topical film made 12 years earlier, Mifune was praised, but Kurosawa's direction was faulted as slow-moving. The only critic touting the film, Judith Crist, called it "an absorbing drama, distinguished ... by the Japanese director's skill in treating a superhuman subject in throbbingly humanistic terms."[8]

Record of a Living Being surpasses Kurosawa's original intent that it be a "social document." Mifune's Nakajima, who has been compared to Shakespeare's King Lear (which later would inspire the director's *Ran* [1985]), is a character that saves the film from being a "museum piece" and making it "live." Donald Richie concludes,

> Kurosawa ... is directing our attention to a curious but central problem. If it is our insecurity which has created our civilization, how very ironic, then, that we—so highly civilized—should be (presumably) on the verge of destroying what we have created by succumbing to the very fear (for the cause of war is fear) which originally was responsible for the now threatened civilization. The father might well then be afraid, might with even more reason be afraid of that fear itself, since he is every one of us.
>
> In this way, the picture becomes very "social" indeed—social in the deepest possible sense. And the "record" becomes the case-history of history, and the "living being" becomes myself.[9]

9. Ikimono no Kiroku (1955)

Director Hiroshi Inagaki had begun his epic "Samurai Trilogy" with *Miyamoto Musashi* [*Samurai I: Musashi Miyamoto*] in 1954. Starring Toshirô Mifune as Musashi ("Takezo"), the film was the second Toho production shot in color and the first using the Eastmancolor process. This 93-minute historical adventure based on Eiji Yoshikawa's novel *Musashi* opens in 1600 at the Battle of Sekigahara, where Takezo and his companion, Matahachi (Rentarô Mikuni), are among those defeated by Tokugawa Ieyasu. Following its Japanese release on September 26, 1954, *Samurai I* won the U.S. Best Foreign Language Academy Award the following year.

Inagaki and cinematographer Jun Yasumoto consistently use fluid camera movement and color for striking narrative as well as aesthetic purposes. Much of *Samurai I* features various shades of green before the "wild" Takezo, thanks to the tough love of Buddhist priest Takuan Osho (Kurôemon Onoe), becomes the disciplined, learned and maturing samurai Musashi Miyamoto, when the color scheme is brilliantly transformed into a much wider palette. Here, these artists deliver a film that would not work nearly as well in the black-and-white format. The musical score, by Ikuma Dan, is also impressive, blending traditional Japanese elements with a lush style reminiscent of earlier epic Hollywood compositions by Austro-Hungarians Max Steiner and Miklos Rozsa (and perhaps influencing subsequent work for Kurosawa by Masaru Satô and the "spaghetti" Western motifs of Italy's Ennio Morricone).

On July 12, 1955, Inagaki's second installment of the trilogy, *Zoku Miyamoto Musashi: Ichijôji no kettô* [*Samurai II: Duel at Ichijoji Temple*], also shot in Eastmancolor, was released in Japan by Toho. (The film would not be released in the United States until October 1967.) This 103-minute episode, featuring more character development, continues with Musashi's (Mifune) efforts to become a "respectable samurai," highlighted by a furious fight between the lone warrior and a large group of treacherous enemies near the site of Ichijôji Temple in Kyoto.

Inagaki asked Shimura to play Sado Nadaoka, a court official who recognizes Miyamoto's triumphant victory over Kojirô Sasaki (Kôji Tsuruta), who desired to become a fencing master under Lord Yagyu in Edo, in the 105-minute conclusion of the Eastmancolor trilogy, *Miyamoto Musashi kanketsuhen: kettô Ganrûjima* [*Samurai III: Duel at Ganryu Island*], in 1955. This third installment features the work of cinematographer Kazuo Yamada.

For good measure, the director also cast Minoru Chiaki as Sasuke the boatman. The duel ends the film with the three Kurosawa favorites (Mifune, Shimura and Chiaki) all in the scene together.

"Mr. Miyamoto, that was splendid," compliments Nadaoka.

"He was the best fencer I will ever encounter," Miyamoto replies before sailing back toward his long-suffering love, Otsu (Kaoru Yachigusa).

In his essay for the Criterion Collection release, Bruce Eder notes,

Samurai III: Duel at Ganryu Island is the last and the best of Hiroshi Inagaki's Trilogy. In contrast to the earlier, more action-oriented *Samurai I* and *II*, this final section shows its hero, Musashi, struggling with questions as much as proponents, the most important of which is: what makes a warrior worthy of renown—strength and the number of victories, or something more?

Hiroshi Inagaki and Toshirô Mifune succeed admirably in capturing the different facets of this man and presenting them in a context accessible to modern viewers. The embellishments to history derived from the novel and screenplay are merely a variation on a maxim put forth by Inagaki's western colleague John Ford: "When the legend becomes fact, print the legend."[10]

Hideko Takamine (left) and Sachiko Hidari (early 1950s) Unique original publicity portrait signed (in Japanese calligraphy and Roman letters) by the prolific and widely admired actress Hideko Takamine (1924–2010), who costars in six films with Takashi Shimura (*San-jaku sagohei* [*Sagohei the Three-footer*, 1944], directed by Tamizo Ishida; *Kita no san-nin* [*Three People of the North*, 1945], directed by Kiyoshi Saeki; *Asu o tsukuru hitobito* [*Those Who Make Tomorrow*, 1946], codirected by Akira Kurosawa; *Aru yo no tonosama* [*Lord for a Night*, 1946], directed by Teinosuke Kinogasa; *Shin, Heike monogatari: Yoshinaka o meguru sannin no onna* [*Three Women Around Yoshinaka*, 1956], directed by Teinosuke Kinugasa; *Arakure* [*Untamed Woman*, 1957], directed by Mikio Naruse), and actress-director Sachiko Hidari (1930–2001), who appeared in films directed by Kon Ichikawa, Tadashi Imai and Yûzo Kawashima, all of whom worked with Shimura.

9. Ikimono no Kiroku *(1955)* 95

Musashi's actual battle with Kojirô Sasake occurred on Ganryû Island, off the coast of Bizen Province, on April 13, 1612. Released in Japan on January 3, 1956, *Samurai III* finally was screened in the United States during November 1967.

Shimura next worked in a major supporting role at Daiei with Machiko Kyô, Fujiko Yamamato and Hideko Takamine for director Teinosuke Kinugasa in *Shin, Heike monogatari: Yoshinaka o meguru sannin no onna* [*Three Women Around Yoshinaka*] (1956), based on the novel by Eiji Yoshikawa. He then returned to Toho to play Hanako's Father in Ishirô Honda's *Wakai ki* [*Young Tree*] (1956) and Nagasawa in director Hideo Suzuki's *Kyatsu o nigasuna* [*I Saw the Killer*] (1956).

Shimura received fifth billing as gang boss Tsunejiro Furuya in director Kajirô Yamamoto's minor Toho yakuza drama *Ankokugai* [*The Underworld*] (1956), shot in moody, *noir*-ish black and white by Seiichi Endo. Toshirô Mifune also appears, but in the small supporting role of a police officer who eventually helps round up Furuya, whose recent stay in a hospital has led to his involvement with a young intern, Yumiko (Kyôko Aoyama), wounded right-hand man, Takao Shoji (top-billed Kôji Tsuruta), who had tried to rape the woman, and the rest of the gang. Yumiko is then free to rejoin her fiancé (Hiroshi Koizumi), and Shoji is confined to a police hospital.

Shimura's performance provides the highpoints of this uneven film. Stuart Galbraith points out, "Shimura, so much the leader in *Seven Samurai*, so wise as the scientist in *Godzilla*, is a delight as a yakuza chief who is also a foolish old man."[11]

On April 27, 1956, the U.S. version of *Gojira*, *Godzilla: King of the Monsters!* was released to major box-office success. In Chicago, 21 neighborhood theaters ran first-run prints, and plans were set for a major publicity campaign on the local Channel 7 television station. At the Fox Ritz Theatre in Los Angeles, promotional manager Myron Talman, formerly of the Paramount and Roxy Theatres in Kansas City, used shapely young ladies in swimming suits holding *Godzilla* posters to grab the attention of filmgoers, claiming that he "did the best job of exploitation on the West Coast."[12]

Shimura and Minoru Chiaki supported Toshirô Mifune in another Toho feature, *Narazu-mono* [*Blackguard*] (1956), directed by Nobuo Aoyagi from the story "*Takurin meshiba*" by Takemi Sasaki. A novel by Kazuo Kikuta provided the material for Toshio Yasumi's screenplay, *Bôkyaku no hanabira* (1957), directed by Toshio Sugie for Toho, with Shimura in a major supporting role.

Kumonosu-jô [*Throne of Blood*] *(1957)*

Shimura, billed third as "Noriyasu Odagura," and Minoru Chiaki, billed sixth as "Yoskiaki Miki," then supported Toshirô Mifune in the starring role of "Taketoki Washizu" in Kurosawa's *Kumonosu-jô* [literally "Castle of the Spider's Web" or *Cobweb Castle* in Japan, and *Throne of Blood* in the West]. Kurosawa, Hideo Oguni, Shinobu Hashimoto and Ryûzû Kikushima's Noh-influenced screenplay is considered a Japanese "transposition" of William Shakespeare's *Macbeth* (1606), previously filmed in expressionistic style from the original play by Orson Welles in 1948. Once again, the four writers holed up at their favorite *ryokan*, each to write individual contributions and then blend them together for the final script. None of them consulted the Shakespeare play, but relied on vivid memories of reading it many years earlier.

Washizu and Miki are two victorious warriors heading back to their lord, Kuniharu Susuki's (Takamaru Sasaki), castle when they meet an Old Ghost Woman (Chieko Naniwa), who foretells that Washizu eventually will rule the fortress until supplanted by Miki's son, Yoshiteru (Akira Kubo). One of the ghost's predictions, that Washizu and Miki will receive their own fiefs, proves true; and Washizu's wife, the devious Lady Asaji (Isuzu Yamada, frightening in Noh-style makeup), incites him to murder the lord (a direct parallel to Lady Macbeth in Shakespeare's play). Asaji becomes pregnant, and Washizu takes another bold step by dispatching an assassin to kill Miki and his son, but Yoshiteru escapes death. Miki's ghost plagues Washizu and, when Asaji's baby is stillborn, she goes insane.

Washizu returns to see the Ghost Woman, and she informs him that he will never lose a battle until Cobweb Forest (Shakespeare's Birnam Wood) approaches Cobweb Castle (Dunsinane). The murdered Miki's forces, commanded by Odagura, camouflaged beneath tree branches and bushes, then advance on the castle; and Washizu's own men, realizing that he killed the lord, impale him during a ferocious hail of arrows.

Stephen Prince writes,

> Kurosawa's movie is a brilliant synthesis of diverse cultural, aesthetic and historical sources, only one skein of which derives from Shakespeare. The film's towering achievement lies in the way Kurosawa seamlessly integrates these and gives them superlative formal expression.[13]

For much of his inspiration, Kurosawa again drew upon the Sengoku Jidai, the century of civil wars in medieval Japan, during which the lack of central rule led to violent conflicts between rival warlords who often treacherously murdered their own confederates. Prince continues, "Washizu ... may enact a story whose outlines are those of *Macbeth*, but he personifies elements of the historical spirit of his own age."[14]

Cobweb Castle is not representative of a single historical type, but founded on fact-based sketches by production designer Yoshiro Muraki, who had his crew build the set on the black, volcanic earth around Mount Fuji. This gives the film the stark style of the pen-and-ink drawings of the Buddhist *sumi-e* tradition, stark compositions with vast, empty spaces symbolic of Kurosawa's deliberately cold aesthetics, not allowing the viewer to empathize with any of the characters.

For the seventh time, Kurosawa relied on the striking black-and-white cinematography of Asakazu Nakai, who most recently had brought so much beauty to the landscapes, particularly the forest scenes, in *Seven Samurai*. Like the earlier film, *Throne of Blood* is a film that works far better in monochrome than it would in color. As Donald Richie pointed out, "There has rarely been a black and whiter black-and-white film. [Kurosawa] purposely restricts himself [to the] simple cut and the simple wipe. There are no fades, no dissolves, nothing soft, nothing flowing."[15]

Stuart Galbraith adds that Kurosawa does utilize one element for "dissolves," actual fog around Mount Fuji that was enhanced with a small amount of white smoke:

> This is seen clearly at the film's beginning and end, when we see a stone marker and the foundations of Cobweb Castle. Fog consumes the markers, and we are suddenly in medieval Japan. As the story shifts back and forth in time, it is the mist that serves as transition, and throughout the picture it is within the murky fog where time and space shift, enhancing its nightmare-like imagery.[16]

Stephen Prince brilliantly sums up Kurosawa's thematic transcendence of his source material:

> Kurosawa ... strips out Shakespeare's political conservatism, refusing to give us the play's reassuring conclusion ... in which a just political authority triumphs. In Kurosawa's film and worldview, the cycle of human violence never ends. Thus the film's many circular motifs describe the real tragedy at the heart of the history that *Throne of Blood* dramatizes. Why do people kill one another so often and through so many ages? Kurosawa had no answer to this question. But he showed us here, through the film's chorus, its circularity, and its Buddhist aesthetics, that there may not be an answer in this world.
>
> The aesthetics and philosophy of *Throne of Blood* take us well beyond Shakespeare, and that's why this is a great *film*. Its accomplishments are not beholden to another medium or artist. Kurosawa gives us his own vision, expressed with ruthless, chilling power, and it's the totality of that vision, its sweep and its uncompromising nature, that moves and terrifies us—and that we are so seldom privileged to see in cinema.[17]

Shimura is featured in the opening and closing scenes, as well as furious chase and combat sequences. His more naturalistic samurai commander provides a contrast to the Noh-masked, scowling, unhappy visages worn by Mifune and Yamada. This is Kurosawa's most frightening film, imbued with a continual creepiness combining medieval Noh theater with a cinematic style recalling that created by Fritz Lang for his German silent epics of the 1920s. Kurosawa and Nakai's use of stark *white* (fog, human bones, the spirit creature) maintains a level of unease throughout the film's 109 minutes.

Masaru Satô's potent score, imbued with ethereal, traditional Japanese elements, also lends to the uncomfortable atmosphere.

Kurosawa also foreshadows major events in *Throne of Blood*, particularly the climactic archery onslaught that finally kills Washizu: Prior to murdering the Great Lord Susuki, he sits in front of a large rack of arrows that foreground the bloodstained wall behind him and his wife. After he moves off camera to slay the lord with his spear, Asaji closely observes and dances around the dried blood, spattered there when the previous lord had committed suicide.

Shimura's character is far more important to the narrative than is his actual performance, though he does enjoy some pivotal, powerful moments when Kurosawa frames him in close-up as Odagura leads his forces toward Cobweb Castle. It is Odagura who hits upon the idea of using the trees to camouflage their successful assault on the fortress. In another overt instance of foreshadowing, Washizu and his faltering forces are deluged with a huge flock of birds (gathered from two large Tokyo pet shops by property master Kôichi Hamamura, who tried in vain to prevent many of them from flying to freedom) deprived of their habitat by Odagura's removal of the trees from Spider's Web Forest.

Hamamura also worked closely with Mifune on the terrifying death scene, in which 20 archers were deployed to fire needle-tipped arrows along wires at the actor, who had carefully to remain on his marks to avoid certain injury. Individual arrows pierced between the beads of his samurai armor to impale boards that had been placed beneath, while entire groups of them pierced the sets around him. Mifune literally risked his life to shoot these sequences (making one wonder to what heights the liability insurance costs rose during the production), and his performance is arguably one of the most courageous ever filmed.

The film premiered in Japan on January 15, 1957, played the Venice Film Festival on September 5, and was released in London during October 1957. Kurosawa, while on a promotional tour of Great Britain, met up with John Ford at the Savoy Hotel, where the Hollywood director was staying with John Wayne while making the British film *Gideon's Day* (released in the U.S. as *Gideon of Scotland Yard* in February 1959).

In August 1945, Ford had "secretly" watched Kurosawa directing Shimura in *The Men Who Tread on the Tiger's Tail*, and now accepted an invitation to attend the London premiere of *Throne of Blood*. In return, he invited Akira and Yôko Kurosawa to the set of *Gideon's Day* at MGM British Studios in Borehamwood, Hertfordshire.

Following *Throne of Blood*, Shimura appeared in 10 more films during 1957. At Toho, he appeared in *Yama to kawa no aru machi* [*A Path Through Mountains and Rivers*], directed by Seiji Maruyama, and supported Toshirô Mifune in Ishirô Honda's excellent *Kono futari ni sache ari* [*Be Happy, These*

9. Ikimono no Kiroku *(1955)*

Akira Kurosawa (center) visits John Ford (right) (October 1957): In August 1945, Captain John Ford, USNR, in Tokyo as part of the U.S. Occupation forces, had "secretly" watched Akira Kurosawa direct Takashi Shimura in *Tora no o wo fumu otoko-tachi* [*The Men Who Tread on the Tiger's Tail*] at Toho Studios. More than 12 years later, the two directors met by chance in the bar at the Savoy Hotel in London, where Kurosawa invited Ford to attend the British premiere of *Throne of Blood*. In return, Ford invited Kurosawa and his wife, Yôko, to the set of *Gideon's Day* (released in the U.S. as *Gideon of Scotland Yard* in 1959) at MGM British Studios in Borehamwood, Hertfordshire. This photograph is the only original studio publicity still of the two directors ever issued.

Two Lovers]. For director Toshio Sugie at Tokyo Eiga, he and Minoru Chiaki again joined forces, for *Sanjûrokunin no jôkyaku*, based on a novel by Yorichika Arima.

Toho released *Arakure* [*Untamed Woman*], Shimura's next collaboration with Mikio Naruse, who assembled a sterling cast also including Hideko Takamine, Ken Uehara, Masayuki Mori, Daisuke Katô and Tatsuya Nakadai. The film's title is apt, as Takemine's protagonist, maligned and abused by men and women alike, continually survives her plight from being abandoned by her mother through a host of bad marriages and other relationships.

Shimura portrays the master of a rice mill, referred to as "our capitalist" by the only man the untamed woman loves (Mori), who unfortunately is married and eventually dies from "a lung ailment." The master is a bit decadent, frequenting the geisha house run by his madam "friend." Shortly after meeting the untamed woman, having been abandoned by her husband (Uehara) following a miscarriage, he "accidentally" grabs her while exiting the bordello. "You have big breasts," he remarks. "They are great."

Two of Shimura's fellow "Seven Samurai," Katô ("Shichiroji" in the earlier film) and Seiji Miyaguchi ("Kyuzo"), lend the film added interest for his and Kurosawa's admirers, as do Bokuzen Hidari ("Farmer Yohei," in a tiny role) and Kokuten Kôdô ("Old Man Gisaku"). Having appeared in an unbilled walk-on for *Seven Samurai*, Nakadai (in the small supporting role of a tailor) here was acting in his eighth film.

Shimura, remaining at Toho, received fourth billing, above Tatsuya Nakadai and Toshirô Mifune, in Hideo Suzuki's *Kiken na eiyu* [*A Dangerous Hero*], appeared as the male lead, Yasunori Igawa, in *Yuunagi*, directed by Shirô Toyoda, and played small supporting roles in Shûe Matsubayashi's *Aoi sanmyaku Shinko no maki* and *Zoku aoi sanmyaku Yukiko no maki*. For his final role of 1957, he was billed fourth in the Toei Company's *Dotanba*, directed by Tomu Uchida.

10

More *Kaijû Tokusatsu* and *Jidai-Geki* for Shimura-san

GREATEST SCIENCE-FICTION PICTURE EVER CONCEIVED BY THE MIND OF MAN—publicity for the U.S. release of *Chikyû Bôeigun* [*The Mysterians*] (1957)

Following his appearances in the first two Godzilla films, Shimura became a popular supporting actor in Toho's *kaijû tokusatsu* genre, playing distinguished roles from 1957 through 1965. Regardless of film content, Shimura played his roles with the same earnest sincerity, never "slumming" or "walking through" pictures that many actors, especially in English-language films in both Hollywood and Great Britain, believed "beneath them." Shimura reasoned that work *was work*, and that an artist had a responsibility to deliver his best effort every time.

Chikyû Bôeigun [*The Mysterians*] (1957)

In *The Mysterians*, Shimura again plays a major supporting character, Dr. Tanjiro Adachi, head astronomer at an observatory near Mt. Fuji, who, along with his young assistant, astrophysicist Rioshi Shiraisi (Yumi Shirikawa), obverses the activities of aliens who attempt to dupe the people of Earth into believing they are pacifists who have arrived only for reasons of survival. Clad completely in white suit and hat, he is clearly set apart from every other character in the film.

Titled *Chikyû Bôiegun* [*Earth Defense Force*] in Japan, this *tokusatsu eiga* intended to get Toho into the cinematic "space race" with other Japanese and Hollywood studios, features an interesting screenplay, by Takeshi Kimura, with strong Cold War overtones. The superpowers and other nations of the world must join forces to combat a common enemy, but when the use of nuclear weapons is mentioned, Dr. Adachi, ever the voice of reason, warns that this must not be done, placing this film squarely in Toho's "no nukes" subgenre. The Mysterians, having escaped to Mars from a celestial body originally existing between the red planet and Jupiter, had long ago destroyed their own home during an atomic war.

A clever thematic and casting contrast is presented when Susumu Fugita, icon of the Japanese fighting man for World War II soldiers, sailors and flyers, plays General Morita, head of the combined military forces, appearing with his Kurosawa costar Shimura, whose Dr. Adachi represents a less extreme approach toward defeating the Mysterians. At a press conference, Adachi tells a group of international journalists, "America and the Soviet Union now face a common foe. Japan's trouble today will be theirs tomorrow. The Earth is one. If we do not unite and prevent the Mysterians' attack, our plight will be irremediable."

Nations across the globe establish Defense Force of the Earth, and representatives gather at Head Quarters to hear General Morita's military strategy. An attack against the Mysterians' impenetrable dome proves futile, and when the use of nuclear weapons is mentioned, Adachi says, "We must not use H-Bombs under any circumstances. It means our ruin."

Just in time, a new, primarily defensive, weapon is developed: the Marcalite FARP (Flying Atomic Ray Projector), a 600-foot diameter lens that will deflect the Mysterians' powerful heat rays, as well as produce potent beams of its own. When the enemy is vanquished, and a few of their craft barely make it back to their satellite space station, Adachi (like Shimura's Dr. Yamane

Chûshingura [The Loyal 47 Ronin] (1958; directed by Kunio Watanabe): Jûbei Ôtake (Takashi Shimura, left) with his son-in-law, Shinzaemon Katsuda (Keizô Kawasaki), in this epic cinematic account of the 1701 Akô Incident, aka "The Treasury of Loyal Retainers," 46 (or 47) master-less samurai who fought to avenge their lord, Asano Naganori, who was forced to commit *seppuku* after attempting to kill Kira Kôzuke-no-suke Yoshinaka at Edo Castle.

before him), observes, "They're trapped in space forever. We must not repeat their error." The success of the two Godzilla features and *Sora no daijkaijû Radon* [*Radon, Giant Monster in the Sky*] (1956), another rampaging beast modeled on a dinosaur, the pterodactyl (and known as "Rodan" in the United States), had convinced producer Tomoyuki Tanaka again to pair Ishirô Honda and Eiji Tsuburaya in the production of a special effects-rich science-fiction ex-

Ôedo shichininshû [*Seven from Edo*] (1958; directed by Sadatsugu Matsuda): Takashi Shimura as the soft-spoken Tokugawa gambling boss Sagayima.

travaganza. During production, after the U.S.S.R. launched *Sputnik 1* into orbit, the two filmmakers added their own early-warning satellites to the film. Tanaka, realizing that the film also needed a *kaijû* to attract larger audiences, inspired the Moguera (Haruo Nakajima, who had suffered so courageously in the Godzilla suit), a giant robot that wreaks considerable havoc before being crushed beneath the destroyed Koyama Bridge.

Chikyû Bôiegun was released in Japan on December 28, 1957, netting Toho a total of $975,000 at the box office. In the U.S., RKO Radio Pictures, titling the film *The Mysterians*, dubbed it into English, but then sold it to Loew's, Inc., who released it through MGM on May 15, 1959, realizing a small profit of $58,000. Reviews were mixed, with the plot considered "confusing" and Tsuburaya's effects drawing most of the praise. Arguably, the original Japanese version, with its thoughtful and lucid screenplay, is one of the very best *kaijû tokusatsu eiga*.

Shimura worked constantly during 1958, appearing in 11 major films, beginning with a small supporting role in director Sadatsugu Matsuda's *Otorijo hanayome* [*Samurai Bride Hunter*], released by the Toei Company. At Daiei, he played Hôkinokami Aoyama in *Eddoko matsuri* (1958), written by Hideo Oguni and directed by Kôji Shima.

He again supported Kazuo Hasegawa, along with Shintarô Katsu, Machiko Kyô and Fujiko Yamamoto, in Kunio Watanabe's adaptation of *Chûshingura* [*The Loyal 47 Ronin*] (1958). One of the most famous stories in Japanese history, *Chûshingura* refers to all fictional accounts of the 1701 Akô Incident, aka "The Treasury of Loyal Retainers," 46 (or 47) master-less samurai who fought to avenge their lord, Asano Naganori, who was forced to commit *seppuku* after attempting to kill Kira Kôzuke-no-suke Yoshinaka at Edo

Castle. In 1703, the *ronin*, led by Ôishi Kuranosuke Yoshio, executed Kira, laid his head at the grave of Asano, and then surrendered, knowing they also would be sentenced to *hara kiri*.

For more than three centuries, this tale has been dramatized in kabuki and *bunraku* theater, stage plays, novels, films, television shows, a ballet and an opera. Watanabe's 166-minute Daieicolor and Daieiscope spectacular followed several silent films (1907–1932), the last an epic, also featuring Kazuo Hasegawa, directed by Teinosuke Kinogasa.

A four-hour sound version was commissioned by the Japanese military in 1941. Adapted by Kenichiro Hara and Yoshikata Yoda from the play *Mayama Chûshingura* and directed by Kenji Mizoguchi, this ponderous film, released just one week before the attack on Pearl Harbor, was a commercial failure.

In *The Loyal 47 Ronin*, Shimura portrays Jûbei Ôtake, father-in-law of Shinzaemon Katsuda (Keizô Kawasaki), one of the *ronin*. He appears in four scenes, two of which show him bathing with several other men, from midpoint until the end. His Jûbei differs greatly from his other characters, and is one of his most hot-headed, often disapproving of his son-in-law's behavior.

The Loyal 47 Ronin, despite its length, slow pace and frequent lack of atmosphere (except when cinematographer Takashi Watanabe moves the camera outdoors or uses visual framing devices), became the number-one box-office draw in Japan during 1958, as well as the second highest-grossing Japanese film of the decade.

The Toei Company released Sadatsugu Matsuda's Cinemascope-and-color, Tokugawa-era *jidai-geki Ôedo shichininshû* [*Seven from Edo*] (1958), in which Shimura plays the soft-spoken Sagamiya, a local gambling boss. Katsukawa (Utaemon Ichikawa) and a group of six other samurai retainers living in poverty moonlight as *yôjinbô* [bodyguards] to protect Sagamiya's operation. Victimized by a political conspiracy hatched by Tatewaki (Isao Yamagata), a corrupt official and rival boss, Katsukawa is banished from the community but eventually returns to defeat the enemy gang and rejoin Sagamiya.

The shortcomings of Yoshitake Hisa's (often two-dimensional) screenplay are compensated by the color of

Uguisu-jô no hanayome [*The Bride in Uguisu Castle*] (1958; directed by Shoji Matsumura): Takashi Shimura as Sir Ogata, the prospective bride's father, in this entertaining Toei *jidai-geki* musical comedy.

Taizô Kawashima's vibrant art direction and Shintarô Kawasaki's fluid camerawork, in this neglected release from a year of memorable Japanese films. The final scene is unforgettable: Katsukawa laments his "responsibility" for the death of Hirahara (Ryûtarô Ôtomo), a fallen comrade, as the remaining six of the "Seven from Edo" and their associates, including Sagamiya, observe him pouring saké over the deceased samurai's wooden grave marker.

Directed for Daiei by Shigeo Tanaka, *Haha* (1958) includes Shimura (as Ijôin) in a fine cast featuring Machiko Kyô and Kuniko Miyake. *Uguisu-jô*

Ten to sen [Point and Line] (1958; directed by Tsuneo Kobayashi): In this Toei *noir* crime drama, Takashi Shimura is in top form as the calm, quiet chief detective Kasai, who refuses to give up on his young colleague's quest for the truth in a murder case previously judged a "double suicide."

no hanayome [The Bride in Uguisu Castle] (1958), a very entertaining *jidai-geki* musical comedy directed for the Toei Company by Shoji Matsumura, casts him in the supporting role of Sir Ogata, father of Princess Matsu, who is expected to marry Lord Matsudaira (Minoru Chiaki) or risk the abolishment of her clan. Matsu has no interest in marriage, so Ogata, saying she has a contagious disease, plants her in a convent. She is kidnapped but rescued by Lord Hikoshiro, whom she truly loves.

Matsumura's screenplay is a balanced blend of comedy and drama, well-represented by Shimura's performance. The musical score by Tadashi Manjôme is also an impressive mixture, fusing Japanese and Middle Eastern melodies with Western-style orchestrations. The comic nature of the film's early scenes turns dramatic after the kidnapping, when the clan's samurai, led by Hikoshiro, defeat the enemy forces of the devious Shinshichiro.

In the excellent *noir* crime drama *Ten to sen [Point and Line]* (1958), directed at Toei by Tsuneo Kobayashi, Shimura plays chief detective Kasai, who aids a young associate, Kiichi Mahara (Hiroshi Minami, in his film debut), intent on proving the facts of a case previously judged a "double suicide." Tenaciously remaining on the case despite constant departmental obstacles, the detectives eventually catch up with Ryoko (Mieko Takamine), an ill woman, who poisoned the mistress of her husband, Tatsuo Yasuda (Isao Yamagata), and Kenichi Sayama (Masahiko Naruse), the man she was with at the time. Tatsudo then conspired with Ryoko to make the killings look like a suicide pact.

Based on a novel by Seichô Matsumoto, *Point and Line*, shot in Ferraniacolor and widescreen by Shizuka Fujii, is lent much of its *noir* atmosphere by Kobayashi's use of flashbacks and montage sequences, and the jazz-inflected musical score of Chûji Kinoshita. Shimura, briefly shifting away from the *jidai-geki* realm to a modern milieu, is in top form as the calm, quiet detective who refuses to give up on his young colleague's quest for the truth.

Shimura again worked with Toshio Sugie at Toho, enjoying billing above Toshirô Mifune, in *Jinsei genkijô—Seishun hen* [*Theater of Life*] (1958), adapted from Shiro Ozaki's novel by Ryuji Shiina and Toshio Yasumi. Then, as his favorite director had done the previous year, Kurosawa came calling.

Kakushi-toride no san-akunin [*The Hidden Fortress*] (1958)

Kurosawa, having just directed two very serious films (*Throne of Blood* and *Donzoko* [*The Lower Depths*] {1958}, based on Maxim Gorky's play and starring Toshirô Mifune), intended his next major project to be "one-hundred percent entertainment" and a "thank you" to Toho for supporting his more artistic, less commercially appealing endeavors. Shot (including locations at Harima, Gotemba and Mt. Fuji) in Tohoscope by Kazuo Yamazaki, this 16th-century adventure bordering on fantasy, described as "Western-style" by co-writer Hideo Oguni, displays Kurosawa's admiration for the work of John Ford.[1] The title, literally translated from the Japanese, is "Three Bad Men in a Hidden Fortress." (*Three Bad Men* [1926], an unforgettable Western, is one of Ford's best silent films.)

Widescreen formats had been in use by U.S. filmmakers since 1953, although few of the "golden age" directors were fond of altering the way they had been composing their shots for decades. Ford, though he preferred to shoot in the original 1:33 ratio and black-and-white, did make impressive use of Vistavision and Technicolor, especially in his Western masterpiece *The Searchers* (1956). In Japan, five years passed before directors began to make use of the compositional opportunities afforded by the Cinemascope image. In 1958, Kurosawa voiced his preference for the wider format; but, often shooting in deep focus, also emphasized why he still liked to film in black-and-white:

> I have been feeling that the standard screen is a little too narrow from the viewpoint of composition, to my way of filming. I find wide screen rather easier for me.... I am not yet contented with the color of Japanese pictures. Color pictures are apt to have a shallower focal length so they do not suit my style of direction.[2]

10. More Kaijû Tokusatsu and Jidai-Geki for Shimura-san 107

Kurosawa and Oguni also were joined by Shinobu Hashimoto in developing the screenplay from an idea by Ryûzô Kishushima, who knew of a still-standing "hidden fortress" built in Kôshû by Shingen Takeda. Production ran from May 27 to December 11, 1958, taking far longer than expected, due primarily to location changes made necessary by three typhoons. As a change of pace, Kurosawa improvised much of the film while shooting, in the mornings developing difficult situations for his characters, and then challenging the other writers to devise ways for them to overcome these obstacles.

Cast as The Old General, Izumi Nagakura, Shimura again joined a fine group of "usual Kurosawa suspects," including Toshirô Mifune (as the heroic General Rokurota Makabe), Minori Chiaki, Susumu Fugita and Kokuten Kôdô. Chiaki and Kamitari Fujiwara portray Tahei and Matashichi, respectively, two greedy peasants with few, if any, positive qualities, but who provide the well-sustained humor distinguishing the film. These performers are ably augmented by the addition of the gorgeous 20-year-old Misa Uehara as Princess Yuki. Kurosawa, choosing not to cast an experienced actress, auditioned several hundred young women before he found this "girl with a fresh and princess-like dignity" who had "miraculous eyes" to play the 16-year-old character.[3]

In his essay for the 2009 Janus Films release, Michael Joshua Brown writes,

> The Hidden Fortress is perhaps the most audience courting of Kurosawa's period films, made in the tradition of mythic tales about stoic warriors, rescued princesses, and sweeping action. And yet through subtle variations on narrative conventions and social themes, and the sheer bravado of Kurosawa's directorial skills, it is as rich as his more directly challenging works.[4]

Shimura again appears for only a few minutes, but his obligatory inclusion by Kurosawa is necessary, featuring a wide emotional range. He enters *laughing*, as the Old General meets with the princess and Rokoruta in a cave near the Hidden Fortress, and exits *crying*, as he and his companions, atop a crag, watch them ride away toward Hayakawa. Susumu Fujita is also a welcome presence, playing General Heiei Tadokoro, initially an enemy of Rokoruta and Yuki, who turns traitor to save their lives and restore the princess to power.

Kurosawa frames the film with the two fools, opening as the camera follows behind them while they flee from disastrous warfare and gravedigging, and closes as they, with a small token of gold in hand, walk toward the camera and beyond. Their comic, cry-baby conduct provides a contrast to Mifune's serious, stern general, whose expressions of disdain often resemble those of his Noh-style Washizu in *Throne of Blood*. Several rousing action scenes, including one of Rokoruta dispatching two enemy samurai during a chase atop his trusty steed, are bolstered by the superb Noh-influenced music of Fumio Hayasaka protégé Masaru Satô.

The Hidden Fortress premiered in Japan on December 28, 1958. A huge commercial hit, it also won a Tokyo Blue Ribbon as Best Picture. In 1959, it was awarded the International Film Critics Prize and the Silver Bear at the ninth Berlin International Film Festival. Edited for its U.S. release in 1960, the film was compared unfavorably to Kurosawa's earlier, more serious efforts such as *Rashômon* and *Seven Samurai*, and did not fare well at the box office.

George Lucas readily admitted that he based *Star Wars* (1977), in part, on *The Hidden Fortress*. (He also was generally influenced by samurai culture and Zen philosophy; and, specifically, transforming *jidai* into "jedi" and, perhaps, using the name of screenwriter Yoshikata Yoda as the basis for the character of "Yoda" in *The Empire Strikes Back* [1980] and subsequent *Star Wars* films. He had inquired about Toshirô Mifune to portray Ben Obi-Wan Kenobi [but reportedly the actor's agent, thinking the production would be shoddy, advised against it], a role that went to Sir Alec Guinness, and considered casting a Japanese actress as Princess Leia [Carrie Fisher].) Michael Joshua Brown notes,

> Kurosawa, unlike Lucas, was intent on having his comic foils display no likable traits. They alter nothing about their avaricious, traitorous ways over the course of the story. Nobility and courage belong to Makabe and the young woman under his protection...[5]

Donald Richie concluded that *The Hidden Fortress* "is what they call an action-drama in the trade, but one so beautifully made, one so imaginative, so funny, so tender, and so sophisticated, that it comes near to being the most lovable film Kurosawa ... ever made."[6]

In Kunio Watanabe's 13th-century historical-religious epic, *Nichiren to moko daishurai* [*Nichiren and the Great Mongol Invasion*] (1958), Shimura is billed 14th, as Yasaburô, an Izu fisherman, who rescues the legendary Buddhist monk Nichiren (Kazuo Hasegawa) from a watery death on "Chopping-board Rock." After surviving another exile and a near-beheading (when lightning strikes the sword of the executioner), Nichiren spreads Buddhism, and a typhoon scuttles a 100,000-strong fleet of Mongol ships set to invade Japan.

Devoid of any Hollywood-style romantic subplots or comedy relief, Watanabe's straightforward, fact-based depiction of Nichiren (an actual Kamakura-period monk, also known as "Rencho," who lived from 1222 to 1282) focuses on his devotion to the *Lotus Sutra* as the one true method to attain enlightenment and salvation through Buddhism, and his predictions involving political strife within Japan and invasions from without. Shimura's Yasaburô is so convincing and pleasant that he leaves the viewer wanting more of him; again, his performance is not as important as his character. Saved from drowning and hidden for 30 days on the Izu Peninsula, Nichiren respectfully tells Yasaburô and his wife that they have made him feel as if "he was back with his father and mother."

10. More Kaijû Tokusatsu and Jidai-Geki for Shimura-san   109

Directed by Kokichi Uchide, *Ken wa shitte ita,* with Shimura in another small part, proved his swansong for 1958. Another 10 roles followed in 1959, beginning with his return to Toei to support Ken Takakura in director Hideo Sekigawa's crime drama *Kêdaemonô no torû michi* [*Beast's Passage*]. Back at Toho, he contributed a cameo to old friend Ishirô Honda's comedy *Tetsuwan tôshu Inao monogatari* [*Inao: Story of an Iron Arm*] (1959).

Nichiren to moko daishurai [*Nichiren and the Great Mongol Invasion*] (1958; directed by Kunio Watanabe): In this historical-religious epic set during the 13th-century, Takashi Shimura portrays Yasaburô, an Izu Peninsula fisherman, who rescues the legendary Buddhist monk Nichiren from a watery death on "Chopping-board Rock."

Another film directed by Mikio Naruse, *Kotan no kuchibue* [*A Whistle in My Heart,* aka *Whistling in Kotan*] (1959), also made for Toho, reteamed Shimura with Masayuki Mori and Bokuzen Hidari. Mori plays the alcoholic father of the Hatanka family, ethnic Ainus in a Hokkaido *kotan* (a village comprised of homes built along a river containing salmon), who face traditional discrimination that contributes to a series of tragedies. Shimura portrays the Japanese Professor Tazawa, the "one person who has never discriminated" against anyone, but whose refusal to accept the hand of an 18-year-old Ainu, Fue Hatanka (Kumi Mizuno), *for* his son leads to the starvation death of "Granny" Ikante (Eiko Miyoshi) and the disappearance of the young woman. Tazawa, guilt-ridden, does attempt to visit Ikante before her passing, and later remains at her grave until he is beckoned away by his son. The conflicted professor is another memorable Naruse role for Shimura.

Thirteen-year-old Yutaka (Ken Kubo [Yamauchi]) then attempts to duel with a racist classmate who has been bullying him at school but is beaten from behind by another delinquent with a baseball bat. After their father is killed by a falling tree while working in a lumber camp, Yutaka, who recovers except for a permanent limp, and his 15-year-old sister, Masu (Ryoko [Yoshiko] Kôda), deprived of their home by a selfish uncle (Kyû Sazanka) who holds the deed, set off down a Hokkaido road to an unknown destination but try to remain positive with a "whistle in their hearts."

Shinobu Hashimoto adapted the screenplay for *A Whistle in My Heart* from a Nubuo Ishimori children's novel dealing with the racism endured by

Hokkaido's Ainus. In 1899, the Japanese government annexed the Ainu homeland, granting them citizenship and, expecting them to assimilate, labeled them "former aborigines." Assimilation meant that they were forced to adopt Japanese names and speak the language. (Until 1997, Japan insisted that there were no "ethnic groups" in the nation. Finally, in 2008, the Ainu were officially recognized as an indigenous people.)

In the film, before the children hit the road as refugees, their cousin, Koji (Kunio Otsuka), explains to Yutaka that bigotry is not confined to any one group but unfortunately universal in the human condition. Also universal in *A Whistle in My Heart* are some of the pieces played on-screen in scenes involving the Kotan school's music teacher. Much like director Keisuke Kinoshita and composer Chûji Kinoshita, who added several Western folk songs to the score for *Twenty-Four Eyes* (1954), also set on Hokkaido, Naruse and Akira Ifukube chose familiar tunes by the American Stephen Foster ("Swanee River"), Scottish Robert Burns ("Auld Lang Syne") and German Ludwig van Beethoven ("Bagatelle for piano in A minor ['Für Elise']") to create a wide-reaching atmosphere. The Eastmancolor and Tohoscope cinematography of Masao Tamai is also impressive.

At Shochiku, Shimura played another detective, "Ichikawa," in *Taiyô ni somuku mono* (1959), directed by Tatsuo Sakai. Back at Toho, he, Misa Uehara and Minoru Chiaki again supported a top-billed Toshirô Mifune, under the familiar direction of Toshio Sugie, in *Sengoku gunto-den* [*The Saga of the Vagabonds*], an action film, written by Kurosawa from a Jûrô Miyoshi story and 1937 Sadao Yamanaka screenplay, involving a Robin Hood–like outlaw band. Kurosawa, anxious to fund his new production company, was more than happy to accept further writing assignments at Toho.

Mifune portrays the swaggering Rokuro, who joins a parcel of rogues led by Jibu (Chiaki) who steal a chest of gold from Lord Taro (Kôji Tsuruta) before it can be delivered to a rural governor. Rokuro then meets Taro, who impresses him enough for a return of the war funds. Taro is accused of stealing the gold by Jiro (Akihiko Hirata), his avaricious brother, and vassal, Hyoe Yamana (Seizaburô Kawazu), so he joins the bandits, known as the Crimson Band, robbing from the rich and giving to the poor. As Saemon Toki, Jiro's father, Shimura makes his obligatory appearance in a Kurosawa project, but quickly is dispatched when Toki's own son gives him a fatal shove off a cliff.

Richly photographed in Tohoscope and Agfacolor by Akira Suzuki, *Saga of the Vagabonds* is a rip-roaring 105-minute adventure. As pointed out by Stuart Galbraith, "The picture ... may not [progress much] beyond simply telling a good ... story, but [is] memorable in a way that similar Cinemascope epics from Hollywood, which emphasized pageantry and little else, are not."[7] Mifune steals the film with his sly comic characterization:

10. More Kaijû Tokusatsu and Jidai-Geki for Shimura-san

Somewhere between *Seven Samurai*'s Kikuchiyo and *Yojimbo*'s Sanjuro, Rokuro is wily, boastful, honorable, subversive.... Later in life, Mifune would almost always play stoic, veteran characters, and to see him clearly relishing such a broad, physical role is a genuine pleasure.[8]

Released in Japan on August 9, 1959, *Saga of the Vagabonds* made its Los Angeles debut on November 23, 1960. U.S. reviewers were primarily impressed, particularly with Mifune, hailed by the *Los Angeles Examiner*'s S. A. Desick as "probably one of the finest actors in the world." But the rest of the cast also was praised, "steeped in skill down to the smallest bit part" (one of which is played by Shimura).[9]

In demand by every top director in Japan, Shimura next worked for Teinosuke Kinugasa in the excellent mystery *Kagero ezu* [*Stop the Old Fox*] (1959). Adapted from a novel by Seichô Matsumoto, the screenplay was co-written by Kinugasa and Minoru Inuzuka.

Billed fifth in an all-star cast led by Toshirô Mifune (as Prince Yamato Takeru), Shimura again was directed by Hiroshi Inagaki, in Toho's *Nippon tanjô* [*Age of the Gods*] (1959), an epic adventure also featuring Setsuko Hara (as Amaterasu, the Sun Goddess). Set in 4th-century Japan, Ryûzô Kikushima and Toshio Yasumi's screenplay depicts the birth of *kami-no-michi* (Shintô), the traditional Japanese religion emphasizing the connection between the present and the ancient past. Shimura portrays the Elder Kumaso.

Director Yoshiaki Banshô billed Shimura second, as Shichimiya, in the romantic drama *Sora kakeru hanayome* [*The High-Flying Bride*] (1959), produced for Shochiku. A role in Kôji Shima's *Shobushi to sono musume* was followed by his final 1959 film, *Beran me-e geisha* [*The Prickly-mouthed Geisha*], directed for Toei by Eiichi Koishi, in which he received third billing as

Beran me-e geisha [*The Prickly Mouthed Geisha*] (1959; directed by Eiichi Koishi): Takashi Shimura engages in some delightful antics as Masagoro Kosugi, prideful carpenter and headstrong father of Koharu (Hibari Misora), in Toei's entertaining comedy involving corporate criminals.

Masagoro Kosugi, prideful carpenter and headstrong father of Koharu (Hibari Misora), a young Edoite geisha who "doesn't like men." Koharu encourages her father to accept a position with the Heiwa Construction Company, whose president, he discovers, is an old friend, even more grouchy and stubborn, who insults him with consistently pretentious behavior.

"Masa" eventually teams up with Kenishi (Shinjirô Ebara), the son of his old friend, to construct a new-style teahouse. Masa builds the model, while Kenishi draws the blueprint, which then is stolen by unscrupulous capitalists who are rounded up by police after the two old friends happily join a furious melee in an office building. Shimura is delightful throughout the film, and his comic antics during the climactic brawl are a highpoint of his performance as the cranky craftsman. The film concludes with the stubborn men again becoming friends, with their children causing a traffic jam as they embark upon wedded life.

Shimura began the new decade by appearing in eight 1960 films in the usual variety of genres. *Karakkaze yarô* [*Afraid to Die*] (1960), a modern yakuza drama directed for Daiei by New Wave pioneer Yasuzô Masumura, cast him as dying mob boss Gohei Hirayama opposite costars Yukio Mishima as gangster Takeo Asahina, just released from Tokyo Prison following an unsuccessful attempt on his life, and Ayako Wakao as his girlfriend, Yoshie Koizumi. Asahina attempts to give up "the life," but ends up shot through the heart (in spectacular style on a downward escalator, grasping clothes meant for their unborn child). Masamura's introduction of Hirayama is unforgettable: Shimura, his entire back tattooed, faces away from the camera and then (like Boris Karloff as the Monster in James Whale's *Frankenstein*, slowly turns around to reveal his face.

Karakkaze yarô [*Afraid to Die*] (1960; directed by Yasuzô Masumura): Takeo Asahina (Yukio Mishimi), dying gang boss Gohei Hirayama (Takashi Shimura) and Susumu Aikawa (Eiji Funikoshi) in Japanese New Wave pioneer Yasuzô Masumura's hard-hitting modern yakuza drama.

10. More Kaijû Tokusatsu and Jidai-Geki for Shimura-san 113

In the World War II action drama *Hawai Middowei daikaikûsen: Teiheiyô no arashi* [*Storm Over the Pacific*] (1960), Shimura once more supports Toshirô Mifune (as Admiral Isoroku Yamaguchi) and Susumu Fugita (as Admiral Yamamoto). The screenplay, co-written by Shinobu Hashimoto and Takeo Kunihiro, covers the Pacific War from the Japanese attack on Pearl Harbor until their navy's defeat at the Battle of Midway, which is spun for maximum propaganda affect over the radio.

The main plot focuses on Lieutenant Koji Kitami (Yôsuke Natsuki), a young navigator-bombardier in the Japanese Naval Air Force, who leads the attack on Pearl Harbor and becomes somewhat disillusioned after being prevented from communicating with his family after the debacle at Midway. Shimura portrays the kindly Tosaku, father of Keiko (*The Hidden Fortress'* Misa Uehara), who is anxious for Kitami to marry his daughter, although military duty continues to intervene.

Mifune, stone-faced throughout the film, has little opportunity to do anything but wear a serious scowl; and his character, based on the historical Tamon Yamaguchi (1892–1942), who is depicted going down with his ship *Hiryû* at Midway, is renamed "Isoroku" after Yamamoto, who isn't called by his first name on screen. *Storm Over the Pacific*, the first color Tohoscope World War II film produced at the studio, is another Eiji Tsuburaya miniature-effects extravaganza, featuring scores of plastic ships and airplanes being blown to bits. The film is heavy on action, some of it unconvincing, but the emphasis on Kitami and the Imperial government's "lies" helps balance the narrative.

On November 29, 1961, Hugo Grimaldi released an abridged version (cut from 118 to 98 minutes, dubbed into English, and sensationally retitled *I Bombed Pearl Harbor*) in the United States. Fifteen years later, Tsuburaya's model work was still so impressive that some footage was reused in the Universal epic *Midway* (1976), featuring an "all-star" cast including Charlton Heston, Henry Fonda and Mifune (as Yamamoto, dubbed by Paul Frees).

Shimura again worked for Mikio Naruse (who codirected with Yûzô Kawashima) in the Toho drama *Yoru no nagara* [*Evening Stream*] (1960), adapted from Naruse and Kawashima's original story by Toshirô Ide and Zenzô Matsuyama. Shot in Tohoscope by Rokurô Nishigaki, the film also features an atmospheric musical score by Masaru Satô.

Kawashima directed the scenes involving youth culture, including Miyako Fujimura (Yôko Tsukasa), Shinobu Sonada (Yumi Shirakawa), and a host of geisha girls; while Naruse handled the more mature material involving restaurant manager (and Miyako's mother) Aya Fujimura (Isuzu Yamada, in her final role for the director) and Koichiro Sonada (Shimura), the amiable owner of the eating establishment where he always dines with the young women. The styles of the two different directors don't always merge successfully, but the main plot of mother and daughter being in love with the same man, the wounded World War II veteran Ita (Tatsuya Mihashi), who eventually leaves his position as cook at the restaurant, and the continual presence of Shimura are among the elements that hold the narrative together.

Before once again answering the call of Kurosawa, Shimura, as Chotaro Masue, appeared in another Toho crime drama, Senkichi Taniguchi's *Otoko tai otoko* [*Man Against Man*] (1960) costarring Toshirô Mifune and Ryô Ikebe as gang colleagues.

11

Akira, Toshirô and Oji-chan

Mr. Shimura is more than just an actor to me. Since I met him, he's been *Oji-chan* ["dear Uncle"] to me.—Akira Kurosawa

Warui yatsu hodo yoku nemuru [*The Bad Sleep Well*] (1960)

In his 2006 essay, "The Higher Depths," Chuck Stephens notes, "A gray flannel ghost story in which the living haunt the dead, *The Bad Sleep Well* remains the least appreciated of Akira Kurosawa's midperiod collaborations with Toshirô Mifune—a fate for which we have only the other Kurosawa-Mifune films to blame."[1]

Kurosawa initially based this *shakai-mono* [social problem film] on "Bad Men's Prosperity," a script dealing with bureaucratic corruption written by his nephew Mike Inoue, but he added equal measures of Shakespeare's *Hamlet* while co-writing the screenplay with his *The Idiot* collaborator Eijirô Hisaita. By the time the script was finished, Kurosawa had holed up at two different inns, at Izu and Hakone, respectively, also welcoming the contributions of Ryûzô Kikushima, Hideo Oguni and Shinobu Hashimoto. Knowing that no studio would allow him to depict an actual story of corporate degeneracy, Kurosawa explained his approach to the material:

> There was so much corruption going on at the time. The investigations were always dropped when some assistant manager would kill himself. That made no sense. What would happen if somebody investigated the corruption and followed it through to the end?[2]

Kurosawa and cinematographer Yuzuru Aizawa planned to begin shooting *The Bad Sleep Well* in black-and-white Tohoscope on March 1, 1960; but, due to the need for extensive rehearsals, production was delayed by 27 days. Like *The Idiot* and *Throne of Blood*, this dark exercise often displays, visually and through the actions of its characters, the expressionist influence of Fritz Lang's German films.

Mifune portrays Itakura, the "illegitimate" son of an industrialist, who switches identities with Kôichi Nishi (Takeshi Katô), to infiltrate the ranks of Dairyu Construction, a company involved in a corrupt government housing conspiracy with Public Corporation. Five years earlier, an employee of Dairyu (Itakura's father) took a fatal fall from the window of a government building, a death officially ruled a "suicide." The film opens with "Nishi's" marriage to Yoshiko Iwabuchi (Kyôko Kagawa), daughter of Public Corporation's vice-president (an almost unrecognizable, inspired Masayuki Mori), an utterly self-absorbed capitalist without a conscience who will stop at nothing, including multiple murders, to protect his interests.

Shimura turns in one of his finest performances, as the greasy Administrative Officer Moriyama, another of the "Bad Who Sleep Well," who eventually discovers Nishi's real identity. This leads to his being kidnapped and locked in the air-raid shelter of a bombed-out World War II munitions plant by Itakura/Nishi. Starved for two days, he yells out and pounds the iron door, then agrees to come clean, but initially lies about where the monetary kickbacks have been stashed. Locked up again, he finally relents, but meets a bad end, as does Itakura/Nishi, after Yoshiko, believing her evil father has agreed to confess to his crimes, reveals their whereabouts. Iwabuchi saves his own skin, but ultimately loses his daughter and son, who reveals his urge to "shoot" the malignant industrialist.

The Bad Sleep Well is a powerful, often genuinely frightening indictment of corporate greed, a film that has gained even greater potency over the six decades since it was made. The director commented,

> This was the first film of Kurosawa Productions, my own unit which I run and finance myself. From this film on, I was responsible for everything. Consequently, when I began, I wondered what kind of film to make. A film made only to make money did not appeal to me—one should not take advantage of an audience. Instead, I wanted to make a movie of some social significance. At last I decided to do something about corruption because it always seemed to me that graft, bribery, etc., at the public level, is one of the worst crimes that there is. These people hide behind the façade of some great company or corporation and consequently no one knows how dreadful they really are, what awful things they do. Exposing them was, I thought, a socially significant act—and so I started the film.[3]

Some of the darkest, moody, *noir*-like scenes involve Wada (Kamatari Fujiwara, in another outstanding portrayal for Kurosawa), former Assistant to the Chief, who is ordered to commit suicide but is saved at the last moment by Itakura/Nishi, who then uses him to frighten another of the "Bad," Contract Officer Shirai, who, believing the "dead" Wada is pursuing him, "loses his mind," declared schizophrenic and confined to an "insane asylum." A highpoint of the film involves Itakura/Nishi forcing the profusely sweating, increasingly paranoiac Wada to watch his own funeral from a distance (shot in deep focus from inside a car by the innovative Yuzuru Aizawa).

The Bad Sleep Well, also featuring Chishû Ryû and Susumu Fugita in supporting roles, did moderate box-office business but was a critical success in Japan. It was a bigger hit at the 1961 Berlin International Film Festival, where it was nominated for the Golden Bear. Shimura and his wife, along with Kyôko Kagawa, flew to West Germany to attend the festival, held from June 23 to July 1. Mifune, his wife and two children also joined them following a holiday in Acapulco. (He had just completed his role as a Zapotec Indian peasant in the Mexican film *Ánimas Trujano*, aka *El hombre importante* [*The Important Man*] {1961}). Mifune enjoyed the status of being an international leading man; but, always carefully learning his dialogue phonetically, was irritated by every producers' insistence that his work be overdubbed by a voice actor during postproduction.)

The Bad Sleep Well wasn't released in the United States until January 22, 1963, after it had 16 of its original 151 minutes trimmed. U.S. critics, especially in New York, were not kind. The curmudgeonly Bosley Crowther of the *Times* called it "an imitation ... of some classic American gangster pictures,"[4] while Stanley Kauffmann, in *The New Republic*, simply wrote it off as "not very good."[5] *The Bad Sleep Well* remains one of Kurosawa's most underrated epics.

Following his comeuppance in the corporate exposé, Shimura costarred with Keiju Kobayashi in director Shûe Matsubayashi's *Gambare! Bangaku* [*Master Fencer Sees the World*] (1960), a Takarazuka Motion Picture production released by Toho. Matsuo Kishi and Kaneto Shindô adapted the screenplay from an original story by Sadao Yamanaka.

Toshio Sugie again directed Shimura, in the supporting role of Honzo Kadokawa, in *Sararîman Chûshingura* [*Salary Man Chushingura*] (1960). Daisuke Katô and Reiko Dan enjoyed major parts, while Toshirô Mifune, as Kazuo Momoi. contributed a cameo.

At Daiei, Shimura (as Sadonokami Honda) joined his frightening *Throne of Blood* colleague Isuzu Yamada in *Sen-hime goten* [*Princess Sen in Edo*] (1960), directed by Kenji Misumi from Fuji Yahiro's original screenplay. He followed this final film of 1960 with 11 the following year.

Shimura again teamed with Toshirô Mifune and director Hiroshi Inagaki for Toho's *Ôsaka-jô monogatari* [*The Story of Osaka Castle*, aka *Daredevil in the Castle*] (1961), an ambitious historical epic with well-balanced humor, also featuring Kyôko Kagawa, Yoshiko Kuga, Isuzu Yamada, Akihiko Hirata and Susumu Fugita. Mifune tackles another "wandering swordsman" character, the boisterous Mohei, who fights for the Toyotomi clan when the opposing 200,000-strong army of Tokugawa Ieyasu attacks Osaka Castle.

Shimura portrays a variation on daimyô Katsumoto Katagiri (1556–1615), whose banishment from the castle is depicted at the beginning of the film. Opposed to fighting the Tokugawa clan, Katagari, loyal to Hideyoshi Toyotomi, remains ineffective during the siege of Osaka (1614–1615). The historical Katagiri's actions at Osaka remain shrouded in mystery, and he died only 20 days after the fall of the castle. (Rumors of his committing *seppuku* were rampant at the time.)

As Mohei, Mifune brings his unique combination of rambunctious humor and impressive physicality to the fore, and the presence of so many "usual Kurosawa suspects" is a most welcome addition. The great "*Gojira* team" of Ikira Ifukube and Eiji Tsubaraya also contribute their expertise to the musical score and special effects, respectively. Infused with Inagaki's energetic style (beautifully paced at 95 minutes) and Kazuo Yamada's vibrant Eastmancolor and Tohoscope cinematography, this underrated, nearly forgotten epic (perhaps lost in the wake of Inagaki's much-heralded *Samurai* trilogy) deserves more attention.

Kimiyoshi Yasuda directed Shimura in Daiei Kyoto's *Harekosode* [*Clear Weather*] (1961), adapted by Yoshikata Yoda and Matsutarô Kawaguchi from the latter's novel. Shimura then was back as Honzo Kadokawa, with Daisuke Katô, Reiko Dan and Toshirô Mifune, in Toshio Sugie's *Sararîman Chûshingura* follow-up, *Zoku sararîman Chûshingura* [*Salary Man Chushingura Sequel*] (1961).

Yôjinbô [*Yojimbo*] (1961)

In *The Emperor and the Wolf*, Stuart Galbraith writes,

> In *Yojimbo* (1961) ("Bodyguard"), Kurosawa toys with the *chanbara* [sword-fighting] genre, amusingly turning it inside out, much like Mifune's self-satisfied title character. Kurosawa had subverted the genre's conventions before, in *Rashômon*, *Seven Samurai* and *The Hidden Fortress*, although playing with the genre had been a secondary concern. By contrast, *Yojimbo*, a black comedy, is a direct response to the mindless *chanbara* Toei, Daei and Nikkatsu were churning out with great success and reckless abandon.[6]

Set in 1860, *Yojimbo* features a *ronin*, Sanjuro Kuwabatake (Toshirô Mifune), who happens upon a windswept, dusty village torn by a mindless civil war. One faction is led by the "horny, old" saké brewer, Tokuemon (Shimura), and backed by his right-hand gangster, Ushitora (Kyû Sazanka); while the other is bossed by a silk merchant, Tazaemon (Kamatari Fujiwara), who is also head of the village, and enforced by his henchman, brothel operator Seibêi (Seizaburô Kawazu). Sanjuro soon realizes that both sides in the conflict are equally without reason and devises his own shattering yet darkly

11. Akira, Toshirô and Oji-chan

comic solution. The cast also includes Tatsuya Nakadai as (the deliberately "snake-like") Unosuke, the "Gunfighter," and Susumu Fujita, in a brief, slyly comical turn as Homma, the "Cowardly but Wise *Yojimbo* Who Skips Town."

Kurosawa created a new, unique visual style and rhythm for *Yojimbo*. Though he already had created ballet-like on-screen movement in his previous films by pairing the physical movements of his actors with fluid camera techniques, here he took that style to a higher plane, coupling the balanced compositions of cinematographer Kazuo Miyagawa (who had shot *Rashômon*) with the telephoto work of cameraman Takao Saitô. *Yojimbo* opens as the camera, moving in medium close-up, follows Sanjuro, first over his right shoulder and then showing his sandals on the dusty road, as he wanders his way toward the anarchic Edo village. Mifune's movements are choreographed perfectly with Masaru Satô's stirring introductory theme.

Many of the scenes take place within the saké tavern of Gonji (Eijirô Tôno), where he and Sanjuro lift the interior shutters, lending right-angle framing devices that provide windows to the action (or lack of it) occurring outside, swept by Kurosawa's famous use of the elements: wind, dust, fire and rain. Gonji is one of two characters left standing at the film's end, when Sanjuro turns, like a Western gunslinger who "has cleaned up the town," to walk back out.

Shimura, having played a corrupt authority figure in Kurosawa's previous film, again proved he could create a thoroughly unpleasant character. His degenerate Tokuemon scowls, cries and shouts, "Somebody do something!" as his precious saké floods out of the large barrels and his sex slave, Nui (Yôko Tsukasa), is taken back to her husband, Kohei (Yoshio Tsuchiya), "the Unlucky Gambler," by Sanjuro. Tokuemon then meets his end (off-screen) at the hand of a *hara kiri*-sword-wielding Hansuke (Ikio Sawamura), the shady town timekeeper. If Nakadai succeeds in carrying out Kurosawa's order to look "like a snake," Shimura does his best to look like a frog. The somewhat exaggerated, grotesque characters played by Shimura, Daisuke Katô (as the rodent-faced Inokichi, Unosuke's older brother), Seizaburô Kawazu (Seibêi), Isuzu Yamada (in her final Kurosawa performance, as Orin, Seibêi's overbearing wife), and Atsushi Watanabe (The Cooper, Coffin-Maker) were inspired by the director's lifelong love of the literature of Charles Dickens.

Along with Kurosawa's genre-bending elements, his other innovations were an incorporation of more graphic special effects (including sword-slashing sounds and a certain amount of bloodletting on screen), plus constant use of Satô's pioneering score. (The music soon was mimicked by Ennio Morricone for Sergio Leone's "Spaghetti Western" unauthorized remake of *Yojimbo*, *Per un pugno di Dollari* [*A Fistful of Dollars*] {1964}, and its popular sequels. Lawsuits eventually were filed, and an out-of-court settlement was reached whereby Kurosawa received 15 percent of Leone's worldwide receipts.)

Sanjuro succeeds in saving a worthy handful of people while the "bads" destroy each other, and he departs, having gained nothing material for himself. The film, described as a "comedy" by Kurosawa, created a new samurai persona for Mifune, who previously had played such characters much closer to historical reality. Here he and the director transformed his former warrior into a far more ambiguous personality: dirty, broke, wearing a tattered kimono, laconic with unclear motivations, and ultimately performing a good deed with no obvious reasoning.

Mifune, at age 41, gave his usual 100 percent in an extremely taxing, physical role, as Sanjuro is brutally beaten by Kunnuki, the Giant *Yojimbo* (Namigoro [Tsunagorô] Rashômon, an actor with actual giantism, appearing in six films from 1958–1961), who carries a huge wooden hammer, and cuts down his sword-brandishing opponents at the astonishing rate of one per second. Mifune's son, Shirô, when speaking about his father's off-screen behavior when playing these difficult roles, recalled an anecdote from Masako Shimura:

> My father and the Shimuras were visiting Kurosawa's house in Komae, and my father got drunk. When they took their leave, my father was driving the Shimuras home. It seems my father [had] wanted to swear at Kurosawa, but the Shimuras persuaded him to hold back until they got beyond a certain railroad crossing. They told him that he could swear then. So my father kept driving, holding it in, but the second they passed the crossing, he let out something like, "Stupid ass!" That's what I heard from Shimura's wife.[7]

Yojimbo, groundbreaking in so many departments, became the highest grossing Kurosawa film to date, and skyrocketed Mifune into the ranks of international stardom. The director summed up the film's thematics:

> The idea is about rivalry on both sides, and both sides are equally bad. We all know what that is like. Here we are, weakly caught in the middle, and it is impossible to choose between evils. Myself, I've always wanted somehow or other to stop these senseless battles of bad against bad, but we're all more or less weak—I've never been able to. And that is why the hero of this picture is different from us. He is able to stand squarely in the middle and stop the fight. And it is this—him—that I thought of first. That was the beginning of the film in my mind.[8]

Stuart Galbraith may put it best:

> *Yojimbo* not only redefined the *chanbara* genre; its influence was felt all over the world, and its basic story and antihero concepts have been reworked in a myriad of genres and countries. For Japanese audiences, *Yojimbo* was unlike anything that had come before. Its overwhelming popularity proved tremendously influential. It begat countless imitations in Japan as well, but none better than the original. The hundreds of imitative *chanbara* films made since have only slightly lessened *Yojimbo*'s startling impact on audiences today.[9]

Hisaya Morishiga, Setsuko Hara, Yôsuke Natsuki, Chiemi Eri and Sô Yamamura costar in Hiroshi Inagaki's *Fundoshi Isha* [*Life of a Country Doctor*] (1961). Ryûzô Kikushima's screenplay, based on a novel by Minoru Mikano, depicts a country doctor adept at surgery but hampered by his wife's gambling addiction. Shimura appears in the small role of Matsuoemon.

Kazuo Ikehiru's *Katsukake Tokijirô* [*The Gambler's Code*] (1961), adapted from Shin Hasegawa's yakuza novel by Masaharu Matsumura and Masao Uno for Daiei, costars Shimura (as honorable gang boss Hacchônawate Tokubei) with Raizô Ichikawa as the title character (who earns the trust of Tokubei) and Michiyo Aratama as Okinu, a pregnant young widow whom he tries to rescue from an insidious rival gang. The film depicts the early days of the yakuza, which emerged during the middle Edo period (1603–1868), specifically those of the *bakuto* variety, gangsters who engaged in illegal gambling activities, at Kumagai, the eighth of 69 stations along the Nakasendô highway connecting Edo with Kyoto. Tokubei, benefiting from the swordsmanship of Tokijirô, remains in control of the Kumagai area.

The Gambler's Code, though featuring majestic mountain locations shot in color and widescreen by cinematographer Kazuo Miyagawa, is a bizarre blend of crime, action and *songs* suddenly incorporated without reason and performed by Ichikawa (1931–1969), a popular kabuki actor-singer who sadly died of cancer at age 37. The flowing fight choreography by Shôhei Miyauchi, shot in long takes with very little editing (refreshing in our current age of over-cutting and CGI animation) is a true highlight. The ending, as Tokijirô walks off down a road into the mountains, appears an *homage* to George Stevens' famous Western *Shane* (1953): The murdered Okinu's young son, who has grown attached to the "reforming" yakuza, but now left with his grandparents, repeatedly calls out, "Uncle!" and finally, "Daddy!" his young voice echoing through the valley.

Ai to honobo to [*Challenge to Live*] (1961), adapted from the Shintarô Ishihara story "Chosen" by Kaneto Shindô and directed by Eizô Sugawa for Toho, features Shimura in an outstanding cast including Tatsuya Mihashi, Yokô Tsukasa, Yumi Shirakawa, Masayuki Mori and Susumu Fugita. Masaru Satô contributed another of his atmospheric scores to this Eastmancolor and Tohoscope production, photographed by Fukuzô Koizumi.

Mosura [*Mothra*] (1961)

The success of the two Godzilla films and *Radon* [*Rodan*] (1956) inspired Tomoyuki Tanaka to produce *Mothra*, another *kaijū tokusatsu eiga* with a screenplay by Shin'íchi Sekizawa, based on the Toho-commissioned novel, *The Luminous Fairies and Mothra*, by Shin'íchirô Nakamura, Takehiko Fukunaga and Yoshie Hotta, serialized in the *Weekly Asahi* newspaper. Modeled on the plot of *King Kong*, the film involves four survivors of the ship *Daini-Gen'you-Maru*, wrecked during a typhoon on Infant Island, who, when returned to Japan, are examined for radiation poisoning. The sailors suggest that juice provided by the natives must have protected them from harm, and two workers from the *Nitto* newspaper, reporter Zenichiro ("Bulldog") Fukuda (popular Japanese comedian Furanki Sakai) and photographer Michi Hanamura (Kyôko Kagawa) reveal that the nation of Rolisica was responsible for atomic testing on the supposedly "uninhabited" island, a story that inspires their enthusiastic and sometimes "furious" news editor (Shimura, portraying a more subtle version of the 1930s Hollywood newspaper boss).

Japan and Rolisica send a joint expedition to Infant Island. On board ship are radiation specialist Dr. Harada (Ken Uehara), anthropologist Dr. Shinίchi Chûjô (Hiroshi Koizumi), Rolisican promoter Clark Nelson [Kurâruku Neruson] (Jerî Itô) and Fukuda, who stows away. On Infant Island, Chûjô, by reading ancient hieroglyphs, discovers the secret of Mothra and the *Shobijin*, tiny twins (actual twin sisters Yumi and Emi Itô, who performed as the singing group *Za Pinattsu* [The Peanuts]) who, along with their fellow natives, worship the Lepidoptera as a god. The scientists and diplomats return home, but the greedy Nelson and his gang remain to kidnap the twins for an exploitation campaign back in Japan.

The *Shobijin* and natives call upon Mothra for help. She hatches from her egg as a giant caterpillar, swims to Japan, sinking a luxury liner and surviving a blanket of napalm on the way. After wreaking havoc, she spins a cocoon on the wreckage of Tokyo Tower. Metamorphosed into a huge moth, she then destroys much of the Rolisican capitol, "New Kirk City," with the wind from the flapping of her wings, before being united with the *Shobijin*.

In a scene featuring a flood bursting through a dam, Fukuda proves himself a true hero by rescuing an accidentally abandoned baby in the middle of a bridge. The avaricious Nelson, who had grown to be loathed by the public, due in large part to an unrelenting press campaign waged by the *Nitto* editor, is gunned down by the police. At one point, Shimura clearly enjoys his performance as his character informs Fukuda that they are no longer newsmen but "social workers."

Although inspired by mythology from an earlier era, much obvious Christian imagery (first seen in the hieroglyphs on Infant Island by Chûjô) is featured during the film's closing moments. Many shouts of "Sayônara!" accompany the *Shobijin* as they head back to the island atop Mothra's head. The one major change from *King Kong* insisted upon by Ishirô Honda was that his film have a happy ending.

Originally the creature was designed to resemble a scientifically accurate, much more horrific, tussock moth, but her features eventually were softened considerably, with most of the destruction from her rampage being accidental. The concept of a divine Lepidoptera can be found in the mythology of the East and the West. The Greek goddess Psyche had been represented as a moth, so depicting a giant monster with godlike qualities didn't seem too unreasonable to the makers of *Mosura* [*Mothra*] the final title of the film, released in Japan on July 30, 1961. Selling nine million-plus tickets, it proved a massive success. The U.S. version, dubbed into English and cut from 101 to 90 minutes, hit screens across the country on May 10, 1962.

Ishin no kagarabi [*Restoration Fire*] (1961; directed by Sadatsugu Matsuda): Takashi Shimura as Yahei Kazuma, whose son, Ando, is forced to commit *seppuku* by Hijikata Toshizô, Vice-Commander of the Shinsengumi, the special police force drawn from the sword schools of Edo during the late Tokugawa shogunate.

The film features a fast pace, with effective cross-cutting by Honda and editor Kazuji Taira, fluid camerawork by Hajime Koizumi, and good performances from Shimura, Kyôko Kagawa and the Itô sisters. U.S. reviewers singled out the Itôs, as well as the Tohoscope color and the special effects of Eiji Tsuburaya.

Hideo Suzuki directed Shimura and a fine cast, including Ryô Ikebe, Michiyo Aratama and Akihiko Hirata, in the black-and-white Tohoscope drama *Kuroi gashû dainibu: Kanryû* [*Structure of Hate*] (1961). Toho also reunited Shimura with Kamatari Fugiwara for Yasuki Chiba's *Futari no musuko* [*Different Sons*] (1961).

Ishin no kagarabi [*Restoration Fire*] (1961), directed by Sadatsugu Matsuda for Toei, casts Shimura as Yahei Kazuma, a maker of footwear whose son, Ando, is forced to commit *seppuku* by Hijikata Toshizô (Chiezô Kataoka), Vice-Commander of the Shinsengumi, the special police force drawn from the sword schools of Edo during the late Tokugawa shogunate (1863–1869), and who fought the Reformists under Aizu Daimyô Matsudaira Katamori in Kyoto. A slow-moving 86-minute drama dragged down by a romantic subplot involving Hijikata and Ofusa (Chikage Awashima), *Restoration* finally catches fire when Shimura appears, lending the film some genuine emotion as the pitiful Yahei, mourning his son and the baby miscarried by his daughter-in-law, Omine (Noriko Kitazawa), refuses to supply a pair of slippers for the Shinsengumi leader.

An interesting connection to Shimura is the film's brief depiction of the Shinsengumi clashing with the pro-Imperial Chôshû and Satsuma clans at the Battle of Toba-Fushimi, in which his grandfather had fought in January 1868. Although it is not shown, the burning of Osaka Castle is mentioned.

Tsubaki Sanjûrô [*Sanjuro*] (1962)

Akira Kurosawa, assisted by Hideo Oguni and Ryûzô Kikushima, had adapted a script for *Sanjuro* from the novel *Hibi heian* by Shugôrô Yamamoto before making *Yojimbo*. The initial characterization of the title figure was a samurai who used his wiles far better than his sword, but after *Yojimbo* became a smash success, Toho asked Kurosawa to rewrite the screenplay so that Mifune again could play the hero. Kurosawa agreed, intending to ask Hiromichi Horikawa to direct the film, but the studio knew it would be far better if the master made it himself. Following a third rewrite, making Sanjûrô an even stronger character, and incorporating only a third of the original draft, Kurosawa was set to direct.

Mifune again portrays the unkempt, capable and cunning Sanjûrô, but he sports a different family name in this stand-alone *jidai-geki* "comic prequel." In both films, he chooses these names from the vegetation he spies growing nearest to him: in *Yojimbo*, it's *"Kuwabutake"* [mulberry field]; in *Sanjuro*, *"Tsubaki"* [camellia]. The character is also quite different in nature: *Yojimbo* depicts him as a nearly superhuman force who, though put through a veritable meat-grinder, triumphs over an entire community of treacherous, murderous fools; while *Sanjuro* presents a down-to-earth, imperfect, yet extremely capable swordsman dealing with a more diverse group.

Tatsuya Nakadai, as Hanbei Muroto, again plays Mifune's deadly enemy, but here he is, not a reptilian gunslinger, but a swordsman intensely loyal to the samurai code who serves as henchman to the city's Superintendent.

Keiju Kobayashi, originally cast in the leading role when Kurosawa had chosen Horikawa to direct the film, instead plays "Kimura, the Captured Samurai in the Closet" of Terada (Akihiko Hirata). He later described what Kurosawa expected from his actors (a comment that reflects the director's overall style, which consistently integrates movements from actors and the camera):

> I thought I'd be nervous but wasn't. [He] wasn't satisfied with just a verbal performance; he wanted us to act with our entire body. Of course, this is not easy. You can see what he's after by watching Mr. Mifune."[10]

Production on *Sanjuro* began on September 25, 1961, with Kurosawa and cinematographers Fukuzô Koizumi and Takao Saitô primarily shooting the film in sequence. Interior scenes at Toho were filmed first, and then the crew began to work at exterior locations (including a shrine at Gotemba) on November 1. Except for one stumbling block, which greatly annoyed Kurosawa (the tedious process of preparing the camellias [artificial elements were combined with leaves from the *sakai* plant, which had to be replaced each morning]), the shoot went smoothly and quickly, wrapping on December 1. *Sanjuro* took less time to make than any other major film of Kurosawa's mature period, and he admitted that he had "great fun" during most of the production.[11]

As a contrast to *Yojimbo*, set in a dusty, windswept village on the plains, *Sanjuro* takes place in a Tokugawa seaside castle town. The film opens with a group of nine young samurai, led by Iori Azaka (Yûzô Kayama), nephew of Chamberlain Mutsuda (Yûnosuke Itô), meeting in a deserted shrine to discuss his uncle's destruction of their petition to end the graft and corruption waged by the town's organized crime structure. Mutsuda's remark, "Perhaps I'm behind it all, you never know. After all, people aren't what they seem to be. *You* have no idea which the bad ones are. It's dangerous, very dangerous," has enraged them. The gathering was organized by Iori after reporting the Chamberlain's response to the Superintendent, who suggested the shrine as the meeting place.

Awakening from a nap in the temple, Sanjûrô enters the room, surprising the nine, who reach for their swords. He obviously has overheard their plans to continue their crusade against corruption, and impresses them by explaining his ideas about the Chamberlain and Superintendent:

> I don't know because I've never met the [Chamberlain]—that is one of the things about eavesdropping ... outsiders can judge a lot better. He's ugly, I hear. Well, that's a good thing. At least he seems honest. He told you he didn't mind being called a fool, is that right? Well, any man who says that isn't likely to be entirely bad. Now the Superintendent. You say that he is honest and sincere. That must mean he is a fine-looking, handsome man, right? But people are not what they seem. The Chamberlain told you that you didn't know who the bad ones were, didn't he? And you don't. I think the Superintendent is behind the whole thing.

Sanjûrô's conjectures describe the theme of the film. Here, Kurosawa again examines illusion versus reality; in Donald Richie's words, "things as they seem, things as they are, and the muddle that comes from confusing them."[12]

The Chamberlain has been kidnapped by the Superintendent and his gang, led by Hanbei, and the young samurai are aided by Sanjûrô in rescuing the Chamberlain's wife (Takako Irie) and daughter (Reiko Dan), as well as the politician himself. Following another spectacular Mifune-Nakadai sword duel (concluding shockingly, with a lightning-fast slice through the heart of Hanbei, unleashing a *geyser* of blood [chocolate syrup and carbonated water propelled by 30 pounds of pressure]), Sanjûrô informs the impressed group of nine (whose leader has called his actions "splendid"):

Shut up. What was so great about that? He was exactly like me—a drawn sword. Your old lady was right. Really good swords are kept in their scabbards. Yours better stay in yours. And don't try to follow me or I'll kill you. Goodbye.

Following a test-screening on December 27, *Sanjuro* was released domestically on January 1, 1962, surpassing *Yojimbo* at the box office to become the highest grossing Japanese film of the year. Produced for $500,000 (U.S.), it raked in $1.25 million in rental fees. Critics also greatly admired the film, and it ranked fifth on *Kinema Junpô*'s "Ben Ten" list for 1962.

Actors Reiko Dan, Masao Shimizu (who plays Kikui) and Mie Hama (whose current Toho film was *Kingu Kongu tai Gojira* [*King Kong vs. Godzilla*]) all flew to Los Angeles to attend the U.S. premiere at the Toho La Brea, where it was included in a June 14–18, 1962, festival of the studio's films. *Sanjuro* garnered Kurosawa some of the finest U.S. reviews (particularly from *Variety* and *The Hollywood Reporter*) of his career. He said,

Personally, I think this film very different from *Yojimbo*. In Japan the audience does too. The youngsters loved *Yojimbo*, but it was the adults who liked *Sanjuro*. I think they liked it because it is the funnier and really the most attractive of the two.[13]

Donald Richie described Kurosawa's artistic intent behind the film:

That final fight, that single heroic slash, followed by the spectacular demise of Nakadai, contains Kurosawa's comment.... That grand *splaaaaat* at the end is a lethal thrust indeed—straight into the heart of conventional *jidai-geki*, and all of the more stupid feudal remains it so appeals to.[14]

After his small part as Kurofuji in *Sanjuro*, Shimura remained at Toho for director Shûe Matsubayashi's *Zoku sararîman shimizu minato* (1962) and *Long Way to Okinawa* (1962), directed by Hideo Suzuki and featuring Akira Takarada, Yuriko Hoshi and Mie Hama. Following a supporting role in Senkichi Taniguchi's wartime adventure *Kurenai no sora* [*Scarlet Sky*] (1962), Shimura returned to the familiar *kaijû tokusatsu* genre for Toho.

Yôsei Gorasu [*Gorath, the Monstrous Star*] (1962)

Shimura plays the familiar supporting role of kindly, wise paleontologist Kensuke Sonada in *Gorath*, another Ishirô Honda-Eiji Tsuburaya *kaijû tokusatsu* extravaganza. Toho's theme of international cooperation continues in Takeshi Kimura's screenplay, based on a story by Jôjirô Okami about the core of a collapsed star whose gravitational force is 6,000 times that of Earth, the planet directly in its rogue trajectory.

To attract a larger audience, producer Tomoyuki Tanaka asked Honda to add a *kaijû* to the story, so one six-minute sequence involving the enormous "Maguma," resembling a walrus and named after magma, the subterranean mixture of molten and semi-molten rock, crystals and gas, was created. Its rampage at the South Pole results when ice is melted by heat from rocket boosters used to help move the Earth out of Gorath's route.

This Tohoscope film premiered in Japan on March 21, 1962, and in the U.S. as *Gorath*, in an inferior, English-dubbed version shorn of the Maguma material, on May 15, 1964. The English-language script was written by John Meredyth Lucas, the adopted son of Michael Curtiz, later known for his work as both writer and director on the *Mannix* (1967–1974) and original *Star Trek* (1967–1969) television series.

Loosely inspired by Herman Melville's *Moby Dick*, *Kujira gami* [*Killer Whale*, aka *The Whale God*] (1962), directed by Tokuzô Tanaka for Daiei, features Shimura, as the elder of Wadaura Village, in stunning black-and-white compositions shot in widescreen by master cinematographer Setsuo Kobayashi. *Kujira gami*, designed by special effects director Chikara Komatsubara, was the first *kaijû* created by Daiei Studios, and is effectively edited into scenes integrating at-sea action with close-ups of the fisherman determined to end its destructive and murderous existence.

The Whale God, rather than featuring one Ahab-like captain obsessed with killing the beast, involves an entire Christian community led by Shimura's old samurai, who promises to reward the spearman who "brings him the snout of the whale" with everything he possesses, including his land, title, and hand of his daughter, Toya (Kyôko Enami), in marriage. And Shimura's character is not all talk, as he joins the rest of the fisherman in

Kujira gami [*Killer Whale*] (1962): Takashi Shimura as the charismatic village elder in this interesting, stunningly photographed (by Setsuo Kobayashi) Japanese variation on Herman Melville's classic novel *Moby Dick*. Designed by special effects director Chikara Komatsubara, the whale was the first *kaijû* character created by Daiei Studios.

their rousing and dangerous maritime mission to destroy the cause of so much misery to their village and many neighboring fishing communities.

Arguably it must have seemed natural that Hiroshi Inagaki eventually contributed his personal version (from a screenplay by Toshio Yasumi) of *Chûshingura* [*The Loyal 47 Samurai*] (1962) to the long history of films on the subject. Toho's Tomoyuki Tanaka, sharing production duties with Inagaki and Sanezumi Fujimoto, intended this lavish, three and one-half hour Eastmancolor, widescreen epic shot by Kazuo Yamada, graced by an all-star cast, featuring production design by Kisaku Itô and Hiroshi Ueda, and another of Akira Ifukube's memorable musical scores, as a top highlight of the studio's 30th anniversary year.

Shimura, as Hyôbu Chisaka, appears amid the formidable cast of more than 100 players, including Yûzô Kayama, Tatsuya Mihashi, Akira Takarada, Yôsuke Natsuki, Seizaburô Kawazu, Daisuke Katô, Ryô Ikebe, Setsuko Hara (in her final film) and Toshirô Mifune (receiving "special guest star" billing as Genba Tawaraboshi, a character who appears on screen for only 15 minutes). Although the historical Hyôbu Chisaka (1638–1700), a high-ranking samurai official with the "outsider" Uesugi clan during the Edo period, died prior to the activities of the "Forty-Seven Ronin," he often appears as a character in fictional accounts of the story, including this film.

Kayama portrays Lord Takuminkami Asano, who must commit *seppuku* after striking the imperial retainer Lord Kôzukenosuke Kira (Chûsha Ichikawa). Asano's chamberlain, Ôishi Kuranosuke (Matsumoto Hakuô), plots secretly for two years until, on January 30, 1703, he and Asano's loyal group of *ronin* attack the mansion of Kira, whom they murder before carrying his decapitated head through the streets, knowing they, too, will be sentenced to commit *seppuku*.

Stuart Galbraith notes,

> At 204 minutes, the film is never less than fascinating, often deeply moving, rich in characterization, with a thrilling climax. It manages to both glorify and criticize the *bushido* and the intractable regimentation of Japanese society. And in sheer production alone, its scope has never been equaled. For Toho, the 1962 *Chûshingura* was a culmination of everything they had built in the postwar era. Never again would they produce a film on this scale.[15]

On October 10, 1963, Toho premiered a severely truncated, 108-minute version of *Chûshingura* at their La Brea theater in Los Angeles, where the screening was attended by Masao Shimizu, Yôko Tsukasa and Kumi Mizuno, all of whom then moved on to the official opening in New York. Subsequently, San Francisco theater owner Edward Landberg, who served as President of the Berkeley Cinema Guild, acquired the U.S. distribution rights to the original 208-minute cut. A successful 41-week run attended by University of California–Berkeley students led to many bookings in other areas of the nation,

11. Akira, Toshirô and Oji-chan

including New York, where the uncut version met with considerable success in October 1966.

Several members of the *Chûshingura* cast also costar in Toho's World War II drama *Taiheiyo no tsubasa* [*Wing of the Pacific*, aka *Attack Squadron!*] (1963), a follow-up to *Storm Over the Pacific* directed by Shûe Matsubayashi and featuring special effects by Eiji Tsuburaya. Toshirô Mifune, as Lieutenant Colonel Senda, is supported by Yûzô Kayama, as Captain Shiro Taki, Susumu Fugita, as Second Fleet Commander Shuichi Itô, and Shimura, as Admiral Kojirô Oikawa. Senda, near the end of the Pacific War, is staunchly against sending Japan's surviving fighter pilots on *kamikaze* missions, instead choosing to form an elite group of airmen to regain supremacy in three locations: Rabaul ("Tenshin"), under the command of Teppei Yano (Makoto Satô); Okinawa ("Ishinbun"), led by Captain Ataka (Yôsuke Natsuki); and the Philippines ("Shinsengumi"), headed by Captain Taki.

The opening scene features both Mifune and Shimura, whose Admiral supports Senda's lone stand against "suicide attacks." "It's cowardly defeatism," Senda states at one point.

Tsubaraya's special effects work, less flamboyant here than in *Storm Over the Pacific*, is also more convincing, as Senda's three groups in the "343 Air Corps" are successful in raising the morale of the Japanese Navy. When the ship *Yamato*, under Commander Ito, is doomed to be sunk by the enemy, four pilots from the remaining combined squadron disobey orders, instead becoming what Senda describes as "not humans, but bombs."

The actual Japanese battleship *Yamato*, commissioned one week after the attack on Pearl Harbor, had served as flagship of the fleet at the Battle of Midway (June 1942), was present at the Battle of the Philippine Sea (June 1944), and saw action at the Battle of Leyte Gulf (October 1944). In April 1945, she was ordered on a "one-way mission" to Okinawa, to defend the island at all costs. On April 7, while commanded by Vice-Admiral Seiichi Itô (1890–1945), and having no air support, she was hit by at least 17 bombs and torpedoes, capsized and exploded. The resulting mushroom cloud could be seen on Kyûshû, one hundred miles distant. Itô, having ordered his escorts to rescue any survivors, chose to go down with the *Yamato* and crew.

The pilots in the "343 Air Corps" were not involved with the actual *Yamato*. In the film, the surviving airmen return to Senda at the Matsuyama base, from where they fly out to sacrifice themselves during a subsequent air battle.

The historical Admiral Koshirô Oikawa (1883–1958) graduated from the Imperial Japanese Naval Academy, receiving his first command in 1911. Twenty years later, he became Director of the IJNA, was promoted to Vice-Admiral in 1933, and supported the 1930 London Naval Treaty, an agreement between the UK, Japan, France, Italy and the U.S., which limited naval armament and regulated submarine warfare. As a full admiral, he was appointed

Minister of the Imperial Japanese Navy (1940–41); hoping to prevent war, he continued to build close ties with the United States and opposed conflict with the Soviet Union. During World War II, he served as a Naval Councilor and Chief of the General Staff, finally resigning in protest in May 1945, when, Emperor Hirohito, knowing that Japan already had lost, refused to consider peace proposals. Oikawa lived in retirement until his death at age 75. In the film, Shimura, again ideally cast, portrays the leader with the level-headed humanity that he exhibited in real life.

An epilogue, depicting young residents sailing from a nearby beach at the time of the film's release, features Mifune's optimistic narration:

> Seventeen years have passed. Peace is here to stay. You've won it for us. Taki! Ataka! Yano!
>
> These youngsters will never know the atrocities of war. They've set out to explore new horizons.
>
> Let the Pacific Ocean remain peaceful, as it was meant to be.

12

Tengoku to jigoku (1963)

> [Toshirô] Mifune was a great actor who could do one thing
> very well; Shimura was a great actor whose versatility was
> seemingly limitless.—Alex Cox, British Film Institute[1]

Fifteen years after directing his first gritty modern crime films, *Drunken Angel* and *Stray Dog*, Akira Kurosawa (collaborating with Hideo Oguni, Eijirô Hisaita, and Ryûzô Kikushima) chose to adapt the 1959 novel *King's Ransom*, an "87th Precinct" paperback mystery by New Yorker Ed McBain (born Salvatore Albert Lombino, and sometimes known as Evan Hunter) into a far more mature police procedural, *Tengoku to jigoku* [*High and Low*]. This gripping narrative, symphonically directed, photographed by Azakazu Nakai and Takao Saitô, and edited by Kurosawa and Reiko Kaneko, involves Kingo Gondo (Toshirô Mifune), a National Shoes business executive refusing to increase profits by selling an inferior product line. Gondo's young boy, Jun (Toshio Egi), is targeted for kidnapping by medical intern Ginjirô Takeuchi (Tsutomu Yamazaki), a mentally disturbed drug addict, who mistakenly grabs Shinichi (Masahiko Shimazu), the son of Gondo's chauffeur, Aoki (Yutaka Sada).

Kurosawa assembled a who's who of his acting "stock company" for the film: Mifune, Kyôko Kagawa, Tatsuya Nakadai, Yoshio Tsuchiya, Susumu Fugita, Takeshi Katô, Nobuo Nakamura, Yûnosuke Itô, Minoru Chiaki, Eijirô Tôno, Kamatari Fugiwara and, billed 11th, Shimura as Chief of the Investigation Section. Though set in post–Occupation Japan (Yokohama, where much of the location work was done), the film acknowledges it roots in U.S. police procedural cinema, particularly the groundbreaking postwar classics *T-Men* (1947), directed by Anthony Mann, and *The Naked City* (1948), directed by Jules Dassin.

Tengoku to jigoku literally translates as "Heaven and Hell," but the "High" and "Low" of the English title refer to the respective environments inhabited by the contestants in this kidnapping and extortion stand-off: Gondo, in his mansion on the "heavenly" hill; and Takeuchi, in his shack located in the dope-infested "hellish" slums. In a 2008 essay, Geoffrey O'Brien points out,

> The real hero may be neither Gondo nor Inspector Tokura [Nakadai] but the bald, blunt, bull-like Head Detective Taguchi [Kenjirô Ishiyama], a working class-hero of the oldest school who can barely hold back his contempt for the weaselly executives of National Shoes when they hang Gondo out to dry; or perhaps Aoki, who suffers not only the loss of his child but the intolerable burden of having him restored at his employer's expense, placing him in the position of having received a gift he can never repay and has destroyed the giver...[2]

Kurosawa, who began production at Toho on September 2, 1962, often shot his scenes with two or three cameras simultaneously. His preference for long takes featuring ensemble acting rehearsed to naturalistic "perfection" can be seen in abundance in *High and Low*, with one single take running nearly 10 minutes. To capture enough workable footage for the finale of this film, set on an actual moving express train (the "Kodama Super Express"), he used a total of *nine* cameras. Donald Richie, who visited the set, wrote,

> Ordinary actors would probably become exhausted, but Kurosawa's actors are not ordinary—they are of a professionalism rare even in Japan. And there is no guesswork about a "peak" performance—actors this professional can give the "peak" whenever the director tells them to.
>
> "Of course," Mifune told me, "as the scenes get longer and longer, it gets harder and harder for us. When we take this scene, one little mistake and we do the whole thing over again. He would probably make it even longer except that the cameras can only hold a thousand feet of film at a time. One mistake and we reload. Still, this is what makes it interesting for us, and that is why anyone who is any good at all longs for a role in a Kurosawa film. We know we have to be perfect."[3]

The end of this film, showing the faces of Gondo and the doomed Taheuchi reflected together in the glass at the prison, blurs the boundaries between "Heaven" and "Hell," with neither man's morality being totally "positive" nor "negative." Like much great art, *High and Low* offers moral ambiguity. As stated by Stuart Galbraith, the dual reflection suggests that

> Kurosawa is saying that each of us is capable of both good and evil, that we choose to be good or bad, or both for that matter. What's important about the reflections in the glass isn't that they become one.... Kurosawa does this to illustrate the thin line, literally and figuratively, that separates them. More precisely, what's shown is how much of Takeuchi is buried within Gondo, and of Gondo within Takeuchi. The great sadness of this scene is Gondo's realization that he's rather like the kidnapper himself.... Choice rather than circumstance is all that separates them. Takeuchi believed his hate is what kept him alive, when in fact it proved his undoing. Gondo, on the other hand, made difficult, agonizing choices in a random, chaotic world where choice is the only thing he has.

12. Tengoku to jigoku (1963)

In the end, Kurosawa says, money and poverty, heaven and hell are meaningless. The film finishes with a shot of Gondo facing the closed shutter, his face reflected in the glass—Gondo confronting himself. Though the film ends in a vaguely hopeful way (suggesting that Gondo has recognized the ugliness within him), it nonetheless concludes on a deeply sad, existential note.[4]

High and Low (or "Heaven and Hell"), running 142 minutes, deals with two different planes of existence, and Kurosawa divides the film into two parts: the first, depicting the botched crime and negotiations with the kidnapper, set primarily within the confines of Gondo's living room; and the second, involving the delivery of the ransom, lengthy investigation and capture of the criminal, on the express train and in various areas across Yokohama. Brilliantly, the director uses separate, distinct styles of cinematography and editing (the first employing long takes kept dynamic by superb writing, acting, camerawork and cutting; and the second involving more kinetic camerawork and cutting) to contrast these two "movements" of this markedly symphonic film. With this work, Kurosawa proves the "infinite" possibilities of great cinema, by consistently multiplying these "divisions of two" by three dimensions (two actual and one suggested).

High and Low is one of the most believable and realistic crime films ever made, often graced with a documentary atmosphere free of the artifice usually generated in this genre, particularly the modern use of unnatural sound and visual effects, extraneous violence and bloodshed. (At times, it is reminiscent of Fritz Lang's *M* [1930], yet another hint of Kurosawa's admiration for the German Expressionist master.)

Shimura's Chief of the Investigation Section enters the film at the 71-minute mark, and intermittently appears as his many officers report their individual progress in locating the kidnapper, who becomes a murderer after providing a rare, 90-percent pure form of heroin to his two accomplices, long-term junkies who perish in a seaside hideout at Enomisha.

An especially memorable statement, summing up the film's depiction of Gondo's capitalist "colleagues," is given by Chief Detective 'Bos'n' Taguchi (Kenjirô Ishiyama), who informs the Chief and his fellow officers, "I met today with the National Shoes executives." As he raises his right hand to scratch his forehead, he displays "the finger" as he adds, "What a bunch of assholes!"

Takeuchi finally is captured when he attempts to purchase more heroin after returning to a popular nightspot (Negishiya Bar, populated by many U.S. G.I.s Kurosawa had hired for the scene) and "Dope Alley," a sequence that adds a particularly squalid touch to the realism of the film. Kurosawa and Masaru Satô's choice of including "'O Sole Mio" (also popularly known as "It's Now or Never" in 1963) on the soundtrack adds powerful counterpoint to the officers' apprehension and handcuffing of the junkie-kidnapper-killer.

High and Low, with exterior scenes also filmed in Enomisha, Kamakura, Kishigoe, Chiyoda-ku and at the Sakawa River, took nearly five months to produce, opening in Japan on March 1, 1963. A widespread critical success, it also became the highest-grossing Japanese film of the year, surpassing both *Yojimbo* and *Sanjuro* by raking in rentals of $1.3 million (U.S.). A United States release followed on November 26, 1963, at the Toho Cinema in New York. A more widespread distribution led to mixed reviews, due to American journalists' inability to understand why such a technically brilliant filmmaker would choose such "inferior" material. Kurosawa's indirect social commentary flew right over their heads.

Shimura again is ideally cast as a cool-headed, respected veteran authority figure; and Tatsuya Nakadai's intelligent and sympathetic characterization of Inspector Tokura, who forges an amiable relationship with the troubled Gondo, provides quite a contrast to those of his arch-villains with Mifune's wandering *ronin* in *Yojimbo* and *Sanjuro*. When Kurosawa was unsure how to end the film, Nakadai thought a brief scene involving Tokura and Gondo discussing the latter's situation following the criminal's sentencing would provide the appropriate closure, but the director devised the brilliant conclusion, with Takeuchi asking Gondo (who again is making his own shoes, competing with his former company), "What are you doing now?"

High and Low includes two technical firsts for Kurosawa: the use of four-track stereophonic sound (the Westrex Recording System) and a brief use of color, a burst of pink smoke seen from the window of Gondo's mansion when the kidnapper burns the two leather cases used to deliver the 30 million-yen ransom. In a nice narrative touch, Gondo joins the police in tracking down the criminal by again becoming the working-class man, using his old shoe-making tools to plant powder (which will burn pink) in the bags. The previous year, Kurosawa had wanted to depict red camellias in the black-and-white *Sanjuro*, but this effect couldn't be achieved successfully; for *High and Low*, the director and his crew, with great difficulty, were able to include this inspired cinematic use of the format.

Masahiro Makino's *Hasshu yukyoden—otoko no sakazuki* [*Gambler Tales of Hasshu: A Man's Pledge*] (1963), costarring Chiezô Kataoka (as Chuji Kunisada, "Japan's Robin Hood" of the Edo period), Shin'ichi [Sonny] Chiba (as a victim of criminals) and Shimura (as Chuji's father), is a minor Toei *jidai-geki* yakuza drama. *Boryokudan* [*Violent Gang*] (1963), a *noir*-like, modern *jitsoroku* [true account] crime film directed by Shigehiro Ozawa for Toiei, again features Shimura as a yakuza boss. Director Eizô Sugawa then brought him back to Toho for *Taiyô wa yondeiru* (1963), costarring Yûzô Kayama and Yôko Fujiyama.

Dai tuzoku [*The Lost World of Sinbad*] (1963), directed in Tohoscope and blazing Eastmancolor by Senkichi Taniguchi, has alternately been titled

12. Tengoku to jigoku (1963)   135

The Adventures of Sinbad, The Great Thief, The Great Bandit, 7th Wonder of Sinbad and, most ridiculously, *Samurai Pirate*. This ludicrous but often entertaining *tokusatsu eiga* stars Toshirô Mifune in a completely earnest performance as the adventurous Sukezaemon Naya ["Sinbad" in the English version], as if he instead was playing one of Kurosawa's serious dramatic characters.

The setting is a mythical Middle Eastern kingdom, but uneasily comprised of Arabic, Chinese, Indian and South Seas cultural elements. Falsely accused of being a pirate, Sukezaemon decides to become one; and, in the process, rescues the realm of old King Raksha (Shimura) and Princess Yaya (Mie Hama) from the evil Premier (Tadao Nakamaru), who has conspired with the Black Pirate (Makoto Satô) to wrest control. Eiji Tsubaraya (who reportedly didn't get along well with the director) again contributes a host of wild visual effects to a Toho fantasy, highlighted by scenes of flaming arrows and a hideous, Gorgon-like witch (Hideyo "Eisei" Amamoto, in drag) who, upon seeing her own reflection, is turned to stone.

Shimura finally makes an appearance, in a drugged, comatose state, two-thirds into this 96-minute film. He eventually rallies to a semblance of life, and then is seen uttering one line of dialogue, inquiring as to the whereabouts of the heroic pirate, as the king reclaims his throne during the closing sequence. As in other films, the producers (Tomoyuki Tanaka and Kenichirô Tsunoda) didn't need an actor of Shimura's caliber to play this character; but merely having him appear, even for a single minute, added some prestige to the project.

Dai tuzoku was a box-office hit in Japan; but, like other *tokusatsu eiga*, became a confusing mess after being dubbed into English by American International Pictures for release as *The Lost World of Sinbad*. Reviewers in the United States, though noting Mifune's "intensity" and the impressive color cinematography, dismissed it as just another "Sinbad" adventure (a label tacked on by AIP, who quickly sold it into television syndication). Stuart Galbraith notes, "Takashi Shimura [is] wasted in a cameo part…. Ironically, more Americans were introduced to Toshirô Mifune through this tacky picture than through all his Kurosawa films combined."[5]

Hirokazu Ichimura directed Shimura in his final role of 1963, Nagisa yo yuki jo, in *Tsukiyo no wataridori*, also featuring Mieko Takamine and Yoshiko Kayama, released by Shochiku on December 24. He managed to appear in just six productions the following year, but one proved a major *kaijû tokusatsu* success, and another one of the greatest of all serious Japanese "horror" films.

Jinsei Gekijo: shin hisha kaku [*Theater of Life—New Hishakaku Story*] (1964), directed by Tadashi Sawashima for Toiei, again drew him into the world of the modern yakuza. *Chi to daiyamondo* [*Blood and Diamonds*] (1964), starring Akira Takarada and Yôsuke Natsuki, a black-and-white Tohoscope crime drama directed by Jun Fukuda, followed.

Aku no monsho [*Brand of Evil*] (1964), a crime drama directed by Hiromichi Horikawa for the Takarazuka Motion Picture Company and released through Toho, cast him in support of Tsutomu Yamazaki, Michiyo Aratama and Kyôko Kishida. Kajirô Yamamoto's color Cinemascope comedy *Tensai sagishi monogatari: Tanuki no hanamachi* (1964) teamed him with Keiju Kobayashi, Keiko Awaji and Yôko Tsukasa.

Ghidorah: The Three-Headed Monster (1964)

Shimura was back in a major *kaijû* supporting role, Dr. Tsukamoto, a distinguished psychiatrist with his own laboratory, in another Honda-Tsuburaya collaboration, *San Daikaijū: Chikyū Saidai no Kessen* [*Three Giant Monsters: The Greatest Battle on Earth*] (1964), a follow-up to the successful *Mosura tai Gojira* [*Mothra vs. Godzilla*, aka *Godzilla vs. the Thing*] (1964). Shiníchi Sekizawa's screenplay features two major subplots that slickly merge: En route to Japan, the plane of Princess Selino Salno of Selgina (Akiko Wakabayashi) explodes, while a meteor lands, attracting the interest of Professor Murai (Hiroshi Koizumi).

Police Detective Shindo (Yôsuke Natsuki) notices the striking resemblance of a rumored "prophet from Venus" to the assumed deceased princess. Attracting large crowds, she correctly predicts the return of both Rodan and Godzilla. She also warns of the arrival of King Ghidorah, who will destroy the Earth unless its nations join forces. Selina's uncle (Shin Ôtomo), continuing his assassination plot, sends his right-hand man, Malmess (Hisaya Itô) and his gang to Japan to make another attempt and steal her priceless golden bracelet. Warned by the *Shobijin* (Emi and Yumi Itô), who are in Tokyo for a television show, Shindo temporarily foils the assassins.

The *Shobijin* remain in Tokyo due to Godzilla's sinking of the cruise ship upon which they were to return to Infant Island. Malmess again tries to kill the princess, whom Shindo believes suffers from "acute amnesia and megalomania," but is prevented by Godzilla and Rodan's duel ravaging of the city. As Dr. Tsukamoto, Shimura plays his role with calm credibility, even when the gang shoots it out in his laboratory and as he watches the titanic struggle between four monsters, including King Ghidorah, who has risen like a phoenix from the meteor, and a new Mothra caterpillar summoned by the *Shobijin*.

The gang eventually is buried in their car when a ray from Ghidorah causes an avalanche, the same occurrence that takes out Malmess after he fires one last shot at the princess, who regains her memory when being wounded. Dr. Tsukamoto explains that her prophetic powers were due to shock caused by the explosion when she escaped from the plane, the defeated Ghidorah is tossed into outer space, and Godzilla and Rodan beat their respective retreats.

Designed by Akira Watanabe, King Ghidorah, a gold, three-headed, bat-winged, twin-tailed dragon based on the *Yamata no Orochi* [eight-branched giant snake] from Japanese mythology, is one of Eiji Tsuburaya's most impressive *kaijû*, requiring one man (Shôichi Hirosi, who previously wore the gorilla suit in *King Kong vs. Godzilla*) to hunch over inside the torso and up to seven in the soundstage rafters to manipulate the necks, wings and double tail. The reliable Haruo Nakajima again played Godzilla.

Toho released the film in Japan on December 20, 1964. A U.S. release by Continental Distributing, titled *Ghidorah the Three-Headed Monster*, dubbed into English and shorn from 92 to 81 minutes, premiered on September 13, 1965, double billed with *Harum Scarum* (1965), one of the most ludicrous vehicles ever yoked on Elvis Presley by avaricious puppet master "Colonel" Tom Parker. In his *New York Times* review, Vincent Canby noted, "This fascination, on the part of contemporary Japanese filmmakers, with the destruction of their land by fantastic, prehistoric forces only 20 years after Hiroshima, might be of interest to social historians."[6]

Kaidan [*Kwaidan*] (1964)

Masaki Kobayashi, famous for his socially significant and emotionally powerful *The Human Condition* (1959–1961) and *Hara Kiri* (1962), made something completely different with *Kwaidan*, an adaptation (by Yôko Mizuki) of four ghost stories from the novel *Kwaidan: Stories and Studies of Strange Things* (1904) and other books by Lafcadio Hearn [aka Koizumi Yokumo] (1850–1904), combining Yoshio Miyajima's fluid Eastmancolor and Tohoscope camerawork with Dai Arikawa's innovative set decoration (much of it hand-painted and shot in an airplane hangar). Geoffrey O'Brien has noted,

> For a film so widely and indelibly remembered, [it] has confounded a surprising number of critics over the years. Ever since its release ... there have been those who have found it too long, too artificial, too self-consciously exotic ... not scary or gory enough to qualify as a horror film. To be sure, this [is] not comparable to any other film, regardless of genre or country of origin, and unique in Kobayashi's oeuvre, defies easy categorization. This is perhaps why it has remained for countless viewers such a singular experience, clinging to memory like an unshakeable dream...[7]

As O'Brien explains, Kobayashi, who had trained as a painter, never intended to "conceal" this artificiality, in an epic in which every element is carefully "made by hand": "Such openly acknowledged artificiality has deep roots in Japanese art, and most prominently in Japanese theatrical traditions."[8] Prior to *Kwaidan*, Keisuke Kinoshita had included painted landscapes in his Fujicolor and Shochiku Grandscope epic, *Narayama bushikô* [*The Ballad of Narayama*] (1958).

Hearn, a "man without a country" who died in Tokyo, had been born to a Greek mother and Irish father in the Ionian Islands, and became known in the Caribbean and Southern United States prior to marrying a samurai-class woman and converting to Buddhism in Japan. In *Kwaidan*, meant for a Western readership, he incorporates several Japanese folk tales, some which he was writing down for the first time, integrating his own European influences along the way. These "mysteries of 'ghostly Japan,'" as O'Brien calls them, also seemed rather exotic to Japanese readers of the Meiji period:

> That era, too, in light of all the cataclysms that followed, had by 1964 acquired its own patina of myth. Myth within myth, then, exoticism within exoticism: for *Kwaidan*, the whole of the past is itself something of a supernatural phenomenon, an unreality to which we remain inescapably tied, a ghost story from which no one can entirely awake.[9]

Three of the four stories depicted in the film involve vows broken by victims of circumstance. The first, "*Kurokami*" ["The Black Hair"] deals with a poor Kyoto swordsman (Rentarô Mikuni) who divorces his wife (Michiyo Aratama) to marry a wealthier woman (Misako Watanabe), only to realize his mistake. Returning to his former love, he is shocked by a horrible discovery. The second, "*Yukionna*" ["The Woman of the Snow"], a fairy tale-like episode, involves a Musashi woodcutter (Tatsuya Nakadai) who marries and has children with Yuki (Keiko Kishi), a woman-ghost who never ages, threatens to kill him and, after 10 years, disappears into a snowstorm.

The third and longest story, "*Miminashi Hôichi no Hanashi*" ["Hoichi the Earless"], features Shimura as Head Priest at a monastery where a young blind *biwa* player (Katsuo Nakamura) is now living. The segment opens with painted and *bunraku* puppet-like enactments of the Battle of Dan-no-ura, a decisive engagement between the Heike and Genji Clans in 1185, and then depicts the spirit of a dead warrior (Tetsurô Tanba) summoning Hoichi to sing his account of the war for the departed court, who need to learn the truth about their fate.

In a film filled with long takes and stunning compositions, Kobayashi fully utilizes the widescreen image when showing the Priest questioning Hoichi about where he secretly goes every evening. Attempting to save Hoichi from a further "draining off of his life," the Priest and his attendant (Yoishi Hayashi) paint the Heart Sutra (the most well-known Buddhist scripture) on his body from head to toe; but, when the spirit again comes for him, his ears are found to be bare. The warrior, grabbing the ears to drag Hoichi back into the world of the dead, tears them off his head. This terrifying event does not kill the young monk-musician, however; and he lives on to "become a very wealthy man" by playing the *biwa* at the monastery. Katsuo Nakamura is completely convincing as Hoichi; and, once again, Shimura is well cast in a benevolent, soft-spoken role.

The fourth and final tale, "*Chawan no naka*" ["In a Cup of Tea"], features a disturbing experience in which a samurai sees a malevolent ghostly reflection (Kei Satô) on the surface of his drink. The film ends with the narrator (Osamu Takizawa) becoming another reflection in his own story.

Following a premiere at the Toho Yurakuza on December 29, 1964, *Kwaidan* was released throughout Japan on January 6, 1965. *Kinema Junpô* gave Yôko Mizuki its Best Screenplay award, while the Cannes Film Festival bestowed the Silver Jury Prize on Kobayashi. In the United States, released on November 22, 1965, it was nominated for the Best Foreign Language Film Academy Award. Unfortunately, after its Los Angeles premiere, the U.S. version was shorn of the entire "Lady of the Snow" segment, removing Tatsuya Nakadai's performance and altering the running time from 183 to only 125 minutes.

Made by Mifune Productions Co., Ltd., for distribution through Toho, *Samurai* [*Samurai Assassin*] (1965), casts the associate producer alongside Keiju Kobayashi, Michiyo Aratama, Eijirô Tôno and Shimura (as Narahisa Ichijô). Directed by Kihachi Okamoto, this political action-drama set at Edo Castle in February 1860 involving Niiro (Mifune), a bastard swordsman and suspected traitor to the House of Ii, was adapted by Shinobu Hashimoto from the book *Samurai Nippon* by Jiromasa Gunji. Shimura appears in only one scene, in which Ichijô turns down Niiro's proposal to marry his daughter, Okiku (Aratama).

Hashimoto's adaptation (which more often *tells* rather than shows) is long on dialogue and short on movement, until the final half hour, when the film finally explodes into an unpleasant flurry of (often excessive) violence. Ordered to slay Einosuke Kurihara (Kobayashi), a good friend first identified as "the real traitor," and then discovered to be innocent, Niiro also unknowingly dispatches and decapitates his own father, carrying the head around on his sword, during the climactic battle at Sakurada Gate.

Mifune had decided to form his own production company after Toho executives, claiming they were leaning mostly toward "Godzilla" and war pictures, suggested that he follow in Kurosawa's footsteps. At a time when a top Japanese star might earn only $5,000 (U.S.) for a major role, Mifune chose to assume significant financial risk in return for accepting work outside Toho, particularly the offers arriving from international producers.

Akahige [*Red Beard*] (1965)

Akira Kurosawa began production on *Red Beard*, a film he intended to be "so magnificent that people would just have to see it," in 1963.[10] During an era in which Western films (the James Bond series) and pop music were all the rage in Japan, the director persuaded Toho to spend $700,000 (U.S. dollars, enough to make 10 feature films) on this three-hour epic about selflessness and criticism of the Japanese class system. Ultimately, *Red Beard* took longer to shoot than *Seven Samurai*.

The screenplay, by Kurosawa, Ryûzô Kikushima, Hideo Oguni and Masato Ide, based on the short-story collection *Akahige shinryôtan* by Shugôrô Yamamoto and set in Edo at the end of the Tokugawa period, tells the story of ambitious young doctor Noburo Yasumoto (Yûzô Kayama). Trained at a Dutch school in Nagasaki, he is assigned to the Koishikawa Public Clinic for the poor run by the older physician Kyojô ["Red Beard"] Niidé (Toshirô Mifune), a man who believes that helping others is the only worthwhile value in life. The greater part of the film deals with the moral duel between the two doctors: the young man's desire for success versus the elder's altruism and dedication to humanity.

Kurosawa had the script ready in early July 1963. Later that month, he began casting the film, with Mifune and Kayama locked in from the start. Mifune is top-billed as the title character, but Kayama's moral transformation as the young doctor dominates the picture. Shimura plays a small supporting character role (Tokubei Izumiya, a wealthy patient Dr. Kyojô uses to help compensate for some of his constant, underfunded charity work), as does Chishû Ryû, (Mr. Yasumoto, one of his many cinematic fathers), Yasujirô Ozu's favorite actor.

Kurosawa began production on December 9, 1963. Three days later, on his 60th birthday, Ozu died, and Kurosawa, accompanied by Kajirô Yamamoto, Yasuki Chiba and Keisuke Kinoshita, took time to attend the great master's funeral. Kurosawa soon became obsessed with the absolute historical accuracy of his new film, down to the smallest detail, including every element of Yoshirô Muraki's production design in the Edo clinic sets, especially the massive hospital gate, which appears only briefly. The director's demands began to seem overblown when he insisted that Mifune, using a caustic blend of chemicals, maintain a certain shade of red for his beard, even though the Tohoscope film was shot (by Asakazu Nakai and Takao Saitô) in black-and-white.

Shooting commenced on December 21, but Kurosawa ran into costly delays, and the production ran through 1964. At various times, Kurosawa, Mifune and Kayama became ill; and the real-life aging of some actors, compared to the lesser passage of time on screen, became a problem. The most obvious casualty of the director's vast extension of the original 50-day shooting schedule was his relationship with Mifune, whose pay did not increase with the delay and total commitment to the role was not fully appreciated. (Mifune, still sporting the bushy beard, resorted to performing in a television commercial to make ends meet.)

12. Tengoku to jigoku (1963)

Kurosawa's introduction of Red Beard is textbook: Just arrived at the clinic, young Dr. Yasumoto is given a "tour" by his (anxious to depart) predecessor, who leads him through the complex to Dr. Niidé's room. The doors are slid open, and (again, appearing to pay homage to James Whale's *Frankenstein*) Kurosawa shoots Mifune with his back to the camera; Niidé then slowly turns around to stare at Yasumoto for some time before finally admitting, "Red Beard." From the first moment he appears, Mifune gives one of his finest, understated performances.

The middle hour of the film is devoted to a flashback, triggered by a landslide (brought on by one of Kurosawa's trademark torrential rainstorms), narrated by Sahachi (Tsutomu Yamazaki), a dying, much-loved patient, who wishes to "confess" the sins of his past to all his friends, who have appreciated all the aid he has given to the community's needy people. A great earthquake, which causes confusion to Sahachi and his wife, who leaves, assuming her husband will think her dead, hits (after Kurosawa uses a change of seasons, from rain to a stunning winter snow, visually heightening the flashback). When the couple (and a baby whose father is *not* Sahachi) are reunited, she, wracked with guilt, commits suicide in his arms.

Buried on the cliff behind his house, under a workshop, her skeleton was unearthed during the landslide, necessitating Sahachi's revelations about the past. The only way he had "to make amends," he explains, was "by being useful to others."

Shimura, whose appearance is one of the "blink and you'll miss him" variety, again provides an important narrative function: not only is his Izumiya one of two wealthy patients Niidé uses to help offset a deadly governmental budget cut of money to treat destitute outpatients; he also asks Red Beard if doctors really affect the recovery of an ill person. Is a good doctor no better than a bad one?

Red Beard, running 185 minutes, finally premiered on May 29, 1965. Initially successful, it was released on a limited, roadshow basis on April 3, and then nationwide at the end of the month. In Japan, the film played to strong box office for several months; critically, it won the Asahi Cultural Prize, "best film" at the Mainichi Film Competition, and *Kinema Junpô*'s Best Film and Best Director awards, among others. The U.S.S.R. bestowed it with the Film Union Prize and Mifune with the Best Actor Award.

The film did not fare as well in the United States, where it was released on January 19, 1966. U.S. audiences and reviewers had become used to the kinetic movement of recent Kurosawa films like *Yojimbo*, *Sanjuro* and *High and Low*, leaving *Red Beard* primarily misunderstood as a mere "art-house hospital drama." Comparisons to MGM's "Dr. Kildare" series of the late 1930s and 1940s are not out of line, however. The ending shows Yasumoto, rather than accepting a post as the shogun's physician, choosing to stay at the clinic.

He walks back under the gate with Niidé, who gives a playful, Dr. Gillespie (Lionel Barrymore)-like grunt. The young doctor, who has learned much from Niidé's grouchy, hardline teachings, grins in Dr. Kildare (Lew Ayres) fashion.

Mifune unfortunately parted ways with Kurosawa following his frustrating *Red Beard* experience. As Stuart Galbraith points out, the actor "would never again appear in a film as great. With very few exceptions, his subsequent roles don't even come close."[11] Thereafter, as Kurosawa's world view became darker and his ability to make films more difficult, Shimura, too, would see less of his greatest collaborator. Fifteen years would pass before they would work together again, one last time.

Matatabi san ning yakuza [*Wanderers: Three Yakuza*] (1965), a two-hour, three-part feudal gangster epic, directed by Tadashi Sawashima and shot in color and Toeiscope by Osamu Furuya for Toei Kyoto, costars Kinnosuke Nakamura and Tatsuya Nakadai, with Shimura in the third-billed role of Kakegawa Bunzo. The opening episode, set in the village of Sawara, features Nakadai as Hatsukari-no-Sentaro, a yakuza on the run from Hasshu agents for avenging the murder of his boss, who becomes involved with a young prostitute after accidentally killing her fiancé in a bamboo forest. The final story involves the boastful, aspiring yakuza Kaze-no-Kyutaro (Nakamura), who is hired by villagers to kill a despised official.

The second, and most dramatically successful, segment involves Bunzo, a dishonest gambler and "reformed" criminal, with a young yakuza, Dani-no-Genta (Hiroki Matsukata), who offers aid during a raging snowstorm. Seeking refuge in the lonely hut of Omiya, the two come to blows after the truth about the older man's attempts to "deliver" money from the abandoned woman's father, a former yakuza, is betrayed by the younger. Angered by this late attempt at reconciliation, Omiya turns Bunzo back out into the blizzard, but Genta follows; pursued by a group of swordsmen, he is driven into an avalanche of snow. This event is foreshadowed when the men first meet: "When I hear that sound, I can't help thinking about the future," admits Bunzo.

After being thrown out of the hut by Omiya, Bunzo tells Genta, "I got what I deserved." The younger gambler, just before "disappearing" into the swirling snow, points out, "It's better to have a dad, even if he's a bad yakuza." Omiya's realization that her father deserves a chance is reflected in Shimura's sympathetic characterization, another of his performances rising above the overall appeal of its host film.

The film's first two wandering yakuza meet definite fates; however (along with the older gangster in the second episode), the third, merely a pretender used by a group of selfish villagers, moves toward redemption by resisting the temptation of a young woman offered to him. The closing scene shows

12. Tengoku to jigoku (1963)

him abandoning his weapons and telltale yakuza hat in a field as he wanders off down a dusty road toward the horizon. Directed by Seiichirô Uchikawa, Sugata Sanshiro [Sanshiro Sugata] (1965), Kurosawa's attempt to placate the Toho executives after the Red Beard production imbroglio, is a direct remake of his 1943 debut film and its 1945 sequel using the original screenplays. Shimura again plays a major character; but, rather than Hansuke Murai, the now 60-year-old actor appears as Police Chief Michitsune Mishima. Fresh from his costarring per-

Matatabi san ning yakuza [Wanderers: Three Yakuza] (1965; directed by Tadashi Sawashima): In this three-part feudal gangster epic, Takashi Shimura costars in the second episode as Kakegawa Bunzo, a dishonest gambler and "reformed" criminal, who teams up with a young yakuza, Dani-no-Genta, who offers aid during a raging snowstorm.

formance in Red Beard, Yûzô Kayama follows in Susumu Fugita's footsteps as Sanshiro, and is supported by Kurosawa regulars Bokuzen Hidari, Daisuke Katô and Toshirô Mifune, as Shôgorô Yano (played by Denjirô Ôkôchi in the original). A Kurosawa-Toho (Tomoyuki Tanaka) coproduction, this 159-minute remake also features a musical score by Masaru Satô.

Toho's Taiheiyô kiseki no sakusen: Kisuka [Kiska] (1965), directed by Seiji Murayama, is another in the studio's series of World War II action dramas featuring an "all-star" cast. Adapted from the story Taiheyo kaisen saidai no Kiseki by Masataka Chihaya, Katsuya Susaki's fact-based screenplay centers on the evacuation of the Aleutian Island of Kiska by the Japanese when faced by an Allied invasion force in August 1943. This small, frozen isle had been captured by a special Imperial Navy landing party, supported by 500 marines, on June 6, 1942, the same day on which the Battle of Midway was fought.

Shimura plays "President of the Military Command" among a formidable array of familiar faces, including Toshirô Mifune, Sô Yamamura, Susumu Fugita, Kô Nishimura, Akihiko Hirata, Yoshio Tsuchiya and Ren Yamamoto. Eiji Tsuburaya, who had begun his career working on wartime propaganda films, once again directed the special effects sequences. Released in Japan on July 4, 1965, the film was re-edited as an English-language version, Kiska, integrating new sequences by Walter Black, first broadcast on U.S. television on August 24, 1973.

13

Tôjôjinbutsu Senmonka Supreme

> Shimura ... played characters who were not bound by any genre with humanism, rugged honesty and dignity; neither a handsome man nor a clown. The wide variety of the characters he played ... is unsurpassable.—National Film Archive of Japan (2015)

Furankenshutain tai chitei kaijû Baragon [Frankenstein Conquers the World] (1965)

Shimura's most brief appearance in a *kaijû tokusatsu eiga* occurs in one scene of Ishirô Honda and Eiji Tsuburaya's incredible *Furankenshutain tai chitei kaijû Baragon* [*Frankenstein vs. Subterranean Monster Baragon*]. As an experimental surgeon in 1945, Shimura is entrusted with the Frankenstein Monster's heart after it is stolen from Dr. Riesendorf (Peter Mann and voice actor Kuzuo Kamakura) in Nazi Germany and transported to Hiroshima aboard a Kriegsmarine U-boat and a Japanese Imperial submarine. Just as the surgeon is about to examine the heart, Little Boy devastates the city with a radioactive mushroom cloud, taking Shimura's role with it.

A Toho-United Productions of America (UPA) coproduction, the film stars Nick Adams (dubbed by voice actor Goro Naya) as Dr. James Bowen, a U.S. scientist who aids the Japanese when a feral boy appears, running wild in the city's streets 15 years later. The remainder of the film is devoted to the mistreatment of the Frankenstein creature (Sumio Nakao and Kôji Furuhata) and his prolonged battle with Baragon (Haruo Nakajima, wearing yet another Tsuburaya suit), an Ankylosaurus-like monster that burrows its way from underground. A classic horror/sci-fi film conclusion, a raging fire, is followed by both combatants swallowed up in an enormous fissure.

Among this ridiculous film's indirect connections to Akira Kurosawa

13. Tôjôjinbutsu Senmonka *Supreme* 145

are Ishirô Honda and the appearances of Shimura and Susumu Fugita (as the Osaka Police Chief). Running 89 minutes, the film, released in Japan on August 8, 1965, also was distributed in an international version (including an additional 3-minute giant octopus ending) and an English-dubbed, 87-minute U.S. edition, titled *Frankenstein Conquers the World*, on July 8, 1966. In 1965, Nick Adams appeared in another non–U.S. horror/sci-fi film, *The House at the End of the World* [U.S. title; *Die, Monster, Die!*] based on H. P. Lovecraft's "The Colour Out of Space," and costarring Boris Karloff.

Shimura appears in another yakuza thriller, *Buraikan jingi* [*Villain's Code*] (1965), a low-budget affair directed by Yûsuke Watanabe and shot in black-and-white by Ichirô Hoshijima for Toei Tokyo. He costars, with Yoshiko Kayama and Chishû Ryû, in Hirokazu Ichimura's *Kono koe naki sakebi* [*The Soundless Cry*] (1965) and, with Kôji Tsuruta and Hideo Murata, in *Kanto hamonjo* [*Expelled from the Kanto Mob*] (1965), an additional yakuza outing, written and directed by Shigehiro Azawa for Toei, who released a total of five titles in its "*Kanto nagaramono*" series. Toei's *Jigoku no hatobâ* [*Pier of Hell*] and *Bâra kêtsu shobû* [*Hoodlum Match*] (both 1965) involve Shimura in more gritty, low-budget yakuza intrigue.

Bangkok no joru [*Night in Bangkok*] (1966) reunited Shimura (as Dr. Yoshino) with Yûzô Kayama (as Shûichi Tsumura) in rich Eastmancolor and Tohoscope, and *Shurushuru* (1966), a black-and-white, standard ratio television production, also featuring his *Kwaidan* costars Tatsuya Nakadai and Michiyo Aratama, marked his small-screen film debut. *Kaerazeru hatoba* [*The Harbor of No Return*] (1966), a Nikkatsu color and Cinemascope crime drama directed by Mio Ezaki and shot by Minoru Yokoyama, casts him as another clever cop, Detective Egusa.

Adapted from a story by Kenji Ôe, *Zesshô* (1966), written and directed by Katsumi Nishikawa for Nikkatsu, includes Shimura in the role of Sôbei Sonoda. More yakuza adventures followed in *Showa saidai no kaoyaku* [*Greatest Boss of the Showa Era*] (1966) and *Noren ichidai: jôkyô* [*Life of a Chivalrous Woman*] (1966). Shochiku's *Sarutobe Sazuke* [*Ninja Spy*] (1966) features him as Hakuunsai Tozawa.

The Daiei drama *Satogashi ga kowareru toki* [*When the Cookie Crumbles*] (1967), adapted from Ayako Sono's novel by Sugako Hashida and directed by Tadashi Imai, includes Shimura in the supporting role of Kudo, opposite Ayako Wakao (as Kyoko Senzaka). From this rather typical outing, he then moved on to one of the most monumental of all stories, the Japanese government's reaction (during the post-atomic, 24-hour period between noon, August 14, and noon, August 15, 1945) to the Allied demand for unconditional surrender, in Toho's *Nihon no ichiban nagai hi* [*Japan's Longest Day*] (1967), produced by Tomoyuki Tanaka and Sanezumi Fujimoto, directed by Kihachi Okamoto and written by Shinobu Hashimoto.

Running 157 minutes, this black-and-white historical exercise, as expected, features an impressive cast, led by Seiji Miyaguchi (as Foreign Minister Shigenoro Togo), Rokkô Toura (Shunichi Matsumoto, Vice-Minister of Foreign Affairs), Chishû Ryû (Prime Minister Kantaro Suzuki), Sô Yamamura (Admiral Mitsumasa Yonai, Minister of the Navy), Toshirô Mifune (General Korechika Anami, Minister of the Army), Yoshio Kosugi (Keisuke Okada, Minister of Public Welfare) and Shimura (Hiroshi Shimomura, Minister of the Board of Information), who appears sporadically throughout the film. *Japan's Longest Day*, like other Hashimoto military scripts, is long on talk, in this case leading to a very pedantic, pseudo-documentary result that, especially to non–Japanese speaking viewers, may become confusing at times.

Hiroshi Shimomura (1875–1957) graduated from the University of Tokyo and served as fourth President of the Japanese Olympic Committee from 1937 to 1942. As usual, Shimura is ideally cast, playing the cool-headed administrator calmly and quietly, among many hawks who want nothing more than to carry on the war, beyond all reason and at any cost.

The "who's who" cast also includes Yoshio Tsuchiya, Daisuke Katô, Yûzô Kayama, Michiyo Aratama, Akira Kubo, Susumu Fugita, Yûnosuke Itô, Ren Yamamoto and Tatsuya Nakadai (voice only). Masaru Satô composed the powerful score. Masaki Kobayashi had been asked to direct the project but understandably turned it down.

Japan's Longest Day was released on August 12, 1967, to commemorate the 22nd anniversary of the actual events (and the 35th anniversary of Toho). Domestically it fared very well as the second-most commercially successful Japanese film of the year. Critically, perhaps due to its packing so much historical detail into two and one-half hours, it won *Kinema Junpô*'s Best Screenplay award for Hashimoto.

Toei's *Gyangu no teio* [*Gyungu II*] (1967), directed by Yasuo Furuhata and costarring Shimura, Noboru Andô and Shin'ichi [Sonny] Chiba, was followed by the television series *Kaze* (1967–1968) for Shochiku and the Tokyo Broadcasting System (TBS). Toei's yakuza genre continued to utilize Shimura as a regular presence: *Ârappoi no ha gômen dazê* [*Pardon My Violent Ways*] (1967), directed by Masaharu Segawa; *Naniwa kyokaku: dokyo shichinin giri* [*Killer of Seven Men*] (1967), by Shigehiro Ozawa; and *Kyokatsu ichidai* (1967), by Masahiro Makino, featuring him as support to Ken Takakura.

The last of these, released under the English title *The Chivalrous Life*, benefits from an interesting screenplay by Isao Matsumoto, Akira Murao and Hideaki Yamamoto involving the efforts against a yakuza gang of the kind businessman Sakamoto (Shimura) to complete a construction project that will bring clean water to his community. Ryuma (Takakura), one of two Imperial Army buddies who collide over this undertaking (his former friend has joined the yakuza), is inspired by his love for a prostitute, who reminds him

13. Tôjôjinbutsu Senmonka *Supreme* 147

of his late mother, and an assassination attempt on Sakamoto, who has developed strong faith in his abilities.

The *Chivalrous Life* is one of the better yakuza films costarring Shimura, whose character is well-developed, sympathetic, and possessing an effective blend of drama and humor. In his first appearance, Sakamoto, witnessing Ryuma attempting suicide by weighing himself down with stones and jumping into a shallow river, remarks matter-of-factly, "What's the point in dying?" as he strolls along the dock. Throughout the film, he also proves to be a very wise

Kyokatsu ichidai [*The Chivalrous Life*] (1967; directed by Masahiro Makino): Kind, honorable businessman Sakamoto (Takashi Shimura), who defies a yakuza gang while attempting to complete a construction project that will bring clean water to his community.

boss to Ryuma, at one point, explaining, "Courage is only good when it's based on reason."

The Chivalrous Life, beautifully shot in color and Toeiscope by Ichirô Hoshijima, is a very well-acted film, including a first-rate group of character actors as a band of beggars who befriend Ryuma and later come to his aid at the construction site, where the yakuza have burned all the trucks owned by Sakamoto. The generally realistic atmospheric is belied only by ludicrous sound effects common to Japanese action and martial-arts films of the period.

Shimura maintained his professional pace throughout the late Sixties, appearing in nine films during 1968. The ambitious, 196-minute Mifune Productions-Ishihara Productions project *Kurobe no taiyo* [*The Sands of Kurobe*] (1968), directed by Kei Kumai (and distributed through Nikkatsu and Toho) is second only to Kurosawa's *Seven Samurai* as the longest epic ever to feature both Toshirô Mifune and Takashi Shimura.

Based on a story by Sôjirô Motoki, the Masato Ide-Kei Kumai screenplay covers the arduous construction of the 3.4-mile long, 610-feet high Kanden Tunnel under Mount Tate in the Japanese Alps, through which equipment was transported for the building of the dam located on the Kurobe River in Toyama Prefecture. In the film, many disasters (natural, political and personal) hamper this massive engineering undertaking (which, between 1956 and 1963, claimed 171 lives and over 51.3 billion yen).

Shot in Eastmancolor and Cinemascope by Mutsuo Tanji, the film employed three art directors (Masayoshi Kobayashi, Hiroshi Yamashita,

Masao Yamazaki) and three assistant directors (Toshi Aoki, Mizuho Doi, Hideo Miyau), as well as an enormous cast, including Mifune, Shimura, Yûjirô Ishihara, Shûji Sano, Masahiko Naruse and Mieko Takamine. *The Sands of Kurobe*, released in Japan on March 1, 1968, and the United States seven months later, also was submitted to the Academy of Motion Picture Arts and Sciences (AMPAS) for consideration as Best Foreign Language Film but was not nominated.

As he often did, Shimura then made a 180-degree turn for his next role: the Fortune Teller in the Fujicolor and Daieiscope horror drama *Botan-dôrô* [*Peony Lantern*] (1968), directed by Satsuo Yamamoto from a Yoshikata Yoda script, based on the novel by Enchô San'yûtei.

Shimura plays the kindly Dr. Junan in director Kimiyoshi Yasuda's *Zatôichi hatashi-jô* [*Zatoichi and the Fugitives*] (1968), in which the famed blind swordsman Zatoichi (Shintarô Katsu) of the late Edo period faces off against the renegade henchmen of Boss Matsugoro (Hôsei Komatsu), a corrupt local official. Created by novelist Kan Shimozawa, Zatoichi, who travels under the guise of *anma* [masseur] and *bakuto* [gambler] but trained in Muraku-school *kenjutsu* [pre–Meiji Restoration] and *iaido* [strong awareness and quick-draw] swordsmanship, is featured in a series of 26 Daiei films (1962–1973), one directed by Katsu (1989) and a television series of 100 episodes (1974–1979).

In *Zatoichi and the Fugitives*, the swordsman informs an enemy, who has threatened to kill him in the night, "Darkness makes no difference to a blindman." He also explains to a young woman that, being unable to see, he does not make the mistake of judging by appearances.

Shimura's doctor serves an important narrative role. An honorable man who treats his patients "without regard for payment," he has been troubled by his estranged son, Ogano (Kyôsuke Machida), who killed a man in Edo five years earlier and now runs with the cruel fugitives who hide out above Matsugoro's silk-weaving factory. Seeking Zatoichi, who is hired by Dr. Junan to provide massages and acupuncture, Matsugoro orders the gang to beat him and kidnap his daughter, Oshizu (Kayo Mikimoto), whom they plan to torture. Zatoichi arrives to dispatch the gang members, ultimately facing only Ogano, whom he cuts down in front of Junan. Oshizu mourns her brother's death, and Zatoichi turns to walk out of the town, Sanjuro-style.

Zatoichi and the Fugitives, the 18th in the Daiei series, featuring some stunning Eastmancolor and Daieiscope compositions by Kazuo Miyagawa, was released in Japan on August 10, 1968. Once again, the blind swordsman's formidable, against-all-odds heroics proved very popular with audiences. One specific sword thrust, used by Zatoichi to dispatch Matsugoro, involves the blade slicing through the wooden door of the silk factory: Shintarô Katsu's performance recalls those of James Cagney in the Warner Bros. crime classics

13. Tôjôjinbutsu Senmonka *Supreme*

Zatiôchi hatashi-jô [*Zatoichi and the Fugitives*] (1968; directed by Kimiyoshi Yasuda): Wise, Dr. Junan (Takashi Shimura, left) aids the famed blind swordsman Zatoichi (Shintarô Katsu) as he battles the renegade henchmen of Boss Matsugoro in this late Edo-period *chanbara*.

Taxi! (1932), directed by Roy Del Ruth, and *White Heat* (1949), directed by Raoul Walsh, in which the great "tough-guy" actor fires lethal bullets through a door.

For its DVD release of *Zatoichi and the Fugitives*, the Criterion Collection aptly noted, "This lean and mean entry [in the series] is packed with coldhearted villainy and rough justice, but it finds its heart in the great Takashi Shimura, who plays a kindly country doctor caught up in a violent world."[1]

Gion matsuri [*Festival of Gion*] (1968), directed by Daisuke Itô and Tetsuya Yamanouchi for Shochiku, casts Toshirô Mifune as Kumaza and Kinnosuke Nakamura as Shinkichi, a peasant cloth-dyer endeavoring to revive Kyoto's traditional *Gion Matsuri* Festival, currently banned during a civil war between clans and roving brigands. Shimura plays the supporting role of Tsuneemon, joined by fellow Kurosawa loyalist Kamatari Fujiwara as Genzô.

The Gion Festival, held in Kyoto from July 1–31 annually, is one of the oldest public celebrations in Japan, first organized in the year 869, when the 56th Emperor, Seiwa, ordered the people to call upon *Susanoo-so-Mikoto*, god of the Yasaka Shrine, to protect them from the evil deity *Gozu Tennô*, responsible for spreading deadly pestilence and plague. Decreed an annual event in 960, it was held faithfully; and, by the Edo period 700 years later, had been increased in influence by the wealthy merchant class.

Although the Askikawa shogunate outlawed religious events in 1533, the people of Kyoto, unconcerned with the overall event itself, did strongly protest the ending of the traditional parade that distinguished the festival. To this day, this procession, the *Yamaboko Junkô*, held on July 17 and 21 in Gion's downtown area, comprises the Festival.

Gion matsuri was released in Japan on November 23, 1968, and as *Festival of Gion* in the United States on February 12, 1969. In 1973, the film was cut from 168 to 123 minutes for a reissue by Toho.

At Toiei, Shimura appeared in the Fujicolor action thriller *Sangyo sapai* [*Industrial Spy*] (1968) for director Eiichi Kudô. At Daiei, he costarred with Yusuke Kawazu in *Onno tobakushi amadera kaichô* [*The Woman Gambler and the Nun*] (1968), directed in Fujicolor by Shigeo Tanaka, and made another familiar contribution to the yakuza genre at Toiei Tokyo, in *Gendai yakuza: yotomono no okite* (1968), directed by Yasuo Furuhata from a screenplay by Akira Murao. Toiei also cast him in one of its World War II dramas, *Ah kaiten tokubetsu kogetikai* [*Human Torpedoes*] (1968), directed in black-and-white Toieiscope by Shigehiro Ozawa and starring Shin'ichi [Sonny] Chiba.

Shimura, as Tetsutarô Fujigami, supports costars Ken Takakura and Tatsuya Mihashi in Toei Tokyo's *Shin Abashiri Bangaichi* [*The Man from Abashiri Jail Strikes Again*] (1968), directed by Masahiro Makino and shot in Fujicolor and Toeiscope by Motoko Tsudoi. The 11th entry in the studio's 18-film "*Shin Abishiri Bangaichi*" series, it was based on a novel about a lonely gangster housed in a prison located at Abishiri on Hokkaido.

Shimura again makes a brief appearance in a sweeping historical epic, *Fûrin kazan* [*Samurai Banners*] (1969), based on Yasushi Inoue's novel, adapted by Shinobu Hashimoto and Takeo Kunihiro, and directed by Hiroshi Inagaki for Mifune Productions and distribution through Toho. Shot in Eastmancolor and Tohoscope by Kazuo Yamada, with a musical score by Masaru Satô, this 165-minute epic is another history-packed Hashimoto epic interspersing lengthy dialogue sequences with bursts of violent action.

Set in feudal Japan (between 1543 and 1562) during the Sengoku period, the narrative deals with Kansuke Yamamoto (Toshirô Mifune), a samurai seeking to unite the nation by any means necessary, including serving Kai Province warlord Takeda Shingen (Kinnosuke Nakamura), the assassination of the neighboring lord and seduction of his widow, Princess Yufu (Yoshiko Sukuma), and various other political and military strategies. The film's climax occurs at the fourth Battle of Kawanakajima in September 1561, when clans led by Takeda and Uesugi Kenshin (Yûjirô Ishihara) of Echigo Province clashed indecisively at Nagano.

On February 1, 1969, Toho released a roadshow version of *Fûrin kazan* and expanded it nationwide two months later. The film became, not only the studio's top-grossing title, but also Japan's number-one overall domestic release of the year. As with previous historical epics scripted by Hashimoto,

13. Tôjôjinbutsu Senmonka *Supreme*   151

it is so heavy on historical detail that few viewers outside Japan have been able to follow the convoluted structure; and so much screen time is devoted to battle scenes that insufficient development is allowed the story's three main characters, played by Mifune, Nakamura and Sukuma. Toho's June 24, 1969, release of the English language version, *Under the Banner of the Samurai*, generated only moderate interest in the United States.

Toiei Tokyo's nine-film "Brutal Tales of Chivalry" yakuza series received what would seem an obligatory appearance by Shimura in Masahiro Makino's *Shôwa zankyô-den: Karajishi jingi* [*Brutal Tales of Chivalry 5*] (1969), scripted by Isao Matsumoto and Hideaki Yamamoto. In this sixth entry, shot in color and Cinemascope by Makoto Tsudoi, star Ken Takakura is supported by Shimura, Ryô Ikebe, Seizaburô Kawazu and Bokuzen Hidari.

Produced for Japanese television, *Otoko janaika* premiered on April 6, 1969, and ran until 1971. Appearing in a supporting role, Shimura was joined by Yumiko Fugita, Shin'ichirô Mikami, Hiroshi Sekiguchi and Jun Tatara.

At Daiei, Shimura supported Michiyo Yasuda, Shintarô Katsu and Kô Nishimura in director Kazuo Mori's *Kanto onna akumyo* [*Unknown Woman of Kanto*] (1969). This "female yakuza" drama, written by Kôji Takada, is a standard programmer that, like many other genre thrillers, finally comes to life during a climatic swordfight sequence.

Shimura landed roles in two more entries in Toiei's 18-film "*Shin Abashiri Bangaishi*" yakuza series. In the first title, *Shin Abashiri Bangaichi: Runinmasaki no ketto* [*New Abashiri Prison Story—Harbor Duel*] (1969), directed by Yasuo Furuhata, he supports Minoru Ôki and Ken Takakura, whose Tsukibana is transferred from Abashiri to Tanigawa Prison, where he is assigned to the "honor factory," incarceration without walls intended to rehabilitate the inmates. Shimura plays president of the company responsible for the new system, which involves hard work but also respect for those willing to give the program a chance. Local residents finally support the president's idea after the prisoners fight a blaze at a noodle shop, where Tsukibana saves a small child. When a yakuza gang attacks Tanigawa, the president and a prison leader are badly wounded, but Tsukibana prevents them from igniting a dynamite charge and is returned to Abashiri.

In between the "*Abashiri Bangaishi*" films, Shimura made his first appearance in Shôchiku's "Tora-san" comedy series as Professor Hyôichirô Suwa in *Otoko wa tsurai yo* [*It's Tough Being a Man*] (1969), directed by Yôji Yamada, who also co-wrote the screenplay with Azuma Morisaki. Yamada created the character of the traveling salesman Torajirô Kuruma ("Tora-san") who, in this debut film, having been shown the door by his late father two decades earlier, now reappears to cause impolite and drunken trouble for his uncle (Shin Morikawa), aunt (Chieko Misaki) and sister, Sakura (Chieko Baishô), as she prepares to marry Suwa's son, Hiroshi (Gin Maeda). Star

Kiyoshi Atsumi also is supported by Chishû Ryû, who makes the first of his more than 40 series appearances as the Buddhist priest Gozen-sama.

Shimura gives a brief but moving performance as Hiroshi's estranged father who, during a speech at the wedding reception, describes himself as an "inadequate parent." Humbly asking for forgiveness by offering sincere well wishes to his son and new daughter-in-law, he is called "Father" by Torajiro.

Premiering in Japan on August 27, 1969, *It's Tough Being a Man* was awarded five stars by *Kinema Junpô*, who joined the Mainichi Film Awards (where Yamada was named Best Director) in bestowing the Best Actor title on Atsumi. Released in the United States as *Am I Trying* on August 18, 1974, the film later was reissued as *Tora San Our Lovable Tramp*.

Toiei Tokyo kept Shimura busy with the yakuza in *Nihon boryoku-dan: kumicho to shikaku* [*Japan's Violent Gangs—The Boss and the Killers*] (1969), the second in its "*Nihon boryoku-dan*" [particularly harmful] quartet, directed by Jun'ya Satô, who co-wrote the screenplay with Fumio Kônami. The next "*Abashiri Bangaishi*" title for Toei, *Shin Abashiri Bangaichi: Saihate no Nagaremono* [*The Vagrant Comes to a Port Town*] (1969), directed by Kiyoshi Saeki, again stars Ken Takakura as Shinichi Tsukibana, model inmate at Hokkaido's Abashiri Prison. Akira Murao's screenplay depicts Tsukibana battling a criminal who muscles in on a local fishery business.

Shimura played the uncredited role of an editor in Toho's *Gekido no showashi "Gunbatsu"* [*The Militarists*] (1970), director Hiromichi Horikawa and screenwriter Ryôzô Kasahara's account of the "dangerous" activities of Hideki Tôjô (Keiju Kobayashi). Shot in Eastmancolor and Tohoscope by Kazuo Yamada, and released in "Hyper Three-Dimensional Stereo" sound,

Otoko wa tsurai yo [*It's Tough Being a Man*, aka *Am I Trying*] (1969; directed by Yôji Yamada): Supporting the star Kiyoshi Atsumi (as Torajirô Kuruma ["Tora-san"]), Takashi Shimura made his first appearance (as Professor Hyôichirô Suwa) in Shôchiku's long-running, award-winning comedy series.

13. Tôjôjinbutsu Senmonka *Supreme* 153

Akira Kurosawa signed "Kumi-Odori Series" first day cover envelopes, Ryûkyû, Okinawa (May 29 & June 30, 1970): "Kumi Odori," a traditional narrative dance established in the capital of Shuri in 1719, was developed to entertain Chinese diplomats who traveled to the Ryûkyûan islands in Okinawa Prefecture. These rare first day cover envelopes, postmarked in Ryûkyû, were signed (in both Japanese calligraphy and Roman letters) by Akira Kurosawa while he was making his bizarre experimental film *Dodes'ka-den* (1970), the first feature he had directed in 13 years not to include Takashi Shimura in the cast. Aside from his uncredited appearance in Hiromichi Horikawa's *Gekido no showashi "Gunbatsu" [The Militarists]*, in which Toshirô Mifune stars as Admiral Isoroku Yamamoto, Shimura took a hiatus from acting that year, the only time he did so in a career lasting nearly five decades.

the film costars Toshirô Mifune as Admiral Isoroku Yamamoto and Yûzô Kayama as reporter Goro Arai, who courts great peril covering the events of World War II.

Aside from his brief appearance in *The Militarists*, Shimura took a hiatus from acting that year, the only time he did so in a career lasting nearly five decades. In the meantime, Akira Kurosawa was making his bizarre experimental film *Dodes'ka-den* (1970), the first feature he had directed in 13 years *not* to include Shimura in the cast. Though he completed the film under budget and ahead of schedule, and it fared well critically, the Japanese public frankly didn't know what to make of the uneven blend of equally bleak and foolish material in *Dodes'ka-den*, which became the only Kurosawa production in 15 years to lose money at the box office. (About 14 months after *Dodes'ka-den* was released in Japan, on December 22, 1971, Kurosawa, unable to secure financing to make any more films, attempted suicide by slashing his own throat and wrists with a razor. Fortunately, the family maid heard him in the bathroom and was able to call for help in time.)

A small part for Shimura in Ishihara Productions' *Yomigaeru daichi* (1971), directed by Noboru Nakamura from Kengo Inomata's screenplay, was accompanied by more familiar territory the following year. Two more entries in Yôji Yamada's "Tora-san" comedy series alternated with another appearance in Toei's yakuza genre: *Gorotsuki mushuku* [*Rogue Wanderer*] (1971), directed by Yasuo Furuhata from a Toshiya Itô-Shin'ichirô Sawai screenplay, has him supporting Ken Takakura and Rin'ichi Yamamoto.

Otoko wa tsurai yo: Torajiro renka [*Tora San's Shattered Romance*] (1971) involves Torajiro (Kiyoshi Atsumi) falling in love with an escapee from a local institution. Fortunately, their marriage plans are ended when his family and the young woman's teacher intercede.

Otoko wa tsurai yo: Torajiro koiuta [*Tora San's Love Call*] (1971), offers Shimura ample screen time playing Professor Hyôichirô Suwa, father-in-law of Sakura (Chiekô Baisho), Torajiro's sister, as "Tora-san" returns home to fall in love again, this time with a widow, only to seek the freedom of the road once more. True to form, Shimura plays a moving scene as Suwa, this time at the memorial service for his wife; and Chishû Ryû again appears in his recurrent role of the priest Gozen-sama. Released in Japan on November 20, 1971, the film won Yamada a tie for Best Director (with Masahiro Shinoda) at the Mainichi Film Awards.

Gokuaku bozu—nomu utsu kau [*The Bloody Priest*] (1971), directed for Toiei by Buichi Saitô from Akira Murao and Kôji Takada's screenplay, brought Shimura back into the yakuza world. The crime drama continued in Toiei's *Gokudo makari touru* [*Gokudo's Notorious Reputation*] (1972), directed by Shigehiro Ozawa and starring Tomisaburô Wakayama as Shimamura Seikichi. The studio also hired Shimura to play Jinpei in the Asahi television series

13. Tôjôjinbutsu Senmonka *Supreme*

Otoko wa tsurai yo Torajiro koiuta [*Tora San's Love Call*] (1971; directed by Yôji Yamada): Torajiro Kuruma (Kiyoshi Atsumi, with hat), Sakura Suwa (Chiekô Baisho), "Tora-san's" sister, and Professor Hyôichiro Suwa (Takashi Shimura) at the memorial service for Suwa's late wife.

Dokkoi daisaku, which premiered on January 8, 1973. Yoshinobu Kaneko, Ryûsei Nakao and Chishû Ryû also appeared over the course of the 1973–1974 season.

Shimura plays Sakubei, a kind craftsman, in Toho's *Shin Zatôichi monogatari: Kasama no chimatsuri* [*Zatoichi's Conspiracy*] (1973), the 25th entry in the "blind swordsman" series, directed by Kimiyoshi Yasuda and shot in Eastmancolor and Tohoscope by Chikashi Makiura. For the first time in a decade, Zatoichi (Shintarô Katsu) returns home, only to encounter an unscrupulous magistrate (Kei Satô) and Shinbei (Eiji Okada), an old "friend," who now has a gang of yakuza involved in his attempt to take over a local rock quarry. This second of Shimura's two "Zatoichi" characterizations is not unlike his first, an honorable widower with a daughter who aids the swordsman in his efforts to save the community from rampant corruption and criminality.

On October 27, 1973, Shimura played Tatewaki Ôtawara in "*Adauchi dai satsujin*," episode two of the Shochiku-Asahi *jidai-geki* television series *Tasukenin hashiru*, directed by Kôki Matsuno and starring Takahiro Tamura as Bunjûrô Nakayama.

He then moved back to the big screen for the small supporting role of Yasuda, father of Makiko Manpyo (Mari Nakayama), in director Satsuo Yamamoto's 211-minute epic *Karei-yaru ichizoku* [*The Family*] (1974), produced by the Geiensha Company for distribution through Toho. The impressive cast also includes Tatsuya Nakadai, Kyôko Kagawa, Machiko Kyô, Kô Nishimura, Akihiko Hirata and Seizaburô Kawazu.

Aside from horseback riding and occasional wrestling in his earlier days, Shimura continued to enjoy working out with a rowing machine and playing golf as leisure activities. Although he was diagnosed with emphysema (brought on by decades of smoking) in 1974, he worked consistently that year, playing Shihei Furukawa in director Kôzaburô Yoshimura's *Ranru no hata* [*The Tattered Banner*], the Pediatrician in Toho's science-fiction thriller *Nosutoradamasu no daiyogen*, directed by Toshio Masuda (and released in the United States as *The Last Days of Planet Earth* in 1979], and a strong supporting role in Sadao Nakajima's crime drama *Karajishi keisatsu* [*Lion Enforcer*].

In February 1974, Akira Kurosawa began shooting the Soviet-Japanese coproduction *Dersu Uzala* (1975), one of the director's most atmospheric and moving films, on location in Siberia, a location to which the ever-more-fragile Shimura likely couldn't have traveled had his friend wanted him for a part. Mosfilm, the Moscow studio which financed the film with Daiei, had suggested Toshirô Mifune for the lead role of nomadic Goldi hunter Dersu Uzala; but, for reasons both ethnic and personal, Kurosawa cast the Russian actor Maksim Munzuk (1910–1999), who gives an extraordinarily naturalistic and charming performance. His achievement is matched by the distinguished Siberian stage and film actor-director Yuriy Solomin as Captain Arseniev, sent to chart unknown territory for the Russian Army, who forges a deep friendship with the capable little Goldi man of the wilderness.

Based on a true account, published in 1923, by the real-life Vladimir Arsenyev (1872–1930) about the remarkable Dersu Uzala (who actually was murdered following a stifling experience living with his friend in a Russian city), the film, set primarily during the years 1902–1907, won two awards at the 9th Moscow International Film Festival (the Golden Prize and the Prix Belgium Fédération Internationale de la Presse Cinématographique [FIPRESCI]), as well as the Best Foreign Language Film Academy Award at the U.S. ceremony in 1976. One of the few Kurosawa directorial efforts in which Shimura does not appear (the second since his brief appearance in *Red Beard*), it is also one of the best, verdantly shot in color Sovscope by Asakazu Nakai, Fyodor Dobronravov and Yuriy Gantman.

In director Jun'ya Satô's Toiei crime thriller *Shinkansen daibakuha* (1975), Shimura plays the Japanese National Railways (JNR) President, supporting costars Ken Takakura and Shin'ichi [Sonny] Chiba. Filmed at locations in Tokyo and on Hokkaido, in color and Toieiscope by Masahiko Iimura, the 152-minute original cut was edited to 115 minutes for its U.S. release as *Bullet Train* on January 1, 1976.

Back on the small screen, Shimura played Bugyô Torii in the "*Ippitsu keijô meimu ga mieta*" episode of the *jidai-geki* television series *Hissatsu shiokiya kagyô* (1975–1976), directed by Kuniya Ôkuma from Yoshiki Hori's script. Returning to the historical epic genre, he then accepted a supporting part in Scenario Kaisha-Toho's *Zoku ningen kakumei* [*Human Revolution II*] (1976), directed by Toshio Masuda from a screenplay by Shinobu Hashimoto.

13. Tôjôjinbutsu Senmonka *Supreme*

Shimura's only screen credit for 1977 involves footage in which he appeared (as Dr. Yamane) 23 years earlier. For release in Italy as *Cozzilla*, director Luigi Cozzi, denied the original *Gojira* rights by Toho, purchased the English-language version of *Godzilla: King of the Monsters!* and, to appease his distributor, hired Armando Valcauda to colorize it. Produced by Cozzi and Renato Barbieri, this extended, 105-minute version, re-edited by Alberto Moro, includes additional music by Franco Bixio, Fabio Frizzi and Vince Tempera.

Shimura also appears in one 1978 film, Takarazuka Eiga-Toho's 154-minute epic drama *Ogin-sama*, directed by Kei Kumai and scripted by Yoshikata Yoda from the Tôkô Kon novel. Marking his final on-screen collaboration with Toshirô Mifune, the production also features Eiji Okada and Kô Nishimura.

By this time, Shimura was quite ill; but, still in demand at age 73, he accepted the major, second-billed role of Sen Rikyu, a characterization requiring the most work (including singing during one sequence) from the actor in many years. Set in 1585 Sakai, a harbor town near Osaka, the film focuses on the relationships between Rikyu, a ceremonial tea master and powerful merchant, Imperial Regent Taiko Hideyoshi (Mifune) and Rikyu's daughter, Lady Ogin (Ryôko Nokano). The great *daimyô* becomes viciously angered by Ogin's conversion to Christianity and Rikyu's opposition to his plans to invade China and Korea.

The film concludes tragically, with Ogin committing suicide, a close-up of the weeping Shimura, and the subtitle, "February 15, 1591: Rikyu Sen killed himself. In September that year, the Korean war began…"

The historical Sen no Rikyû (1522–1591), also an accomplished poet, had the most widespread influence, based in Zen Buddhism, on *chanoyu*, the Japanese "Way of Tea" ceremony. In 1579, he became a tea master for Oda Nobunaga, followed by his being named to a similar post for Toyotomi Hideyoshi three years later. Rikyû's daughter, Okame, married Sen Shôan, stepson to Rikyû from his second marriage. In 1591, Rikyû, having clashed over several matters with Hideyoshi, committed *seppuku* per his lord's orders. The last act of his life was presiding over an elaborate tea ceremony. He addressed his "suicide note," a poem, to the dagger with which he killed himself. The harsh-tempered Hideyoshi (as he is effectively portrayed by the intense Mifune) later expressed regret for ordering the suicide.

Stuart Galbraith provides a fine analysis of Shimura's performance style in *Ogin-sama*:

> Shimura is an excellent Rikyû. Generally, he is very mannered, but the warmth and wisdom of the character come through in several key scenes, particularly as his family spends one last night together before Ogin takes her life. There is also an excellent moment when Hideyoshi informs Rikyû that he has just executed one of the tea master's disciples. Rikyû has been whittling at a piece of wood and continues doing so as the horrible news is recounted. Finally, he can stand it no more and, shuddering mid-whittle, nearly collapses. For a character so deliberate with every move—much like

the tea ceremony itself—this bubbling of emotion is powerful, and Shimura pulls it off with great effect.

Ultimately Rikyû's story, while subservient to Ogin's tale of love and faith, is a kind of Japanese *Man for All Seasons*. The clashes between Mifune and Shimura are generally well done, if not exceptionally so.... In their last film together, 30 years after Mifune's debut in *Snow Trail*, Mifune and Shimura continue to surprise audiences in their scenes together.[2]

The original June 24, 1978, Japanese release of *Ogin-sama* ran 154 minutes, but was shorn of four minutes for the subtitled U.S. version, *Love and Faith*. A subsequent release was edited to 116 minutes.

Shimura returned to Shochiku's "Tora-san" comedy series as Hyôichirô Suwa in *Otoko wa tsurai yo: Uwasa no Torajirô* [*Talk of the Town Tora-san*] (1978), directed by Yôji Yamada, who again co-wrote the screenplay with Yoshitaka Asama. Once more becoming embroiled in family affairs, Torajirô (Kiyoshi Atsumi), believing that his brother-in-law's boss is planning to kill himself, attempts to avert the catastrophe. While riding a city bus, he meets up with Suwa, who offers to share his home, and then becomes exhausted by the young rascal's indefatigable nature.

In his fourth performance as the widowed scholar, Shimura, during a series of charming adventures with his new companion, is at his most sincere and likeable. His mastery of subtle humor is a frequent highlight: While imparting to Torajirô such practical wisdom as "nothing is fun when you get old," Suwa ironically is enjoying some of the most pleasant experiences since the passing of his beloved wife.

The sustained development of Shimura's characterization over the course of four "Tora-san" films is a testament both to his acting and the talented

Otoko wa tsurai yo Uwasa no Torajirô [*Talk of the Town Tora-san*] (1978): In his fourth performance as the widowed scholar, Professor Hyôichiro Suwa, Takashi Shimura (right), during a series of charming adventures with Torajirô Kuruma (Kiyoshi Atsumi), is at his most sincere. His mastery of subtle humor is a highlight: While imparting practical wisdom to "Tora-san," Suwa enjoys some of the most pleasant experiences since the passing of his beloved wife.

13. Tôjôjinbutsu Senmonka *Supreme*

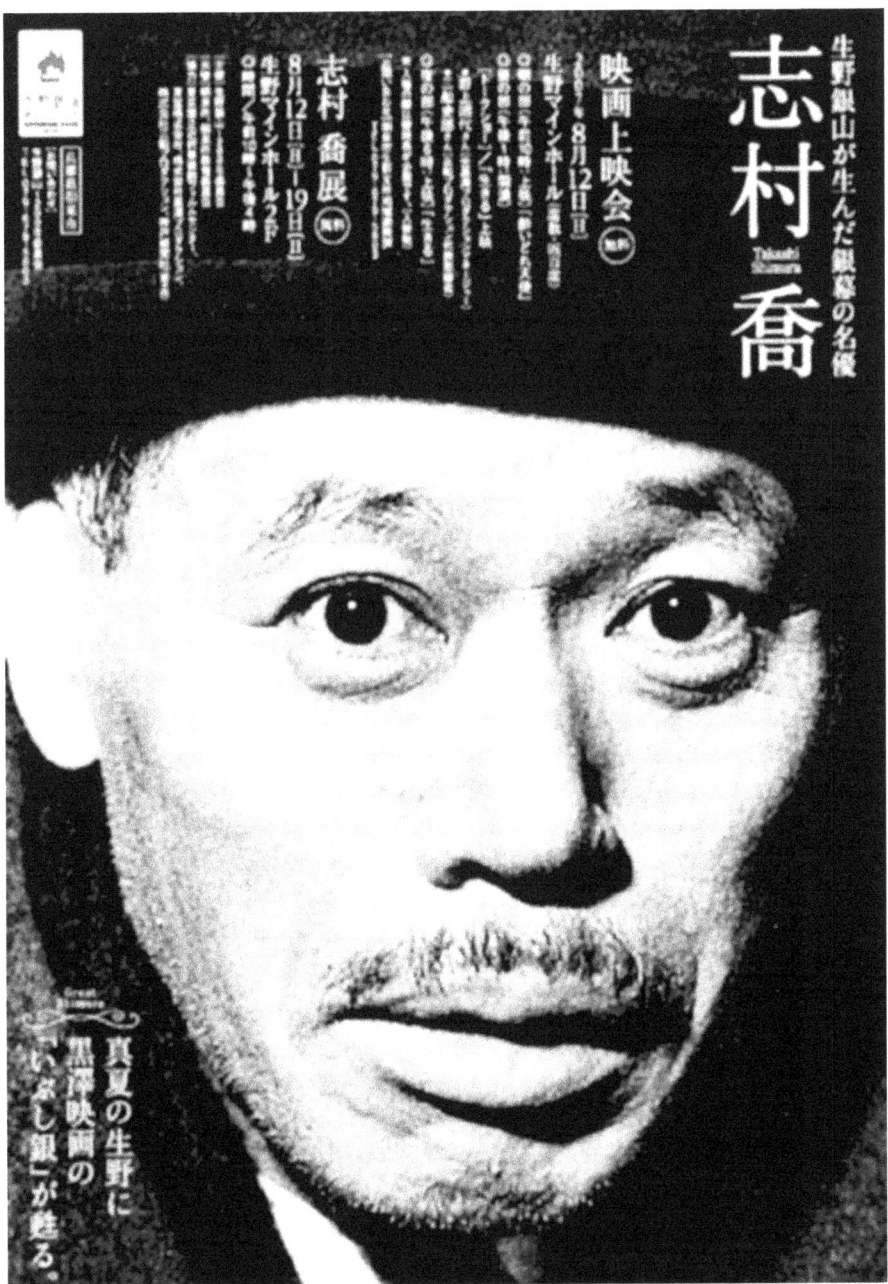

Takashi Shimura Film Festival, Ikuno, Japan (2007): This Japanese "chirasi" mini-poster advertised a cinematic tribute to Takashi Shimura held at his birthplace of Ikuno, Hyôgo, on the 25th anniversary of his death.

direction and writing of Yamada. At Japan's 1979 Academy Prize ceremony, Atsumi was nominated for Best Actor and Yamada for Best Director, for their respective work on this film and the previous series entry, *Otoko wa tsurai yo: Torajirô Wagamichi o Yuku* [*Stage Struck Tora-san*] (1978).

Toiei's World War II epic *Dôran* (1980), directed by Shirô Moritani from Nobuo Yamada's screenplay, stars Ken Takakura, Takahiro Tamura and Kunie Tanaka, with Shimura appearing in the supporting role of Kosuke Miyagi. Kei Kumai directed the Toho production *Tempyo no iraka* [*Ocean to Cross*] (1980), featuring Katsuo Nakamura, Mieko Takamine and Shimura, for its premiere on the Tokyo Broadcasting System (TBS). In the four-part NHK television comedy series *A un* (1980), Shimura joined a fine cast, including Furanki Sakai, Jitsuko Yoshimura and Kyôko Kishida.

Kagemusha (1980)

For his samurai epic *Kagemusha*, based on important Sengoku-period historical events, including an incident in which an entire clan was killed in battle, Akira Kurosawa took his cast and crew to a host of rugged locations, including Himeji Castle; Kumamoto Castle; Iga Ueno Castle in Mie Prefecture; Gotemba, Shizuoka; and Yuhara Plain, Hokkaido. Since the late 1970s, inspired by his studies of 15th-century Japan, the director had wanted to make the film, but couldn't find a studio, including Toho, willing to invest the budget to finance its necessarily grand scope.

Eventually, in a first for a company outside Japan, 20th Century–Fox, headed by Alan Ladd, Jr., was persuaded by George Lucas and Francis Ford Coppola, who had met with Kurosawa in San Francisco during July 1978, to provide additional financing ($1.5 million U.S.) in exchange for the international distribution rights. As Lucas admitted, he used the continued spectacular success of *Star Wars* (1977) as a strong persuasion tactic.

Once more Kurosawa, who had persuaded Ishirô Honda to fill his old position as assistant director, called upon another longtime collaborator, his favorite actor, though Shimura now was suffering from an advanced stage of emphysema. The director had him put on a special flight to shoot his scenes on location; but, upon seeing his old friend, "was afraid he would break."[3]

Tatsuya Nakadai stars in the dual role, Shingen Takeda, Lord of the Takeda Clan, and his double, Kagemusha (The Shadow Warrior), a poor thief chosen to impersonate the *daimyô* just prior to and after his death. Shintarô Katsu, of "Zatoichi" fame, originally had been cast as Shingen, but was fired during the first day of shooting, after angering Kurosawa with his general movie-star pomposity and specific attempts to shoot his performance on videotape using his own camera crew.

13. Tôjôjinbutsu Senmonka *Supreme* 161

Shimura portrays Gyobu Taguchi, Deputy of Oda Nobunaga (Daisuke Ryû), Lord of the Oda Clan, whom Kurosawa called Shingen's "most eminent rival" in real life. The director explained,

> Had Shingen lived and captured control of Kyoto—and hence Japan—Japanese history would assuredly have been very different. Once Nobunaga ruled the country, he was assassinated, and it was only then that Japan came into the hands of the Tokugawa family. It was a fateful moment in Japanese history.[4]

Shimura's one scene depicts Taguchi arriving to check on the health of "Shingen," an effort to assess the viability of an impending attack on the Takedas by the Odos.

Kurosawa, as he had done with Toshirô Mifune during the making of *Red Beard*, again, with unreasonable demands, angered a major collaborator, this time Masaru Satô, who had provided the director with outstanding film scores since *Throne of Blood* 23 years earlier. Unwilling to replace his music to suit the director's personal tastes, Satô quit, and the entire score was composed to Kurosawa's liking by Shin'ichirô Ikebe, who, at that point, had only written the scores for three feature films. (Unfortunately, at no point in *Kagemusha* does Ikebe's music match up to anything in Satô's vast catalog.)

The 179-minute, Japanese version of *Kagemusha*, which premiered on April 26, 1980 (Shimura was well enough to attend with Masako), was trimmed to 162 for its international release. Included in the footage that hit the cutting-room floor was Shimura's scene; and, aside from the May 14, 1980, audience at the Cannes Film Festival, no one outside Japan saw his final big-screen performance until it was restored for video release in 2005. At Cannes, the full-length version won the Palm d'Or, while the 162-minute cut was nominated for Best Foreign Language Film and Best Art Direction at the Academy Awards.

Interestingly, Michael Rich, an American who served as an assistant director on the film, claimed,

> The … fact is that Kurosawa himself cut the film from its Japan release length … no one else touched *Kagemusha*. Because of its expense and length of production, it was rushed into release in Japan to make back some of Toho's investment as soon as possible. As a result, Kurosawa did not have sufficient time to cut the film to his liking. He considers the longer version a "rough cut" of the film which unfortunately got shown…[5]

Whatever the reason, after specifically including a character in the screenplay for Shimura, Kurosawa (whose friend's footage was restored after the director's death) deliberately removed it.

Shimura made his final professional appearance in writer-director Seijirô Kôyama's *Nihon Philharmonic Orchestra: Honoo no dai gogakusho* (1981), produced by NR Kikaku for distribution by Nikkatsu. Too ill to accept any further work, he passed away from chronic pulmonary emphysema at Keio University Hospital in Tokyo on February 11, 1982. His remains were cremated, and his ashes presented to Masako.

Conclusion

In 2010, a collection of materials from Shimura's film career was donated to the Film Center at the National Museum of Modern Art (now the National Film Archive of Japan) in Tokyo. From August 18–December 23, 2015, an exhibition, "Film Actor Takashi Shimura," celebrating the 110th anniversary of his birth, was open to the public from 11:00 a.m. to 6:00 p.m. daily, excepting Mondays and designated holidays.

The "Takashi Shimura Memorial Hall," featuring an exhibit of artifacts and photographs, also was established at the location of his birthplace in Asago-shi, Hyogo Prefecture, and housed in one of the remaining, preserved six buildings of the original 18 in the Meiji-era Ikuno Mine staff quarters. It is a major tourist attraction of the area and, in 2007, a Takashi Shimura Film Festival was held there.

Though Shimura made a major mark in 21 of the 30 features directed by his top collaborator and good friend Akira Kurosawa, he also worked for other filmmakers in the Japanese pantheon, including Hiroshi Inagaki (19 films as director), Masahiro Makino (18 as director), Ishirô Honda (13 as director), Senkichi Taniguchi (nine as director), Toshio Sugie (eight as director), Mikio Naruse (eight as director and/or writer), Yôji Yamada (three as director and writer), Kon Ichikawa (two as director), Yasuzô Masamura (one as director), Masaki Kobayashi (one as director) and Kenji Mizoguchi (at least one as director). Along with so many major talents behind the cameras, he also shared the screen with a who's who of Japan's finest performers.

Aside from his major colleagues in Kurosawa's "stock company," he appeared (from five to 26 times) with Shin'ichi [Sonny] Chiba, Isao Yamagata, Furanki Sakai, Shintarô Katsu, Setsuko Wakayama, Mieko Takamine, Hideko Takamine, Kenji Sahara, Chishû Ryû, Ken Uehara, Ken Takakura, Machiko Kyô, Yûzô Kayama, Yôsuke Natsuki, Akira Takarada, Kôji Tsuruta, Ren Yamamoto and Akihiko Harata. He appeared in 24 films on which Haruo Nakajima, "Godzilla" himself, worked as a "suit actor," extra or stuntman. Admirers of *kaijû tokusatsu eiga* always will appreciate that he contributes

Conclusion

Asago City Old Ikuno Mine in Hyogo Prefecture, where the Takashi Shimura Museum is housed in one of six buildings preserved from the staff quarters used during the Meiji era (1868–1912).

his distinguished presence to the rampaging adventures of Gojira, Radon, the Moguera, Mosura, Kujira Gami, Ghidorah, the Maguma, Baragon and "Frankenstein."

Shimura brought honor and humanity even to minor roles, and to characters who would have been primarily two-dimensional if portrayed by actors less talented and versatile. From ages 29 to 76, he worked in films during six decades, and did not miss a single year, appearing in at least 270 films in 47 consecutive years (1934–1981).

His characters often possess a high degree of ambiguity; and usually his "open" criminals (gamblers, yakuza bosses) have more positive, likable qualities than do his more socially accepted capitalist businessmen and authority figures. His "heroic" characters (doctors, police detectives, scientists, military leaders, diplomats, priests), though some are quite benevolent, frequently display their human faults and frailties.

Shimura truly was a cinematic chameleon, able to play a wide array of characters possessing great dramatic and comic range. He also ranks among the world's finest actors to have played a long list of actual historical figures.

Like any true artist, he was able to accomplish much with a general "less is more" performance style, often speaking softly while wielding a large samurai sword and maintaining a strong moral compass. To name only two of his

Takashi Shimura Memorial Hall at the location of his birthplace in Asago-shi, Hyogo Prefecture, housed in one of the remaining, preserved six buildings in the Meiji-era Ikuno Mine's staff quarters. It is a major tourist attraction of the area.

finely etched portrayals, Kanji Watanabe in *Ikiru* and Kambei Shimada in *Seven Samurai* (vastly different characters, yet both eminently admirable) are two of world's cinema's greatest acting achievements.

Professionally, Shimura was consistently encouraging and helpful to his colleagues, particularly instrumental in providing much-needed support to the young Toshirô Mifune, the actor who eventually became the nation's top leading man and international movie star. Personally, he was a private, disciplined gentleman, reserved, gentle, a devoted husband with no outward vices who was deeply respected and admired by those with whom he associated, both within and without the art and industry of the cinema. In many ways, living the positive aspects of his ancestors' samurai code, he was not unlike Kambei Shimada, a rare and honorable role model, to be sure.

Perhaps his dying Kanji Watanabe in *Ikiru* simply sums up Takashi Shimura's artistic philosophy the best:

It is too late.... No, it isn't too late. It isn't impossible.... I *can* do something if I really want to.

Appendix A
Takashi Shimura Filmography

Following is the most complete listing of *verified* theatrical-release films featuring Takashi Shimura ever published in either printed or electronic form. Multiple sources have been used in a meticulous research effort, especially to corroborate information and insure as much accuracy as possible.

Each original Japanese title is followed by an English title [in brackets] *if* the film subsequently was released officially in the United States. (If the film is "unofficially" known by an English translation, that title is included in the credits.)

The date accompanying each title is when the film was first released in Japan. The films are listed in chronological order of release. If only the year of release (rather than the specific date) is available, those titles are listed at the end of each respective year (unless the order of its release within that year is known).

If the film subsequently was released in the United States, that date is included in the credits. All films are in the sound format unless indicated otherwise.

Ren'ai-gai itchôme (September 6, 1934)

Credits: Director: Taizo Kamisuna; Screenplay: Kennosuke Morooka; Story: Minoru Nakano; Cinematographer: Ken Azuma; Format/Aspect Ratio: Black-and-White, Silent [1.37:1]; Production Company: Shinko Kinema; English Title: *Number One, Love Street*; Running Length: 8 reels.
Cast: Kenji Asada (Movie Director), Eiko Azuma (Osachi's Mother), Yûkichi Kamishiro (Ryôsaku Takashima, Jobless Bachelor), Hikaru Kicchôji [Mitsuhiko Okazaki] (Keikichi Egi, Jobless Bachelor), Masaki Môri (Reporter), Kaoru Nakano (Fumiko Ôhama), Takashi Shimura (Osachi's Father), Kaoru Wakaba (Chief Editor), Naoyo Yamagata (Osachi, Daughter of Goldfish Seller).

Umon torimonochô: Harebare gojûsantsugi–Ranma hen (December 31, 1935)

Credits: Director: Matsuo Yamamoto; Cinematographer: Kingo Nomura; Format/Aspect Ratio: Black-and-White, Silent [1.37:1]; Production Company: Arashi Kanjurô Production; Running Length: 6 reels.

Cast: Kanjûrô Arashi (Umon "Mutturi" Kondô), Keinosuke Tôyama ("Oshaberi" Denroku), Mon'ya Onoe ("Bata" no Keishirô), Akiko Shiraishi (Oshizu), Mitsuko Mori (Omitsu), Kensaku Hara (Jûzô), Takashi Shimura (Santa).

Chûji uridasu (1935)

Credits: Director, Screenplay and Story: Mansaku Itami; Cinematographer: Shigeru Miki; Format/Aspect Ratio: Black-and-White [1.37:1]; Sound: Sadatoshi Kono; Production Company: Shinko Kinema Oizumi Company, Ltd.

Cast: Tokumaro Dan (Yosako), Asataro Ichikawa (Chuji Nagaoka), Kunio Kaga [Kuninosuke Funanami] (Chiyomatsu), Mineko Môri (Osato), Keiko Takatsu (Omachi), Shinobu Araki, Ryônosuke Azuma, Kensaku Haruji, Junko Kinugasa, Taisuke Matsumoto, Shôroku Onoe, Takashi Shimura, Ryûnosuke Tsukigata.

Umon torimonochô: Harebare gojûsantsugi–Saiketsu hen (January 10, 1936)

Credits: Director: Matsuo Yamamoto; Screenplay: Shiro Hakushu, Ryô Takei; Story: Mitsuzô Sasaki; Cinematographer: Kingo Nomura; Format/Aspect Ratio: Black-and-White [1.37:1]; Production Company: Arashi Kanjiro Production; Distributor: Shinko Kinema.

Cast: Junosuke Arashi, Kanjûrô Arashi, Tokusaburo Arashi, Tarô Bandô, Hanako Beppu, Kensaku Hara, Kensaku Haruji, Kakô Ichikawa, Kiyoko Izumi, Kiyoshi Kasuga, Takeo Kawasaki, Hisao Kikumoto, Tasaburo Matsumoto, Ryûzaburô Matumoto, Mitsuko Mori, Mon'ya Onoe, Takashi Shimura, Akiko Shiraishi, Aizo Tamashima, Keinosuke Tôyama.

Naniwa erejî [*Osaka Elegy*] (May 28, 1936)

Credits: Director and Screen Story: Kenji Mizoguchi; Producer: Masaichi Nagata; Screenplay: Yoshikata Yoda, Tadashi Fujiwara; Based on the Story "Mieko" by Saburo Okada; Cinematographer: Minoru Miki; Format/Aspect Ratio: Black-and-White [1.37:1]; Assistant Cinematographer: Kunitarô Yoneyama; Editor: Tatsuko Sakane; Musical Score: Kôichi Takage; Sound: Hisashi Kase, Yasume Mizoguchi; Lighting Technician: Tatsuro Horikoshi; Production Company: Daiichi Eiga; U.S. release: January 31, 1979; Running Time: 90 minutes.

Cast: Isuzu Yamada (Ayako Murai), Seiichi Takagawa (Junzo Murai), Chiyoko Ôkura (Sachiko Murai), Shinpachirô Asaka (Hiroshi Murai), Benkei Shiganoya (Sonosuke Asai), Yôko Umemura (Sumiko Asai), Kensaku Hara (Susumu Nishimura), Shizuko Takizawa (Mine Fukuda, the Maid), Eitarô Shindô (Yoshizo Fujino), Kunio Tamura (Dr. Yoko), Takashi Shimura (Inspector), Mitsuzo Tachibana (Famizaburo Matsushita), Kasuke Koizume, Kiyoko Ôkubo.

Shura hakkô: Dai-san-pen (July 31, 1936)

Credits: Directors: Masahiro Makino, Nubuo Nakagawa; Producer: Masahiro Makino; Screenplay: Kenji Hata; Based on the Novel by Rifû Yukimoto; Cinematographer: Shihei Masaki; Format/Aspect Ratio: Black-and-White [1.37:1];

Production Company: Makino Talkie Seisaku-jo; Distributor: Chidori Kogyo; Running Time: 68 minutes.
Cast: Junko Hara, Jun'nosuke Hayama, Tsukie Matsuura, Eizaburô Sakauchi, Takashi Shimura.

Chûretsu nikudan sanyûshi (November 29, 1936)

Credits: Director and Producer: Masahiro Makino; Cinematographer: Keizo Yanagi; Format/Aspect Ratio: Black-and-White [1.37:1]; Production Company: Makino Kyoiku Eiga Seisaku-jo.
Cast: Ryûzaburô Mitsuoka, Yôichi [Kôichirô] Mizuhara, Eizaburô Sakauchi, Katsuji Shimazu, Takashi Shimura.

Akagaki Genzô (December 13, 1936)

Credits: Director: Yoshio Hirao; Supervisor: Masahiro Makino; Cinematographer: Ihachi Ômori; Format/Aspect Ratio: Black-and-White [1.37:1] Sound: Masahiro Makino; Production Company: Makino Talkie Seisaku-jo; Running Time: 38 minutes.
Cast: Tokumaru Dan, Kuniko Hanano, Tsukie Matsuura, Fumio Okura, Kunitarô Sawamura, Eitarô Shimizu, Takashi Shimura, Susumu Sorori, Yoshida Naramaru [Yamatonojô Yoshida] (voice only).

Akanishi Kakita (1936)

Credits: Director and Screenplay: Mansaku Itami; Story: Naoya Shiga; Cinematographer: Hiroshige Urushiyama; Format/Aspect Ratio: Black-and-White [1.37:1]; Musical Score: Nakaba Takahashi; Assistant Directors: Masaki Môri, Kiyoshi Saeki, Minoru Sano; Sound: Masataka Ikedo, Shigeharu Tsukagoshi, Nobuo Yamauchi; Production Company: Kataoka Chiezo Productions; English Title: *Capricious Young Man*; Running Time: 77 minutes.
Cast: Chiezô Kataoka (Akanishi Kakita/Kai Harada), Shôsaku Sugiyama (Tetsunosuke Matsumae), Sôjin Kamiyama (Aki), Yôko Umemura (Masaoka), Mineko Mori (Onami), Takashi Shimura (Taranoshin Tsunomata), Takeo Kawasaki (Monban), Misao Seki (Sabaemon of Irifuneya), Eiko Higashi (Princess), Michisaburo Segawa (Date Hyobu), Eiko Azuma, Sayoko Kasumi, Kensaku Hara.

Mitokomon kaikokuki (1937)

Credits: Director: Tomiyasu Ikeda; Cinematographer: Seishi Tanimoto; Format/Aspect Ratio: Black-and-White [1.37:1]; Production Company: Nikkatsu Kyoto.
Cast: Kaichi Yamamoto, Tsumanaburô Bandô, Chiezô Kataoka, Kikutaro Onoe, Ryôsuke Kagawa, Minoru Takase, Michisaburo Segawa, Takashi Shimura, Kajô Onoe, Seinosuke Hayashi, Ryûnosuke Nanjô, Shizuko Takizawa.

Seishun gonin otoko: Zempen (January 10, 1937)

Credits: Director and Producer: Masahiro Makino; Screenplay: Rintarô Ôfuna; Story: Hachirô Satô; Cinematographer: Shinjiro Izumi; Format/Aspect Ratio:

Black-and-White [1.37:1]; Supporting Director: Hiroshi Seimaru; Production Company: Makino Talkie Seisaku-jo; Running Length: 8 reels.
Cast: Chieko Kanazawa, Hiroko Makino, Yôichi [Kôichirô] Mizuhara, Eizaburô Sakauchi, Ryôko Satomi, Katsuji Shimazu, Takashi Shimura, Kunio Tamura, Sanshirô Tsubaki, Sumie Tsuki.

Seishun gonin otoko: Kôhen (January 24, 1937)
Credits: Directors: Masahiro Makino, Hiroshi Seimaru; Producer: Masahiro Makino; Screenplay: Rintarô Ôfuna; Story: Hachirô Satô; Cinematographer: Shinjirô Izumi; Format/Aspect Ratio: Black-and-White [1.37:1]; Production Company: Makino Talkie Seisaku-jo; Running Length: 7 reels.
Cast: Chieko Kanazawa, Yôichi [Kôichirô] Mizuhara, Ryôko Satomi, Takashi Shimura, Kunio Tamura, Sanshirô Tsubaki, Sumie Tsuki.

Jiraiya (December 31, 1937)
Credits: Director: Masahiro Makino; Screenplay and Story: Yoshitake Hisa; Cinematographer: Hideo Ishimoto; Format/Aspect Ratio: Black-and-White [1.37:1]; Musical Score: Gorô Nishi; Sound: Yukio Kaihara; Production Company: Nikkatsu; Running Time: 56 minutes.
Cast: Chiezô Kataoka (Jiraiya), Reiko Hoshi (Princess Tsunade), Gorô Kawabe, Takashi Shimura (Gundayu Yao), Matsunosuke Fukui (Heitayû Yanami), Shojiro Ichikawa (Terutaka-Sarashina), Hidemichi Ishikawa (Kakunoshin Sakurai), Kiyoshi Kagawa (Dansuke), Sayoko Kasumi (Omaki), Hirorô Kato (Shôsaku), Fumie Miyoshi (Ochiyo), Yôichi Mizahara (Isobei Tengan), Ryûnosuke Nanjô (Hanbei Hikosaka), Kinko Narimiya (Ohide), Kajô Onoe (Tenzen Igarashi), Michisaburo Segawa (Orochimaru), Shuntaro So (Tarômaru), Ryôsuke Kagawa, Kunitaro Bando.

Chikemuri Takadanobaba (December 31, 1937)
Credits: Directors: Hiroshi Inagaki, Masahiro Makino; Cinematographers: Hideo Ishimoto, Rokusaburô Mitsui; Format/Aspect Ratio: Black-and-White [1.37:1]; Production Company and Distributor: Nikkatsu; Running Time: 57 minutes.
Cast: Tsumasaburô Bandô (Yasubei Nakayama), Tokumaru Dan (Genjihei Segawa), Komako Hara (Osai), Shunaburo Iba (Yengan), Momonosuke Ichikawa (Kumako) Ryôsuke Kagawa (Rokuzaemon Sugano), Takashi Shimura (Takusan), Chiyoko Ôkura (Otae).

Kurama Tengu (March 15, 1938)
Credits: Directors: Masahiro Makino, Sadatsugu Matsuda; Screenplay: Keinosuke Uekasa; Cinematographer: Kazuo Miyagawa; Format/Aspect Ratio: Black-and-White [1.37:1]; Musical Score: Nakaba Takahashi; Production Company: Nikkatsu Kyoto; Distributor: Nikkatsu; Running Time: 52 minutes.
Cast: Goro Abe (Isami Kondo), Kanjûrô Arashi (Kurama Tengu),Kunitaro Bando (Teizo Miyabe), Tokumaro Dan (Kurohime no Kichibei), Sannosuke Fujikawa (Priest at Shôgetsu-in), Fujiko Fukamizu (Okichi, Daughter of Choshichi),

Kensaku Hara (Soshi Okita), Komako Hara (Kurayami no Okane), Komako Hara (Kurayami no Okane), Momotaro Hata (Shinkichi), Ryôsuke Kagawa (Harimanokami Akimoto), Kajô Onoe (Toshizô Hijikata), Kunitarô Sawamura (Kogoro Katsura), Michisaburo Segawa (Choshichi/Hayabusa), Takashi Shimura (Kichinosuke Saigô), Shuntaro So (Sugisaku).

Shamisen yakuza (June 1, 1938)

Credits: Director: Toshizô Kinugasa; Screenplay: Hassaku Suzukano; Story: Matsutarô Kawaguchi; Cinematographer: Rokusaburô Mitsui; Format/Aspect Ratio: Black-and-White [1.37:1]; Musical Score: Nakaba Takahashi; Production Company: Nikkatsu Kyoto.
Cast: Satoko Chikamatsu (Osan), Sannosuke Fujikawa (Yasaburô Kineya), Tominosuke Hayama (Zenroku), Kichinosuke Ichikawa (Kinsuke), Shojiro Ichikawa (Yagirô), Ryôsuke Kagawa (Shichibei), Taichiro Okura (Jinsai, Doctor), Kikutaro Onoe (Yaichi Kineya), Tôka Onoe (Kanta), Kunitarô Sawamura (Fujirô Nakamura), Takashi Shimura (Heisuke), Hanako Suehiro (Otami), Shizuko Takizawa (Otoku, Shichibei's Wife), Hidemichi Ishikawa, Midori Komatsu.

Yami no kagebôshi [Shadows of Darkness] (July 14, 1938)

Credits: Director: Hiroshi Inagaki; Screenplay: Nariharu Iinuma; Cinematographer: Kazuo Miyagawa; Format/Aspect Ratio: Black-and-White [1.37:1]; Musical Score: Gorô Nishi; Sound: Toshio Nakamura; Running Time: 52 minutes.
Cast: Sannosuke Fujikawa (Yobei), Kanae Kobayashi (Oshima), Midori Komatsu (Oraku), Kaoru Nakano (Okiku), Saganji Ôkawara (Senkichi), Teruo Shimada (Goichi), Shizuko Takizawa (Okume), Yukiko Todoroki (Oyuki), Kunitaro Bando, Tsumasaburô Bandô, Seinosuke Hayashi, Momonosuke Ichikawa, Shojiro Ichikawa, Hidemichi Ishikawa, Ryôsuke Kagawa. Ryûtarô Matsumoto, Taichiro Okura, Kunitarô Sawamura, Takashi Shimura, Reizaburô Yamamoto.

Akagaki Genzô (November 17, 1938)

Credits: Director: Tomiyasu Ikeda; Screenplay and Story: Tomiyasu Ikeda [Kôyô Takigawa]; Cinematographer: Shigeo Yoshimi; Format/Aspect Ratio: Black-and-White [1.37:1]; Musical Score: Yoshio Shiraki; Production Company: Nikkatsu Kyoto; Running Length: 9 reels.
Cast: Tsumasaburô Bandô (Genzo Akagaki), Kogiku Hanayagi (Chizue), Kensaku Hara (Takeshiro Sakaya), Kobunji Ichikawa (Riemon Torii), Momonosuke Ichikawa (Yogoro Kanzaki), Katsuhiko Isokawa (Tsunehei, Old Servant), Ryôsuke Kagawa (Isabei Shioyama), Kaoru Nakano (Omaki, Shioyama's Wife), Kikuhei Okada [Masahiro Nagata] (Isuke Maebara), Tôka Onoe (Kamaroku), Takashi Shimura (Jozaemon Sakaya), Kunio Tamura (Senta, Newspaper Seller), Chiyoko Ôkura (Osugi, Maid).

Yajikita dôchûki (December 1, 1938)

Credits: Director: Masahiro Makino; Screenplay and Story: Hideo Oguni; Cinematographer: Hideo Ishimoto; Format/Aspect Ratio: Black-and-White

[1.37:1]; Editor: Nobuo Miyamoto; Musical Score: Masao Koga; Sound: Yukio Kaihara; Production Company: Nikkatsu Kyoto.

Cast: Satoko Chikamatsu (Otsuta), Tokumaro Dan (Magician), Etchan (Sankichi), Komako Hara (Okuni), Taeko Hira (Oyuki), Ryôsuke Kagawa (Kôchinokami Tôyama), Chiezô Kataoka (Kinshiro Tôyama), Shigeo Kusunoki (Yajirobei), Dick Mine (Kitahachi), Kaoru Nakano (Ogin), Kajô Onoe (Senta), Michisaburo Segawa (Denshichi), Kyôji Sugi (Jirokichi, nezumi-kozô), Sannosuke Fujikawa, Tomiko Hattori, Seinosuke Hayashi, Hidemichi Ishikawa, Gorô Kawabe, Midori Komatsu, Michiyakko, Takashi Shimura.

Shusse taikoki, Mazô, Jigoku no mushi (1938)

Credits: Director: Hiroshi Inagaki; Screenplay and Story: Itarô Yamagami; Cinematographer: Kazuo Miyagawa; Format/Aspect Ratio: Black-and-White [1.37:1]; Musical Score: Gorô Nishi; Production Company: Nikkatsu Kyoto; Distributor: Nikkatsu; Running Time: 103 minutes.

Cast: Kanjûrô Arashi, Ryûnosuke Tsukigata, Kikutaro Onoe, Gorô Kawabe, Kensaku Hara, Michisaburo Segawa, Ryôsuke Kagawa, Haruyo Ichikawa, Kazuko Yoshida, Kobunji Ichikawa, Kajô Onoe, Takashi Shimura, Goro Abe, Jiro Tomei.

Zoku mazô-Ibara Ukon (January 14, 1939)

Credits: Director: Hiroshi Inagaki; Story: Kaitaro Haegawa [Fubô Hayashi]; Cinematographer: Kazuo Miyagawa; Format/Aspect Ratio: Black-and-White [1.37:1]; Musical Score: Gorô Nishi; Production Company: Nikkatsu Kyoto; Running Time: 65 minutes.

Cast: Tsumanaburô Bandô (Ukon Ibara/Kyinosuke Kajio), Kensaku Hara (Hanbei Ushida), Kobunji Ichikawa (Yamashironokami Wakisaka), Ryôsuke Kagawa (Choan Murai), Sayoko Kasumi (Sonoe), Goro Kawabe (Echizen'nokami Ôoka), Junko Kinugasa (Ogen), Mayumi Kofuji (Otae), Kunitarô Sawamura (Kanroku Watanuki), Michisaburo Segawa (Genban Ôsako), Shizuko Takizawa (Oshizu), Hiroko Tomoe (Otame), Kunitaro Bando, Tokumaro Dan, San'nosuke Fujikawa, Tominosuke Hayama, Katsuhiko Isokawa, Hiroro Kato, Kanae Kobayashi, Jo Kume, Shizuo Maeda, Ichirô [Ikkô] Ôkuni, Taichiro Okura. Kajô Onoe, Takashi Shimura.

Edo no akutarô (May 4, 1939)

Credits: Director: Masahiro Makino; Screenplay and Story: Yoshitake Hisa; Cinematographer: Hideo Ishimoto; Format/Aspect Ratio: Black-and-White [1.37:1]; Musical Score: Gorô Nishi; Production Company: Nikkatsu Kyoto; Running Length: 12 reels.

Cast: Kanjurô Arashi, Kensaku Hara, Reiko Hoshi, Kobunji Ichikawa, Takashi Shimura, Yukiko Todoroki.

Oshidori utagassen [Singing Lovebirds] (December 14, 1939)

Credits: Director: Masahiro Makino; Screenplay: Koji Edogawa; Cinematographers: Akira Mimura, Kazuo Miyagawa; Format/Aspect Ratio: Black-and-White

[1.37:1]; Editor: Nubuo Miyamoto; Musical Score: Tokujiro Okubo, Masao Yoneyama; Set Decorator: Shigekichi Hasegawa; Assistant Director: Morihisa Haneda; Recording Director: Sadamitsu Ishihara; Stunt Designer: Reijiro Adachi; Production Company and Distributor: Nikkatsu; Running Time: 69 minutes.
Cast: Chiezô Kataoka (Reisaburo Asai), Ryôsuke Kagawa (Soshichi Kagawaya), Takashi Shimura (Kyosai Shimura), Mitsuru Toyama (Man-emon Toyama), Kajô Onoe (Roku-be of Dogu-ya, Antique Dealer), Hidemichi Ishikawa (Matsusuke Matsuda), Eizaburo Kusunoki (Sugiura), Ryutaro Chikamatsu (Hinokiyama), Matsunosuke Fukui (Takebayashi), Minoru Fujisaki (Yanagawa), Shirô Osaki (Tsubaki), Mitsuo Kobayashi (Sankichi), Heizaburo Fujimura (Young Master of Charcoal Shop), Daihachiro Takebayashi (Young Master of Grocer), Junosuke Arashi (Young Master of Liquor Shop), Makitaro Bando (Young Master of Rice Shop), Sanpei Ishimaru (Young Master of Dry Food Shop), Shôjiro Kawase (Medical Doctor), Haruyo Ichikawa (Oharu, Daughter of Kyosai), Fujiko Fukamizu (Fujio, Daughter of Man-emon), Dick Mine (Minezwa Tanba-no-kami), Tomiko Hattori (Otomi, Daughter of Kagawaya).

Tsubanari ronin (December 30, 1939)

Credits: Director: Ryohei Arai; Screenplay: Yoshitake Hisa; Story: Kikuo Tsunoda; Cinematographer: Chojiro Arakai; Format/Aspect Ratio: Black-and-White [1.37:1]; Musical Score: Gorô Nishi; Production Company: Nikkatsu Film.
Cast: Tsumasaburô Bandô, Kensaku Hara, Momotaro Hata, Haruyo Ichikawa, Kobunji Ichikawa, Omezo Ichikawa, Ryôsuke Kagawa, Akemi Kawakami, Takeo Minato, Kôtarô Nirei, Kikuhei Okada, Ichirô Okuni, Kinitarô Swamura, Michisaburo Segawa, Reinosuke Segawa, Kazushi Seto, Go Shimoyama, Takashi Shimura, Ryoichi Takeuchi, Joji Tani, Kunihito Tsukihashi, Kichijirô Ueda.

Shunjû ittôryû (1939)

Credits: Director and Screenplay: Santarô Marune; Cinematographer: Seishi Tanimoto; Format/Aspect Ratio: Black-and-White [1.37:1]; Musical Score: Nakaba Takahashi; Production Company: Nikkatsu Kyoto; Distributor: Nikkatsu; Running Time: 74 minutes.
Cast: Chiezô Kataoka (Miki Hirate), Kunitarô Sawamura (Sasagawa no Shigezo), Kansaku Hara (Ganryu Tadaki), Ryôsuke Kagawa (Jin'an, Doctor), Takashi Shimura (Jûbei Tamon), Shôjirô Asano (Katsuzaemon Murase) Taeko Hira (Omine), Kobunji Ichikawa (Sukegoro Iioka), Sayoko Kasumi (Okiku, Tadahei's Wife), Junko Kinugasa (Oyuki, Shigezo's Wife), Midori Komatsu (Aged Janitor at Temple), Kôtarô Nirei (Kiyotaki no Sakichi), Kunio Tamura (Sugayama no Tadahei), Yukiko Todoroki (Osei, Shigezô's Sister), Goro Abe.

Miyamoto Musashi: Dai-san-bu-Kenshin ichiro (April 18, 1940)

Credits: Director: Hiroshi Inagaki; Screenplay: Hiroshi Inagaki, Hiroshi Makimoto; Story: Eiji Yoshikawa; Cinematographer: Kazuo Miyagawa; Format/Aspect Ratio: Black-and-White [1.37:1]; Musical Score: Gorô Nishi; Production Company: Nikkatsu Kyoto; Running Time: 68 minutes.

Cast: Tokumaro Dan, Kobunji Ichikawa, Ryôsuke Kagawa, Chiezô Kataoka, Gorô Kawabe, Chikako Miyagi, Michisaburo Segawa, Takashi Shimura, Ryûnosuke Tsukigata.

Phantom Castle (October 10, 1940)

Credits: Director: Kyotaro Saga; Format/Aspect Ratio: Black-and-White [1.37:1].
Cast: Kensaku Hara, Takashi Shimura, Kimiko Tachibana, Otome Tsukinomiya.

Zoku Shimizu minato (1940)

Credits: Director: Masahiro Makino; Screenplay: Hideo Oguni; Format/Aspect Ratio: Black-and-White [1.37:1]; Production Company: Nikkatsu; Alternate Title: *Shimizu minato daisan yume dôchû*.
Cast: Chiezô Kataoka (Katsuhiko Ishida/Mori no Ishimatsu), Takashi Ogawa (Jirochô Shimizu), Yukiko Todoroki (Fumiko Kuroda/Ofumi), Torazo Hirosawa, Kunitarô Sawamura, Takashi Shimura.

Oda Nobunaga (1940)

Credits: Director: Masahiro Makino; Cinematographer: Hideo Ishimoto; Format/Aspect Ratio: Black-and-White [1.37:1]; Musical Score: Nakaba Takahashi; Production Company: Nikkatsu Kyoto; Distributor: Nikkatsu; Alternate Title: *Fûunji Nobunaga*; Running Time: 91 minutes.
Cast: Chiezô Kataoka (Nobunaga Oda), Takashi Shimura, Eiji Takagi, Goro Abe.

Umi wo wataru sairei (May 4, 1941)

Credits: Director: Hiroshi Inagaki; Screenplay: Shintarô Mimura; Cinematographer: Hideo Ishimoto; Format/Aspect Ratio: Black-and-White [1.37:1]; Musical Score: Gorô Nishi; Sound: Toshirô Sasaki; Production Company: Nikkatsu; Running Time: 92 minutes.
Cast: Tokumaro Dan, Fujiko Fukamizu, Haruyo Ichikawa, Kobunji Ichikawa, Sashô Ichikawa, Hidemichi Ishikawa, Ryôsuke Kagawa, Kiyoshi Kasuga, Junko kinugasa, Mitsuo Kobayashi, Ryusei Koike, Eijirô Kusunoki, Ryû Kuze, Hirotoshi (Kôju) Murata, Kôtarô Nirei, Kajô Onoe, Shirô Osaki, Kazushi Seto, Go Shimoyama, Takashi Shimura, Noburo Taki, Jôtarô Togami, Mitsuru Toyama, Otome Tsukinomiya, Kichijirô Ueda, Katsusaburo Ukita, Chiyoko Ôkura.

Sugata naki fukushû (July 8, 1941)

Credits: Director: Sadatsugu Matsuda; Screenplay: Yoshitake Hisa; Cinematographer: Rokusaburô Mitsui; Format/Aspect Ratio: Black-and-White [1.37:1]; Production Company: Nikkatsu Kyoto; Running Length: 15 reels.
Cast: Kobunji Ichikawa, Ryôsuke Kagawa, Chikako Miyagi, Takashi Shimura, Denmei Suzuki, Shintarô Takiguchi, Otome Tsukimiya, Chiyoko Ôkura.

Edo saigo no hi (1941)

Credits: Director and Screenplay: Hiroshi Inagaki; Cinematographer: Hideo Ishi-

moto; Format/Aspect Ratio: Black-and-White [1.37:1]; Production Company: Nikkatsu Kyoto; Distributor: Nikkatsu; Running Time: 72 minutes.
Cast: Kensaku Hara, Ryôsuke Kagawa, Takashi Shimura.

Miyamoto Musashi: Ichijoji ketto (March 25, 1942)

Credits: Director and Screenplay: Hiroshi Inagaki; Producer: Mikio Takahashi; Story: Eiji Yoshikawa; Cinematographer: Hideo Ishimoto; Format/Aspect Ratio: Black-and-White [1.37:1]; Editor: Shigeo Nishida; Musical Score: Gorô Nishi; Production Company: Nikkatsu Kyoto; Running Time: 86 minutes.
Cast: Chiezô Kataoka (Musashi Miyamoto), Chikako Miyagi (Otsu), Shinpachirô Asaka, Sannosuke Fujikawa, Kaoru Futaba, Haruyo Ichikawa, Ryôsuke Kagawa, Gorô Kawabe, Takashi Shimura.

Hahakogusa (June 4, 1942)

Credits: Director: Tomotaka Tasaka, Screenplay and Story: Shinobu Koito; Cinematographer: Saburô Isayama; Format/Aspect Ratio: Black-and-White [1.37:1]; Musical Score: Gen Uchida; Production Company: Shôchiku Uzumasa; Distributor: Shiro-kei; Running Length: 13 reels.
Cast: Masao Hayama, Akiko Kazami, Isamu Kosugi, Eitarô Ozawa, Takashi Shimura, Hisako Takihana, Reiko Ueda.

Sugata Sanshirô [*Sanshiro Sugata*] (March 25, 1943)

Credits: Director and Screenplay: Akira Kurosawa; Producer: Keiji Matsuzaki; Executive in Charge of Production: Jin Usami; Based on the novel by Tsuneo Tomita; Cinematographer: Akira Mimura; Format/Aspect Ratio: Black-and-White [1.37:1]; Processing: Toho Developing; Editor: Akira Kurosawa; Negative Cutter: Toshio Gotô; Musical Score: Seiichi Suzuki; Art Director: Masao Tozuka; Chief Assistant Director: Toshio Sugie; Assistant Director: Seki Nakamura; Script Supervisor: Yukie Kikuchi; Sound: Tomohisa Higuchi; Art Crew: Tsukasa Kondo; Lighting Technician: Masaki Ônuma; Stills Photographer: Akira Ôtani; Judo Instructors: Keishichi Ishiguro, Kinnosuke Sato; Locations: Kyoto; Production Company: Toho Eiga Company, Ltd.; Distributor: Film Distribution, Inc.; U.S. Release Date: April 28, 1974; Running Time: 97 minutes; 1952 Reissue Running Time: 80 minutes, (U.S. Release) 79 minutes.
Cast: Denjirô Ôkôchi (Shogoro Yano), Susumu Fugita (Sanshiro Sugata), Yukiko Todoroki (Sayo Murai), Ryûnosuke Tsukigata (Gennosuke Higaki), Takashi Shimura (Hansuke Murai, Sayo's Father), Ranko Hanai (Osumi Kodana), Sugisaku Aoyama (Tsunetami Iinuma), Ichirô Sugai (Police Chief Mishima), Yoshio Kosugi (Master Soburo Monma, Jujitsu Teacher and Osumu's Father), Kokuten Kôdô (Buddhist Priest), Michisaburo Segawa (Wada), Akitake Kôno (Yoshimaro Dan), Sôji Kiyokawa (Yujiro Toda), Kunio Mita (Kohei Tsuzaki), Akira Nakamura (Toranosuke Niizeki), Eisaburo Sakauchi (Nemeto), Hajime Hikari (Torakichi).

Himetaru kakugo (November 18, 1943)

Credits: Director: Eisuke Takizawa; Screenplay: Matsuo Kishi, Mikio Naruse, Eisuke Takizawa, Yûsaku Yamagata [all as Eichi Nariyama]; Cinematographer:

Jôji Ohara; Format/Aspect Ratio: Black-and-White [1.37:1]; Editor: Toshio Gotô; Musical Score: Noboru Itô; Art Director: Tôtetsu Hirakawa; Sound: Masao Kurabe; Sound Editor: Hisashi Shimonaga; Lighting Technician: Iwaharu Hiraoka; Production Manager: Toshio Sugie; Production Company: Toho Eiga; Distributor: Shiro-kei; Running Time: 73 minutes.
Cast: Kenzô Asada (Motohiko), Susumu Fugita (Navy Officer), Yuriko Hanabusa (Tama), Kazuo Hasegawa (Fumio Abe), Toshiko Hatori (Toyoko), Kimie Hayashi (Asa), Tsugurô Kanemitsu (Yamagishi), Tamae Kiyokawa (Detective Woman), Isao Numasaki (Shintaro Takenaka), Ichirô Ryûzaki (Narita), Masao Shimizu (Toshio Ômura), Takashi Shimura (Ryôkichi Ishikawa), Eitarô Shindô (Shibata), Yônosuke Toba (Morita), Hiroshi Tsukiji (Tamizô), Isuzu Yamada (Oshizu), Fumio Hara, Zenpei Saga, Eizaburô Sakauchi, Ichirô Sugai.

Kaigun (December 8, 1943)

Credits: Director: Tomotaka Tasaka; Screenplay: Tsutomu Sawamura, Tomotaka Tasaka; Story: Bunroku Shishi [Toyoo Iwata]; Cinematographer: Saburô Isayama; Format/Aspect Ratio: Black-and-White [1.37:1]; Musical Score: Gen Uchida; Production Company: Shôchiku Eiga; Distributors: Beni-kei, Shiro-kei; Running Time: 132 minutes.
Cast: Kazuko Aoyama, Shigeo Araki, Shinobu Araki, Kandô Arashi, Yôko Benisawa, Satoko Chikamatsu, Toichi Doki, Hisae Fujieda, Enji Hajime, Yasumi Hara, Michio Hino, Ren Hokkai, Takeo Iizuka, Masahiko Inoue, Sumitaka Kanda, Eijirô Kataoka [Teruo Shimada], Shoko Kazami, Isamu Kosugi, Masami Maehata, Ikuro Matoba, Mitsuko Mito, Binnosuke Nagao, Eitarô Ozawa, Chishû Ryû, Yutaka Sada, Misao Seki, Takashi Shimura, Munenori Suganuma, Kenji Tachibana, Hisako Takihana, Kenzô Tanaka, Yuji Tani, Haruhiko Terada, Eijirô Tôno, Yôko Umemura, Okuryo Yamanoue, Akira Yamauchi.

Haha no kinembi (1943)

Credits: Director: Yasushi Sasaki; Screenplay: Kôgo Noda, Shin'ichi Yanagawa, Takao Yanai; Based on the Story "Ginkonshiki" by Takamaru Sasaki; Cinematographer: Suketarô Inokai; Format/Aspect Ratio: Black-and-White [1.37:1]; Musical Score: Tadashi Manjôme; Art Director: Motoji Kojima; Production Company: Shochiku Ofuna; Running Time: 86 minutes.
Cast: Shigenobu Chiyo, Yôsuke Hanzawa, Toshio Ichise, Chôko Iida, Kimiko Inoue, Kôichi Itô, Hiroko Katsuya, Katsumi Kubota, Masami Maehata, Kôji Mitsui, Mitsuko Miura, Seiji Nishimura, Toshiko Onoya, Shin Saburi, Takashi Shimura, Chiyo Shin, Akira Takakura, Shin Tokudaiji, Yoshindo Yamaji.

Katô hayabusa sento-tai [*Colonel Katô's Falcon Squadron*] (March 9, 1944)

Credits: Kajirô Yamamoto; Producer: Haruo Mura; Screenplay: Kajirô Yamamoto, Kenta Yamazaki; Cinematographer: Akira Mimura; Format/Aspect Ratio: Black-and-White [1.37:1]; Musical Score: Seiichi Suzuki; Production Designer: Takashi Matsuyama; Art Director: Sô Matsuyama; Assistant Director: Ishirô Honda; Sound: Tomohisa Higuchi; Special Effects Supervisor: Eiji Tsuburaya;

Lighting Technician: Kakuzô Nishikawa; Production Company and Distributor: Toho Company; Running Time: 110 minutes.
Cast: Susumu Fugita (Colonel Tateo Katô), Minoru Takada, Denjirô Ôkôchi, Takashi Shimura, Yatarô Kurokawa, Katsuhiko Haida, Takuzô Kumagai.

Ichiban utsukushiku [*The Most Beautiful*] (April 13, 1944)

Credits: Director and Screenplay: Akira Kurosawa; Planning: Motohiko Ito; Producer: Jin Usami; Cinematographer: Jôji Ohara; Format/Aspect Ratio: Black-and-White [1.37:1]; Processing: Toho Developing; Musical Score: Seiichi Suzuki; Music Producer: Hisashi Iuchi; Production Designer: Teruaki Abe; Assistant Directors: Hiromichi Horikawa, Jin Usami; Sound Effects: Hisashi Shimonaga; Lightning Technician: Masaki Ônuma; Stills Photographer: Taizo Shin; Fife and Drum Band Instructor: Hisa Iuchi; Locations: Hiratsuka; Production Company: Toho Company, Ltd.; Distributor: Film Distribution, Inc.; U.S. Release Date: May 1987; Running Time: 85 minutes.
Cast: Takashi Shimura (Chief Goro Ishida), Sôji Kiyokawa (Soichi Yoshikawa, Chief of General Affairs Section), Ichirô Sugai (Ken Shinda, Chief of Labor Section), Takako Irie (Noriko Mizushima, Dorm Mother), Yôko Yaguchi (Tsuru Watanabe, President of Women Workers), Sayuri Tanima (Yuriko Tanimura, Vice President of the Women Workers), Sachiko Ozaki (Sachiko Yamazaki), Shizuko Nishigaki (Fusae Nishioka), Asako Suzuki (Asako Suzumura), Haruko Toyama (Masako Koyama), Aiko Masu (Tokiko Hiroda), Kazuko Hitomi (Kazuko Futomi), Shizuko Yamada (Hisae Yamaguchi), Itoko Kôno (Sue Okabe), Toshiko Hadori (Toshiko Hattori), Emiko Rei (Chie Shima), Haruko Mii (Haruko Kawai), Minori Toyohara (Minori Yoyota), Eiko Hirayama (Yoshiko Shirayama), Harue Yamashita (Kiyo Mishima), Mineko Mashiro (Mineko Bando), Isuzu Miyakawa (Shizue Miyazaki), Michiko Aikawa (Michiko Ayukawa), Teruko Kato (Teruko Sato), Aritake Kôno (Fife and Drum Band Instructor), Unpei Yokoyama (Dormitory Worker), Chieko Nakakita (Student Worker), Korumi Tanima (Factory Worker).

Shibaidô (May 11, 1944)

Credits: Director: Mikio Naruse; Screenplay: Toshio Yasumi; Based on the Novel by Kôen Hasegawa; Cinematographer: Kinya Ogura; Format/Aspect Ratio: Black-and-White [1.37:1]; Musical Score: Yasuji Kiyose; Art Director: Satoru Chûko; Production Company: Toho Company; English Titles: *The Way of Drama*; *Actor's Way*; Running Time: 82 minutes.
Cast: Roppa Furukawa, Kazuo Hasegawa, Isuzu Yamada, Tomosaburô Ii, Ranko Hanai, Atsushi Watanabe, Eitarô Shindô, Takashi Shimura, Toshiko Itô, Sôji Kiyokawa, Yônosuke Toba.

San-jaku sagohei (July 6, 1944)

Credits: Director: Tamizo Ishida; Producer: Teppei Himuro; Screenplay: Shintarô Mimura; Cinematographer: Tatsuo Tomonari; Format/Aspect Ratio: Black-and-White [1.37:1]; Musical Score: Shigekazu Kurihara; Art Director: Kôhei Shima; Sound: Kenji Murayama; Lighting: Sôichi Yokoi; Production Company:

Toho Company; Distributor: Film Distribution; English Title: *Sagohei the Three-footer*; Running Time: 74 minutes.
Cast: Hideko Takamine (Otae), Yatarô Kurokawa (Dembei Ujiie), Ken'ichi Enomoto ("Three-Footer" Sagohei), Takashi Shimura (Yasukichi Ito), Unpei Yokoyama (Inozuke Yamada), Toshiko Itô (Maki), Sôji Kiyokawa (Kai Harada), Eizaburo Onoe (Herself).

Nichijô no tatakai (1944)

Credits: Director: Yasujirô Shimazu; Screenplay: Hideo Oguni; Cinematographer: Asakazu Nakai; Format/Aspect Ratio: Black-and-White [1.37:1]; Production Designer: Takashi Matsuyama; Production Company and Distributor: Toho Company; English Title: *The Daily Battle*; Running Time: 72 minutes.
Cast: Shin Saburi, Tsutomu Odaka, Susumu Fugita, Takashi Shimura, Ichirô Sugai.

Tokkan ekichô (March 29, 1945)

Credits: Director: Torajirô Saitô; Producer: Teppei Himuro; Screenplay: Satoshi Kisaragi, Toshio Shimura; Based on the Comic by Ichio Matsushita; Cinematographer: Mikiya Tachibana; Format/Aspect Ratio: Black-and-White [1.37:1]; Musical Score: Noboru Itô; Art Director: Keiji Kitagawa; Sound: Kenji Murayama; Production Company: Toho Eiga Company, Ltd.; Distributor: Shiro-kei; English Title: *The Brash Stationmaster*; Running Time: 62 minutes.
Cast: Saburô Boya, Fusako Fujima, Roppa Furukawa, Yuriko Hanabusa, Eiichi Horii, Morihide Ishida, Akira Kishii, Itoko Kôno, Sachiko Matani, Takashi Shimura, Michitaro Shirikawa, Minoru Takase, Atsushi Watanabe, Hisako Yamane, Dekao Yokoo.

Ai to chikai (July 26, 1945)

Credits: Directors: In-kyu Ch'oe, Tadashi Imai; Screenplay: Ryuichiro Yagi; Cinematographer: Kazuo Yamazaki; Format/Aspect Ratio: Black-and-White [1.37:1]; Production Company: Toho Company; English Title: *Love and Pledge*.
Cast: Minoru Takada (Shiraishi), Chieko Takehisa (Shiraishi's Wife), Takashi Shimura (Murai's Father, Principle), Eun-gi Dog (Second Lieutenant Murai), Shin-jae Kim (Murai's Widow), Yu-ho Kim (Yeong-lyong).

Kita no san-nin (August 5, 1945)

Credits: Director: Kiyoshi Saeki; Producer: Tomoyuki Tanaka; Screenplay: Yûsaku Yamagata; Cinematographer: Asakazu Nakai; Format/Aspect Ratio: Black-and-White [1.37:1]; Production Companies: Film Public Corporation, Toho Company; Distributor: Toho Company; English Title: *Three People of the North*; Running Time: 72 minutes.
Cast: Setsuko Hara (Sumiko Ueno), Hideko Takamine (Yoshie Matsumoto), Hisako Yamane (Akiko Goto), Susumu Fugita (Kakuta), Shin Saburi (Iwao Hara), Akitake Kôno (Isao Mochizuki), Takashi Shimura (Masaki), Haruo Tanaka (Ishii), Kenzô Asada (Uchimura), Hajime Hikari (Kawashima), Toshiko Hajima (Miyo), Chieko Nakakita (Matsu), Sachiko Ozaki (Yone), Toshi Komori.

Koi no fuunji (September 6, 1945)
Credits: Director and Screenplay: Kajirô Yamamoto; Producer: Teppei Himuro; Cinematographer: Mitsuo Miura; Format/Aspect Ratio: Black-and-White [1.37:1]; Art Director: Sô Matsuyama; Sound: Tomoyuki Higuchi; Lighting Technician: Chôshirô Ishii; English Title: *Misfortunes of Love*; 1953 Release Title: *Kaidanji* [*Energetic Boy*].
Cast: Susumu Fugita, Setsuko Hara, Takashi Shimura, Ken'ichi Enomoto, Eitarô Shindo, Toshiko Hattori, Teiichi Yanagida.

Tora no o wo fumu otoko-tachi [*The Men Who Tread on the Tiger's Tail*] (1945/April 24, 1952 [banned for eight years])
Credits: Director and Screenplay: Akira Kurosawa; Producer: Motohiko Itô; Based on Plays by Nobomitsu Kanze and Gohei Namiki; Cinematographer: Takeo Itô; Format/Aspect Ratio: Black-and-White [1.37:1]; Processing: Toho Development; Editor [Negative Cutter]: Toshio Gotô; Musical Score: Tadashi Hattori; Production Designer: Kazuo Kubo; Sound: Kaeji Hasebe; Sound Effects: Ichirô Minawa; Lighting Technician: Iwaharu Hiraoka; Stills Photographer; Koichi Shikida; Unit Production Manager: Jin Usami; Script Supervisor: Hachiko Toi; Production Company and Distributor: Toho Company, Ltd.; U.S. Release Date: February 28, 1960 [Brandon Films, Inc.]; Running Time: 59 minutes.
Cast: Denjirô Ôkôchi (Benkei), Susumu Fugita (Togashi), Ken'ichi Enomoto (Porter), Masayuki Mori (Kamei), Takashi Shimura (Kataoka), Akitake Kôno (Ise), Yoshio Kosugi (Suruga), Hanshirô Iwai [Shubo Nishina] (Yoshitsune), Dekao Yokoo (Hidachibo), Yasuo Hisamatsu (Kajiwara's Messenger), Sôji Kiyokawa (Togashi's Messenger).

Minshu no teki (April 25, 1946)
Credits: Director: Tadashi Imai; Producer: Sôjirô Motoki; Screenplay: Yûsaku Yamagata, Toshio Yasumi; Cinematographer: Hiroshi Suzuki; Format/Aspect Ratio: Black-and-White [Spherical 1.37:1]; Processing: Kinuta Laboratories, Tokyo; Production Designer: Takashi Matsuyama; Sound Recordist: Kenji Murayama; Lighting Technician: Chôshirô Ishii; English Title: *An Enemy of the People*.
Cast: Susumu Fugita, Akitake Kôno, Ureo Egawa, Takashi Shimura, Ichirô Sugai.

Asu o tsukuru hitobito [*Those Who Make Tomorrow*] (May 6, 1946)
Credits: Directors: Akira Kurosawa, Hideo Sekigawa, Kajirô Yamamoto; Producers: Keiji Matsuzaki, Sôjirô Motoki, Ryô Takei, Tomoyuki Tanaka; Screenplay: Yûsaku Yamagata, Kajirô Yamamoto; Cinematographers: Takeo Itô, Taiichi Kankura, Mitsuo Miura; Format/Aspect Ratio: Black-and-White [Spherical 1.37:1]; Musical Score: Noburo Itô; Production Designers: Takeo Kita, Keiji Kitagawa; Sound: Masatoshi Karahima, Isamu Suzuki; Lighting Technicians: Kenzo Ginya, Iwaharu Hiraoka, Sôichi Yokoi; Production Company and Distributor: Toho Company; Running Time: 82 minutes.
Cast: Susumu Fugita (Fugita), Hideko Takamine (Takamine), Kenji Susukida (Gintaro Okamoto, Father), Masayuki Mori (Seizo Hori, Chauffeur), Chieko Takehisa

(Kin Okamoto, Mother), Takashi Shimura (Theatre Manager), Yônosuke Toba (Okamoto's Colleague), Masao Shimizu (Section Chief), Hyô Kitazawa, Kenzô Asada (Kume), Ichirô Chiba (Matsui, Light Man), Sumie Tsubaki (Chiyoko Hori, Chauffeur's Wife), Sayuri Tanima (Shizumi, Dancing Girl), Sachiko Mitani (Haruko, Dancing Girl), Itoko Kôno (Fumie, Actress), Chieko Nakakita (Yoshiko Okamoto, Elder Sister), Yuriko Hamada (Tokiko, Second Dancing Girl), Mitsue Tachibana (Aiko Okamoto, Younger Sister), Michiko Kayama (Kimiko, Dancing Girl).

Juichinin no jogakusei (August 22, 1946)

Credits: Director: Motoyoshi Oda; Producer: Tomoyuki Tanaka; Screenplay: Toshio Yasumi; Cinematographer: Taiichi Kankura; Format/Aspect Ratio: Black-and-White [Spherical 1.37:1]; Processing: Kinuta Laboratories, Tokyo; Musical Score: Shigeru Tsuda; Production Designer: Teruaki Abe; Sound Recordist: Kunie Maruyama; Lighting Technician: Shoichi Tahata; Production Company and Distributor: Toho Company; English Title: *Eleven Girl Students*.

Cast: Yatarô Kurokawa, Yuriko Hamada, Chieko Nakakita, Takashi Shimura.

Waga seishun ni kuinashi [*No Regrets for Our Youth*] (October 29, 1946)

Credits: Director: Akira Kurosawa; Producer: Keiji Matsuzaki; Screenplay: Akira Kurosawa, Eijirô Hisaita, Keiji Matsuzaki; Cinematographer: Asakazu Nakai; Format/Aspect Ratio: Black-and-White [Spherical 1.37:1]; Processing: Toho Film Laboratory; Editor: Akira Kurosawa; Musical Score: Tadashi Hattori; Production Designer/Art Director: Keiji Kittagawa; Production Manager: Ryô Takei; Chief Director: Hiromichi Horikawa; Assistant Directors: Ko Horiuchi, Akitoshi Maeda; Sound: Isamu Suzuki; Sound Effects Editor: Ichirô Minawa; Lighting Technician: Chôshirô Ishii; Stills Photographer: Goichi Araki; Script Supervisor: Yukie Kikuchi; Locations: Kyoto University, Yoshida Hills, Kyoto; Waseda University, Tokyo Loyal Court, Tokyo; Production Company: Toho Company; Distributor: Toei Company; U.S. Release Date: June 6, 1980 [Libra Films]; Running Time: 110 minutes.

Cast: Setsuko Hara (Yukie Hagihara), Susumu Fugita (Ruykichi Noge), Denjirô Ôkôchi (Professor Yagihara, Yukie's Father), Haruko Sigamura (Madame Noge, Ryukichi's Mother), Eiko Miyoshi (Madame Yagihara, the Professor's Wife), Kokuten Kôdô (Mr. Noge, Ryukichi's Father), Akitake Kôno (Itokawa), Takashi Shimura (Police Commissioner "Poison Strawberry" Dokuichigo), Taizo Fukami (Minister of Education), Masao Shimizu (Professor Hakozaki), Haruo Tanaka, Ichirô Chiba, Isamu Yonekura, Noburo Takagi, Hiroshi Sano (Students), Kazu Hikari (Detective), Hisako Hara (Itokawa's Mother), Shin Takemura (Professor), Tateo Kawasaki (Servant), Fusako Fujima (Old Woman), Sayuri Tanima, Itoko Kôno, Chieko Nakakita (Ladies).

Aru yo no tonosama (1946)

Credits: Director: Teinosuke Kinugasa; Format/Aspect Ratio: Black-and-White [1.37:1]; English Title: *Lord for a Night*.

Cast: Kazuo Hasegawa, Hideko Takamine, Susumu Fugita, Denjirô Okochi, Isuzu Yamada, Chôko Iida, Mitsuko Yoshikawa, Takashi Shimura, Ichirô Sugai, Sôji Kiyokawa, Eitarô Shindo, Masao Shimizu, Hyô Kitazawa, Tamae Kiyokawa, Kikuko Hanaoka.

Yottsu no koi no monogatri [*Four Love Stories*] (March 11, 1947)

Credits: Directors: Kajirô Yamamoto, Kenta Yamazaki, Teinosuke Kinugasa, Mikio Naruse, Shirô Toyoda; Producers: Keiji Matsuzaki, Sôjirô Motoki, Tomoyuki Tanaka; Screenplay: Akira Kurosawa, Hideo Oguni, Kenta Yamazaki, Toshio Yasumi; Cinematographers: So Kawamura, Seiichi Kitsuke, Asakazu Nakai, Takeo Itô; Format/Aspect Ratio: Black-and-White [Spherical 1.37:1]; Musical Score: Fumio Hayasaka, Shigekazu Kurihara; Production Designers: Keiji Kitagawa, Takashi Matsuyama; Art Directors: Minoru Esaka, Hidetetsu Hirakawa; Sound: Michio Okazaki; Production Company and Distributor: Toho Company; Running Time: 112 minutes.
Cast: Ryô Ikebe (Masao), Yoshiko Kuga (Yukiko), Michiyo Kogure (Mitsuko), Isao Numasaki (Arita), Ken'ichi Enomoto (Kin-chan), Setsuko Wakayama (Nami-chan), Yuriko Hamada (Mariko), Akitake Kôno (Tomizo), Kenzô Asada (Prosecutor), Yuriko Hanabusa (Kayo), Tokue Hanazawa (Tsutada), Yasuo Hisamatsu (Sankichi), Chôko Iida (Black Market Woman), Ko Ishida (Student), Tokuji Kobayashi (Bar Owner), Masao Shimizu (Detective), Takashi Shimura (Masao's Father), Eitarô Shindô (Dancho), Ichirô Sugai (Yoshioka), Haruko Sugimura (Yukiko's Mother), Chieko Takehisa (Newspaper Sales Woman), Fudeko Tanaka (Sansho), Shiro Tomosaka (Student), Taiko Fukumoto, Mari Hata, Tamotsu Kawasaki, Takeo Kitamura, Itoko Kuwano, Shizuko Nagaoka, Teiko Nakamura, Tadashi Okabe, Tôgô Yamamoto, Sadaichi Yanagida, Isamu Yonekura.

Chikagai nijuyojikan (1947)

Credits: Directors: Tadashi Imai, Kiyoshi Kusuda, Hideo Sekigawa; Producer: Tomoyuki Tanaka; Screenplay: Takeo Chiaki, Yûsaku Yamagata, Toshio Yasumi; Cinematographers: Shunichirô Nakao, Koji Nakazawa; Format/Aspect Ratio: Black-and-White [1.37:1]; Processing: Kinuta Laboratories, Tokyo; Musical Score: Fumio Hayasaka; Art Director: Shigeru Miyamori; Sound: Noboru Yoshioka; Lighting Technician: Shoichi Tahata; Production Company and Distributor: Toho Company; English Title: *24 Hours of a Secret Life*.
Cast: Hideo Saito, Yuriko Hamada, Itoko Kôno, Ichiro Sugai, Sô Yamamura, Chieko Higashiyama, Takashi Shimura.

Ginrei no hate [*Snow Trail*] (August 5, 1947)

Credits: Director: Senkichi Taniguchi; Producer: Tomoyuki Tanaka; Screenplay: Akira Kurosawa, Senkichi Taniguchi; Cinematographer: Junichi Segawa; Format/Aspect Ratio: Black-and-White [Spherical 1.37:1]; Processing: Kinuta Laboratory, Tokyo; Editors: Akira Kurosawa, Senkichi Taniguchi; Negative Cutter: Yoshiki Nagasama; Musical Score: Akira Ifukube; Art Director: Taizô Kawashima; Production Chief: Noboru Nezu; Chief Assistant Director: Jin Usami; Assistant Directors: Mikio Komatsu, Kihachi Okamoto; Property Master: Shoji Kamiho;

Sound: Shoji Kameyama; Sound Effects Editor: Ichirô Minawa; Assistant Cameramen: Masashi Aramaki, Hiroshi Komatsu, Tadashi Sato; Cinematographer (Second Unit): Takeo Itô; Assistant Cameramen (Second Unit): Yuzuru [Jo] Aizawa, Taheshi Nakamachi, Yoshio Teshirogi; Lighting Technician: Mitsuhara Harata; Assistant Lighting Technicians: Rokuro Ishikawa, Kozaburo Mikami; Lighting Technician (Second Unit): Kuichirô Kushida; Stills Photographer: Ikuo Kobayashi; Script Supervisor: Yoshie Yaguchi; Alternate Title: *To the End of the Snow-Capped Mountains*; Locations: Mount Habuka, Hokkaido; Production Company and Distributor: Toho Company, Ltd.; Running Time: 89 minutes.

Cast: Toshirô Mifune (Eijima), Takashi Shimura (Nojiro), Yoshio Kosugi (Takasugi), Akitake Kôno (Honda), Setsuko Wakayama (Haruko), Kokuten Kôdô (Haruko's Grandfather), Fusatarô Ishijima (Shikanoyu Hotel Owner), Haruko Toyama (Maid A), Chizuko Okamura (Maid B), Toshio Kasai, Ko Ishida (Students), Eizaburo Sakauchi (Investigation Chief), Taizô Fukami (Chief Detective), Fumio Ômachi (Detective), Kenzô Asada (Reporter), Nobumitsu Morozuki (Kiuemon), Tokubei Hanazawa, Fumiyoshi Kumagawa, Mitsuo Tsuda (Lumberjacks).

Haru no mezame [*Spring Awakens*] (November 2, 1947)

Credits: Director: Mikio Naruse; Producer: Sôjirô Motoki; Screenplay: Mikio Naruse, Toshio Yasumi; Cinematographer: Shunichirô Nakao; Format/Aspect Ratio: Black-and-White [Spherical 1.37:1]; Processing: Kinuta Laboratories, Tokyo; Editor: Yoshiki Nagasawa; Musical Score: Nubuo Iida; Production Designer: Keiji Kitagawa; Assistant Director: Teruo Nomura; Sound Recordist: Masao Fujiyoshi; Sound Effects Editor: Yoshitatsu Sonoda; Gaffer: Arao Wakatsuki; Production Company and Distributor: Toho Company; Running Time: 89 minutes.

Cast: Tatsuya Ishiguro (Shûji Hirobe), Yoshiko Kuga (Kumiko Hirobe), Takashi Shimura (Kenzô Ogura), Yuriko Hanabusa (Akiko Tanai), Chôko Iida (Tama Takemura), Sachiko Murase (Masa Hirobe), Minako Himada, Chiyoko Hosokawa, Taeko Kitajima, Yoshiko Shimamura, Yumiko Ôtori (Schoolgirls), Otowa Haruno (Kei Ogura), Ruriko Hitomi (Hashimoto's Sister), Kazumasa Hoshino (Nobuyoshi Noshiro), Fusatarô Ishijima (Male Teacher B), Yaeko Izumo (Female Teacher B), Hiroshi Kondô (Kunio Takemura), Ayako Kunii (Kyôko Machii), Akiko Kusama (Fusako Hirobe), Itoko Kôno (Kazuko Ogura), Tsuruko Mano (Female Teacher A), Mayuri Mokushô [Kumiko Kitsui] (Hanae Takemura), Miyoko Nishiguchi (Ohatsu), Tazuko Shigi (Tomie), Hiroyuki Sugi (Hiroshi Ogura), Fudeko Tanaka (Taki Tai), Ichiro Tetsu (Male Teacher A), Haruko Sugimura, Mitsuami Yoshioka, Hideo Ôtsuka.

Daini no jinsei (February 3, 1948)

Credits: Director: Hideo Sekigawa; Screenplay: Yasutarô Yagi; Cinematographer: Taiichi Kankura; Format/Aspect Ratio: Black-and-White [Spherical 1.37:1]; Processing: Kinuta Laboratories, Tokyo; Musical Score: Akira Ifukube; Production Designer: Teruaki Abe; Sound Recordist: Shôji Kameyama; Lighting Technician: Junro Ishikawa; Production Company and Distributor: Toho Company.

Cast: Sô Yamamura, Takashi Shimura, Kamatari Fujiwara, Michiko Araki.

Yoidore tenshi [Drunken Angel] (April 27, 1948)

Credits: Director: Akira Kurosawa; Producer: Sôjirô Motoki; Screenplay: Akira Kurosawa, Keinosuke Uekusa; Cinematographer: Takeo Itô; Format/Aspect Ratio: Black-and-White [Spherical 1.37:1]; Processing: Toho Film Laboratory; Editor and Negative Cutter: Akikazu Kôno; Musical Score: Fumio Hayasaka; Song ("Jungle Boogie"): Akira Kurosawa (lyrics), Ryoichi Hattori (music); Musicians: Toho Orchestra, Toho Modernnyaz, Ôsuke Itô (guitar); Production Designer: Takashi Matsuyama; Assistant Art Director: Yoshirô Muraki; Chief Assistant Director: Tsuneo Kobayashi; Sound: Wataru Konuma; Sound Effects Editor: Ichirô Minawa; Lighting Technician: Kinzo [Kinji] Yoshizawa; Stills Photographer: Masao Soeda; Script Supervisor: Sumiko Nakao; Production Dates: mid–November 1947 to March 10, 1948; Production Company and Distributor: Toho Company; U.S. Release Date: December 30, 1959 [Brandon Films]; Running Time: 98 minutes [Original Director's Cut: 150 minutes]; U.S. Release Running Time: 102 minutes.
Cast: Takashi Shimura (Sanada), Toshirô Mifune (Matsunaga), Reizaburô Yamamoto (Okada), Michiyo Kogure (Nanae), Chieko Nakakita (Miyo), Noriko Sengoku (Gin), Shizuko Kasagi (Singer), Eitarô Shindô (Takahama), Masao Shimizu (Oyabun), Taiji Tonoyama (Shop Proprietor), Yoshiko Kuga (Schoolgirl), Chôko Iida (Bâya), Ko Ukubuta (Punk), Akira Tani (Yakuza Follower), Sachio Sakai (Guitar Player), Tateo Kawasaki (Flower Shop Proprietor), Mayuri [Kumiko] Mokushô (Daughter at Flower Shop), Toshiko Kawakubo, Haruko Toyama, Yukie Nanbu, Yôko Sugi (Dancers), Sumire Shiroki (Anego), Senkichi Ômura.

Onna no issho (January 25, 1949)

Credits: Director: Fumio Kamei; Producers: Toshirô Ide, Takero Itô; Screenplay: Yôko Mizuki, Toshio Yasumi; Based on the Novel by Kaoru Morimoto; Cinematographer: Yoshio Miyajima; Format/Aspect Ratio: Black-and-White [Spherical 1.37:1]; Processing: Kinuta Laboratory, Tokyo; Musical Score: Nobuo Iida; Production Designer: Teruaki Abe; Sound Recordist: Ariaki Hosaka; Production Companies: Fujimoto Productions, Toho Company; Distributor: Toho Company; Running Time: 101 minutes.
Cast: Tamotsu Kawasaki, Takashi Shimura, Masao Mishima, Eizo Tanaka.

Shizukanaru kettô [The Quiet Duel] (March 13, 1949)

Credits: Director: Akira Kurosawa; Producers: Hisao Ichikawa, Sôjirô Motoki; Screenplay: Akira Kurosawa, Senkichi Taniguchi; Based on a Play by Kazuo Kikuta; Cinematographer: Sôichi Aisaka; Format/Aspect Ratio: Black-and-White [Spherical 1.37:1]; Processing: Daiei Laboratory, Tokyo; Editor: Masanori Tsujii; Musical Score: Akira Ifukube; Art Director: Koichi Imai; Sound: Mitsuo Hasegawa; Lighting Technician: Tsunekichi Shibata; Stills Photographer: Isamu Shima; Production Companies: Daiei Studios, Film Art Association; Distributor: Daiei Motion Picture Company; U.S. Release Date: November 30, 1979 [Brandon Films]; Running Time: 95 minutes.
Cast: Toshirô Mifune (Dr. Kyoji Fujisaki), Takashi Shimura (Dr. Konosuke Fujisaki), Miki Sanjô (Misao Matsumoto), Kenjirô Uemura (Susumu Nakada),

Chieko Nakakita (Takiko Kanada), Noriko Sengoku (Apprentice Nurse Rui Minegishi), Jyonosuke Miyazaki (Corporal Horiguchi), Isamu Yamaguchi (Patrolman Nosaka), Shigeru Matsumoto (Boy with appendicitis), Hiroko Michida (Nurse Imai), Kan Takami (Laborer), Kisao Tobita (Boy with typhoid), Shigeyuki Miyajima (Officer), Tadashi Date (Father of Boy with appendicitis), Etsuko Sudo (Mother of Boy with appendicitis), Seiji Izumi (Policeman), Masateru Sasaki (Old Soldier), Ken'ichi Miyajima (Dealer), Yosuke Kudo (Boy), Yakuko Ikegami (Gaudy Woman), Wakayo Matsumura (Student Nurse), Hatsuko Wakahara (Mii-chan).

Jigoku no kifujin (March 15, 1949)

Credits: Director: Motoyoshi Oda; Producer: Tomoyuki Tanaka; Screenplay: Akira Kurosawa, Motosada Nishiki; Cinematographer: Shunichirô Nakao; Format/Aspect Ratio: Black-and-White [1.37:1]; Musical Score: Ryôichi Hattori; Art Director: Minoru Esaka; Sound: Michio Okazaki; Lighting Technician: Kinzo Yoshizawa; Production Companies: Matsuzaki Productions, Toho Company; Distributor: Toho Company; English Title: *Lady from Hell*; Running Time: 72 minutes.

Cast: Michiyo Kogure (Mrs. Mibu), Eitarô Ozawa (Fujimura), Ichirô Ryûzaki (Nango), Minoru Takada (Doi), Takashi Shimura (Chief of Police), Shin Tokudaiji (Yoshioka), Akitake Kôno (Tachibana).

Mori no Ishimatsu [*Ishimatsu of the Forest*] (June 4, 1949)

Credits: Director: Kôzaburô Yoshimura; Screenplay: Kaneto Shindô; Format/Aspect Ratio: Black-and-White [1.37:1]; Production Company: Shôchiku Eiga; Running Time: 97 minutes.

Cast: Susumu Fugita (Ishimatsu), Yukiko Todoroki (Ofuji), Chôko Iida, Reikichi Kawamura, Chishû Ryû, Takashi Shimura.

Nora inu [*Stray Dog*] (October 17, 1949)

Credits: Director: Akira Kurosawa; Producer: Sôjirô Motoki; Associate Producers: Akira Kurosawa, Senkichi Taniguchi, Kajirô Yamamoto; Screenplay: Akira Kurosawa, Ryûzô Kikushima; Cinematographer: Asakazu Nakai; Assistant Camera: Kazuo Yamada; Format/Aspect Ratio: Black-and-White [Spherical 1.37:1]; Processing: Toho Developing Company; Editors: Toshio Gotô, Yoshi Sugihara; Negative Cutter: Toshio Gotô; Musical Score: Fumio Hayasaka; Production Designer: Takashi Matsuyama; Assistant Art Director: Yoshirô Muraki; Production Manager: Seinosuke Hirai; Chief Assistant Director: Ishirô Honda; Assistant Director: Zenshu Koizumi; Sound: Fumio Yanoguchi; Sound Effects Editor: Ichirô Minawa; Lighting Technician: Chôshirô Ishii; Choreographer: Yoji Ken; Script Supervisor: Hachiko Toi; Double for Mifune: Ishirô Honda; Locations: Ameya Yokocho Market, Ueno, Tokyo; Korakeun Stadium, Tokyo; Production Companies: Film Art Association, Shintoho Film Distribution Committee; Distributor: Toei Company; U.S. Release Date: August 31, 1963; Running Time: 122 minutes.

Cast: Toshirô Mifune (Detective Murakami), Takashi Shimura (Chief Detective Sato), Keiko Awaji (Harumi Namaki, Showgirl), Eiko Miyoshi (Harumi's

Mother), Noriko Sengoku (Ogin, the Pickpocket), Fumiko Homma (Wooden Tub Shop Woman), Eijirô Tôno (Wooden Tub Shop Man), Reikichi Kawamura (Officer Ichikawa), Isao Kimura (Shinjuro Yusa), Yasushi Nagata (Investigation Chief Abe), Minoru Chiaki (Girlie Show Director), Teruko Kishi (Pickpocket), Ichirô [Hajime] Sugai (Yayoi Hotel Owner), Gen Shimizu (Police Inspector Nakajima), Hiroshi Yanagiya (Police Officer), Hajime Izu (Criminal Identification Officer), Masao Shimizu (Nakamura, Husband of a Victim), Kokuten Kôdô (Old Landlord), Yûnosuke Itô (Bluebird Theatre Manager), Akira Ubukata (Police Doctor), Fujio Nagahama (Sakura Hotel Manager), Isao Ikukaka (Sei-san, Bellhop), Shiro Mizutani (Punkster), Eizo Tanaka (Old Doctor), Kazuko Ihonbashi (Sato's Wife), Haruko Tôgô (Azuma Hotel Madame), Haruko Toyama (Kintaro Geisha), Asô Mie [Mitsue Yasuseki] (Pinball Parlor Woman), Rikie Sanjô (Manager's Wife), Chôko Iida (Kogetsu Hotel Manager), Ishirô Honda (Fleeing Villain), Reizaburô Yamamoto (Honda), Haruo Nakajima, Hajime Taniguchi (Men in Bar Flight—scenes deleted), Reikichi Kawamura, Yasushi [Kiyoshi] Nagata, Kappei Matsumoto.

Onna koroshi abura jigoku (October 31, 1949)

Credits: Director: Akira Nobuchi; Format/Aspect Ratio: Black-and-White [1.37:1]; Production Company and Distributor: Daiei Motion Picture Company.
Cast: Kôtarô Bandô, Takashi Shimura, Misako Tokiwa, Sumiko Hidaka, Shinobu Araki, Ryûonosuke Tsukigata, Sadako Sawamura, Daisuke Katô, Kichijirô Ueda.

Ore wa yojinbo (February 19, 1950)

Credits: Director: Hiroshi Inagaki; Producer: Mitsuo Makino; Screenplay: Mansaku Itami; Cinematographer: Takeo Itô; Format/Aspect Ratio: Black-and-White [Spherical 1.37:1]; Editor: Shintarô Miyamoto; Musical Score: Akira Ifukube; Lighting Technician: Tsuruzô Nishikawa; English Title: *I'm the Bodyguard*; Running Time: 89 minutes.
Cast: Chiezô Kataoka, Ryûnosuke Tsukigata, Achako Hanabishi, Daisuke Katô, Kunitarô Sawamura, Reiko Kitami, Takashi Shimura.

Ma no ogon (February 19, 1950)

Credits: Director: Senkichi Taniguchi; Producer: Sojiro Motoki, Tomoyuki Tanaka; Screenplay: Takeo [Kenrô] Matsuura, Senkichi Taniguchi; Cinematographer: Michio Takahashi; Format/Aspect Ratio: Black-and-White [Spherical 1.37:1]; Musical Score: Akira Ifukube; Production Company and Distributor: Daiei Studios; Running Time: 111 minutes.
Cast: Masayuki Mori, Jûkichi Uno, Michiko Hoshi, Ichirô Izawa, Eijirô Tôno, Takashi Shimura.

Pen itsuwarazu boryoku no machi [*Streets of Violence: The Pen Never Lies*] (February 26, 1950)

Credits: Director: Satsuo Yamamoto; Screenplay: Yasutarô Yagi, Yûsaku Yamagata; Cinematographer: Eikichi Uematsu; Format/Aspect Ratio: Black-and-

White [1.37:1]; Musical Score: Ichirô Saitô; Production Company and Distributor: Daiei Motion Picture Company; Running Time: 111 minutes.
Cast: Takashi Shimura (Sagawa), Tôru Abe, Midori Ariyama, Shin Date, Kamatari Fujiwara, Taizô Fukami, Eiji Funakoshi, Yuriko Hanabusa, Tokue Hanazawa, Yasumi Hara, Kiyoko Hirai, Ryô Ikebe, Hajime Izu, Takashi Kanda, Tamotsu Kawasaki, Hatae Kishi, Akitake Kôno, Junji Masuda, Kappei Matsumoto, Bontarô Miake, Masao Mishima, Jun'nosuke Miyazaki, Mitsuyo Nagashima, Yasushi Nagata, Shin'yô Nara, Jun Negami, Isao Numasaki, Eitarô Ozawa, Ichirô Ryûzaki, Hideo Saito, Miki Sanjô, Masao Shimizu, Kenji Susukida, Osamu Takizawa, Eizo Tanaka, Jun Tatara, Taiji Tonoyama, Kenjirô Uemura, Jûkichi Uno, Isamu Yamaguchi, Reizaburô Yamamoto, Shirô Ôsaka.

Shûbun, aka *Skandaru* [*Scandal*] (April 26, 1950)

Credits: Director: Akira Kurosawa; Producer: Takashi Koide; Planning Producer: Sôjirô Motoki; Screenplay: Akira Kurosawa, Ryûzô Kikushima; Cinematography: Toshio Ubukata; Format/Aspect Ratio: Black-and-White [Spherical 1.37:1]; Processing: Kametaro Kamida; Editor: Akira Kurosawa; Negative Cutter: Yoshi Sugihara; Musical Score: Fumio Hayasaka; Art Director: Tatsuo Hamada; Costume Designer: Bunjiro Suzuki; Hair Stylist: Toku Sakuma; Chief Assistant Director: Teruo Hagiyama; Assistant Directors: Keizaburô Kobayashi, Yasu Nakahira, Yoshiko Nihonmatsu, Hotaro Nomura; Sound: Saburô Ômura; Special Effects: Keiji Kawakami; Lighting Technician: Masao Katô; Stills Photographer: Kazuzo Kajimoto; Equipment: Takamasa Kobayashi; Script Supervisor: Hideo Morishita; Display: Fushitaro Moriya; Production Company and Distributor: Shochiku Company; U.S. Release Date: July 17, 1964; Running Time: 105 minutes.
Cast: Toshirô Mifune (Ichirô Aoye), Yoshiko [Shirley] Yamaguchi (Miyako Saijo), Yôko Katsuragi (Masako Hiruta), Noriko Sengoku (Sumie), Sakae [Eitarô] Ozawa (Hori), Takashi Shimura (Attorney Otokichi Hiruta), Shin'ichi Himori (Editor Asai), Ichirô Shimizu (Arai), Fumiko Okamura (Miyako's Mother), Masao Shimizu (Judge), Tanie Kitabayashi (Yasu Hiruta), Sugisaku Aoyama (Dr. Kataoka), Kokuten Kôdô (Old Man A), Kichijirô Ueda (Old Man B), Bokuzen Hidari (Drunk), Taiji Tonoyama (Aoye's Friend), Junji Masuda (News Reporter), Kôji Mitsui (Cameraman A), Yasuko Gotô.

Ikari no machi [*The Angry Street*] (May 14, 1950)

Credits: Director: Mikio Naruse; Producer: Tomoyuki Tanaka; Screenplay: Mikio Naruse, Motosoda Nishiki; Based on the Novel by Fumio Niwa; Cinematographer: Masao Tamai; Format/Aspect Ratio: Black-and-White [1.37:1]; Processing: Kinuta Laboratories, Tokyo; Editor: Yoshiharu Bandô; Musical Score: Nobuo Iida; Production Designer: Minoru Esaka; Executive in Charge of Production: Teruo Maki; Assistant Director: Masayoshi Kawanishi; Sound: Chôshichirô Mikami; Gaffer: Hyakumi Shima; Production Company: Tanaka Productions; Distributor: Toho Company; Running Time: 105 minutes.
Cast: Jûkichi Uno (Munehisa Mori), Yasumi Hara (Shigetaka Sudô), Yuriko Hamada (Chizuru Tagami), Setsuko Wakayama (Masako Sudô), Yoshiko Kuga (Tsuneko

Fukuda), Mayuri [Kumiko] Mokushô (Kimiko Miyabe), Takashi Shimura (Kimiko's Father), Ichirô Sugai (Tokunaga), Kan Yanagiya (Ken Doigaki), Mitsue Tachibana (Midori), Mie Asô (Sarii), Chieko Higashiyama (Sudô's Grandmother), Sachiko Murase (Sudô's Mother), Keiko Kishi (Kumiko's Mother), Isao Kimura (Jôji), Fujio Nagahama, Isao Ubukata, Hiroshi Kondô, Kiyoshi Kamoda, Ko Ishida, Sachio Sakai, Tadashi Okabe, Hiroshi Imaizume, Ichirô Tetsu.

Rashômon (August 26, 1950)

Credits: Director: Akira Kurosawa; Executive Producer: Masaichi Nagata; Associate Producer: Minoru Jingo; Screenplay: Akira Kurosawa, Shinobu Hashimoto; Based on the Stories "*Rashômon*" and "*Yabu no naka*" ["In a Grove"] by Ryûnosuke Akutagawa; Cinematographer: Kazuo Miyagawa; Assistant Cameramen: Kanichi Aoki, Kenichi Araki, Fujio Morita; Format/Aspect Ratio: Black-and-White [Spherical 1.37:1]; Processing: Daiei Laboratory, Tokyo; Editor: Akira Kurosawa; Musical Score: Fumio Hayasaka; Production Designer: Takashi [Shu] Matsuyama; Set Decorator: H. Motsumoto; Chief Assistant Director: Tai Katô; Assistant Directors: Tokuzô Tanaka, Mitsuo Wakasugi; Sound: Iwao Ôtani; Sound Assistant: Tsuchitarô Hayashi; Lighting Technician: Kenichi Okamoto; Lighting Assistant: Genken Nakaoka; Dolly Grip: Hiroshi Shibata; Script Supervisor: Teruyo Nogami; Press Agent: Francois Vila; Locations: Komyoji Temple, Kyoto; Nara; Production Company and Distributors: Daiei Motion Picture Company; U.S. Release Date: December 26, 1951 (RKO Radio Pictures); Running Time: 88 minutes.
Cast: Toshirô Mifune (Tajômaru, the Bandit), Machiko Kyô (Masako Kanazawa, the Samurai's Wife), Masayuki Mori (Takehiro Kanazawa, the Samurai), Takashi Shimura (The Woodcutter). Minoru Chiaki (The Priest), Kichijirô Ueda (The Commoner), Noriko Honma (The Medium), Daisuke Katô (The Policeman), Anthony La Penna (Priest [voice]).

Yoru no hibotan (December 8, 1950)

Credits: Director: Yasuki Chiba; Producer and Screenplay: Naoyuki Hatta; Cinematographer: Hiroshi Suzuki; Format/Aspect Ratio: Black-and-White [1.37:1]; Musical Score: Fumio Hayasaka; Art Director: Tomoo Shimogawara; Assistant Director: Umetsugu (Umeji) Inoue; Running Time: 105 minutes.
Cast: Hajime Izu (Ryûsuke Oguma), Hyô Kitazawa (Dr. Tanigawa), Chigira Miyuki (Hatsumi), Ichirô Ryûzaki ("Tetsu" Mimura), Yukiko Shimazaki (Taiko), Jun Tazaki (Yoshioka), Yumeji Tsukioka (Miki Natsukawa), Kyota Fuyuki, Yûnosuke Itô, Yôtarô Katsumi, Sôzaburô Kikuchi, Yôyô Kojima, Kokuten Kôdô, Ranko Sawa, Takashi Shimura, Harue Wakahara, Reizaburô Yamamoto, Kô Yamamura.

Tenya wanya (1950)

Credits: Director: Minoru Shibuya; Format/Aspect Ratio: Black-and-White [1.37:1]; Musical Score: Akira Ifukube; English Title: *Crazy Uproar*; Running Time: 96 minutes.
Cast: Chikage Awashima, Kamatari Fujiwara, Takashi Shimura, Kôji Tsuruta.

Ginza Sanshiro (1950)

Credits: Director: Kon Ichikawa; Producer: Nobuo Aoyagi; Screenplay: Naoyuki Hatta, Noriyuki Yata; Story: Tsuneo Tomita; Cinematographer: Jun Yasumoto; Format/Aspect Ratio: Black-and-White [Spherical 1.37:1]; Editor: Shin Yoshida; Musical Score: Nobuo Iida; Production Designer: Kazuo Ogawa; Chief Assistant Director: Goro Kadono; Sound Recordist: Kihachiro Nakai; Production Companies: Aoyagi Productions, Shintoho Film Distribution Committee; Distributor: Toho Company; English Title: *A Ginza Veteran*; Running Time: 82 minutes.

Cast: Chôko Iida, Gen Shimizu, Yôtarô Katsumi, Yûnosuke Itô, Atsuko Ichinomiya, Susumu Fugita, Reikichi Kawamura, Takashi Shimura.

Datsugoku [Escape from Prison] (1950)

Credits: Director: Kajirô Yamamoto; Format/Aspect Ratio: Black-and-White [1.37:1]; Production Company: Film Art Association; Distributor: Daiei Motion Picture Company.

Cast: Mieko Takamine, Takashi Shimura, Eitarô Ozawa, Toshirô Mifune.

Ai to nikushimi no Kanata e [Beyond Love and Hate] (January 11, 1951)

Credits: Director: Senkichi Taniguchi; Screenplay: Akira Kurosawa, Senkichi Taniguchi; Based on the Story "Fugitive" by Kotaro Samukawa; Cinematographer: Masao Tamai; Format/Aspect Ratio: Black-and-White [1.37:1]; Musical Score: Akira Ifukube; Production Designer: Tatsuo Kita; Sound: Masao Fujiyoshi; Lighting Technician: Kuichirô [Kyuichiro] Kishida; Production Company: Film Art Association; Distributor: Toho Company; Running Time: 107 minutes.

Cast: Ryô Ikebe, Mitsuko Mito, Toshirô Mifune, Takashi Shimura, Eitarô [Sakae] Ozawa, Kichijirô Ueda.

Aika [Elegy] (February 22, 1951)

Credits: Director: Kajirô Yamamoto; Producers: Kazuhei Hoshino, Sôjirô Motoki; Screenplay: Hideo Oguni, Kajirô Yamamoto; Based on the Story "Saint Woman" by Hideo Oguni; Cinematographer: Asakazu Nakai; Format/Aspect Ratio: Black-and-White [Spherical 1.37:1]; Musical Score: Urato Watanabe; Production Designer: Takashi Matsuyama; Sound: Masanobu Miyazaki; Lighting Technician: Kuichirô [Kyuichiro] Kishida; Associate Director: Ishirô Honda; Production Manager: Hiroshi Nezu; Production Companies: Film Art Association, Toho Company; Distributor: Toho Company; Running Time: 110 minutes.

Cast: Kyoko Yoshizawa (Shizuko Toki), Ken Uehara, Mieko Takamine, Toshirô Mifune, Takashi Shimura, Haruna Kaburagi, Yoshio Kosugi, Sugisaku Aoyama, Sachio Sakai, Tokuji Kobayashi, Isao Kimura, Sadako Sawamura, Bokuzen Hidari, Eiko Miyoshi, Masaru Kamiyama.

Hakuchi [The Idiot] (May 23, 1951)

Credits: Director: Akira Kurosawa; Producer: Takashi Koide; Screenplay: Akira Kurosawa, Eijirô Hisaita; Based on the Novel by Fyodor Dostoevsky; Cine-

matographer: Toshio Ubukata; Format/Aspect Ratio: Black-and-White [Spherical 1.37:1]; Editor: Akira Kurosawa; Assistant Editor: Yoshi Sugihara; Musical Score: Fumio Hayasaka; Production Designer: Takashi [Shu] Matsuyama; Set Decorator: Ushitarô Shimada; Camera Operator: Asakazu Nakai; Chief Assistant Director: Yoshitarô Shimada; Settings: Genzô Komiya, Shohei Sekine; Sound: Yoshisaburo Imo; Lighting Technician: Akio Tamura; Locations: Hokkaido; U.S. Release Date: April 30, 1963; Running Time: 166 minutes [Original Director's Cut: 265 minutes].
Cast: Setsuko Hara (Taeko Nasu), Masayuki Mori (Kinji Kameda), Toshirô Mifune (Denkichi Akama), Yoshiko Kuga (Ayako), Takashi Shimura (Ono, Ayako's Father), Chieko Higashiyama (Satoko, Ayako's Mother), Eijirô Yanagi (Tohata), Minoru Chiaki (Mutsuo Kayama, the Secretary), Noriko Sengoku (Takako), Kokuten Kôdô (Jumpei), Bokuzen Hidari (Karube), Eiko Miyoshi (Madame Kayama), Chiyoko Fumiya (Noriko), Mitsuyo Akashi (Madame Akama), Daisuke Inoue (Kaoru), Jun Yokoyama, Atsumi Nakama, Kunio Miyogi, Shôichi Kofujita [Kotôda], Yôichi Ohsugi [Osugi], Keiko Izumi, Haruko Chichibu.

Kedamono no yado (June 8, 1951)

Credits: Director: Tatsuo [Tatsuyasu] Osone; Producer: Kôichirô Ogura; Screenplay: Akira Kurosawa, Shinya Fujiwara; Based on the Story *"Mizumi Nobara"* ["The Rose on the Lake"] by Shinya Fujiwara; Cinematographer: Kiyoshi Kataoka; Format/Aspect Ratio: Black-and-White [Spherical 1.37:1]; Musical Score: Mitsuo Katô; Art Director: Haruhide Kuwano; Production Company: Shochiku-Kyoto Co., Ltd.; Distributors: Shochiku Company; English Title: *The Den of Beasts*; Running Time: 85 minutes.
Cast: Takashi Shimura, Keiko Kishi, Kôji Tsuruta, Ichirô Arishima.

Aoi shinju (August 3, 1951)

Credits: Director and Screenplay: Ishirô Honda; Producer: Sôjirô Motoki; Cinematographer: Tadashi Iimura; Format/Aspect Ratio: Black-and-White [1.37:1]; Musical Score: Tadashi Hattori; Production Designer: Takashi Matsuyama; Chief Assistant Director: Kihachi Okamoto; Sound Recordist: Chôshichirô Mikami; Lighting Technician: Kuichirô Kishida; Script Girl: Kimi Honda; Production Company and Distributor: Toho Company; English Title: *The Blue Pearl*.
Cast: Yuriko Hamada, Reizaburô Yamamoto, Ryô Ikebe, Kokuten Kôdô, Yukiko Shimazaki, Takashi Shimura.

Mesu inu (August 10, 1951)

Credits: Director: Keigo Kimura; Screenplay: Keigo Kimura, Masahige Narusawa; Cinematographer: Yasuichirô Yamazaki; Format/Aspect Ratio: Black-and-White [1.37:1]; Art Director: Atsuji Shibata; Production Company and Distributor: Daiei Studios; English Title: *Bitch*; Running Time: 100 minutes.
Cast: Machiko Kyô (Emmy), Takashi Shimura (Horie), Yoshiko Kuga (Yukiko), Tanie Kitabayashi (Tami), Daisuke Katô (Matoba), Kamatari Fujiwara (Matsuda), Jun Negami (Keiichi Shirakawa), Shin Karino (Kitamura), Bontarô Miake (Nogami), Harue Tone (Asami).

Hopu-san: sararîman no maki (October 19, 1951)

Credits: Director: Kajirô Yamamoto; Producer: Sanezumi Fujimoto; Screenplay: Toshirô Ide, Kajirô Yamamoto; Cinematographer: Asakazu Nakai; Format/ Aspect Ratio: Black-and-White [Spherical 1.37:1]; Processing: Kinuta Laboratories, Tokyo; Musical Score: Toriro Miki; Production Designer: Keiji Kitagawa; Chief Assistant Director: Hisanobu Marubayashi; Sound Recordist: Hisashi Shimonaga; Lighting Technician: Shigeru Mori; Production Company and Distributor: Toho Company.
Cast: Keiju Kobayashi. Eiko Miyoshi, Eijirô Tôno, Hizuru Takachiho, Takashi Shimura, Sadako Sawamura, Tatsuya Iahiguro, Daisuke Inoue, Toranosuke Ogawa.

Bakurô ichidai [The Life of a Horse-Trader] (December 7, 1951)

Credits: Director: Keigo Kimura; Screenplay: Keigo Kimura, Masashige Narusawa; Based on the Novel by Masao Nakayama; Cinematographer: Shigeyoshi Mine; Format/Aspect Ratio: Black-and-White [Spherical 1.37:1]; Musical Score: Fumio Hayasaka; Art Director: Atsuji Shibata; Production Company and Distributor: Daiei Motion Picture Company; Running Time: 113 minutes.
Cast: Toshirô Mifune (Yonetaro Katayama), Machiko Kyô (Yuki), Takashi Shimura (Rokutaro Kosaka), Ichirô Sugai (Ogasawara), Bokuzen Hidari (Gosaku), Yoshio Kosugi (Jinzo), Haruyo Ichikawa (Haruno), Hikaru Hoshi (Teiji Shimazaki), Kyôji Sugi (Magohachi), Mantarô Ushio (Senzo), Kumeko Urabe (Onobu).

Nusumareta koi (1951)

Credits: Director: Kon Ichikawa; Screenplay: Kon Ichikawa, Natto Wada; Story: Kyôtarô Namiki [Jirô Kagami]; Cinematographer: Minoru Yokoyama; Format/Aspect Ratio: Black-and-White [Spherical 1.37:1]; Musical Score: Akira Ifukube; Production Companies: Aoyagi Productions, Shintoho Film Distribution Committee; English Title: *Stolen Love*; Running Time: 102 minutes.
Cast: Michiko Kato, Asami Kuji, Masayuki Mori, Takashi Shimura.

Araki Mataemon: Kettô kagiya no tsuji [Vendetta of Samurai] (January 3, 1952)

Credits: Director: Kazuo Mori; Producer: Sôjirô Motoki; Screenplay: Akira Kurosawa; Cinematographer: Kazuo Yamazaki; Format/Aspect Ratio: Black-and-White [Spherical 1.37:1]; Musical Score: Gorô Nishi; Production Designer: Takashi Matsuyama; Sound: Masanobu Miyazaki; Lighting Technician: Kuichirô Kishida; Production Companies: Daiei Studios, Toho Company; Distributor: Toho Company; Running Time: 82 minutes.
Cast: Toshirô Mifune (Mataemon Araki), Takashi Shimura (Jinzaemon Kawai), Daisuke Katô (Rokusuke), Bokuzen Hidari (Old Man), Yuriko Hamada, Akihiko Katayama, Minoru Chiaki, Shin Tokudaiji, Toranosuke Ogawa.

Nangoku no hada [The Skin of the South] (February 8, 1952)

Credits: Director and Screenplay: Ishirô Honda; Producer: Saburo Nosaka, Kimitake Ohashi; Cinematographer: So Kawamura; Format/Aspect Ratio: Black-

and-White [Spherical 1.37:1]; Processing: Kinuta Laboratories, Tokyo; Musical Score: Yasushi Akutagawa; Production Designer: Akira Watanabe; Sound Recordist: Yoshio Nishikawa; Special Effects Supervisor: Eiji Tsuburaya; Script Girl: Kimi Honda; Production Company and Distributor: Toho Company.
Cast: Hajime Izu, Yôko Fujita, Takashi Shimura, Kamatari Fujiwara, Yoshio Kosugi.

Muteki [*Foghorn*] (March 3, 1952)

Credits: Director: Senkichi Taniguchi; Producer: Tomoyuki Tanaka; Screenplay: Senkichi Taniguchi, Toshio Yasumi; Based on the Novel by Jirô Osaragi; Cinematographer: Masao Tamai; Format/Aspect Ratio: Black-and-White [1.37:1]; Musical Score: Ichirô Saitô, Nobuo Iida; Production Designer: Takashi [Shu] Matsuyama; Sound: Ariaki Hosaka; Lighting Technician: Tsuruzô Nishikawa; Production Company and Distributor: Toho Company; Running Time: 99 minutes.
Cast: Yoshiko [Shirley] Yamaguchi (Chiyo [Hana]), Toshirô Mifune (Chiyokichi), Robert H. (Bob) Booth, Takashi Shimura, Fuyuki Murakami, Noriko Sengoku, Sôjin Kamiyama.

Saikaku ichidai onna [*The Life of Oharu*] (April 17, 1952)

Note: Although this film is usually included in Takashi Shimura's filmography, he does not conspicuously appear in the finished film, directed by Kenji Mizoguchi.

Sengoku burai [*Sword for Hire*] (May 22, 1952)

Credits: Director: Hiroshi Inagaki; Producer: Tomoyuki Tanaka; Screenplay: Hiroshi Inagaki, Akira Kurosawa; Based on the Novel by Yasushi Inoue; Cinematographer: Tadashi Iimura; Format/Aspect Ratio: Black-and-White [Spherical 1.37:1]; Musical Score: Ikuma Dan; Production Designer: Takeo Kita; Assistant Director: Katsuya Shimizu; Sound: Shôji Kameyama; Lighting Technician: Tsuruzô Nishikawa; Stills Photographer: Matsuo Yoshizaki; Production Company and Distributor: Toho Company; U.S. Release Distributors: Topaz Film Company (November 15, 1956), Joseph Brenner Associates (September 4, 1957); Running Time: 135 minutes.
Cast: Toshirô Mifune (Hayatenosuke Sasa), Rentarô Mikuni (Jurata Tachibana), Danshiro Ichikawa (Yakeiji Kagami), Yoshiko [Shirley] Yamaguchi (Oryo), Shinobu Asaji (Kano), Bob Booth (Narrator), Takashi Shimura, Yoshio Kosugi, Sugisaku Aoyama, Eijirô Higashino [Tôno], Ryôsuke Kagawa, Kokuten Kôdô, Kichijirô Ueda, Eiko Miyoshi, Haruo Nakajima.

Bijo to touzoku (September 23, 1952)

Credits: Director and Screenplay: Keigo Kimura; Based on the Novel by Ryûnosuke Akutagawa; Format/Aspect Ratio: Black-and-White [Spherical 1.37:1]; Production Company: Daiei Studios; Distributor: Daiei Motion Picture Company; English Title: *Beauty and the Thieves*; Running Time: 80 minutes.
Cast: Machiko Kyô (Sakin), Masayuki Mori (Kuroki no Taro), Rentarô Mikuni

(Kuroki no Jiro), Minoru Ciaki (Takeichi no Takamaru), Yûnosuke Itô (Dohachi), Tanie Kitabayashi (Mrs. Inokumi), Yûko Mochizuki (Kotora), Takashi Shimura (Yoshimichi), Ichirô Sugai (Mr. Inokuma), Eijirô Tôno (Jurota), Bokuzen Hidari.

Ikiru (October 9, 1952)

Credits: Director: Akira Kurosawa; Producer: Sôjirô Motoki; Screenplay: Akira Kurosawa, Shinobu Hashimoto; Hideo Oguni; Cinematographer: Asakazu Nakai; Assistant Camera: Takao Saitô; Format/Aspect Ratio: Black-and-White [Spherical 1.37:1]; Editor: Kôichi Iwashita; Musical Score: Fumio Hayasaka; Production Designer: Takashi [Shu] Matsuyama; Assistant Art Director: Yoshirô Muraki; Hair Stylist: Sadako Okada; Unit Production Manager: Teruo Maki; Chief Assistant Director: Hisanobu Marubayashi; Assistant Director: Teruo Maru; Sound Recordist: Fumio Yanoguchi; Sound Effects Editor: Ichirô Minawa; Lighting Technician: Shigeru Mori; Stills Photographer: Masao Soeda; Accountant: Akira Araki; Advisor to the Director: Hiromichi Horikawa; Script Supervisor: Teruyo Nogami; Production Company and Distributor: Toho Company; U.S. Release Date: March 25, 1956 [Brandon Films]; Running Time: 143 minutes.

Cast: Takashi Shimura (Kanji Watanabe, Chief of Citizen's Section), Shin'ichi Himori (Kimura, Assistant, Citizen's Section), Haruo Tanaka (Sakai, Assistant, Citizen's Section), Minoru Chiaki (Noguchi, Assistant, Citizen's Section), Miki Odagiri (Toyo Odagiri, Employee), Bokuzen Hidari (Ohara, Assistant, Citizen's Section), Minosuke Yamada (Subordinate Clerk Saito), Kamatari Fujiwara (Sub-Section Chief Ono), Makoto Kobori (Kiichi Watanabe, Kanji's Older Brother), Nobuo Kaneko (Mitsuo Watanabe, Kanji's Son), Nobuo Nakamura (Deputy Mayor), Atsushi Watanabe (Patient), Isao Kimura (Intern), Masao Shimizu (Doctor), Yûnosuke Itô (Novelist), Kumeko Urabe (Tatsu Watanabe, Kiichi's Wife), Eiko Miyoshi, Noriko Honma, Kin Sugai (Petitioning Housewives), Yatsuko Tan'ami (Madame of Bar), Yoshie Minami (The Maid), Kyôko Seki (Kazue Watanabe, Mitsuo's Wife), Kusuo Abe (City Assemblyman), Tomo Nagai, Fuyuki Murakami, Hirayoshi Aono (Newspapermen), Seiji Miyaguchi (Yakuza Boss), Daisuke Katô, Hiroshi Hayashi, Sachio Sakai (Yakuza), Toranosuke Ogawa (Park Section Chief), Akira Sera (Worker in General Affairs), Ichirô Chiba (Policeman), Akira Tani (Bar Owner), Yôkô Kajima (Worker in Sewage Section), Haruko Toyama (Woman at Dance Hall), Toshiyuki Ichimura (Pianist), Harue Kuramoto (Dancer), Lasa Saya (stripper), Junpei Natsuki (Hand-Washing Cancer Patient), Taizô Fukami, Katao Kawasaki, Keiichirô Katsumoto, Fujio Nagahama, Mie Asô.

Oka wa hanazakari (November 18, 1952)

Credits: Director: Yasuki Chiba; Producer: Sanezumi Fujimoto; Screenplay: Toshirô Ide, Yôko Mizuki; Based on the Novel by Yojirô Ishizaka; Cinematographer: Asakazu Nakai; Format/Aspect Ratio: Black-and-White [1.37:1]; Musical Score: Ryôichi Hattori; Art Director: Takashi Matsuyama; Production Company and Distributors: Toho Company.
Cast: Michiyo Kogure (Nobuko Takabatake), Sanae Takasugi (Asako Shirakawa),

Ryô Ikebe (Masaya Nozaki), Yôko Sugi (Miwako Kozuki), Sô Yamamura (Ryôzô Noro), Chieko Nakakita (Hisao Iwamoto), Ken Uehara (Haruo Ishiyama), Maso Shimizu (Yuzo Takabatake), Hisako Takihana (Kayo), Takashi Shimura (Kenkichi Kimura), Ken Mitsuda (Yamada), Sadako Sawamura (Ayako Kanzaki), Kumeko Urabe (Okuni).

Minato e kita otoko [*The Man Who Came to Port*] (November 27, 1952)
Credits: Director: Ishirô Honda; Producer: Tomoyuki Tanaka; Planning Producer: Yasuaki Sakamoto; Screenplay: Ishirô Honda, Masahige Narusawa; Based on the Story "Dance of the Stormy Waves" by Shinzo Kajino; Cinematographer: Taiichi Kankura; Format/Aspect Ratio: Black-and-White [1.37:1]; Musical Score: Ichirô Saitô; Production Designer: Tatsuo Kita; Chief Assistant Director: Jun Fukuda; Sound: Masao Fujiyoshi; Special Effects Supervisor: Eiji Tsuburaya; Lighting Technician: Shigeru Mori; Stills Photographer: Masao Fukuda; Script Girl: Kimi Honda; Production Company and Distributor: Toho Company; Running Time: 88 minutes.
Cast: Toshirô Mifune (Goro Niinuma), Takashi Shimura (Okabe), Hiroshi Koizumi (Shingo Nishizawa), Asami Kuji (Sonoko), Bokuzen Hidari (Kan-jii), Yuriko Tashiro (Akemi), Yaeko Izumo (O-Hide), Kamatari Fujiwara (Takasaki-Shochou), Seijirô Onda (Miake), Ren Imaizumi (Yamashita), Senkichi Ômura (Harada), Ren Yamamoto, Shôichi Hirose, Massaki Tachibana, Kenô Echigo, Sachio Sakai, Teruhiko Suzuki, Yasuhisa Tsutsumi, Shigeo Katô, Akira Yamada, Etsuo Saijô, Akira Sera, Junpei Natsuki, Akira Kitchôji, Yoko Ueno, Tsuruko Umano, Yutaka Oka, Akira Tani.

Fuun senryobune (December 16, 1952)
Credits: Director and Screenplay: Hiroshi Inagaki; Story: Shintarô Mimura; Cinematographer: Jun Yasumoto; Format/Aspect Ratio: Black-and-White [Spherical 1.37:1]; Processing: Kinuta Laboratories, Tokyo; Production Designer: Takeo Kita; Sound Recordist: Masanobu Miyazaki; Lighting Technician: Tsuruzô Nishikawa; Production Company and Distributor: Toho Company; Running Time: 93 minutes.
Cast: Kazuo Hasegawa, Tomoemon Otani, Danshirô Ichikawa, Hiroshi Nihon'yanagi, Daisuke Katô, Yoshiko [Shirley] Yamaguchi, Eijirô Tôno, Takashi Shimura.

Hoyo [*The Last Embrace*] (March 11, 1953)
Credits: Director: Masahiro Makino; Producer: Tomoyuki Tanaka; Screenplay: Motosoda Nishiki, Haruo Umeda, Toshio Yasumi (idea); Cinematographer: Tadashi Iimura; Format/Aspect Ratio: Black-and-White [1.37:1]; Musical Score: Yasushi Akutagawa; Production Designer: Kazuo Ogawa; Sound: Ariaki [Yumei] Hosaka; Lighting Technician: Tsuruzô Nishikawa; Production Company and Distributor: Toho Company; Running Time: 87 minutes.
Cast: Yoshiko [Shirley] Yamaguchi (Yukiko Nogami), Toshirô Mifune (Shinkichi/Hayakawa), Takashi Shimura (Watanabe, alias Nabesan), Akihiko Hirata

(Yamaoka, alias Sandaime), Hiroshi Koizumi (Yoshikawa, alias Sampei), Sachio Sakai (Uchimura, alias Saboten), Ren Yamamoto (Numaguchi, alias Kurochan), Seiji Miyaguchi, Katsumi Tezuka (Gangsters), Toyoko Takegawa (Madame Natsuko), Yô Shiomi (Mitsutaro).

Yoru no awari (April 8, 1953)

Credits: Director: Senkichi Taniguchi; Producer: Sojirô Motoki; Screenplay: Ryûzô Kikushima; Cinematographer: Kazuo Yamada; Format/Aspect Ratio: Black-and-White [Spherical 1.37:1]; Processing: Kinuta Laboratories, Tokyo; Musical Score: Yasushi Akutagawa; Production Designer: Takashi Matsuyama; Sound Recordist: Yoshio Nishikawa; Production Company and Distributor: Toho Company.

Cast: Ryô Ikebe (Shinji Kizaki), Mariko Okada (Miyo), Takashi Shimura (Yoshikawa), Aiko Mimasu (Sayoko), Sadako Sawamura (Tsuneko), Sachiko Murase (Madame), Kamatari Fujiwara (Police), Fujio Nagahama (Yamamoto, Tsuneko's Husband), Masao Shimizu Matsuno).

Taiheiyô no washi [*Eagle of the Pacific*] (October 21, 1953)

Credits: Director: Ishirô Honda; Executive Producer: Iwao Mori; Producer: Sôjirô Motoki; Screenplay: Shinobu Hashimoto; Cinematographer: Kazuo Yamada; Format/Aspect Ratio: Black-and-White [Spherical 1.37:1]; Processing: Kinuta Laboratories, Tokyo; Musical Score: Yûji Koseki; Editor: Kôichi Iwashita; Production Designers: Iwao Akune, Takeo Kita; Production Supervisor: Tatsuo Kuroda; Chief Assistant Director: Mikio Komatsu; Second Unit Director: Motoyoshi Oda; Sound Recordist: Masanobu Miyazaki; Special Effects Staff Supervisor: Motoyoshi Oda; Director of Special Effects: Eiji Tsuburaya; Special Effects Art Director: Akira Watanabe; Chief Cameraman of Special Effects: Sadamasa Arikawa; Special Effects Opticals: Hiroshi Mukoyama; Fire Stunts: Haruo Nakajima; Lighting Technician: Masaki [Masayoshi] Ônuma; Script Girl: Kimi Honda; Production Company and Distributor: Toho Company; Alternate English Title: *Operation Kamikaze*; Running Time: 119 minutes.

Cast: Denjirô Ôkôchi (Grand Admiral Isoroku Yamamoto), Hiroshi Nihon'yanagi (Commander Furukawa), Masao Shimizu (Commander Kashima), Eijirô Yanagi (Premier Admiral Mitsumasa Yonai), Minoru Takada (Prince Fumimaro Konoe), Ichirô Sugai (Admiral Koshirô Oikawa), Takshi Shimura (Colonel A, Staff Officer of the Army), Takamaru Sasaki (Chief of Staff, Combined Fleet), Bontarô Miake (Commander of the Task Force), Rentarô Mikuni, Keiju Kobayashi, Hajime Izu (Staff Officers), Toshirô Mifune (First Lieutenant Tomonaga), Haruo Nakajima (Pilot in Flaming Zero), Shin Ôtomo, Toranosuke Ogawa, Minosuke Yamada, Fuyuki Murakami, Katsumi Tezuka, Heihachirô Ôkawa, Yoshio Kosugi, Koreya Senda, Sachio Sakai, Yasuhisa Tsutsumi, Tadashi Okabe, Yutaka Oka, Akira Sera, Shizuo Ikeda, Takuzô (Jirô) Kumagai, Seijirô Onda, Kazuo Suzuki.

Shichinin no Samurai [*Seven Samurai*] (1954)

Credits: Director: Akira Kurosawa; Producer: Sôjirô Motoki; Screenplay: Akira Kurosawa, Shinobu Hashimoto, Hideo Oguni; Cinematographer: Asakazu Nakai; Assistant Camera: Takao Saitô; Format/Aspect Ratio: Black-and-White

[Spherical 1.37:1]; Processing: Toho Laboratories; Editor: Akira Kurosawa; Editing Manager: Hiroshi Nezu; Negative Cutter: Koichi Iwashita; Musical Score: Fumio Hayasaka; Assistant to Composer: Masaru Satô; Production Designer: Takashi [Shu] Matsuyama; Art Director: Sô Matsuyama; Assistant Art Director: Yoshirô Muraki; Costume Designers: Mieko Yamaguchi [Kyoto Costume]; Makeup Artist: Junjirô Yamada; Hair Stylist: Midori Kakajô; Production Supervisor: Hiroshi Nezu; Assistant Directors: Sakae Hirosawa, Hiromichi Horikawa, Toshi Kaneko, Masaya Shimizu, Yasuyoshi Tajitsu; Art Consultants: Seison Maeda, Kôhei Ezaki; Property Master: Kôichi Hamamura; Sound Recordist: Fumio Yanoguchi; Sound Assistant: Masanaro Uehara; Sound Effects Editor: Ichirô Minawa; Stunts: Haruo Nakajima; Lighting Technician: Shigeru Mori; Assistant Lighting Technician: Mitsuo Kaneko; Stills Photographer: Masao Fukuda; Archery Advisors: Shigeru Endo, Ienori Kaneko; Fencing Advisor: Yoshio Sugino; Folklore Researcher: Kôhei Ezaki; Accountant: Yuji Hamada; Script Supervisor: Teruyo Nogami; Production Assistant: Takeharu Shimada; Acting Office: Toshio Nakane; Locations: Izu Peninsula, Shizuoka; Production Company and Distributor: Toho Company; Alternate U.S. Title: *The Magnificent Seven*; U.S. Release Date: November 19, 1956; Running Time: 207 minutes.
Cast: *The Seven Samurai*: Toshirô Mifune (Kikuchiyo, the Would-be Samurai), Takashi Shimura (Kambei Shimada, Leader of the Seven Samurai), Yoshio Inaba (Gorobei Katayama, the Wise Warrior), Seiji Miyaguchi (Kyuzo, the Master Swordsman), Minoru Chiaki (Heihachi, the Cheerful Samurai), Daisuke Katô (Shichiroji, Kambei's Old Friend), Isao [Ko] Kimura (Katsushiro Okamoto, Kambei's Young Disciple); *The Peasants*: Keiko Tsushima (Shino), Yukiko [Yukio] Shimazaki (Rikichi's Wife), Kamatari Fujiwara (Farmer Manzo, Shino's Father), Yoshio Kosugi (Farmer Mosuke), Bokuzen Hidari (Farmer Yohei), Yoshio Tsuchiya (Farmer Rikichi), Kokuten Kôdô [Kuninori Todo] (Old Man Gisaku), Eijirô Tôno (Thief), Kichijirô Ueda (Captured Bandit Scout), Jun Tatara (First Coolie), Atsushi Watanabe (Bun Vendor), Toranosuke Ogawa (Grandfather of Gono Family); Isao Yamagata, Masanobu Ôkubo, Minoru Itô, Haruya Sakamoto, Gorô Sakurai, Kiyoshi Kamoda, Masahide Matsushita, Kaneo Ikeda (Samurai), Sôjin Kamiyama (Blind Minstrel), Gen Shimizu (Samurai Who Kicks Farmers), Keiji Sakakida (Gosaku), Shinpei Takagi (Bandit Chieftain), Shin Ôtomo (Bandit Second-in-Command), Shuno Takahara (Samurai with Gun), Hiroshi Sugi (Tea Shop Owner), Hiroshi Hayashi (Weak Ronin), Sachio Sakai (Second Coolie), Sôkichi Maki (Strong-Looking Samurai), Ichirô Chiba (Buddhist Priest), Noriko Sengoku (Wife of Gono Family), Fumiko Homma, Matsue Ono, Tsurue [Tazue] Ichimanji, Masako Ôshiro, Kyôko Ozawa, Misao Suyama, Toriko Takahara (Women Farmers), Etsuo Saijô, Hideo Shibuya, Shôichi Hirose, Kôji Uno, Masaaki Tachibana, Kamayuki Tsubono, Taiji Naka, Chindanji Miyagawa, Shigemi Sunagawa, Akira Tani, Akio Kusama, Ryûtarô Amami, Jun Mikami, Haruo Nakajima (Bandits), Senkichi Ômura, Takashi Narita (Bandits Who Escape), Sanpei Mine, Ippei Kawagoe, Jirô Suzukawa, Junpei Natsuki, Kyôichi Kamiyama, Haruo Suzuki, Gorô Amano, Akira Kitchôji, Kôji Iwamoto, Akira Yamada, Kazuo Imai, Eisuke Nakanishi, Toku Ihara, Hideo Ôtsuka, Tokio Ôkawa [Shû Ôe], Yasumasa [Yasuo] Ônishi, Megeru Shimoda, Masayoshi Kawabe, Shigeo Katô, Yoshikazu Kawamata, Ren Yamamoto (Farmers), Takuzo

Kumagai [Jirô Kumagaya] (Gisaku's Son), Hiroshi Akitsu (Gono Husband), Yasuhisa Tsutsumi, Tsuneo Katagiri (Farmers in Front of Gono), Takeshi Seki (Third Coolie), Haruko Toyama (Gisaku's Daughter-in-Law), Tsuroko Mano (Woman Farmer in Front of Gono), Michiko Kadono, Toshiko Nakano, Shizuko Azuma, Keiko Mori, Michiko Kawabe, Yûko Togawa, Yayoko Kitano (Farmers' Wives), Takeshi Katô, Tatsuya Nakadai, Ken Utsui (Samurai Wandering Through Town).

Jirochô sangokushi: kaitô-ichi no abarenbô (June 8, 1954)

Credits: Director: Masahiro Makino; Producer: Sôjirô Motoki; Screenplay: Genzo Murakami, Nobuaki Okawa, Toshiya Okihara; Cinematographer: Tadashi Iimura; Format/Aspect Ratio: Black-and-White [1.37:1]; Musical Score: Seiichi Suzuki; Art Director: Takeo Kita; Sound: Yoshio Nishikawa; Lighting: Tsuruzô Nishikawa; Production Company and Distributor: Toho Company; English Titles: *Jetocho Sangokushi VIII: The Toughest Guy on Seaside Street, Jirocho of Three Provinces—Lone Thunder on Coast Highway*; *Last of the Wild One*; Running Time: 103 minutes.

Cast: Hisaya Morishige, Akio Kobori, Fubuki Koshiji, Seizaburô Kawazu, Kyôko Aoyama, Michitarô Mizushima, Jun Tazaki, Hiroshi Koizumi, Takashi Shimura, Kichijirô Ueda.

Asakusa no yoru (July 14, 1954)

Credits: Director and Screenplay: Kôji Shima; Planning Producer: Yasuaki Sakamoto; Kazuo Tsukaguchi; Based on the Novel by Matsutarô Kawaguchi; Format/Aspect Ratio: Black-and-White [1.37:1]; Musical Score: Seitarô Ômori; Art Director: Mikio Naka; Production Company: Daiei Studios; Distributor: Daiei Eiga.

Cast: Kôji Tsuruta (Susumu Yamaura), Machiko Kyô (Setsuko Takashima), Ayako Wakao (Namie Takashima), Jun Negami (Tozuki), Osamu Takizawa (Tozuki's Father), Hideo Takamatsu (Komakichi), Takashi Shimura (Komazo), Bontarô Miake (Teacher Akiyama), Hikaru Hoshi (Sakutaro Yumi), Kokuten Kôdô (Gosuke), Kumeko Urabe (Otaka), Ryûji Shinagawa (Ikeya).

Kimi Shinitamo koto nakare (August 31, 1954)

Credits: Director: Seiji Maruyama; Producer: Tomoyuki Tanaka; Screenplay: Seiji Maruyama, Dai Nishijima; Story: Shin'ichirô Nakamura; Cinematographer: Masao Tamai; Format/Aspect Ratio: Black-and-White [Spherical 1.37:1]; Processing: Kinuta Laboratories, Tokyo; Musical Score: Fumio Hayasaka; Production Designer: Yasuhide Kato; Sound Recordist: Masao Fujiyoshi; Lighting Technician: Ichirô Inohara.

Cast: Ryô Ikebe, Yôko Sugi, Takashi Shimura, Setsuko Wakayama, Yoshio Tsuchiya.

Haha no hatsukoi (September 17, 1954)

Credits: Director: Seiji Hisamatsu; Producers: Reiji Miwa, Kazuo Takimura; Screenplay: Noriyuki Yata; Cinematographer: Mitsuo Miura; Format/Aspect

Ratio: Black-and-White [Spherical 1.37:1]; Processing: Kinuta Laboratories, Tokyo; Musical Score: Toshiro Mayuzumi; Production Designer: Tomoo Shimagawara; Production Company: Tokyo Eiga Company, Ltd.; Distributor: Toho Company; English Title: *Mother's First Love*.
Cast: Keiko Kishi, Kyôko Kagawa, Hiroshi Koizumi, Ken Uehara, Kuniko Miyake, Yatsuko Tan'ami, Takashi Shimura.

Shin kurama tengu daiichi wa: Tengu shutsugen (October 6, 1954)
Credits: Director: Nobuo Aoyagi; Screenplay: Takeo [Kenrô] Matsuura; Cinematographer: Kazuo Yamazaki; Format/Aspect Ratio: Black-and-White [Spherical 1.37:1]; Processing: Kinuta Laboratories, Tokyo; Musical Score: Toriro Miki; Production Designer: Kazuo Ogawa; Sound Recordist: Shôichi Fujinawa; Lighting Technician: Masaki (Masayoshi) Ônuma; Production Company and Distributor: Toho Company.
Cast: Akio Kobori, Mariko Okada, Takashi Shimura, Kamatari Fujiwara, Yuriko Hamada, Jun Fujimaki.

Gojira [*Godzilla*] (November 3, 1954)
Credits: Director: Ishirô Honda; Producer: Tomoyuki Tanaka; Executive Producer: Iwao Mori; Screenplay: Ishirô Honda, Takeo Murata; Story: Shigeru Kayama; Cinematographer: Masao Tamai; Format/Aspect Ratio: Black-and-White [Spherical 1.37:1]; Processing: Kinuta Laboratories, Tokyo; Editor: Kazuji [Taichin] Taira; Musical Score: Akira Ifukube; Production Designers/Art Directors: Satoru Chûko, Takeo Kita; Executive in Charge of Production: Teruo Maki; Chief Assistant Director: Kôji Kajita; Second Assistant Director: Susumu Takebayashi; Sound Recordist: Hisashi Simonoga; Sound Assistants: Nobuyuki Tanaka, Norio Tone; Sound Effects Editor: Ichirô Minawa; Special Effects Director: Eiji Tsuburaya; Special Effects Cinematographer: Sadamasa Arikawa; Special Effects Lighting: Kuichirô Kishida; Assistant Cameramen: Yôichi Manoda, Sokei Tomioka, Hajime Tsuburaya, Yuzuru Aizawa; Matte Work: Hiroshi Mukoyama; Special Effects Wire Work: Fumio Nakadai; Production Manager: Yasuaki Sakamoto; Monster Builder: Teizô Toshimitsu; Special Effects Art Director: Akira Watanabe; Opticals: Yaka Yuki; Special Effects Technical Advisor: Fuminori Ôhashi; Stunt Choreographer: Haruo Nakajima; Lighting Technician: Chôshirô Ishii; Lighting Assistants: Shinji Kojima, Shoshichi Kojima; Assistant to Akira Ifukube: Sei Ikeno; Supervisors (Gojira's Tail): Fumio Nakadai, Shôji Okawa; Locations: Tokyo, Toba; U.S. Release Date: May 7, 2004; Running Time: 96 minutes.
Cast: Akira Takarada (Hideto Ogata), Momoko Kôchi (Emiko Yamane), Akihiko Hirata (Daisuke Serizawa-hakase), Takashi Shimura (Kyohei Yamane-hakase), Fuyuki Murakami (Professor Tanabe), Sachio Sakai (Newspaper Reporter Hagiwara), Toranosuke Ogawa (President of Company), Ren Yamamoto (Masaji Sieji), Hiroshi Hayashi (Chairman of Diet Committee), Seijirô Onda (Parliamentarian Oyama), Tsuruko Mano (Mrs. Sieji), Takeo Oikawa (Chief of Emergency Headquarters), Toyoaki Suzuki (Shinkichi Sieji), Kokuten [Kuninori] Kôdô (The Old Fisherman), Tadashi Okabe (Professor Tanabe's Assistant), Kin Sugai (Ozawa-san), Ren Imaizumi (Radio Operator), Junpei Natsuki (Power

Substation Engineer), Katsumi Tezuka (Gojira/Hajiwara's Editor), Haruo Nakajima (Gojira/Power Station Worker), Yasuhisa Tsutsumi (Soldier), Jiro Suzuki (Gojira), Saburô Iketani (News Reporter), Shizuko Azuma (Partygoer), Shizuko Higashi (Angry Woman at Diet), Kiyishi Kamata (Partygoer's Escort), Kenji Sahara (Young Lover on the Sound), Keiji Sakakida (Mayor Inada), Tamae Sengo (Mother), Ryosaku Takasugi (Gojira), Ishirô Honda (Power Station Worker Whose Hand Throws the Switch).

Shin kurama tengu daini wa: Azuma-dera no ketto (November 10, 1954)

Credits: Director: Nobuo Aoyagi; Producer: Goro Kontaibo; Screenplay: Takeo [Kenrô] Matsuura; Cinematographer: Kazuo Yamazaki; Format/Aspect Ratio: Black-and-White [Spherical 1.37:1]; Processing: Kinuta Laboratories, Tokyo; Musical Score: Toriro Miki; Production Design: Kazuo Ogawa; Sound Recordist: Shôichi Fujinawa; Lighting Technician: Masaki [Masayoshi] Ônuma; Production Company and Distributor: Toho Company.

Cast: Akio Kobori, Mariko Okada, Takashi Shimura, Jun Fujimaki, Kamatari Fujiwara, Norihei Miki, Takamaru Sasaki.

Bazoku geisha (November 15, 1954)

Credits: Screenplay: Kôji Shima; Based on the Novel by Shôhei Hino; Cinematographer: Michio Takahashi; Format/Aspect Ratio: Black-and-White [1.37:1]; Musical Score: Ichirô Saitô; Art Director: Mikio Naka; Production Company: Daiei Studios; Distributor: Daiei Eiga.

Cast: Machiko Kyô (Nobukichi), Kiyoko Hirai (Oine), Nijiko Kiyokawa (Kiyoka), Chieko Murata (Oyasu), Takashi Shimura (Kotaro Yamabe), Reiko Shirai (Umemaru), Hideo Takamatsu (Kojuro Ichikawa).

Mekura neko (March 1, 1955)

Credits: Director: Masahiro Makino; Producer: Kazuo Takimura; Screenplay: Sanshiro Tezuka; Cinematographer: Akira Mimura; Format/Aspect Ratio: Black-and-White [Spherical 1.37:1]; Processing: Kinuta Laboratories, Tokyo; Musical Score: Kyôsuke Kami; Production Designer: Kiyoshi Shimizu; Sound Recordist: Yoshio Nishikawa; Lighting Technician: Susumu Irie; Production Company: Takimura Productions; Running Time: 101 minutes.

Cast: Hiroshi Koizumi, Jun Tukazi, Takashi Shimura, Michitarô Mizushima, Michiyo Aratama, Eitarô Shindô.

Gojira no gyakushû [*Godzilla Raids Again*] (1955)

Credits: Director: Motoyoshi Oda; Producer: Tomoyuki Tanaka; Screenplay: Takeo Murata, Shigeaki Hidaka; Story: Shigeru Kayama; Story, U.S. Version: "The Volcano Monsters" by Ib Melchoir and Ed Watson; Cinematographer: Seiichi Endô; Format/Aspect Ratio: Black-and-White [Spherical 1.37:1]; Processing: Kinuta Laboratories, Tokyo; Editors: Kasuji Taira, (U.S. version) Hugo Grimaldi; Musical Score: Masaru Satô; Production Designers: Teruaki Abe,

Takeo Kita; Executive in Charge of Production: Kazo Baba; Chief Assistant Director: Eiji Awaya; Sound Recordist: Masonobu Miyasaki; Re-recording Mixer: Ichirô Minawa; Sound Effects Editor (U.S. Version): Alvin Sarno; Director of Special Effects: Eiji Tsuburaya; Special Effects Art Director: Akira Watanabe; Matte Work: Hiroshi Mukoyama; Special Effects Assistant Camera: Sadamasa Arikawa; Visual Effects Producer: Edward Nassour; Assistant Camera: Koichi Takano; Lighting Technician: Masaki Ônuma; Stunt Choreographer: Haruo Nakajima; Stock Music Composers (U.S. Version): Hershel Burke Gilbert, Paul Sawtell, Bert Shefter; Music Editor (U.S. Version): Rex Lipton; Dubbing Director (U.S. Version): Hugo Grimaldi; Voice Dubbing: Multiple Characters (U.S. Version): Paul Frees; Production Company and Distributor: Toho Company; Alternate Title: *Counterattack of the Monsters*; U.S. Release Title: *Gigantis the Fire Monster*; Running Time: 82 minutes.
Cast: Hiroshi Koizumi (Shoichi Tsukioka), Setsuko Wakayama (Hidemi Yamaji, Koehi's Daughter), Minoru Chiaki (Kôji Kobayashi), Takashi Shimura (Kyohei Yamane-hakase), Masao Shimizu (Zoologist Dr. Tadokoro), Seijirô Onda (Captain Terasawa of Osaka Defense Corps), Sônosuke Sawamura (Hokkaido Branch Manager Shingo Shibeki), Yoshio Tsuchiya (Tajima, Member of Osaka Defense Corps), Mayuri Mokusho (Radio Operator Yasuko Inouye), Minosuke Yamada (Chief of Civil Defense), Yukio Kasama (Koehi Yamaji, President of the Fishery), Senkichi Ômura (Small Escaped Convict), Ren Yamamoto (Commander of Landing Craft), Shin Ôtomo (Convict Leader), Takeo Oikawa (Osaka Municipal Police Commissioner), Shôichi Hirose, Shin Yoshida (Convicts), Jinpei Natsuki (Escaped Convict), Teruko Mita (Japanese Restaurant "Yayoi" Madam), Katsumi Tezuka (Angirasu), Haruo Nakajima (Gojira), Miyoko Hoshino (Singer of Cabaret), Toku Ihara, Tadao Nakamaru, Masaaki Tachibana (Policemen), Takuzô [Jiro] Kumagai (Captain of *Hokkai-maru*), Marvin Miller (Narrator [voice]), Hideo Shibuya, Shigemi Sunagawa (Visitors of Cabaret), Kôji Uno (Shibeki's Assistant), Paul Frees (voice), Keye Luke (Shoichi Tsukioka [voice]), George Takei (Commander of Landing Craft [voice]), Shirô [Hirotoshi] Tsuchiya, Shokichi Maki.

Mugibue [*Love Never Fails*] (May 3, 1955)

Credits: Director: Shirô Toyoda; Producer: Tomoyuki Tanaka; Screenplay: Ichirô Ikeda; Based on the Novel by Saisei Murô; Cinematographer: Mitsuo Miura; Format/Aspect Ratio: Black-and-White [Spherical 1.37:1]; Processing: Kinuta Laboratories, Tokyo; Editor: Yoshiharu Bandô; Musical Score: Ikuma Dan; Production Designer: Yasuhide Kato; Sound Recordist: Masao Fujiyoshi; Lighting Technician: Junro Ishikawa; Production Company and Distributor: Toho Company; English Title: *The Grass Whistle*; Running Time: 99 minutes.
Cast: Akira Kubo (Nobuo), Kyôko Aoyama (Odama), Fubuki Koshiji (Omatsu), Takashi Shimura (Nobuo's Father), Kamatari Fujiwara (Saito), Hiroshi (Yoichi) Tachikawa. Bokuzen Hidari, Yuriko Hamada, Chieko Nakakita, Eiko Miyoshi.

Otoko arite [*No Time for Tears*] (May 10, 1955)

Credits: Director: Seiji Maruyama; Producer: Goro Kontaibo; Screenplay: Ryûzô Kikushima; Cinematographer: Masao Tamai; Format/Aspect Ratio: Black-and-

White [Spherical 1.37:1]; Processing: Kinuta Laboratories, Tokyo; Editor: Shûichi Anbara; Musical Score: Ichirô Saitô; Production Designer: Kazuo Ogawa; Chief Assistant Director: Kôji Kajita; Sound: Ariaki Hosaka; Lighting Technician: Chôshirô Ishii; Production Company and Distributor: Toho Company; Running Time: 109 minutes.
Cast: Takashi Shimura (Tatsurô Shimamura), Toshirô Mifune (Mitsuo Yano), Mariko Okada (Michiko Shimamura), Yû Fujiki (Hiroshi Onishi), Shizue Natsukawa (Kinue Shimamura), Masao Shimizu (Segawa, Newspaper Reporter), Gen Shimizu (Koike, Owner of Sparrows), Yoshio Tsuchiya (Maruyama), Tateo Kawasaki (Undertaker), Takashi Itô (Teruo Shimamura), Daisuke Katô (Magazine Reporter), Seijirô Onda (Umpire Who Gets Slapped), Michiko Kawa, Keiko Mori (Michiko's Friends).

Sanjusan go sha otonashi (May 31, 1955)

Credits: Director: Senkichi Tanaguchi; Producer: Tomoyuki Tanaka; Screenplay: Ichirô Ikeda, Senkichi Taniguchi; Cinematographer: Kazuo Yamada; Format/Aspect Ratio: Black-and-White [Spherical 1.37:1]; Musical Score: Yasushi Akutagawa; Production Designer: Iwao Akune; Sound Recordist: Yoshio Nishikawa; Lighting Technician: Tsuruzô Nishikawa; Production Company and Distributor: Toho Company; English Title: *No Response from Car 33*.
Cast: Ryô Ikebe, Yôko Tsukasa, Akihiko Hirata, Momoko Kôchi, Yoshio Tsuchiya, Takashi Shimura.

Shin kurama tengu daisanbu (June 14, 1955)

Credits: Director: Toshio Sugie; Producer: Goro Kontaibo; Screenplay: Takeo [Kenrô] Matsuura; Cinematographer: Taiichi Kankura; Format/Aspect Ratio: Black-and-White [Spherical 1.37:1]; Processing: Kinuta Laboratories, Tokyo; Musical Score: Masaru Satô; Production Designer: Satoru Chûko; Sound Recordist: Ariaki Hosaka; Lighting Technician: Kuichirô Kishida; Production Company and Distributor: Toho Company.
Cast: Akio Kobori, Akira Takarada, Takashi Shimura, Kamatari Fujiwara, Machiko Kitagawa, Yoshio Tsuchiya.

Muttsuri Umon torimonocho (July 6, 1955)

Credits: Director: Kajirô Yamamoto; Producer: Ryô Takei; Screenplay: Tai Katô, Kajirô Yamamoto; Cinematographer: Seiichi Endô; Format/Aspect Ratio: Black-and-White [Spherical 1.37:1]; Processing: Kinuta Laboratories, Tokyo; Musical Score: Urato Watanabe; Production Designer: Takeo Kita; Sound Recordist: Masanobu Miyazaki; Lighting Technician: Masaki [Masayoshi] Ônuma; Production Company and Distributor: Toho Company.
Cast: Kanjûrô Arashi, Ken'ichi Enomoto, Takashi Shimura, Kingorô Yanagiya, Kichijirô Ueda.

Geisha Konatsu: Hitori neru yo no Konatsu (July 13, 1955)

Credits: Director: Nobuo Aoyagi; Screenplay: Haruo Umeda; Based on the Novel by Seiichi Funabasi; Cinematographer: Isamu Ashida; Format/Aspect Ratio:

Black-and-White [1.37:1]; Musical Score: Nobuo Iida; Production Designer: Shinobu Muraki; Production Company: Toho Company; English Title: *The Tears of Geisha Konatsu*.
Cast: Mariko Okada (Natsuko Kamioka, Konatsu), Haruko Sugimura (Raku Kamioka), Takashi Shimura (Sakuma), Hisaya Morishige (Kawashima), Chieko Nakakita (Nobuchiyo), Yu Fujiki (Yamada), Atsuko Ichinomiya (Yumi), Machiko Kitagawa (Hanayu), Toshie Kusunoki (Tsuyue), Chizu Murasaki (Wakako), Kumeko Otowa (Oyone), Sadako Sawamura (Kimiso's Madame).

Sugata naki mokugekisha (September 28, 1955)

Credits: Director and Screenplay: Shigeaki Hidaka; Producer: Tomoyuki Tanaka; Story: Keisuke Watanabe; Cinematographer: Mitsuo Miura; Format/Aspect Ratio: Black-and-White [1.37:1]; Musical Score: Toriro Miki; Art Director: Kazuo Ogawa; Sound: Yoshio Nishikawa; Gaffer: Rokuro Ishikawa; Running Time: 91 minutes.
Cast: Hiroshi Koizumi (Detective Funaki), Fubuki Koshiji (Chiyo, Maid), Asumi Kuji (Ayako Shingû), Sachiko Murase (Motoko), Seijirô Onda (Tajima), Takashi Shimura (Inspector Kasai), Eitarô Shindô (Heijiro Gondo), Shin Tokudaiji (Takayuki Uozumi), Ken Yamauchi [Ken Kubo] (Joji Ogata), Kokuten Kôdô.

Asagiri (November 8, 1955)

Credits: Director: Seiji Maruyama; Producer: Tomoyuki Tanaka; Screenplay: Katsuhito Inomata; Story: Tomoji Abe; Cinematography: Masao Tamai; Format/Aspect Ratio: Black-and-White [1.37:1]; Musical Score: Ichirô Saitô; Art Director: Yasuhide Kato; Sound: Masao Fujiyoshi; Lighting: Ichirô Inohara; Production Company: Toho Company; English Title: *Morning Fog*; Running Time: 94 minutes.
Cast: Akira Kubo, Mariko Okada, Shinji Yamada, Kyôko Aoyama, Yoko Tsukasa, Tatsuyoshi Ehara, Takashi Shimura.

Ikimono no Kiroku [*Record of a Living Being,* aka *I Live in Fear*] (November 22, 1955)

Credits: Director: Akira Kurosawa; Producer: Sôjirô Motoki; Screenplay: Hideo Oguni, Shinobu Hashimoto; Story: Akira Kurosawa, Fumio Hayasaka; Cinematographer: Asakasu Nakai; Format/Aspect Ratio: black-and-white [Spherical 1.37:1]; Processing: Toho Developing Company; Editor: Akira Kurosawa; Negative Cutter: Chozo Kobata; Musical Score and Conductor: Masaru Satô; Composer (Song "Cherry Pink Mambo"): Hachirô Matsui; Production Designer: Yoshirô Muraki; Costume Designer: Miyuki Suzuki; In Charge of Production: Hiroshi Nezu; Chief Assistant Director: Hisanobu Marubayashi; Assistant Directors: Takeo Nakamura, Samaji Nonagase, Ken Sano, Yasuyoshi Tajitsu; Assistant Art Director: Oyako Katô; Property Master: Kiyoshi Toda; Hair Designer: Junjirô Yamada; Sound Recordist: Fumio Yanoguchi; Sound Effects Editor: Ichirô Minawa; Assistant Camera: Takao Saitô; Lighting Technician: Kuichirô Kishida; Assistant Lighting Technician: Shozo Hada; Stills Photographer: Masao Fukuda; Hair Stylist: Sadako Okada; Script Supervisor: Teruyo

Nogami; Production Company and Distributor: Toho Company; Alternate Title: *What the Birds Knew*; U.S. Release Date: January 25, 1967 [Brandon Films]; Running Time: 103 minutes.
Cast: Toshirô Mifune (Kiichi Nakajima), Takashi Shimura (Dr. Harada, Counselor of the Domestic Court), Minoru Chiaki (Jiro Nakajima, Kiichi's Second Son), Eiko Miyoshi (Tayo Nakajima, Kiishi's Wife), Kyôko Aoyama (Sue Nakajima, Kiichi's Second Daughter), Haruko Tôgô (Yoshi Nakajima, Kiichi's First Daughter), Noriko Sengoku (Kimie Nakajima, Ichiro's Wife), Akemi Negishi (Asako Kuribayashi, Kiichi's Current Mistress), Hiroshi Tachikawa (Ryoichi Sayama, Kiichi's Son by a Former Mistress), Kichijirô Ueda (Mr. Kuribayashi, Asako's Father), Eijirô Tonô (The Old Man from Brazil), Yutaka Sada (Ichiro Nakajima, Kiichi's First Son), Kamatari Fujiwara (Okamoto), Ken Mitsuda (Judge Araki), Gen [Masao] Shimizu (Yamazaki, Yoshi's Husband and Chief of Mint Factory), Atsushi Watanabe (Ishida, a Factory Worker), Kiyomi Mizunoya (Satoko, Kiichi's First Mistress), Toranosuke Ogawa (Hori, the Lawyer), Nobuo Nakamura (Psychologist), Bokuzen Hidari (Landowner), Saoko Yonemura (Taeko), Yoshio Tsuchiya (Worker at Factory Following Fire), Akira Tani (First Man in Custody), Kokuten Kôdô (Workers' Older Family Member), Kazuo Katô (Susumu, Hanada's Son), Senkichi Ômura (Second Man in Custody), Fumiko Homma (Family Member of Workers), Kyorô Sakurai (Worker at Factory), Haruo Nakajima (Minor Role).

Miyamoto Musashi kanketsuhen: kettô Ganrûjima [*Samurai III: Duel at Ganryu Island*] (January 1, 1956)
Credits: Director: Hiroshi Inagaki; Producer: Kazuo Takamura; Screenplay: Hiroshi Inagaki, Tokuhei Wakao; Based on the Novel by Eiji Yoshikawa and the Play by Hidejî Hôjô and; Cinematographer: Kazuo Yamada; Format/Aspect Ratio: Eastmancolor [1.37:1]; Processing: Toho Developing Company; Editor: Kôichi [Hirokazu] Iwashita; Musical Score: Ikuma Dan; Production Designer: Kisaku Itô; Production Manager: Hideyuki Suga; Chief Assistant Director: Jun Fukuda; Assistant Art Director: Hiroshi Ueda; Sound: Masanobu Miyazaki; Lighting Technician: Tsuruzô Nishikawa; Production Company: Toho Company; Alternate Title: *Bushido*; Sequel to *Miyamoto Musashi* [*Samurai I: Musashi Miyamoto*] (1954) and *Zoku Miyamoto Musashi: Ichijôji no kettô* [*Samurai II: Duel at Ichijoji Temple*] (1955); U.S. Release Date: November 1967; Running Time: 105 minutes.
Cast: Kôji Tsuruta (Kojiro Sasaki), Toshirô Mifune (Musashi Miyamoto [Takezo]), Kaoru Yachigusa (Otsu), Michiko Saga (Omitsu), Mariko Okada (Akami), Takashi Shimura (Sado Nagaoka the Court Official), Minoru Chiaki (Sasuke, the Boatman), Takamaru Sasaki (Omitsu's Father), Daisuke Katô (Toji Gion), Haruo Tanaka (Kumagoro, Horse Dealer and "Tough Guy"), Kichijirô Ueda (Priest Ogon), Kokuten Kôdô (Old Priest Nikkan), Ikio Sawamura (Innkeeper), Akihiko Hirata (Seijuro Yoshioka), Kenjin Iida (Jotaro), Michiyo Kogure (Yohino), Mitsuko Mito (Oko), Sachio Sakai (Matahachi Honiden), Eijirô Tôno (Baiken Shishido), Haruo Nakajima (Minor Role), Nakajirô Tomita, Sônosuke Sawamura, Minosuke Yamada, Sôjî Kiyokawa, Masako Sakurai, Yutaka Oka,

Tominosuke Hayama, Kumeko Otowa, Yaeko Izumo, Noriko Honma, Etsuo Saijô, Tateo Kawasaki, Fumindo Matsuo, Ren Yamamoto, Fuminori Ôhashi, Haruko Toyama, Hideo Shibuya, Katsumi Tezuka, Keiichirô Katsumoto, Shirô [Hirotoshi] Tsuchiya, Masao Masuda, Yu Agetsu, Senkichi Ômura, Shôichi ["Solomon"] Hirose, Kurôemon Onoe.

Shin, Heike monogatari: Yoshinaka o meguru sannin no onna (January 15, 1956)

Credits: Director: Teinosuke Kinugasa; Executive Producer: Masaichi Nagata; Planning Producers: Matsutaro Kawaguchi, Hideo Matsuyama; Screenplay: Teinosuke Kinugasa, Masahige Narusawa; Based on the Novel by Eiji Yoshikawa; Cinematographer: Kôhei Sugiyama; Format/Aspect Ratio: Color [1.37:1]; Musical Score: Ichirô Saitô; Art Director: Atsuji Shibata; Sound Recordist: Yukio Kaihara; Gaffer: Kenichi Okamoto; Production Company: Daiei Kyoto; Distributor: Daiei Eiga; English Title: *Three Women Around Yoshinaka*; Running Time: 121 minutes.

Cast: Kazuo Hasegawa (Jirô-Yoshinaka Kiso), Machiko Kyô (Tomoe), Fujiko Yamamoto (Yamabuki), Hideko Takamine (Fuyuhime), Takashi Shimura (Sanemori Saito), Yatarô Kurokawa (Higuchi), Denjirô Ôkôchi (Tayubo), Eijirô Yanagi (Matsudono). Eitarô Shindô (Ninomiya), Shunji Natsume (Nishiura), Toshio Hosokawa (Imai), Ryôsuke Kagawa (Yorimori Taira), Bontarô Miake (Wada), Tokiko Mita (Shinobu), Tamao Nakamura (Kugô no hime), Kimiko Tachibana (Nara), Toyo (Toyoko) Takahashi (Tomoe no Tsukibito), Hisao Toake (Nekoma), Shôsaku Sugiyama, Yoshindo (Yoshito) Yamaji, Mitsusaburô Ramon, Kokuten Kôdô.

Wakai ki [*Young Tree*] (January 22, 1956)

Credits: Director: Ishirô Honda; Producer: Jin Usami; Screenplay: Ishirô Honda, Ichirô Ikeda; Cinematographer: Kazuo Yamazaki; Format/Aspect Ratio: Black-and-White [Spherical 1.37:1]; Processing: Kinuta Laboratories, Tokyo; Musical Score: Nobuo Iida; Production Designer: Teruaki Abe; Sound Recordist: Chôshichirô Mikami; Lighting Technician: Ichirô Inohara; Production Company and Distributor: Toho Company.

Cast: Kyôko Aoyama (Hiroko Koizumi), Shinji Yamada (Tatsuo Hotta), Shûji Sano (Mr. Shinohara), Hiroshi (Yoichi) Tachikawa (Jirôzaemon Baba), Keiko Miya (Kuniko Sawazaki), Nijiko Kiyokawa (Katsuko, Hiroko's Aunt), Takashi Shimura (Hanako's Father), Keiko Mori (Hanako Hasegawa), Michiko Kawa (Harue Ôhata), Sadako Sawamura (Kuniko's Mother), Daisuke Inoue (Masa-don), Nakajirô Tomita (Milk Delivery Shop Owner), Misako Asuka (Misako Yabe), Takashi Itô (Yasuo), Atsuko Ichinomiya (Hanako's Mother), Yaeko Izumo (Woman at Next Door), Akemi Ueno (Hiromi Ôishi), Reiko Wakamizu (Hisako Sugiyama), Yûko Togawa (Teacher), Yasuhisa Tsutsumi, Senkichi Ômura, Akira Tani, Tsuruko Mano, Michiko Kadono, Toshio Nakano, Jirô Suzukawa, Keiji Sakakida.

Kyatsu o nigasuna (January 29, 1956)

Credits: Director: Hideo Suzuki; Producer: Jin Usami; Screenplay: Takeo Murata, Hideo Suzuki; Cinematography: Mitsuo Miura; Format/Aspect Ratio: Black-and-White [1.37:1]; Musical Score: Yasushi Akutagawa; Production Designer: Kazuo Ogawa; Sound Recordist: Shôichi Fujinawa; Production Company and Distributor: Toho Company; English Title: *I Saw the Killer*.

Cast: Isao [Ko] Kimura (Takeo Fujisaki), Keiko Tsushima (Kimiko Fujisaki), Takashi Shimura (Nagasawa), Sônosuke Sawamura (Okamoto), Yoshio Tsuchiya (Shiraishi), Akira Sera (Harajima), Ichirô Chiba (Kamihashi), Yasuhisa Tsutsumi (Morishita), Yutaka Sada (Matsunaga), Haruko Tôgô, Ikio Sawamura, Tateo Kawasaki, Sachio Sakai, Seiji Miyaguchi.

Ankokugai [*The Underworld*] (February 26, 1956)

Credits: Director: Kajirô Yamamoto; Producer: Sôjirô Motoki; Screenplay: Tokuhei Wakao; Story: Ryûzô Kikushima; Cinematographer: Seiichi Endô; Format/Aspect Ratio: Black-and-White [1.37:1]; Editor: Yoshitami Kuroiwa; Musical Score: Ikuma Dan; Production Designer: Iwao Akune; Unit Production Manager: Kazuo Baba; Chief Assistant Director: Jun Fukuda; Sound: Shôichi Fujinawa; Lighting Technician: Tsuruzô Nishikawa; Production Company and Distributor: Toho Company; Running Time: 99 minutes.

Cast: Kôji Tsuruta (Takao Shoji), Kyôko Aoyama (Yumiko), Akemi Negishi (Natsue), Hiroshi Koisumi (Yumiko's fiancé), Takashi Shimura (Tsunejiro Furuya), Toshirô Mifune (Chief Inspector Kumuda), Seiji Miyaguchi, Minosuke Yamada, Seijirô Onda, Akira Sera, Matsue Ono, Katsumi Tezuka, Shin Yoshida, Akira Yamada, Etsuo Saijô, Haruya Sakamoto, Ren Imaizumi, Kôji Iwamoto, Ryûtarô Amami, Shôichi Hirose, Jun Mikami, Kôji Sawa, Oeko Kuroiwa, Akemi Ueno, Haruo Nakajima, Reiko Wakasui, michiko Kawa, Isamu Takahashi, Takuya Yuki.

Godzilla, King of the Monsters! (U.S. Release: April 27, 1956)

Credits: Directors: Ishirô Honda, Terry O. Morse; Producer: Tomoyuki Tanaka; Producers (U.S. Material): Edward B. Barison, Richard Kay, Harry Rybnick; Executive Producer (U.S. Material): Joseph E. Levine; Screenplay: Ishirô Honda, Takeo Murata; Adaptation: Al C. Ward; Original Story: Shigeru Kayama; Format/Aspect Ratio: Black-and-White [Spherical 1.37:1]; Cameraman: Masao Tamai; Cinematographer (U.S. Footage): Guy Roe; Supervising Editor: Terry O. Morse; Assistant Editor: Terry Morse, Jr.; Musical Score: Akira Ifukube; Production Designer: Satoru Chûko; Art Director: Takeo Kita; Set Decorator: George Rohr; Assistant Director: Ira Webb; Sound: Hisashi Shimonaga, Arthur B. Smith; Special Photographic Effects: Eiji Tsuburaya, Kuichiro Kishida, Hiroshi Mukoyama, Akira Watanabe; Production Companies: Toho Company, Jewell Enterprises, Inc.; Distributors: Embassy Pictures, TransWorld Releasing Corporation; Running Time: 80 minutes.

Cast: Raymond Burr (Steve Martin), Takashi Shimura (Dr. Yamane), Momoko Kôchi (Emiko), Akira Takarada (Ogata), Akihiko Hirata (Dr. Serizawa), Sachio Sakai (Hagiwara), Fuyuki Murakami (Dr. Tabata), Ren Yamamoto (Seiji), Toyoaki Suzuki (Shinkichi), Tadashi Okabe (Dr. Tabata's Assistant), Toranosuke Ogawa (President of Company), Frank Iwanaga (Security Officer), Mikel Conrad (George Lawrence), James Hong (Ogata/Serizawa [voices]), Ren Imaizumi (Radio Operator), Kokuten Kôdô (Old Man on Hill on Oto Island), Tsuruko

Mano (The Boy's Mother), Lee Miller (Man in Line at Airport), Haruo Nakajima, Ryosaku Takasugi, Katsumi Tezuka (Godzilla), Takeo Oikawa (Chief of Emergency Headquarters), Kenji Sahara (Man on Boat), Sammee Tong (Dr. Yamane [voice]), Paul Frees (Voice), Hiroshi Hayashi, Kin Sugai.

Narazu-mono (May 10, 1956)

Credits: Director: Nobuo Aoyagi; Producer: Tomoyuki Tanaka; Screenplay: Takeshi Kimura, Haruyuki Nakata; Based on the Story *"Takurin meshiba"* ["Takurin Dining Room"] by Takemi Sasaki; Cinematographer: Seiichi Endô; Format/Aspect Ratio: Black-and White [1.37:1]; Musical Score: Masaru Satô; Production Designers: Iwao Akune, Takeo Kita; Sound: Yoshio Nishikawa; Lighting Technician: Tsuruzô Nishikawa; Production Company and Distributor: Toho Company; English Title: *Blackguard*; Running Time: 95 minutes.
Cast: Toshirô Mifune (Kanji), Mariko Okada (Haruko), Yumi Shirakawa (Yuki), Takashi Shimura (Juzo), Minoru Chiaki (Sobei), Hisroshi [Yoichi] Tachikawa (Furukawa), Nijiko Kiyokawa (Otaki), Kamatari Fujiwara (Tsuda), Yoshio Kosugi (Yusaku), Ikio Sawamura (Nezumi), Akira Sera (Shimpei), Choji Oka, Senkichi Ômura.

Bôkyaku no hanabira (January 3, 1957)

Credits: Director: Toshio Sugie; Producer: Ichirô Satô; Screenplay: Toshio Yasumi; Based on the Novel by Kazuo Kikuta; Cinematographer: Taiichi Kankura; Format/Aspect Ratio: Eastmancolor [Spherical 1.37:1]; Processing: Kinuta Laboratories, Tokyo; Musical Score: Yûji Koseki; Production Designer: Shinobu Muraki; Sound Recordist: Shin Watarai; Lighting Technician: Mitsuo Kaneko; Production Company and Distributor: Toho Company; Running Time: 102 minutes.
Cast: Ryô Ikebe, Hiroshi Koizumi, Mitsukô Kusabae, Yôko Tsukasa, Yumi Shirakawa, Takashi Shimura, Akira Kubo, Kyôko Anzai, Keiko Awaji.

Kumonosu-jô [*Throne of Blood*] (January 15, 1957)

Credits: Director: Akira Kurosawa; Producers: Akira Kurosawa, Sôjirô Motoki; Screenplay: Akira Kurosawa, Hideo Oguni, Shinobu Hashimoto, Ryûzô Kikushima; Inspired by the Play *Macbeth* by William Shakespeare; Cinematographer: Azakazu Nakai; Format/Aspect Ratio: Black-and White [Spherical 1.37:1]; Editor: Akira Kurosawa; Negative Cutter: Chozo Obata; Musical Score: Masaru Satô; Production and Costume Designer: Yoshirô Muraki; Makeup Artist: Masanori Kobayashi; Hair Stylists: Yoshiko Matsumoto, Junjirô Yamada; Production Supervisor: Hiroshi Nezu; Chief Assistant Directors: Hiromichi Horikawa, Mimachi Norase; Assistant Directors: Yoshimitsu Banno, Ken Sano, Shoya Shimizu, Yasuyoshi Tajitsu, Michio Yamamoto; Property Master: Kôichi Hamamura; Art Supervisor: Kôhei Ezaki; Assistant Art Director: Yoshifumi Honda; Props: Kaneko; Sound Recordist: Fumio Yanoguchi; Sound Effects Editor: Ichirô Minawa; Assistant Sound: Masanao Uehara; Special Effects: Eiji Tsuburaya; Assistant Camera: Takao Saitô; Lighting Director: Kuichirô Kishida; Assistant Lighting Technician: Shozo Hada; Stills Photographer: Masao

Fukuda; Costumer: Taiki Mori [Kyoto Costume Company, Ltd.]; Horseback Riding Instructors: Shigeru Endo, Einori Kaneko; Accountant: Ikemichi Hashimoto; Script Supervisor: Teruyo Nogami; Locations: Gotemba, Izu Peninsula and Mount Fuji, Shizuoka; Tamagawa River, Tokyo; Production Companies: Kurosawa Production Co., Toho Company; Distributor: Toho Company; French Adaptation (Original Version with Subtitles): Fabrice Arduini, Keiko Tsubai; U.S. Release Date: November 22, 1961 [Brandon Films]; Running Time: 110 minutes.

Cast: Toshirô Mifune (Taketori Washizu), Isuzu Yamada (Lady Asaji Washizu, His Wife), Takashi Shimura (Noriyasu Odagura), Akira Kubo (Yoshiteru Miki), Yôichi [Hiroshi] Tachikawa (Kunimaru Tsuzuki), Minoru Chiaki (Yoshiaki Miki), Takamaru Sasaki (Kuniharu Tsuzuki), Kokuten Kôdô (Military Commander), Kichijirô Ueda (Washizu's Workman), Eiko Miyoshi (Old Woman at the Castle), Chieko Naniwa (Old Ghost Woman), Nakajirô Tomita (Second Military Commander), Yû Fujiki, Sachio Sakai, Shin Ôtomo, Yoshio Tsuchiya. Senkichi Ômura (Washizu Samurai), Yoshio Inaba (Third Military Commander), Takeo Obukawa (Miki Party Member), Akira Tani, Ikio Sawamura, Yutaka Sada (Washizu Soldiers), Seijirô Onda (Second Miki Party Member), Shinpei Takagi, Masao Masuda. Shirô Tsuchiya, Takeo Matsushita, Jun Ôtomo (Commanders), Akifumi [Shôbun] Inoue, Asao Koike, Kyoro Sakurai, Kaneyuki Tsubono (Servants), Takeshi Katô (Guard Killed by Washizu), Hitoshi [Kin] Takagi (Tsuzuki Guard), Michiya Higuchi (Tsuki Guard), Fuminori Ôhashi (Samurai), Isao Kimura, Seiji Miyaguchi, Nobuo Nakamura (Phantom Samurai). Gen Shimizu, Mitsuo Asano, Asao Koike.

Yama to kawa no aru machi (February 12, 1957)

Credits: Director: Seiji Maruyama; Producer: Sanezumi Fujimoto; Screenplay: Zenzô Matsuyama; Story: Yôjirô Ishizaka; Cinematographer: Rokurô Nishigaki; Format/Aspect Ratio: Black-and White [1.37:1]; Musical Score: Urato Watanabe; Production Designer: Kyoe Hamagami; Sound Recordist: Yoshio Nishikawa; Lighting Technician: Ichirô Inohara; Production Company and Distributor: Toho Company; English Title: *A Path Through Mountains and Rivers*.

Cast: Izumi Yukimura, Keiko Tsushima, Hiroshi Koizumi, Shinji Yamada, Akira Takarada, Ranko Hanai, Takashi Shimura.

Kono futari ni sachi are [*Be Happy, These Two Lovers*] (February 19, 1957)

Credits: Director: Ishirô Honda; Producer: Shirô Horie; Screenplay: Zenzô Matsuyama; Cinematographer: Hajime Koizumi; Format/Aspect Ratio: Black-and White [Spherical 1.37:1]; Processing: Kinuta Laboratories, Tokyo; Musical Score: Yoshinao Nakada (Nakata); Production Designer: Tatsuo Kita; Unit Production Manager: Kenichirô Tsunoda; Sound: Ariaki Hosaka; Lighting Technician: Sôichi Yokoi; Production Company and Distributor: Toho Company; Running Time: 97 minutes.

Cast: Hiroshi Koizumi, Yumi Shirakawa, Keiko Tsushima, Toshirô Mifune, Kamatari Fujiwara, Takashi Shimura, Shizue Natsukawa, Yuriko Hanabusa,

Tamae Kiyokawa, Takeo Oikawa, Hirota Kisaragi, Yoshifumi Tajima, Sumiko Koizumi, Yû Fujiki.

Sanjûrokunin no jôkyaku (April 16, 1957)

Credits: Director: Toshio Sugie; Screenplay: Masato Ide, Masaharu Segawa; Based on the Novel by Yorichika Arima; Cinematographer: Kôzô Okazaki; Format/Aspect Ratio: Black-and White [Spherical 1.37:1]; Processing: Kinuta Laboratories, Tokyo; Musical Score: Yoshiyuki Kozu; Production Designers: Takeshi Kanô, Kôhei Shima; Sound Effects Editor: Hisashi Shimonaga; Sound Recordist: Fumio Yanoguchi; Lighting Technician: Kazuo Shimomura; Production Company: Tokyo Eiga Company, Ltd.; Distributor: Toho Company; Running Time: 96 minutes.
Cast: Hiroshi Koizumi (Ichiro Watanabe, Detective), Keiko Awaji (Mitsuko Yanagisawa), Chikage Ôgi (Conductress Sachiko), Takashi Shimura (Yamagami, Detective), Makoto Satô (Kondô, Robbery and Murder), Minoru Chiaki (Motohashi, Drug Salesman), Shin [Nobu] Morikawa (Hoshiyama), Setsuko Wakayama (Hiroko Watanabe, Ichirô's Wife), Bin Amatsu (Detective Anzai), Ken'ichi Miyajima (Old Bus Driver Sasaki), Ichirô Nakatani (Yamaoka), Sachio Sakai (Bus Driver Sasane), Takamaru Sasaki (Police Inspector Kaburagi), Akira Sera (Kishi), Jun Tatara (Manzo), Sen Yano (Aoyama), Toki Shiozawa.

Arakure [*Untamed Woman*] (May 22, 1957)

Credits: Director: Mikio Naruse; Producer: Tomoyuki Tanaka; Screenplay: Yôko Mizuki; Based on the Novel by Shusei Tokuda; Cinematographer: Masao Tamai; Format/Aspect Ratio: Black-and White [Spherical 1.37:1]; Processing: Kinuta Laboratories, Tokyo; Editor: Eiji Ooi; Musical Score: Ichirô Saitô; Production Designer: Yasuhide Kato; Executive in Charge of Production: Teruo Maki; Assistant Director: Masayoshi Kawanishi; Sound: Chôshichirô Mikami; Lighting: Kuichirô Kishida; Historical Research: Shôhachi Kimura; Production Company and Distributor: Toho Company; Running Time: 121 minutes.
Cast: Hideko Takamine (Oshima), Ken Uehara (Her First Husband), Daisuke Katô (Her Second Husband), Masayuki Mori (Her Lover), Mitsuko Miura (Oyu, Her Rival), Tatsuya Nakadai (Shinkichi, the Young Tailor), Eijirô Tôno, Chieko Nakakita, Takashi Shimura, Seiji Miyaguchi, Takeshi Sakamoto, Teruko Kishi, Noriko Honma, Haruo Tanaka, Masahiko Tsugawa, Sadako Sawamura, Kokuten Kôdô, Akira Tani, Natsuko Kahara, Yatsuko Tan'ami, Bokuzen Hidari, Senkichi Ômura, Yutaka Sada, Kan Hayashi, Atsushi Hirana, Hiroshi Imaizumi, Yaeko Izumo, Michiko Kawa, Tame Kiyokawa, Tsuruko Mano, Teruko Mita, Tsuneo Miura, Zekô Nakamura, Yutaka Nakayama, Seijirô Onda, Kumeko Otowa, Gorô Sakurai, Noriko Sengoku, Akira Sera, Yasuhisa Tsutsumi, Unpei Yokoyama, Sadaya Yuki.

Kiken na eiyu [*A Dangerous Hero*] (July 30, 1957)

Credits: Director: Hideo Suzuki; Producer: Masakatsu Kaneko; Screenplay: Eizô Sugawa, Mikiyuki Hasegawa; Cinematographer: Asakazu Nakai; Format/Aspect Ratio: Black-and White [1.37:1]; Musical Score: Yasushi Akutagawa;

Production Designer: Kyoe Hamagami; Sound: Shôichi Fujinawa; Lighting Technician: Ichirô Inohara; Production Company and Distributor: Toho Company; Running Time: 94 minutes.
Cast: Shintarô Ishihara, Yôko Tsukasa, Eitarô Ozawa, Takashi Shimura, Tatsuya Nakadai, Toshirô Mifune, Seiji Miyaguchi, Hisaya Itô, Chieko Nakakita, Ken Mitsuda, Keiko Kishi, Ichirô Shimizu, Ren Yamamoto, Fumindo Matsuo, Ikio Sawamura, Shirô Tsuchiya.

Yuunagi (September 15, 1957)

Credits: Director: Shirô Toyoda; Producer: Ichirô Satô; Screenplay: Toshio Yasumi; Cinematographer: Jun Yasumoto; Format/Aspect Ratio: Color [1.37:1]; Processing: Kinuta Laboratories, Tokyo; Musical Score: Yasushi Akutagawa; Production Designer: Kisaku Itô; Lighting Technician: Toshio Takashima; Production Company: Takarazuka Eiga Company, Ltd.; Distributor: Toho Company.
Cast: Chikage Awashima (Norie Shima), Ayako Wakao (Ryoko Shima), Takashi Shimura (Yasunori Igawa), Ryô Ikebe (Kosuke Igawa), Noriko Sengoku (Okyo), Seizaburô Kawazu (Genzo Itsui), Etsuko Ichihara (Otae), Yasuko Nakada (Hama Goto), Chieko Naniwa (Okura), Eitarô Ozawa (Shoji Ikeda), Jun Tatara (Okami), Yasuhisa Tsutsumi.

Aoi sanmyaku Shinko no maki (October 27, 1957)

Credits: Director: Shûe Matsubayashi; Producers: Sanezumi Fujimoto, Masakatsu Kaneko; Screenplay: Toshirô Ide; Based on the Novel by Yôjirô Ishizaka; Cinematographer: Jôji Ohara; Format/Aspect Ratio: Color [1.37:1]; Musical Score: Ryôichi Hattori; Art Director: Shinobu Muraki; Lighting Technician: Tsuruzô Nishikawa; Production Company: Toho Company; Running Length: 10 reels.
Cast: Hisao Toake (Takeda), Yôko Tsukasa (Yukiko Shimazaki), Izumi Yukimura (Shinko Terasawa), Keiko Awaji, Kamatari Fujiwara, Rumi Konishi, Akira Kubo, Mitsukô Kusabue, Yeako Mizutani, Keiko Mori, Fuyuki Murakami, Rumiko Sasa, Takashi Shimura, Hiroshi [Yôichi] Tachikawa, Akira Takarada.

Zoku aoi sanmyaku Yukiko no maki (November 19, 1957)

Credits: Director: Shûe Matsubayashi; Producers: Sanezumi Fujimoto, Masakatsu Kaneko; Screenplay: Toshirô Ide; Based on the Novel by Yôjirô Ishizaka; Cinematographer: Jôji Ohara; Format/Aspect Ratio: Color [1.37:1]; Musical Score: Ryôichi Hattori; Art Director: Shinobu Muraki; Lighting Technician: Tsuruzô Nishikawa; Production Company: Toho Company; Running Length: 11 reels.
Cast: Hisao Toake (Takeda), Yôko Tsukasa (Yukiko Shimazaki), Izumi Yukimura (Shinko Terasawa), Ichirô Arishima, Keiko Awaji, Kamatari Fujiwara, Atsuko Ichinomiya, Rumi Konishi, Akira Kubo, Yaeko [Yoshie] Mizutani, Keiko Mori, Fuyuki Murakami, Chieko Nakakita, Sachio Sakai, Rumiko Sasa, Takashi Shimura, Hiroshi [Yôichi] Tachikawa, Yoshifumi Tajima, Akira Takarada.

Dotanba (November 24, 1957)

Credits: Director: Tomu Uchida; Screenplay: Shinobu Hashimoto, Tomu Uchida;

Cinematographer: Shizuka Fujii; Format/Aspect Ratio: Black-and-White and Toeiscope [2.35:1]; Editor: Fumio Sôda; Musical Score: Taiichirô Kosugi; Production Designer: Mikio Mori; Chief Assistant Director: Shoichi Shimazu; Assistant Camera: Yoshikazu Yamazawa (Yamasawa); Production Company: Toei Tokyo; Distributor: Toei Company; Running Time: 109 minutes.
Cast: Shinjirô Ebara (Ehara), Eiji Okada, Eijirô Tôno, Takashi Shimura, Jiro Takagi, Takashi Kanda, Chôko Iida, Kokuten Kôdô.

Chikyû Bôeigun [*The Mysterians*] (December 28, 1957)

Credits: Director: Ishirô Honda; Producer: Tomoyuki Tanaka; Producers (English Version): Kaeko Sakamoto, Eric P. Sherman; Executive Producer (English Version): John Sirabella; Assistant Producer (English Version): Mami Odaka; Screenplay: Takeshi Kimura; Story: Jôjirô Okami, Shigeru Kayama; Cinematographer: Hajime Koizumi; Format/Aspect Ratio: Eastmancolor and Tohoscope [2.35:1]; Processing: Tokyo Laboratory, Ltd.; Editor: Kôichi Iwashita; Musical Score: Akira Ifukube; Production Designer: Teruaki Abe; Production Manager: Yasuaki Sakamoto; Assistant Director: Kôji Kajita; Sound Recordist: Masanobu Miyazaki [Perspecta Stereo]; Sound Effects: Ichiro Minawa; Dubbing Supervisor (English): Jay Bonafield; Dubbing Scenarists (English): Carlos Montalbán, Peter Riethof; Casting: Kaeko Sakamoto; Director of Special Effects: Eiji Tsuburaya; Special Effects Photographers: Hidesaburo Araki, Sadamasa Arikawa; Special Effects Art Director: Akira Watanabe; Stunt Coordinator: Haruo Nakajima; Combination Shots: Hiroshi Mukoyama; U.S. Release Date: May 15, 1959; Running Time: 85 minutes.
Cast: Kenji Sahara (Joji Atsumi), Yumi Shirakawa (Etsuko Shiraishi), Momoko Kôchi (Hiroko Iwamoto), Akihiko Hirata (Ryoichi Shiraishi), Takashi Shimura (Dr. Tanjiro Adachi), Susumu Fugita (General Morita), Hisaya Itô (Captain Seki), Yoshio Kosugi (Commander Sugimoto), Fuyuki Murakami (Dr. Nobu Kawanami), Yoshio Tsuchiya (Leader of the Mysterians), Minosuke (The Secretary of Defense Hamamoto), Tetsu Nakamura (Dr. Koda), Heihachirô Ôkawa (Person at Board Meeting), Takeo Oikawa (Announcer on TV), Haruya Katô, Senkichi Ômura, Yasuhiro Shigenobu (Doomed Villagers), Harold Conway (Dr. DeGracia), Yutaka Sada (Police Captain Miyamoto), Hideo Mihara (General Emoto), Rikie Sanjô (Etsuko's Mother), Sôji Ubukata (Dr. Noda), Mitsuo Tsuda, Kamayuki Tsubono (Persons at Defense Meeting), Ren Imaizumi (Adachi's Assistant Hayami), Shin Ôtomo (Policeman Kawada), Takuzô [Jirô] Kumagai (Colonel Ito), Akio Kusama (Chief of Police Station Togawa), Shoichi Hirose (Detective in Etsuko's House), Tadao Nakamaru (First Lieutenant Yamamoto), Rinsaku Ogata (Policeman Ogata), George Furness [Jôji Fânesu] (Dr. Svenson), Haruo Nakajima (Moguera), Katsumi Tezuka, Hideo Unagami (Mysterians), Saburô Kadowski, Masayoshi Kawabe (Policemen), Keiichirô Katsumoto, Jirô Misuaki (Detectives), Mitsuo Matsumoto (Reporter of Newspaper), Eisuke Nakanishi (Detective in Etsuko's House); U.S. Version: Byron Morrow (General), Enver Altenbay (Reporter), Joe Cappelletti [Joey Capps] (Commander voice), Michael Forest (Sugimoto voice), Alf Kjellin (Yamamoto voice), William Knight (Hanamoto voice), Steve Kramer (Morita voice), Dave Mallow (Red Mysterian voice), Michael McConnohie (Adachi voice), Bob

Papenbrook [John Smallberries] (Miyamoto voice), Michelle Ruff (Hiroko voice), Eric P. Sherman [Erik Blackthorn] (Immerman voice), Melodee M. Spevack (Etsuko's Mother voice), Doug Stone (Kawanami voice), Kirk [Sparky] Thornton (Ryoichi voice), Lesli Todd (Etsuko voice), Paul Frees (Dr. Tanjiro Adachi voice).

Ohtori-jo no hanayome (January 1958)

Credits: Director: Sadatsugu Matsuda; Format/Aspect Ratio: Eastmancolor and Toeiscope [2.35:1]; Production Company: Toei Company; English Title: *Samurai Bride Hunter*; Running Time: 86 minutes.

Cast: Yumiko Hasegawa (Okinu), Kunio Kaga (Akiyama), Eijirô Kataoka (Seikichi), Masao Mishima (Lord Matsudaira), Hitomi Nakahara (Omitsu), Eitarô Shindô (Nagano), Kyôji Sugi (Gosuke), Kenji Susukida (Oshima), Jun Yazaki (Higaki), Ryûtarô Ôtomo (Gentaro), Harue Akagi, Ushio Akashi, Hideo Azuma, Kensaku Hara, Ryôei Itô, Akiko Kagami, Yûgi Kamishirô, Takashi Kanda, Kenji Kusumoto, Tsukie Matsuura, Reiko Miyama, Tokinosuke Nakamura, Takashi Shimura, Kinnosuke Takamatsu, Shizuko Tanaka, Kazuo Tokita, Shigetoshi Yoda, Ikko Okuni.

Edokko matsuri (February 12, 1958)

Credits: Director: Kôji Shima; Producer: Shôzaburô Asai; Screenplay: Hideo Oguni; Cinematographer: Yukimasa Makita; Format/Aspect Ratio: Color and Sharpscope [2.35:1]; Editor: Shigeo Nishida; Musical Score: Seitarô Ômori; Production Designer: Yoshizo Kamisato; Sound: Yukio Kaihara; Gaffer: Shonojo Kato; Production Company: Daiei Kyoto; Running Length: 11 reels.

Cast: Kazuo Hasegawa (Tasuke Isshin), Hiroshi Kawaguchi (Takechiyo), Hitomi Nozoe (Otoyo), Michiko Ai (Onaka), Teruyo Asagumo (Oryu), Okuzan Asao (Gen'an), Saburô Date (Nobutada Matsudaira), Seishirô Hara (Iganokami Hori), Sumire Harukaze (Osen), Narutoshi Hayashi (Imposter of Tasuke), Sentarô Izumi (Tadaaki Abe), Ryôsuke Kagawa (Kôzukenosuke Honda), Yatarô Kurokawa (Tajimanokami Yagyû), Tsukie Matsuura (Kasuga no tsubone), Bontarô Miake (Katsuzô), Ganjirô Nakamura (Hikozaemon Ôkubo), Tamao Nakamura (Tae), Shôzô Nanbu (Hidetada, Shôgun), Shintarô Nanjo (Masamori Hotta), Takashi Shimura (Hôkinokami Aoyama), Kinzô Shin (Kinai Sasao), Rieko Sumi (Oren), Musei Tokugawa (Narrator), Masaya Tsukida (Shôkichi), Hiroshi Ueda (Head of Monks), Ichirô Amano, Shinobu Araki, Ryônosuke Azuma, Jun Fujikawa, Yôichi Funaki, Toshihiko Gô, Yûshi Hamada, Kôichi Katsuragi, Midori Komatsu, Hajime Koshikawa, Tetsu Mikami, Naohiko Negishi, Ichirô Takakura, Kazue Tamaki.

Chûshingura [*The Loyal 47 Ronin*] (April 1, 1958)

Credits: Director: Kunio Watanabe; Producer: Masaichi Nagata; Planning Producers: Toshio Kageyama, Hisakazu Tsuji; Screenplay: Fuji Yahiro, Toshio Tamikado, Masaharu Matsumura, Kunio Watanabe; Cinematographer: Takashi Watanabe; Format/Aspect Ratio: Daieicolor and Daieiscope [2.35:1]; Processing: Tôyô Genzôshô; Musical Score: Ichirô Saitô; Art Director: Yoshizô

Kamisato; Costume Designers: Yuko Kurosawa, Shima Yoshizane; Sound Recordist: Masao Ôsumi; Gaffers: Shinichi Ito, Hiroya Katô; Production Company and Distributor: Daiei Studios; Running Time: 166 minutes.
Cast: Kazuo Hasegawa (Kuranosuke Ôishi), Shintarô Katsu (Genzô Akagaki), Kôji Tsuruta (Kin'emon Okano), Raizô Ichikawa (Takuminokami Asano), Machiko Kyô (Orui, Spy), Fujiko Yamamoto (Yôsen in), Michiyo Kogure (Dayû Ukihashi), Chikage Awashima (Riku Ôishi), Ayako Wakao (Orin, Carpenter's Daughter), Osamu Takizawa (Kôzukenosuke Kira), Yatarô Kurokawa (Denpachirô Tamon), Eiji Funakoshi (Tsunanori Uesugi), Keizô Kawasaki (Shinzaemon Katsuta), Eitarô Ozawa (Hyôbu Chisaka), Takashi Shimura (Jûbei Ôtake), Ganjirô Nakamura (Gorobei Kakimi), Chieko Higashiyama (Otaka, Ôishi's Mother), Tamao Nakamura (Midori, Asano's Chambermaid), Michiko Ai (Karumo, Prostitute), Riko Hasegawa (Kobai), Noriko Hodaka (Yûgiri), Kazuko Wakamatsu (Osugi, Shioyama's Maidservant), Aiko Mimasu (Notsubone Toda), Jun Negami (Sagaminokami Tsuchiya), Narutoshi (Naritoshi) Hayashi (Yasubei Horibe), Hiroshi Kawaguchi (Chikara Ôishi), Kenji Sugawara (Awajinokami Wakisaka), Bontarô Miake (Masagorô, Carpenter), Mantarô Ushio (Kinta, Townsfolk), Masao Shimizu (Dewanokami Yanagisawa), Jun Tazaki (Ikkaku Shimizu), Sônosuke Sawamura (Kazusanokami Sôda), Kinzô Shin (Kurobei Ôno), Yoshirô Kitahara (Jûjirô Hazama), Hideo Takamatsu (Yajirô Sekine), Kappei Matsumoto (Yosobei Kajikawa), Gen Shimizu (Chûzaemon Yoshida), Yûsaku Terashima (Tachû Matsubara), Saburô Boya (Genkichi, Townsfolk), Ichirô Ryuzaki (Izaemon Shioyama), Ryôsuke Kagawa (Gengoemon Kataoka), Hisako Takihana (Emoshichi Yatô's Mother), Teruyo Asagumo (Maki, Shioyama's Wife), Yôko Uraji (Yae, Katsuta's Wife), Akiko Hasegawa (Okû, Ôishi's Daughter), Kimiko Tachibana (Oyae, Waitress), Yôko Wakasugi (Oguruma, Prostitute), Setsuko Hama (Yûnagi, Prostitute), Teruko Ômi (Oume, Waitress), Kazuko Ichikawa (Chonmaru, Dancing Girl), Keiko Fujita (Momji, Prostitute), Shinobu Araki (Yahei Horibe), Ryuichi Ishii (Tadashichi Takebayashi), Shôsaku Sugiyama (Kazuemon Fuwa), Saburô Date (Jûheiji Sugino), Ryônosuke Azuma (Master Samurai in Headquarters), Mitsusaburô Ramon (Riemon Torii, Kira's Man), Eigorô Onoe (Yaichirô Niimi, Kira's Man), Shôzô Nanbu (Hikoemon Yasui), Fujio Harumoto (Ukyôdayû Tamura), Ichirô Izawa (Isuke Maebara), Tatsuo Hanabu (Heiemon Mugi), Ryûji Shinagawa (Gengo Ôtaka), Shôji Umewaka (Emoshichi Yatô), Toshio Chiba (Heihachirô Yamaoka), Shintarô Saijo (Sakyônosuke Date), Ichirô Amano (Mankichi, Man in Restaurant), Kin'ya Ichikawa (Townsman), Yôichi Funaki (Yogorô Kanzaki), Kazue Tamaki (Kanroku Chikamatsu), Seishirô Hara (Heihachirô Kobayashi), Daisuke Fujima (Densuke Kurahashi), Yasuhiko Shima (Kyûnoshin Aoki), Yûshi Hamada (Palanquin Bearer), Kôichi Katsuragi (Sôemon Hara), Ryûzaburô Mitsuoka (Yoichiemon Sudô, Kira's Man), Okuzan Asao (Jûnai Onodera), Ichirô Takakura (Matanojô Shiota), Fumihiko Yokoyama (Kichiemon Terasaki), Jun Fujikawa (Magoshirô Soeta, Kira's Man), Kan Ueda (Newspaper Seller), Yukio Horikita (Shinpachirô Yamayoshi, Kira's Man), Sumao Ishihara (Clerk in Headquarters), Masayoshi Kikuno (Heidayû Waku), Tadashi Iwata (Jirôzaemon Mimura), Tokio Oki (Government Official Inspector-General), Kiyoshi Kasuga, Yû Sakarai, Takaji (Ryûji) Fukui (Kira's Men), Keiko Koyanagi, Reiko Kongô.

Appendix A

Ôedo shichininshû [*Seven from Edo*] (April 30, 1958)
Credits: Director: Sadatsugu Matsuda; Producer: Hiroshi Okawa; Planning Producers: Tatsuo Sakamaki, Naoya Taguchi, Kimiharu Tsujino; Screenplay: Yoshitake Hisa; Cinematographer: Shintarô Kawasaki; Format: Color and Toeiscope [2.35:1]; Musical Score: Shirô Fukai; Art Director: Taizô Kamashima; Sound Recordist: Sadamitsu Ishihara; Lighting Technician: Ken'ichi Tenabe; Production Company and Distributor: Toei Company; Running Time: 92 minutes.
Cast: Utaemon Ichikawa (Katsukawa), Ryûtarô Ôtomo (Hirahara), Chiyonosuke Azuma (Murase), Hashizô Ôkawa (Akizuki), Isao Yamagata (Tatewaki), Kenji Susukida (Manabe), Takashi Shimura (Sagamiya), Hiroko Sakuramachi (Ichi). Kogiku Hanayagi (Somekichi), Shinobu Chihara (Rengetsu), Hiromi Hanazono (Osen), Sentarô Fushimi (Sagara), Koinosuke Onoe (Nitta), Kyonosuke Nango (Murayama), Kunio Kaga (Kaizuka), Jun Usami (Matsuno).

Haha (May 5, 1958)
Credits: Director: Shigeo Tanaka; Producer: Haruo Kawasaki; Planning Producer: Masaichi Nagata; Screenplay: Ryôzô Kasahara; Cinematographer: Michio Takahashi; Format: Color; Musical Score: Yûji Koseki; Production Designer: Shigeo Mano; Assistant Director: Masao Segawa; Gaffer: Sachio Itô; Stills Photographer: Tadao Miyazaki; Production Manager: Kiishi Satake; Sound: Mitsuo Hasegawa; Production Company: Daiei Tokyo; Running Time: 111 minutes.
Cast: Aiko Mimasu (Kiyo Yuasa), Nobue Akitsuki (Eriko), Keiko Fujita (Model C), Eiji Funakoshi (Hiroshi Takayama), Fujio Harumoto (Kimura), Yoko Hayama (Sakie Takayama as a Child), Noriko Hodaka (Yukiko Yuasa), Yosuke Irie (Young Worker A), Harue Itakura (Chieko Yuasa as a Child), Naoyasu Itô (Hooligan B), Ichirô Izawa (Tsunoda), Junko Kanô (Chieko Yuasa), Toyomi Karita (Hitomi), Yoshiaki Katô (Eizô Yuasa as a Child), Hiroshi Kawaguchi (Eizô Yuasa), Kanji Kawahara (Principal), Yasuko Kawakami (Setsuko Omachi), Atsuko Kindaichi (Bride), Yoshirô Kitahara (Fireman), Nobusuke Kobayashi (Jirô), Machiko Kyô (Takako Ômachi), Hiroko Machida (Young Mother), Osamu Maruyama (Middle-aged Worker), Naoko Matsudaira (Model F), Bontarô Miake (Senkichi Yuasa), Ken Mitsuda (Hiroshi Ômachi), Kenji Miyajima (Gohei), Manabu Morita (Tomioka), Chieko Murata (Mrs. Hamada), Ikuko Môri (Model E), Fumio Nakae (Young Worker C), Akira Natsuki (Manager), Jun Negami (Ryotaro Yuasa), Naohiko Negishi (Junior High Student B), Michiko Ono (Kaoru Yuasu), Saburô Sakai (Villager C), Kazuhiro Sanada (Saburô), Kaoru Shimizudani (Model D), Takashi Shimura (Ijûin), Ryûji Shinagawa (Seiji Yuasa), Nobuko Shingû (Shirakawa), Kenji Sugawara (Asahara), Yasushi Sugita (Sugishita), Rieko Sumi (Mrs. Mimura), Yoshio Tabata (Sailor), Kikuko Tachibana (Villager B), Miyako Tachibana (Model A), Isao Takada (Junior High Student A), Hideo Takamatsu (Matsuda), Eiichi Takamura (Villager A), Hideko Takano (Maid at Ijûin's), Mitsuko Takesato (Abe), Jirô Tamiya [Goro Shibata] (Kinoshita), Kazuyoshi Tateno (Junior High Student C), Kisao Tobita (Young Worker B), Kazuma Tsuda (Seiji Yuasa as a Child), Masaya Tsukida (Hooligan A), Jôji Tsurumi (Takasaki), Kazuko Tsuruta (Kazuko), Kôji Tsuruta (Yamakawa), Ayako Wakao (Miss Mochizuki), Tetsuya Watanabe (Hooligan C), Hiroko Yajima (Model B), Fujiko Yamamoto (Yamanaka), Yuko

Yashio (Sakie Takayama), Tadashi Date, Yoshihiro Hamaguchi, Tatsuo Hanabu, Hikaru Hoshi, Kuniko Miyake, Hotimi Nozoe, Kumeko Urabe.

Uguisu-jô no hanayome [*The Bride in Uguisu Castle*] (June 22, 1958)
Credits: Director and Screenplay: Shoji Matsumura; Producer: Yurin Nakamura; Cinematographer: Makoto Tsudoi; Format: Color and Toeiscope [2.35:1]; Musical Score: Tadashi Manjôme; Art Director: Choshiro Katsura; Sound: Toshirô Sasaki; Lighting Technician: Hiroshi Watada; Production Company and Distributor: Toei Company; Running Time: 87 minutes.
Cast: Minoru Chiaki (Lord Matsudaira), Takashi Shimura (Sir Ogata, Father of Princess Matsu), Ushio Akashi, Shûsuke Daimonji, Kensuke Hara, Yachiyo Kirishima, Kenji Kusumoto, Tsukie Matsuura, Otabe Michimaro, Masao Mishima, Hitomi Nakahara, Chieko Naniwa, Shintarô Nasu, Satomi Oka, Keiko Okawa, Hiroko Sakuramachi, Akiko Santo, Shin Tokudaiji, Michiko Tsukiyama, Namiji Umemura, Isao Yamagata, Yoshiko Yashioji, Entatsu Yokoyama, Keiko Yukishiro, Ryûtarô Ôtomo.

Ten to sen [*Point and Line*] (November 11, 1958)
Credits: Director: Tsuneo Kobayashi; Producer: Noboro Nezu; Screenplay: Matao Ide; Based on the Novel by Seichô Matsumoto; Cinematographer: Shizuka Fujii; Format: Ferraniacolor and Toeiscope [2.35:1]; Editor: Fumio Sôda; Musical Score: Chûji Kinoshita; Production Designer: Tatsu Tanabe; Assistant Director: Masuichi Iizuka; Sound Recordist: Masanobu Ôtani; Gaffer: Yasunojô Kawasaki; Production Company: Toei Tokyo; Distributor: Toei; Alternate English Title: *The Dead End*; Running Time: 85 minutes.
Cast: Hiroshi Minami (Kiichi Mihara), Isao Yamagata (Tatsuo Yasuda), Mieko Takamine (Ryoko), Yoshi Katô (Jutaro Toriumi), Takashi Shimura (Kasai), Ushio Akashi (Hasegawa), Takashi Kanda (Sayama's Brother), Akitake Kôno (Tsuchiya), Junji Masuda (Sasaki), Masao Mishima (Ishida), Masahiko Naruse (Kenichi Sayama), Chiaki Tsukioka (Yaeko), Tokue Hanazawa, Yûji Hori, Akiko Kazami, Kôji Kiyomura, Mitsue Komiya, Toshie Kusunoki, Sanae Mitsuoka, Yasushi Nagata, Akemi Nara, Masao Oda.

Jinsei gekijô [*Theater of Life*] (November 23, 1958)
Credits: Director: Toshio Sugie; Producer: Ichirô Satô; Screenplay: Ryuji Shiina, Toshio Yasumi; Based on the Novel by Shiro Ozaki; Cinematographer: Taiichi Kankura; Format/Aspect Ratio: Color and Tohoscope [2.35:1]; Musical Score: Yoshiyuki Kozu; Production Designer: Shinobu Muraki; Sound: Toshiya Ban, Masanobu Miyazaki; Lighting Technician: Toshio Takashima; Production Company and Distributor: Toho Company; Literal English Title: *Theater of Life: Youth Version*; Running Time: 111 minutes.
Cast: Ryô Ikebe, Hisaya Morishige, Takashi Shimura, Mitsukô Kasube. Hisako Takihana, Eijirô Tôno, Hiroshi (Yoichi) Tacikawa, Toshirô Mifune, Hideyo Amamoto, Hisao Dazai, Yû Fujuki, Hisaya Itô, Machiko Kitagawa, Yoshio Kosugi, Fuyuki Murakami, Rikie Sanjô, Ikio Sawamura, Yoshifumi Tajima.

Kakushi-toride no san-akunin [The Hidden Fortress] (December 28, 1958)

Credits: Director: Akira Kurosawa; Producers: Akira Kurosawa, Sanezumi Fujimoto; Screenplay: Ryûzô Kikushima, Hideo Oguni, Shinobu Hashimoto, Akira Kurosawa; Cinematographer: Kazuo Yamazaki [Ichio Yamazeki]; Assistant Camera: Takao Saitô; Format/Aspect Ratio: Black-and-White and Tohoscope [Anamorphic 2.35:1]; Processing: Tokyo Laboratory, Ltd.; Editor: Akira Kurosawa; Negative Cutter: Chozo Kobata; Musical Score: Masaru Satô; Production Designer: Yoshirô Muraki; Assistant Art Director: Shinko Kato; Costume Designer: Masahiro Katô [Kyoto Costume]; Hair Stylists: Yoshiko Matsumoto, Junjirô Yamada; Property Master: Kôichi Hamamura; Lighting Technician: Ichirô Inohara; Assistant Lighting Technician: Sei Arai; Chief Assistant Director: Mimachi Yanagase; Assistant Directors: Yasuyoshi Tajitsu, Yoshimitsu Sakano [Banno], Kan Sano, Yoichi Matsue, Masahiro Takase; Sound: Fumio Yanoguchi [Perspecta Stereo]; Sound Assistant: Yoshiro Miyamoto; Sound Mixer: Hisashi Shimonaga; Sound Effects Editor: Ichirô Minawa; Stills Photographer: Masao Fukuda; Horseback Riding Instructors: Shigeru Endo, Ienori Kaneko; Choreographer: Yoji Ken [Nichigeki]; Swordplay Instructor: Yoshio Sugino; Script Supervisor: Teruyo Nogami; Accountant: Kôichi Noguchi; Acting Office: Yûichi Yoshitake; Production Supervisor: Hiroshi Nezu; Production Assistant: Takushi [Takuyuki] Inoue; Production Company and Distributor: Toho Company; Alternate English Title: *Three Bad Men in a Hidden Fortress*; U.S. Release Date: October 6, 1960; Running Time: 126 minutes.

Cast: Toshirô Mifune (General Rokurota Makabe), Minoru Chiaki (Tahei), Kamatari Fujiwara (Matashichi), Susumu Fugita (General Heiei Tadokoro), Takashi Shimura (The Old General, Izumi Nagakura), Misa Uehara (Princess Yuki), Eiko Miyoshi (Old Lady-in-Waiting), Toshiko Higuchi (Farmer's Daughter Bought from a Slave Trader), Yû Fujiki (Barrier Guard), Yoshio Tsuchiya (Samurai on Horse), Kokuten Kôdô (Old Man in Front of Sign), Takeshi Katô (Fleeing, Bloody Samurai), Kôji Mitsui (Guard), Toranosuke Ogawa (Magistrate of the Bridge Barrier), Kichijirô Ueda (Slave Trader), Nakajirô Tomita, Yoshifumi Tajima (Potential Slave Buyers), Ikio Sawamura (Gambler), Sachio Sakai, Akira Tani (Captured Foot Soldiers), Makoto Satô, Niyoshi Kumaya, Shoichi ["Solomon"] Hirose, Takuzô [Jirô] Kumagai, Ichirô Chiba (Yamana Foot Soldiers), Yoshio Kosugi, Haruo Nakajima, Senkichi Ômura, Ryû Kuze (Akisuki Soldiers), Yutaka Sada (Guard at Bridge Barrier), Takeo Oyabigawa (Guard at Pass Barrier), Tadao Nakamaru (Young Man), Etsuro Saijô, Masayoshi Nagashima (Yamana Samurai), Fuminori Ôhashi (Samurai Who Buys Horse), Rinsaku Ogata (Second Young Man), Shin Ôtomo, Minoru Itô, Haruo Suzuki, Shigekatsu Kanazawa, Hiroyoshi Yamaguchi, Haruya Sakamoto (Samurai on Horseback), Nichigeki Dancing Team (Female Dancers), Kazuo Hinata, Shigemi Sunagawa.

Nichiren to môko daishûrai [Nichiren and the Great Mongol Invasion] (October 1, 1958)

Credits: Director and Screenplay: Kunio Watanabe; Producer: Masaichi Nagata; Planning Producer: Tsujii Hisakazu; Cinematographer: Takashi Watanabe; Format/Aspect Ratio: Color and Daieiscope [Anamorphic 2.35:1]; Musical Score:

Yuichi Yamada; Lighting Technician: Yuki Nakaoka; Production Company and Distributor: Daiei Film; Running Time: 145 minutes.
Cast: Kazuo Hasegawa (Nichiren), Takashi Shimura (Yasaburo), Shintarô Katsu (Shijo Kingo), Raizô Ichikawa (Hôjô Tokimune), Narutoshi Hayashi, Shoji Umewaka, Yatarô Kurokawa.

Ken wa shitte ita (1958)

Credits: Director: Kokichi Uchide; Screenplay: Renzaburô Shibata; Aspect Ratio: Toeiscope [2.35:1]; Production Company and Distributor: Toei; English Titles: *A Sword and Love, The Sword Knows*; Running Time: 90 minutes.
Cast: Hiromi Hanazono, Kunio Kaga, Eijirô Kataoka, Hitomi Nakahara, Kinnosuke Nakamura, Keiko Okawa, Takashi Shimura, Eitarô Shindô, Ryûnosuke Tsukigata, Harumi Urazato, Kasho Nakamura, Sôji Kiyokawa, Yasushi Nagata, Juro Hoshi, Hanshiro Iwai.

Tetsuwan toshu Inao monogatari (March 21, 1959)

Credits: Director: Ishirô Honda; Producer: Sadao Sugihara; Screenplay: Yoshio Hasuike, Ryûzô Kikushima; Cinematographer: Seiichi Endô; Format/Aspect Ratio: Black-and-White and Tohoscope [2.35:1]; Processing: Kinuta Laboratories, Tokyo; Musical Score: Yûji Koseki; Production Designer: Tatsuo Kita; Sound Recordist: Chôshichirô Mikami; Sound Effects Editor: Masanobu Miyazaki; Lighting Technician: Toshio Takashima; Executive in Charge of Production: Tasuo Kuroda; Production Company and Distributor: Toho Company; English Title: *Inao: Story of an Iron Arm*; Running Time: 106 minutes.
Cast: Tatsuyoshi Ehara (Naoshi Kurihara), Kamatari Fujiwara (Gentarô Matsuda), Toshiko Higuchi (High School Girl B), Yuriko Hoshi (High School Girl A), Kazuhisa Inao (Himself), Takashi Itô (Inao as a Child), Akemi Kato (Nurse), Kanta Kisaragi (Kunizo), Tokurô Konishi (Himself), Takuzô (Jirô) Kumagai (Doctor), Kô Mishima (Masao Matsuda), Fuyuki Murakami (Mr. Shudô), Chieko Nakakita (Oyoshi Matsuda), Chieko Naniwa (Kameno Inao), Yutaka Sada (Owner of Daikokuya Inn), Sachio Sakai (Sadayuki Inao), Akiko (Michiko) Sawamura (Emiko Inao), Masanori Shimura (Himself), Takashi Shimura (Kyûsaku Iano), Yumi Shirakawa (Setsuko Sugiura), Hajime Shirata (Fan), Katsumi Tezuka (Yoshikawa), Haruko Tôgô (Hisako Inao), Ran Yamamoto (Teruhisa Inao), Keiko Yanagawa (Noriko Matsuda), Mitsuo Yoshida (Inao as a High School Student), Yutaka Nakayama, Kyorô Sakurai.

Kotan no kuchibue [A Whistle in My Heart] (March 29, 1959)

Credits: Director: Mikio Naruse; Producer: Tomoyuki Tanaka; Executive in Charge of Production: Teruo Maki; Screenplay: Shinobu Hashimoto; Based on the Novel by Nubuo Ishimori; Cinematographer: Masao Tamai; Format/Aspect Ratio: Eastmancolor and Tohoscope [2.35:1]; Editor: Eiji Ooi; Musical Score: Akira Afukube; Production Designer: Satoru Chûko; Assistant Director: Kôji Kajita; Sound: Masao Fujiyoshi, Asashi Shimonaga; Gaffer: Chôshirô Ishii; Production Company and Distributor: Toho Company; Alternate English Title: *Whistling in Kotan*; Running Time: 126 minutes.

Cast: Ken Kubo [Yamauchi] (Yutaka), Ryoko [Yoshiko] Kôda (Masu), Masayuki Mori (Hatanka), Akira Takurada (Art Teacher), Kumi Mizuno (Fue), Takashi Shimura (Tazawa), Kyû Sazanka (Uncle), Bokuzen Hidari (School Janitor), Eiko Miyoshi ("Granny" Ikante), Akira Kubo, Yoshifumi Tajima, Yoshio Tsuchiya, Kunio Ôtsuka, Chieko Nakakita, Fuyuki Murakami, Akira Sera, Yutaka Sada, Shôko Seki, Shirô Tsuchiya, Yoshiko Matsuba, Atsuko Ichinomiya, Masaaki Tachibana, Yôichirô Kitigawa, Akio Kasuma, Shigeo Katô, Masayoshi Kawabe, Kôichi Satô, Kôji Uruki, Toku Ihara, Akiko Takebe, Masami Yamazaki, Sumio Takahashi, Yoshiko Yoshino, Hiroshi Kodama.

Taiyô ni somuku mono (June 21, 1959)

Credits: Director: Tatsuo Sakai; Producers: Tsuneyasu Matsumoto, Hiroshi Moroishi; Screenplay: Tatsuo Asano, Masaharu Segawa, Shin'ichi Sekizawa; Story: Ichirô Kashihara; Cinematographer: Tomoichi Kuramochi; Format: Black-and White; Editor: Mitsuzû Miyata; Musical Score: Seiichi Suzuki; Art Director: Hiroshi Mizutani; Sound: Kaichi Watanabe; Lighting Technician: Yoichiro Ichinose; Production Company: Shochiku Kyoto; Running Length: 6 reels.

Cast: Jin'ichi Amano (Senkichi, Ken's Stepfather), Jô Azumi (Ôshita), Kakuko Chino (Hiroko, Ichikawa's Daughter), Fumio Hayashi (Sugiura), Keiko Hibino (Mayako, Madame at Bar), Isao Ichikawa (Harada), Yasunori Irikawa (Sato), Tatsuya Ishiguro (Gondô, Police Chief), Tokuji Kobayashi (Morikawa), Wakako Kunitomo (Moyo, Madame at Bar), Kyoko Kusajima (Hamano's Mother), Asao Matsumoto (Matsumura, Inspective), Machiko Mizuhara (Sumiko, Tokunaga's Wife), Mitsuo Nagata (Nkajima, Section Manager), Hideshi Nakahara (Ken Yasui), Satoshi Nishida (Ônuki, Detective), Yoshihiko Nozaki (Yamaguchi), Kikutaro Onoe (Nodori, Policeman), Kenji Sawai (Kiyoshi Hamano), Gen Shimizu (Haneda, Committeeman), Takashi Shimura (Ichikawa, Detective), Naoki Sugiura (Tsuchiya, Detective), Shinji Takano (Nomura, Newspaper Reporter), Haruo Tanaka (Tokunaga, Detective), Kinuyo Tanaka (Fumi, Ichikawa's Wife), Kiyoko Tsuji (Tsuchiya's Mother), Hironobu Uno (Hisao, Ichikawa's Son).

Sengoku gunto-den [*The Saga of the Vagabonds*] (November 23, 1959)

Credits: Director: Toshio Sugie; Producers: Sanezumi Fujimoto, Kazuo Nishino; Screenplay: Akira Kurosawa, Sadao Yamanaka; Story: Jûrô Miyoshi; Cinematographer: Akira Suzuki; Format/Aspect Ratio: Color and Tohoscope [2.35:1]; Musical Score: Ikuma Dan; Production Designer: Takeo Kita; Production Company and Distributor: Toho Company; Running Time: 115 minutes.

Cast: Toshirô Mifune (Rokuro Kai), Kôji Tsuruta (Taro Toki), Yôko Tukasa (Tazu), Misa Uehara (Princess Koyuki), Takashi Shimura (Saemon Toki), Minoru Chiaki (Jibu), Akihiko Hirata (Jiro Hidekuni), Seizaburô Kawazu (Hyoe Yamana), Yoshifumi Tajima (Jiro's Vassal), Yoshio Kosugi, Kenzô Tabu, Akira Tani, Ren Yamamoto, Sachio Sakai, Shin Ôtomo, Tadao Nakamaru, Haruo Nakajima.

Kagero ezu (September 27, 1959)

Credits: Director: Teinosuke Kinugasa; Screenplay: Minoru Inuzuka, Teinosuke

Kinugasa; Based on the Novel by Seichô Matsumoto; Cinematographer: Kimio Watanabe; Format: Color and Daieiscope [2.35:1]; Musical Score: Ichiro Saito; Production Designer: Yoshinobu Nishioka; English Title: *Stop the Old Fox*; Production Company and Distributor: Daei Studios; Running Time: 117 minutes.
Cast: Raizô Ichikawa (Shinosuke Shimada), Fujiko Yamamoto (Tomi/Toyoharu), Osamu Takizawa (Nakano), Michiyo Kogure (Omiyo no kata), Eijirô Yanagi (Ogosho), Seizaburô Kwazu (Mizuno), Takashi Shimura (Ryoan), Yatarô Kurokawa (Matazaemon Shimada), Michiko Ai (Kikuawa), Tokiko Mita (Kasumi).

Nippon tanjô (November 1, 1959)

Credits: Director: Hiroshi Inagaki; Producers: Sanezumi Fujimoto, Tomoyuki Tanaka; Screenplay: Ryûzô Kikushima, Toshio Yasumi; Based on the Legends "*Kojiki*" and "*Nihon Shoki*"; Cinematographer: Kazuo Yamada; Format/Aspect Ratio: Agfacolor and Tohoscope [2.35:1]; Processing: Tokyo Laboratory, Ltd., Editor: Hitoshi Hira; Musical Score: Akira Ifukube; Production Designers: Kisaku Itô, Hiroshi Ueda; Executive in Charge of Production: Katsutaro Kawakami; Chief Assistant Director: Teruo Maru; Sound: Yoshio Nishikawa, Hisashi Shimonaga; Lighting Technician: Shoshichi Kojima; Director of Special Effects: Eiji Tsuburaya; Special Effects, Optical Photography: Hidesaburo [Shuzaburo] Araki; Art Director of Special Effects: Akira Watanabe; Director of Special Effects Photography: Sadamasa Arikawa; Special Effects Lighting: Kuichirô Kishida; Matte Process: Hiroshi Mukoyama; Stills Photographer: Matsuo Yoshizaki; Choreographer: Enjaku Kiyokata; Production Company and Distributor: Toho Company; English Titles: *Birth of Japan, The Three Treasures, Age of the Gods*; U.S. Release Date: December 20, 1960; Running Time: 182 minutes.
Cast: Toshirô Mifune (Prince Yamato Takeru), Yôko Tsukasa (Princess Oto Tachibana), Akihiko Hirata (Kibino Takehiko), Kyôko Kagawa (Princess Miyazu), Kôji Tsuruta (Younger Kumaso), Takashi Shimura (Elder Kumaso), Setsuko Hara (Amaterasu, the Sun Goddess), Kumi Mizuno (Azami), Misa Uehara (Princess Kushinada), Kinuyo Tanaka (Princess Yamato), Akira Kubo (Prince Iogi), Akira Takarada (Prince Wakatarashi), Ganjirô Nakamura (Emperor), Eijirô Tôno (Ootomo), Jun Tazaki (Ootomo's Kurohiko), Ken'ichi ["Enoken"] Enomoto, Ikio Sawamura, Ichirô Arishima, Norihei Miki (Gods of Yaoyorozu), Hideyo Amamoto (Spectator at God's Dance), Shizuko Muramatsu (Goddess Izanami), Kichijirô Ueda (Kume's Yahara), Akira Sera (Anazuchi), Minosuke Yamada (Okuri of Kunizo), Michiyo Tamaki (Ehime), Haruko Sugimura (Narrator), Kakuko Murata (Obaki's Mother), Chieko Nakakita (Tenazuchi), Nobuo Otowa (Goddess of Anenouzume), Hajime Izu (Prince Oousu), Bokuzen Hidari (God Amenominaka), Yû Fujiki (Okabi), Jun'ichirô Mukai (Moroto), Kôzô Nomura (Ootomo Makeri), Hisaya Itô (Ootomo Kodate), Ko Mishima (Yakumo), Yoshio Kosugi (Inaba), Keiju Kobayashi (God Amatsumaura), Daisuke Katô (God Fudetama), Hiroyuki Wakita (God Izanagi's Son), Kingoro Yanagiya (God of Omoikane), Taro Asahiyo (God of Tachikara), Akira Tani, Keiko Muramatsu, Yasuhisa Tsutsumi, Katsumi Tezuka, Shôichi Hirose, Yutaka Sada, Shin Ôtomo, Senkichi Ômura, Tadashi Okabe, Gorô Sakurai, Fuyuki Murakami, Mitsuo Tsuda, Ryû Kuze, Masayoshi

Nagashima, Akira Kitano, Shirô Tsuchiya, Nadao Kirino, Fumindo Matsuo, Masao Masuda, Takuzô [Jirô] Kumagai, Koji Uemura, Yasuhiro Shigenobu, Haruya Sakamoto, Rinsaku Ogata, Izumi Akimoto, Hiroyoshi Yamaguchi, Akira Yamada, Kôji Iwamoto, Yoshiko Ieda, Midori Kishida. Michiko Kawa, Misako Asuka, Toshiko Higuchi, Teruko Mita, Harumi Ueno, Harold Conway.

Sora kakeru hanayome (1959)

Credits: Director: Yoshiaki Banshô; Screenplay: Ryôzô Kasahara; Cinematographer: Tishio Ubukata; Format: Color; Production Company and Distributor: Shôchiku Eiga; English Title: *The High-Flying Bride*; Running Time: 75 minutes.

Cast: Ineko Arima (Marume Scichimiya), Takashi Shimura (Shichibei), Hisao Toake (Yoshitarô), Sadako Sawamura (Sayoko), Sadaji Takahashi (Jirô Akiyama), Akiko Koyama (Kazue Shiomi).

Shobushi to sono musume (November 10, 1959)

Credits: Director: Kôji Shima; Producer: Kazuyoshi Takeda; Screenplay: Masato Ide; Format: Black-and-White; Running Time: 110 minutes.
Cast: Takashi Shimura.

Kêdamonô no torû michi (1959)

Credits: Director: Hideo Sekigawa; Screenplay: Susumu Saji; Cinematographer: Hanjirô Nakazawa; Format: Black-and-White; Musical Score: Chûji Kinoshita; Production Company: Toei; English Title: *Beast's Passage*.
Cast: Ken Takakura, Katsuo Nakamura, Mitsue Komiya, Isao Kimura, Takashi Shimura, Yoshiko Sakuma, Rin'ichi Yamamoto.

Beran me-e geisha (1959)

Credits: Director: Eiichi Koishi; Screenplay: Kazuo Kasahara, Ryôzô Kasahara; Cinematographer: Shôei Nishikawa; Format/Aspect Ratio: Color and Toeiscope [2.35:1]; Musical Score: Masao Yoneyama; Production Company: Toei Tokyo; Distributor: Toei Company; English Title: *The Prickly Mouthed Geisha*; Running Time: 86 minutes.
Cast: Hibari Misora (Koharu), Shinjirô Ebara [Ehara] (Kenishi), Takashi Shimura (Masagoro Kosugi), Hisao Toake, Mitsuko Miura, Taiji Tonoyama.

Karakkaze yarô [*Afraid to Die*] (March 23, 1960)

Credits: Director: Yasuzo Masumura; Producer: Masaichi Nagata; Planning Producer: Hiroaki Fujii; Screenplay: Hideo Ando, Ryuzo Kikushima; Cinematographer: Hiroshi Murai; Format/Aspect Ratio: Color and Daieiscope [2.35:1]; Editor: Tatsuji Nakashizu; Musical Score: Tetsuo Tsukahara; Production Designers: Takesaburô Watanabe; Production Company and Distributor: Daei Studios; Alternate English Title: *Man of the Biting Wind*; Running Time: 96 minutes.
Cast: Yukio Mishima (Takeo Asahina), Ayako Wakao (Yoshie Koizumi), Keizô Kawasaki (Shoichi Koizumi), Eiji Funakoshi (Susumu Aikawa), Takashi Shimura

(Gohei Hirayama), Yaeko [Yoshie] Mizutani (Masako Katori), Michiko Ono [Toshiko Hasegawa] (Ayako Takatsu), Shigeru Kôyama (Masa), Jun Negami (Yusaku Sagara), Reizaburô Yamamoto (Daizaburo), Mayumi Kurata, Ken Mitsuda, Mantarô Ushio.

Hawai Middowei daikaikûsen: Teiheiyô no arashi [*Storm Over the Pacific*, aka *I Bombed Pearl Harbor*] (April 26, 1960)

Credits: Directors: Shûe Matsubayashi, (English Version) Hugo Grimaldi; Producer: Tomoyuki Tanaka; Producer (English Version): Hugo Grimaldi; Executive Producers (English Version): Riley Jackson, Robert Patrick; Screenplay: Shinobu Hashimoto, Takeo Kunihiro; Cinematographer: Kazuo Yamada; Format/Aspect Ratio: Eastmancolor and Tohoscope [2.35:1]; Processing: Toyo Laboratories; Editors: Kôichi Iwashita, (English Version) Hugo Grimaldi; Musical Score: Ikuma Dan; Production Designers: Takeo Kita, Kiyoshi Shimizu; Executive in Charge of Production: Katsutaro Kawakami; Chief Assistant Directors: Kôji Kajita, Yasuyoshi Tajitsu; Assistant Director: Yasuyoshi Kazane; Sound Recordists: Masanobu Miyazaki, Yoshio Nishikawa; Sound Effects: Hisashi Shimonaga; Sound Effects Editor: Ichirô Minawa; Special Effects Director: Eiji Tsuburaya; Chief Assistant Special Effects Director: Teruyoshi Nakano; Special Effects Cinematographer: Sadamasa Arikawa; Special Effects Art Director: Akira Watanabe; Optical Photography: Hidesaburo [Shuzaburo] Araki; Production Company and Distributor: Toho Company; U.S. Release Date: November 29, 1961 [Parade Releasing Organization]; Running Time: 118 minutes; U.S. Release Running Time: 98 minutes.
Cast: Yôsuke Natsuki (Lieutenant Koji Kitami), Toshirô Mifune (Admiral Isoroku Yamaguchi), Kôji Tsurata (Lieutenant Tomonari), Makoto Satô (Lieutenant Matsuura), Aiko Mimasu (Sato), Jun Tazaki (Captain), Takashi Shimura (Tosaku), Misa Uehara (Keiko, Kôji's Sweetheart), Susumu Fugita (Admiral Yamamoto), Keiju Kobayashi, Tatsuya Mihashi, Hiroshi Koizumi, Akira Takarada, Seizaburô Kawazu, Ken Uehara, Ken'ichi ["Enoken"] Enomoto, Akiko Hirata, Tadao Nakamaru, Yoshio Tsuchiya, Kô Mishima, Hisaya Itô, Hiroshi Tachikawa, Yoshio Kosugi, Sachio Sakai, Ren Yamamoto, Tetsu Nakamura, Senkichi Ômura, Yutaka Sada, Shin Ôtomo, Fuyuki Murakami, Yoshifumi Tajima, Shunichi Segi, Kendo Yashiki, Jun Funado, Yutaka Oka, Nadao Kirino, Akira Oka, Koji Ishikawa, Haruo Nakajima, Hiroshi [Yû] Sekita, Daisuke Katô, Ryô Ikebe, Akira Kubo, Takuzô [Jirô] Kumagai, Gentaro Nakajima, Masaki Shinohara, Paul Frees (multiple voices [English-dubbed version]).

Yoru no nagara [*Evening Stream*] (July 12, 1960)

Credits: Director: Mikio Naruse, Yûzô Kawashima; Producers: Mikio Naruse, Sanezumi Fujimoto; Screenplay: Zenzô Matsuyama, Toshirô Ide; Story: Mikio Naruse, Yûzô Kawashima; Cinematographers: Jun Yasumoto, Tadashi Iimura; Format/Aspect Ratio: Color and Tohoscope [2.35:1]; Processing: Kinuta Laboratories, Tokyo; Editor: Eiji Ooi; Musical Score: Ichirô Saitô; Production Designers: Tatsuo Kita, Takashi Matsuyama; Executive in Charge of Production: Hidehisa Suga; Assistant Directors: Masanobu Nishikiori, Samaji Nonagase;

Sound Recordists: Masao Fujiyoshi, Ariaki Hosaka; Sound Effects Editor: Hisashi Shimonaga; Gaffers: Choshiro Ishii, Toshio Takashima; Costume Researcher: Yoshio Ueno; Production Company and Distributor: Toho Company; Alternate English Title: *The Lovelorn Geisha*; Running Time: 111 minutes.

Cast: Yôko Tsukasa (Miyako Fujimura), Isuzu Yamada (Aya Fujimura), Akira Takarada (Takiguchi), Yumi Shirakawa (Shinobu Sonoda), Takashi Shimura (Koichiro Sonoda), Yaeko [Yoshie] Mizutani (Kintaro), Mitsuko Kusabue (Masae Ichihana), Yoriko Hoshi (Akemi), Etsuko Ichihara (Beniko), Machiko Kitagawa (Komachi), Tadao Nakamaru (Makoto Takamizawa), Teruko Nagaoka (Kaoru Sonoda), Masumi Okada (English Teacher), Michiko Yokoyama (Mari), Tatsuya Mihashi, Aiko Mimasu, Fubuki Koshiji, Fuyuki Murakami, Kazuo Kitamura, Toki Shiozawa, Jun Hongô, Yoshiko Ieda, Masaharu Iimuro, Masayoshi Kawebe, Yoshie Kihira, Kiyoshi Kodama, Rumi Konishi, Mieko Kurenai, Yoshiko Kôda, Hiromi Mineoka, Kumeko Otowa, Yasuhiko Saijô, Rikie Sanjô, Chie Sugiura, Masaaki Tachibana, Isao Tsuzuki, Akira Yamada, Kunio Ôtsuka.

Otoko tai otoko [*Man Against Man*] (August 14, 1960)

Credits: Director: Senkichi Taniguchi; Screenplay: Ichirô Ikeda, Ei Ogawa; Cinematographer: Rokurô Nishigaki; Format/Aspect Ratio: Eastmancolor and Tohoscope [2.35:1]; Processing: Kinuta Laboratories, Tokyo; Musical Score: Masaru Satô; Production Designer: Yoshirô Muraki; Chief Assistant Director: Takeshi ["Ken"] Matsumori; Sound: Shôichi Fujinawa [Perspecta Stereo]; Sound Effects Editor: Masanobu Miyazaki; Lighting Technician: Tsuruzô Nishikawa; Production Company and Distributor: Toho Company; U.S. Release Date: March 17, 1961; Running Time: 116 minutes.

Cast: Toshirô Mifune (Kaji), Ryô Ikebe (Kikumori), Takahi Shimura (Chotaro Masue), Yûzô Kayama (Toshio Masue), Jun Tazaki (Boss Tsukamoto), Akihiko Hirata (Torimi), Yumi Shirakawa (Mineko Nishijo), Akemi Kita (Harumi), Yuriko Hoshi (Natsue), Yutaka Sada (Wada), Shôichi ["Solomon"] Hirose (Genpachi), Yoshifumi Tahima (Taro), Ikio Sawamura (Santa), Sachio Sakai (Shinchan), Shin Ôtomo (Kitagawa), Ren Yamamoto (Igarashi), Nadao Kirino (Tsuchiya), Tadao Nakamaru (Machida), Hideyo Amamoto (Killer), Yoshio Tsuchiya (Detective Yoshizawa), Michiko Kawamoto (Tome), Fumindo Matsuo (Doctor), Haruo Nakajima (Casino Customer).

Warui yatsu hodo yoku nemuru [*The Bad Sleep Well*] (September 15, 1960)

Credits: Director: Akira Kurosawa; Producers: Akira Kurosawa, Tomoyuki Tanaka; Screenplay: Akira Kurosawa, Hideo Oguni, Eijirô Hisaita, Ryûzô Kikushima, Shinobu Hashimoto; Suggested by an Unproduced Screenplay by Mike Inoue; Cinematographer: Yuzuru Aizawa; Assistant Cameraman: Takao Saitô; Format/Aspect Ratio: Black-and White and Tohoscope [2.35:1]; Processing: Kinuta Laboratories, Tokyo; Editor: Akira Kurosawa; Assistant Editor: Reiko Kaneko; Musical Score: Masaru Satô; Production Designer: Shoji Kurihara; Costume Designer: Shoji Kurahara [Kyoto Costume]; Chief Assistant Director: Shirô Moritani; Assistant Directors: Yoshimitsu Sakano [Banno], Kazuko Kawakita, Yôichi

Matsue, Kiyoshi Nishimura; Assistant Art Director: Jun Sakuma; Property Master: Kôichi Hamamura; Hair Stylists: Tomoko Asami, Junjirô Yamada; Sound Recordist: Fumio Yanoguchi [Perspecta Stereo]; Sound Assistant: Masanao Uehara; Sound Mixer: Hisashi Shimonaga; Sound Effects Editor: Ichirô Minawa; Lighting Technician: Ichirô Inohara; Assistant Lighting Technician: Sei Arai; Stills Photographer: Masao Fukuda; Transportation Coordinator: Ginzo Osumi; Production Supervisor: Hiroshi Nezu; Production Assistant: Hidehiko Eguchi; Script Supervisor: Teruyo Nogami; Production Companies: Kurosawa Production Co., Toho Company; Distributor: Toho Company; U.S. Release Date: January 22, 1963; Running Time: 151 minutes.
Cast: Toshirô Mifune (Kôichi Nishi), Masayuki Mori (Public Corporation Vice President Iwabuchi), Kyôko Kagawa (Yoshiko Nishi, His Daughter), Tatsuya Mihashi (Tatsuo Iwabuchi, His Son), Takashi Shimura (Public Corporation Administrative Officer Moriyama), Kô Nishimura (Public Corporation Contract Officer Shirai), Takeshi Katô (Foreign Car Dealer Itakura, the Real Koishi Nishi), Kamatari Fujiwara (Public Corporation Assistant-to-the-Chief Wada), Chishû Ryû (Public Prosecutor Nonaka), Seiji Miyaguchi (Prosecutor Okakura), Kôji Mitsui (Reporter A), Ken Mitsuda (Public Corporation President Arimura), Nobuo Nakamura (Legal Adviser), Susumu Fugita (Detective), Kôji Minamibara (Prosecutor Horiuchi), Gen Shimizu (Miura, Managing Director of the Construction Company, Who Commits Suicide), Yoshifumi Tajima (Reporter B), Someshô Matsumoto (Construction Company President Hatano), Yoshio Tsuchiya (ADA Secretary), Kyû Sazanka (Construction Company Executive Director Kaneko), Kin Sugai (Tomoko Wada), Natsuko Kahara (Mrs. Furuya), Nobuko Tashiro (Mrs. Moriyama), Atsuko Ichinomiya (Mrs. Ariyama), Toshiko Higuchi (Wada's Daughter), Jun Kôndô (Reporter D), Yutaka Sada (Wedding Receptionist), Ikio Sawamura (Taxi Driver), Kisashi [Hisa] Yokomori (Reporter C), Kunie Tanaka (Hitman), Gorô Sakurai (Prosecutor), Ryôji Shimizu (Public Corporation Management Section Worker), Sôji Ubukata, Shirô Tsuchiya (Construction Company Employees), Kyôko Ozawa, Hiromi Mineoka (Iwabuchi Maids), Akemi Ueno (Safety Deposit Box Rental Receptionist).

Gambare! Bangaku [*Master Fencer Sees the World*] (October 16, 1960)

Credits: Director: Shûe Matsubayashi; Producers: Sanezumi Fujimoto, Hisao Ichikawa; Screenplay: Matsuo Kishi, Kaneto Shindô; Story: Sadao Yamanaka; Cinematographer: Kôzô Okazaki; Format/Aspect Ratio: Color and Tohoscope [2.35:1]; Editor: Shûichi Anbara; Production Designer: Yasuhide Kato; Supervising Sound Editor: Yoshio Nishikawa; Lighting Technician: Kazuo Shimomura; Production Companies: Takarazuka Motion Picture Company, Ltd., Toho Company; Distributor: Toho Company; Alternate English Title: *Perils of Bangaku*; U.S. Release Date: April 7, 1961.
Cast: Keiju Kobayashi, Takashi Shimura, Hiroshi Koizumi, Reiko Dan, Yukiko Shimazaki, Tôru Abe, Asao Uchida.

Sararîman Chûshingura (December 25, 1960)

Credits: Director: Toshio Sugie; Producer: Sanezumi Fujimoto; Screenplay: Ryôzô

Kasahara, Yasuo Ihara (idea); Cinematographer: Taiichi Kankura; Format/Aspect Ratio: Eastmancolor and Tohoscope [2.35:1]; Processing: Kinuta Laboratories, Tokyo; Editor: Chozo Kobata; Musical Score: Yoshiyuki Kozu; Production Designer: Yoshirô Muraki; Production Manager: Boku Morimoto; Chief Assistant Director: Susumu Kodama; Sound: Chôshichirô Mikami; Sound Effects Editor: Hisashi Shimonaga; Lighting Technician: Mitsuo Kaneko; Stills Photographer: Kazuhiko [Isei] Tanaka; Production Company and Distributor: Toho Company; English Title: *Salary Man Chushingura;* Running Time: 100 minutes.
Cast: Misaya Morishige (Yoshio Oishi), Daisuke Katô (Jyusaburo Onodera), Keiju Kobayashi (Heitaro Teraoka), Yôko Tsukasa (Keiko), Reiko Dan (Konami), Sonomi Nakajima (Yasuko Hosobe), Mitsukô Kasabue (Saiko), Michiyo Aratama (Geisha Kayoji), Akira Takarada (Kohei Hayano), Yôsuke Natsuki (Riki Oishi), Tatsuya Mihashi (Sadagoro), Asami Kuji (Ritsuko Oishi), Eijirô Tôno (Gonosuke Kira), Ichirô Arishima (Kube Ono), Kyû Sazanka (Koichi Bannai), Takashi Shimura (Honzo Kadokawa), Eijirô Yanagi (Naoyoshi Ashikaga), Shin Ôtomo (Hara), Kiyoshi Kodama (Okano), Tatsuyoshi Ehara (Isogai), Yû Fujiki (Akagaki), Mutoshi Yanami (Takebayashi), Ikio Sawamura (Kurabayashi), George Riker (Henri Richard), Kingorô Yanagiya (Owner of Soba Restaurant Yamashita), Ryô Ikebe (Takuni Asano), Toshirô Mifune (Kazuo Momoi).

Sen-hime goten (1960)

Credits: Director: Kenji Misumi; Screenplay: Fuji Yahiro; Cinematographer: Yasukazu Takemura; Format: Color; Musical Score: Ichirô Saitô; Production Company and Distributor: Daiei Studios; English Title: *Princess Sen in Edo;* Running Time: 97 minutes.
Cast: Fujiko Yamamoto (Princess Sen), Kojirô Hongô (Kihachiro Tahara), Katsuhiko Kobayashi (Manjiro Kobayashi), Tamao Nakamura (Okatsu), Isuzu Yamada (Kisaragi), Ganjirô Nakamura (Ieyasu Tokugawa), Takashi Shimura (Sadonokami Honda), Osamu Takizawa (Tajimanokami Yagyu), Ryûzô Shimada (Dewanokami Sakazaki), Toshio Chiba (Jubei Kuroki), Yôichi Funaki (Bichûnokami Kobori), Jôji Tsurumi (Yoshinosuke), Tokiko Mita (Yuri), Reiko Fujiwara [Namiji Yamato] (Kin'ya Sadoshima), Ikuko Môri (Ayame), Ryôsuke Kagawa (Gemban Ikeda), Ryônosuke Azuma (Kamon'nokami Ii), Gen Shimizu (Fujiuchi), Shinobu Araki (Jigen), Yasuhiko Shima (Hidetada Tokugawa), Hisako Takihana (Satsuki), Kumeko urabe (Omaki), Ryoko Kamo (Kogiku), Junko Mikawa (Momonoi), Kimiko Tachibana (Hanagiri), Rumiko Komachi (Chigusa), Setsuko Hama (Yayoi), Kanae Kobayashi (Ogen), Yôko Wakasugi (Sagiri), Teruko Ômi (Mikasa), San'emon Arashi (Tonomo Honda), Kôichi Kuzuki (Utanokami Sakai), Shôzô Nanbu (Sahei Hikoshima) Seishirô Hara, Saburô Date, Yû Sakurai, Sentarô Godai, Ichiro Takakura, Masayoshi Kikuno, Tadashi Iwata, Tokio Oki, Yûshi Hamada, Kôichi Aihara, Gen Kimura, Tokurin Takeda, Hidehiko Ishikura, Yasuchika Araki, Masao Nishikawa, Kiyoko Fujikawa.

Ôsaka-jô monogatari [*The Story of Osaka Castle,* aka *Daredevil in the Castle*] (January 3, 1961)

Credits: Director: Hiroshi Inagaki; Producer: Tomoyuki Tanaka; Screenplay: Hiroshi Inagaki, Tegeshi Kimura; Based on the Novel by Genzo Murakami;

Cinematographer: Kazuo Yamada; Format/Aspect Ratio: Eastmancolor and Tohoscope [2.35:1]; Processing: Tokyo Laboratory, Ltd.; Editor: Kôichi Iwashita; Musical Score: Akira Ifukube; Production Designer: Hiroshi Ueda; Chief Assistant Director: Masahiro Takase; Sound: Yoshio Nishikawa; Lighting Technician: Shoshichi Kojima; Director of Special Effects: Eiji Tsuburaya; Special Effects Assistant: Teruyoshi Nakano; Special Effects Art Director: Akira Watanabe; Directors of Special Effects Photography: Sadamasa Arikawa, Sokei Tomioka; Special Effects Lighting: Kuichirô Kishida; Optical Photographers: Yukio Manoda, Taka Yuki; Matte Process: Hiroshi Mukoyama; Stills Photographer: Matsuo Yoshizaki; Production Company and Distributor: Toho Company; U.S. Release Date: June 6, 1961 [Frank Lee International, Inc.]; Running Time: 95 minutes. **Cast**: Toshirô Mifune (Mohei), Kyôko Kagawa (Ai), Yuriko Hoshi (Senhime), Yoshiko Kuga (Kobue), Isuzu Yamada (Yodogami), Yôsuke Natsuki (Chomonshu Kimura), Jun Tazaki (Teikabo Tsutsumi), Danko Ichikawa (Saizo Muin), Akihiko Hirata (Hayatonosho [Hayato] Susukida), Takashi Shimura (Katagiri), Koedako Kuroiwa (Nobuo), Tetsurô Tanba (Sadamasa Ishikawa), Tadao Nakamaru (Hyogo), Ryôsuke Kagawa (Michiiku Itamiya), Yû Fujiki (Danuemon Hanawa), Seizaburô Kawazu (Harunaga Ono), Susumu Fugita (Katsuyasu Sakakibara), Hanshirô Iwai (Hideyoshi Toyotomi), Sachio Sakai (Kai Hayami), Yoshio Kosugi (Gidayu Fujimoto), Kichijirô Ueda (Jinbei, Equipment Shop Owner), Chieko Nakakita (Kyoko of Yae), Haruko Tôgô (Ono Woman), Hideyo Amamoto (Interpreter), Jun'ichirô Makai (Kumoi), Shôji Ikeda (Chusho Nanjo), Shirô Tsuchiyo (Tosho Horita), Akira Tani (Rice Shop Owner), Shin Ôtomo (Itamiya Manager), Katsumi Tezuka (Shuma Ono), Hans Horneff, Bill Bassman (Portuguese Sailors), Ren Yamamoto, Senkichi Ômura, Ikio Sawamura, Kôji Uno, Yasuhisa Tsutsumi, Haruo Nakajima, Toshiko Nakano, Osman Yusuf, Shigeki Ishida, Jirô [Takuzô] Kumagai, Ryû Kuze, Tadashi Okabe, Yû Sekita.

Harekosode (January 9, 1961)

Credits: Director: Kimiyoshi Yasuda; Producer: Kazuyoshi Takeda; Screenplay: Yoshikata Yoda; Based on the Novel by Matsutarô Kawaguchi; Cinematographer: Senkichirô Takeda; Format: Black-and-White; Musical Score: Seitarô Omori; Art Director: Yoshizo Uesato; Sound: Tsuchitarô Hayashi; Production Company: Daiei Kyoto; Distributor: Daiei Eiga; English Title: *Clear Weather*; Running Time: 84 minutes.
Cast: Kazuo Hasegawa, Yumeji Tsukioka, Yachiyo Ôtori, Jun Negami, Takashi Shimura, Yoshiaka Hanayagi.

Zoku sararîman Chûshingura (February 25, 1961)

Credits: Director: Toshio Sugie; Producer: Sanezumi Fujimoto; Screenplay: Ryôzô Kasahara; Based on an Idea by Yasuo Ihara; Cinematographer: Taiichi Kankura; Format/Aspect Ratio: Eastmancolor and Tohoscope [2.35:1]; Musical Score: Yoshiyuki Kozu; Production Designer: Yoshirô Muraki; Sound: Chôshichirô Mikami; Lighting Technician: Mitsuo Kaneko; Stills Photographer: Kazuhiko Tanaka; Production Company and Distributor: Toho Company; English Title: *Salary Man Chushingura Sequel*; Running Time: 110 minutes.

Cast: Hisaya Morishige (Yoshio Oishi), Daisuke Katô (Jyusaburo Onodera), Keiju Kobayashi (Heitaro Teraoka), Yôko Tsukasa (Keiko), Reiko Dan (Konami), Sonomi Nakajima (Yasuko Hosobe), Mitsukô Kasabue (Saiko), Michiyo Aratama (Geisha Kayoji), Akira Takarada (Kohei Hayano), Yôsuke Natsuki (Chikara), Tatsuya Mihashi (Sadagoro), Asami Kuji (Ritsuko), Ichirô Arishima (Kube Ono), Eijirô Tôno (Gonosuke Kira), Kyû Sazanka (Koichi Bannai), Takashi Shimura (Honzo Kadokawa), Kiyoshi Kodama (Okano), Tatsuyoshi Ehara (Isogai), Yû Fujuki (Akagaki), Mutoshi Yanami (Takebayashi), Ikio Sawamura (Kurabayashi), Kingorô Yanagiya (Owner of Soba Restaurant Yamashita), Toki Shiozawa (Hostess A), Ayumi Sonoda (Geisha A), Toshirô Mifune (Kazuo Momoi).

Yôjinbô [*Yojimbo*] (April 25, 1961)

Credits: Director, Associate Producer and Story: Akira Kurosawa; Executive Producers: Tomoyuki Tanaka, Ryûzô Kikushima; Screenplay: Akira Kurosawa, Ryûzô Kikushima; Cinematographer: Kazuo Miyagawa; Assistant Camera: Takao Saito; Format/Aspect Ratio: Black-and-White and Tohoscope [Anamorphic 2.35:1]; Processing: Toho Developing Company; Editor: Akira Kurosawa; Assistant Editor: Raiko Kaneko; Musical Score: Masaru Satô; Production Designer/Costume Designer: Yoshirô Muraki; Costumer: Masahiro Katô [Kyoto Isho]; Hair Stylists: Yoshiko Matsumoto, Junjirô Yamada; Chief Assistant Director: Shirô Moritani; Assistant Director: Masanobu Deme; Property Master: Kôichi Hamamura; Assistant Art Director: Yoshifumi Honda; Sound Recordists: Chôshichirô Mikami, Hisashi Shimonaga [Perspecta Stereo]; Sound Mixer: Masanobu Miyazaki; Assistant Sound: Zen Shida; Sound Effects Editor: Ichirô Minawa; Lighting Technician: Chôshirô Ishii; Assistant Lighting Technician: Shôji Kaneko; Stills Photographer: Masao Fukuda; Costumer: Masahiro Katô; Transportation Coordinator: Ginzo Osumi; Choreographer: Hiroshi Kanesu; Swordplay Technique: Ryû Kuze; Swordplay Instructor: Yoshio Sugino; Script Supervisor: Teruyo Nogami; Production Supervisor: Hiroshi Nezu; Assistant Production Supervisor: Shigeru Nakamura; Production Companies: Kurosawa Production Company, Toho Company; Distributor: Toho Company; U.S. Release Date: September 13, 1961 [Seneca International, Ltd.]; Running Time: 110 minutes.

Cast: Toshirô Mifune (Sanjuro Kuwabutake), Tatsuya Nakadai (Unosuke, Gunfighter), Yôko Tsukasa (Nui), Isuzu Yamada (Orin), Daisuke Katô (Inokichi, Unosuke's Older Brother), Seizaburô Kawazu (Seibêi, Brothel Operator, Orin's Husband), Takashi Shimura (Tokuemon, the Saké Brewer), Hiroshi Tachikawa (Yoichiro, Orin and Seibei's Son), Yôsuke Natsuki (Kohei's Rebellious Son Who Longs for a Short and Exciting Life), Eijirô Tôno (Gonji, Tavern Keeper), Kamatari Fujiwara (Tazaemon, the Silk Merchant and Head of the Village), Ikio Sawamura (Hansuke, the Corrupt Official), Atsushi Watanabe (The Cooper, Coffin-Maker), Susumu Fugita (Homma, the Cowardly but Wise *Yojimbo* Who Skips Town), Kyû Sazanka (Ushitora, Tokuemon's Gang Boss), Kô Nishimura (Ronin Kuma), Takeshi Katô (Ronin Kobuhachi), Ichirô Nakatani (First Samurai), Sachio Sakai (First Foot Soldier), Akira Tani (Kame), Namigoro [Tsunagorô] Rashômon (Kannuki, the Giant *Yojimbo*), Yoshio Tsuchiya (Kohei, the Unlucky Gambler), Gen Shimizu (Magotaro), Yutaka

Sada (Matsukichi), Shin Ôtomo (Kumosuke), Shôichi ["Solomon"] Hirose (Ushitora Follower), Hideyo Amamoto (Yahachi), Shôji Ôki (Sukeju), Fuminori Ôhashi (Second Samurai), Hiroshi Yoseyama (Farmer), Senkichi Ômura (Traveler), Fumiko Homma (Farmer's Ex-Wife), Ryusuke Nishio, Naoya Kusama, Nadao Kirino, Jun Ôtomo, Jun'ichirô Kukai, Fumiyoshi Kamagaya, Rinsaku Ogata (Seibei Followers), Shinpei Takagi, Akio Kusama, Yasuzô Ogawa, Hiroshi Takagi, Haruya Sakamoto, Fumio Kogushi (Ushitora Followers), Ichirô Chiba (Second Foot Soldier), Yoko Terui, Hiromi Mineoka, Michiko Kawa (Women at Seibei's House).

Fundoshi isha (1961)

Credits: Director: Hiroshi Inagaki; Producer: Tomoyuki Tanaka; Screenplay: Ryûzô Kikushima; Based on the Novel by Minoru Nakano; Cinematographer: Kazuo Yamada; Format/Aspect Ratio: Black-and-White and Tohoscope [2.35:1]; Musical Score: Ikuma Dan; Production Company and Distributor: Toho Company; English Title: *Life of a Country Doctor*; U.S. Release Date: May 1961; Running Time: 116 minutes.

Cast: Hisaya Morishige (Keisai Koyama), Setsuko Hara (Iku, Wife of Keisai), Yôsuke Natsuki (Hangoro), Chiemi Eri (Osaki), Sô Yamamura (Dr. Meikai Ikeda), Mutoshi Happa (Security Guard), Noriko Honma (Sugi), Seiji Ikeda (Merchant), Shigeki Ishida (Ushi), Haruya Katô (Sanshita, Yakuza Wanna-be), Yoshio Kosugi (Gonsuke), Jiro Kumagaya (Government Official), Tsuruko Mano (Farmer's Wife), Fumindo Matsuo (Merchant), Jun'ichirô Mukai (Matahachi), Fuyuki Murakami (Seamon), Kakuko Murata (Patient's Wife), Masayoshi Nagashima (Farmer), Chieko Nakakita (Matsu), Ichirô Nakatani (Genta), Yutaka Sada (Kanji), Etsuo Saijô (Medicine Salesman), Gorô Sakurai (Man Carrying Passengers Across the River), Ikio Sawamura (Horse Monger), Gen Shimizu (Kiuemon), Takashi Shimura (Matsuoemon), Haruo Suzuki (Vice-President), Yoshifumi Tajima (Seibei), Toshio Takakura (Takeo), Mayumi Tamura (Miyo), Akira Tani (Kitisuke), Hisao Toake (Nagasakiya), Yasuhisa Tsutsumi (Yoshikichi), Kôji Uno (Farmer), Unpei Yokoyama (Boat Pilot).

Katsukake Tokijirô [*The Gambler's Code*] (June 14, 1961)

Credits: Director: Kazuo Ikehiru; Producer: Sadao Zaizen; Screenplay: Masaharu Matsumura, Masao Uno; Based on the Novel by Shin Hasegawa; Cinematographer: Kazuo Miyagawa; Format/Aspect Ratio: Color and Daieiscope [2.35:1]; Musical Score: Ichirô Saitô; Editor: Kôji Taniguchi; Art Director: Yoshinobu Nishioka; Assistant Director: Toshiaki Kunihara; Set Designer: Yoshiki Miwa; Sound: Shôichi Kondô; Fight Choreographer: Shôhei Miyauchi; Gaffer: Genken Nakaoka; Stills Photographer: Masamitsu Nishiji; Color Timer: Shôzô Tanaka; Executive in Charge of Production: Tooru Yoshioka; Production Company and Distributor: Daei; Running Time: 87 minutes.

Cast: Raizô Ichikawa (Katsukake Tokijirô), Michiyo Aratama (Okinu), Takashi Shimura (Hacchônawate Tokubei), Haruko Sugimura (Oroku), Ryûzô Shimada (Mutsuda no Sanzô), Fujio Suga (Tomeda no Sukegorô), Yoshio Inaba (Shôten), Shigeru Aoki (Tarôkichi), Toshio Chiba (Akada Sanjûrô), Shinobu Araki (Gen-emon), Hisako Takihana (Otowa), Gen Shimizu, Mitsugu Terajima, Fujio Murakami, Sumao Ishihara, Ichirô Takakura, Jun Fujikawa, Hajime Koshikawa, Gen Kimura, Tokio Oki, Kôichi Aihara, Esuko Kamiwaki, Kyôko Higashiyama.

Ai to honoho to (June 17, 1961)

Credits: Director: Eizô Sugawa; Producer: Sanezumi Fujimoto; Screenplay: Kaneto Shindô; Based on the Story "Chosen" by Shintarô Ishihara; Cinematographer: Fukuzô Koizumi; Format/Aspect Ratio: Eastmancolor and Tohoscope [2.35:1]; Processing: Kinuta Laboratories, Tokyo; Musical Score: Masaru Satô; Production Designer: Iwao Akune; Sound Recordist: Masanao Uehara; Sound Effects Editor: Masanobu Miyazaki; Lighting Technician: Mitsuo Kaneko; Production Company and Distributor: Toho Company; English Title: *Challenge to Live*; U.S. Release Dates: February 1962; April 7, 1964; Running Time: 99 minutes.

Cast: Tatsuya Mihashi (Izaki), Yôko Tsukasa (Saeko Sawada), Yumi Shirakawa (Keiko Takamine), Masayuki Mori (Sawada), Susumu Fugita (Niimura), Kumi Mizuno (Kazuko Uchimi), Akira Kubo (Kunihiko Uchimi), Takashi Shimura (Yoshii), V. S. Shes (Prime Minister Mesacin), Chanty Zebey (Effran), Schuan (Mafia), Eitarô Ozawa (Ministry of Foreign Affairs), Kyôko Kishida (Geisha), Akihiko Hirata (Kyo Sawada), Eijirô Tôno (Kudo), Tatsuo Matsumura (Lawyer Agawa), Torahiko Hamada (Writer), Yûsuke Takita (Editor).

Mosura [*Mothra*] (July 31, 1961)

Credits: Director: Ishirô Honda, (English version) Lee Kresel; Producer: Tomoyuki Tanaka, (English version) David D. Horne; Screenplay: Shin'ichi Sekizawa, (English version) Peter Fernandez, Robert Myerson; Based on the Novel *The Luminous Fairies and Mothra* by Shin'ichirô Nakamura, Takehiko Fukunaga and Yoshie Hotta; Cinematographer: Hajime Koizumi; Format/Aspect Ratio: Eastmancolor [2.35:1]; Processing: Far East Laboratories, Tokyo; Editing: Kazuji Taira; Musical Score: Yûji Koseki; Composer (Song "Mosura No Uta"): Susumu Ike; Art Directors: Teruaki [Kimei] Abe, Takeo Kita; Production Manager: Shin Morita; Assistant Director: Samaji [Masaji] Nonagase; Sound Recordists: Shôichi Fujinawa, Masanobu Miyazaki [Perspecta Stereo]; Special Cinematography Director: Eiji Tsuburaya; Special Cinematography: Sadamasa Arikawa (Photography);Yukio Manoda Optical Photography), Kuichirô Kishida (Lighting), Akira Watanabe (Art), Hiroshi Mukoyama (Special Effects), Kan Narita (Production Manager); Lighting: Toshio Takashima; Production Company and Distributor: Toho Company; U.S. Release Date: May 10, 1962 [Columbia Pictures Corporation]; Running Time: 101 minutes; U.S. Release Running Time: 90 minutes.

Cast: Furanki Sakai (Senichiro "Sen-chan" Fukuda, aka "Bulldog"), Hiroshi Koizumi (Dr. Shin'ichi Chûjô), Kyôko Kagawa (Photographer Michi Hanamura), Yumi Itô, Emi Itô (Shobijin), Jerry [Jeri] Itô (Kurâruku Neruson), Ken Uehara (Dr. Harada), Akihiko Hirata (Doctor), Kenji Sahara (Helicopter Pilot), Seizaburô Kawazu (General), Takashi Shimura (News Editor), Yoshio Kosugi (Ship Captain), Yoshifumi Tajima (Military Advisor), Ren Yamamoto, Haruya

Katô, Rinsaku Ogata (Ship Survivors), Ko Mishima (Ship Survivor [scenes deleted]), Tetsu Nakamura, Hiroshi Takagi, Kôji Iwamoto, Toshio Miura, Akira Wakamatsu, Hiroshi Akitsu (Nelson's Henchmen), Shôichi Hirose, Toshihiko Furuta (Dam Workers), Yasuhisa Tsutsumi (Woodcutter), Teruko Mita (Rest House Owner's Wife), Mitsuo Tsuda, Tadashi Okabe, Akio Kusama (Surveyors), Masamitsu Tayama (Shinji Chûjô), Yutaka Nakayama (Radio Communicator), Osman Yusuf [Joni Yusefu] (Nelson's Rolisican Henchman), Obel Wyatt [Ôberu Waiatto] (Dr. Roff), Harold Conway [Harorudo Esu Kon′uei] (Rolisican Ambassador), Robert Dunham [Robâto Danhamu] (Police Chief of New Kirk City), Akira Yamada (Island Worshipper), Kôji Uno, Mitsuo Matsumoto, Hiroyuki Satake (Police Officers), Wataru Ômae, Kazuo Hinata (Officials), Keisuke Matsuyama (Shipmate), Kôji Kamimura (Bit), Katsumi Tezuka (Neck of Mosura Larva), Takeo Nagashima, Kô Hayami (Island Dancers), Hideo Shibuya [Shinpei Mitsui] (Journalist), Yutaka Oka (Captain of Transport), Kazuo Imai (Announcer), Haruo Nakajima (Head of Mosura Larva), Gorô Sakurai (Member of Task Force), Junnosuke Suda, Akira Kitchôji, Toshiko Nakano, Tsurue Ichimanji (scenes deleted), Yoshio Katsube, Ryôji Shimizu, Yôichirô Kitagawa [Ryûchi Hosokawa], Junpei Natsuki, Toku Ihara, Yû [Hiroshi] Sekita, Masaaki Tachibana, Tatsuo Sakai, Nanako Yamada, Nichigeki Danshingu Ch▨mu.

Kuroi gashû dainibu: Kanryû [*Structure of Hate*] (November 12, 1961)

Credits: Director: Hideo Suzuki; Producer: Reiji Miwa; Screenplay: Tokuhei Wakao; Based on the Novel by Seichô Matsumoto; Cinematographer: Yuzuru Aizawa; Format/Aspect Ratio: Black-and-White and Tohoscope [2.35:1]; Musical Score: Ichirô Saitô; Production Designer: Yasuhide Kato; Sound Recordist: Ariaki Hosaka; Sound Effects Editor: Hisashi Shimonaga; Lighting Technician: Ichirô Inohara; Production Company and Distributor: Toho Company; Running Time: 96 minutes.
Cast: Ryô Ikebe, Michiyo Aratama, Akihiko Hirata, Tetsurô Tanba, Takashi Shimura, Seiji Miyaguchi.

Futari no musuko [*Different Sons*] (November 12, 1961)

Credits: Director: Yasuki Chiba; Executive Producer: Sanezumi Fujimoto; Screenplay: Zenzô Matsuyama; Cinematographer: Masao Tamai; Format/Aspect Ratio: Eastmancolor and Tohoscope [2.35:1]; Processing: Kinuta Laboratories, Tokyo; Editor: Eiji Ooi; Musical Score: Akira Ifukube; Production Designer: Iwao Akune; Chief Assistant Director: Mikio Komatsu; Sound Recordist: Toshiya Ban; Sound Effects Editor: Hisashi Shimonaga; Lighting Technician: Toshio Takashima; Production Company and Distributor: Toho Company; U.S. Release: October 19, 1962; Running Time: 95 minutes.
Cast: Akira Takarada (Kensuke), Yûzô Kayama (Shoji), Kamatari Fujiwara (Father), Yôko Fujiyama (Daughter), Daisuke Inoue (Salesman), Yûko Mochizuki (Mother), Rumiko Sasa (Girl), Yumi Shirakawa (Kensuke's Wife), Senkichi Ômura (Salesman), Yû Fujiki, Mie Hama, Chisako Hara, Hiroshi Koizumi,

Yutaka Sada, Sachio Sakai, Ikio Sawamura, Takashi Shimura, Masami Taura, Haruko Tôgô.

Ishin no kagarabi [*Restoration Fire*] (1961)

Credits: Director: Sadatsugu Matsuda; Format/Aspect Ratio: Color and Toeiscope [2.35:1]; Production Company and Distributor: Toei Company; Running Time: 86 minutes.
Cast: Chikage Awashima (Ofusa), Chiezô Kataoka (Hijikata Toshizo), Noriko Kitazawa (Omine), Kenji Kusumoto (Okita Soji), Akitake Kôno (Heikichi), Satomi Oka (Oshino), Eiji Okada (Yamanami Keisuke), Koinosuke Onoe (Okabe Hoyama), Kôtarô Satomi (Ando Kazuma), Takashi Shimura (Yahei), Haruo Tanaka (Yasuzo), Jôtarô Togami (Saito Hajime).

Tsubaki Sanjûrô [*Sanjuro*] (January 1, 1962)

Credits: Director and Associate Producer: Akira Kurosawa; Executive Producers: Tomoyuki Tanaka, Ryûzô Kikushima; Screenplay: Akira Kurosawa, Hideo Oguni, Ryûzô Kikushima; Based on the Story "*Hibi Heian*" ["Peaceful Days"] by Shûgorô Yamamoto; Cinematographers: Fukuzô Koizumi, Takao Saitô; Format/Aspect Ratio: Black-and-White and Tohoscope [Anamorphic 2.35:1]; Processing: Kinuta Laboratories, Tokyo; Editor: Akira Kurosawa; Assistant Editor: Reiko Kaneko; Musical Score: Masaru Satô; Production Designer/Costume Designer: Yoshirô Muraki; Assistant Art Director: Tsuneo Shimura; Property Master: Shoji Jinko; Costumes: Shoji Kurahara [Kyoto Costume]; Hair Stylists: Yoshiko Matsumoto, Junjirô Yamada; Chief Assistant Director: Shirô Moritani; Assistant Directors: Masanobu Deme, Yoichi Matsue, Yoshikune Wada; Assistant Cameras: Kazutani Hara, Katsuhiro Kato; Lighting Technician: Ichirô Inohara; Assistant Lighting Technician: Isao Hara; Sound Recordists: Wataru Konuma, Hisashi Shimonaga [Perspecta Stereo]; Sound Assistant: Jin Sashida; Sound Effects: Ichirô Minawa; Stills Photographer: Masao Fukuda; Fencing Adviser: Ryû Kuze; Script Supervisor: Teruyo Nogami; Transportation: Isamu Miwano; Production Supervisor: Hiroshi Nezu; Production Assistant: Shigeru Kishima; Production Companies: Kurosawa Production Co., Toho Company; Distributor: Toho Company; U.S. Release Date: May 7, 1963; Running Time: 96 minutes.
Cast: Toshiro Mifune (Sanjûrô Tsubaki), Tatsuya Nakadai (Hanbei Moroto), Keiju Kobayashi (Kimura, the Captured Samurai in the Closet), Yûzô Kayama (Iori Izaka, Leader of the Nine Young Samurai), Reiko Dan (Chidori, Matsuda's Daughter), Takashi Shimura (Kurofuji), Kamatari Fujiwara (Takebayashi), Takako Irie (Mrs. Matsuda, the Chamberlain's Wife), Masao Shimizu (Kikui, the Superintendent), Yûnosuke Itô (Matsuda, the Chamberlain); *Young Samurai*: Akira Kubo (Morishima, the Younger Brother), Hiroshi Tachikawa (Kawahara), Yoshio Tsuchiya (Hirose), Kunie Tanaka (Yasukawa), Tatsuyoshi Ehara (Sekiguchi), Akihiko Hirata (Terada), Kenzô Matsui (Yata), Tatsuhiko Hari (Morishima); Toranosuke Ogawa (Sandyu, of the Kobuto Family), Sachio Sakai (Ashigaru), Toshiko Higuchi (Koiso), Yutaka Sada (Kikui Samurai), Shin Ôtomo, Shôichi Hirose, Minoru Itô, Kôji Uruki, Hiroyoshi Yamaguchi, Fuminori Ôhashi.

Zoku sararîman shimizu minato (March 7, 1962)

Credits: Director: Shûe Matsubayashi; Producer: Sanezumi Fujimoto; Screenplay: Ryôzô Kasahara; Cinematographer: Rokurô Nishigaki; Format/Aspect Ratio: Color and Tohoscope [2.35:1]; Processing: Kinuta Laboratories, Tokyo; Editor: Kôichi Iwashita; Musical Score: Yoshiyuki Kozu; Production Designer: Kyoe Hamagami; Chief Assistant Director: Katsumi Iwauchi; Sound Recordist: Fumio Yanoguchi; Sound Effects Editor: Hisashi Shimonaga; Lighting Technician: Tsuruzô Nishikawa; Production Company and Distributor: Toho Company; Running Time: 90 minutes.
Cast: Hisaya Morishige, Asami Kuji, Keiju Kobayashi, Daisuke Katô, Norihei Miki, Yôko Tsukasa, Eijirô Tôno, Yuriko Hanabusa, Yôsuke Natsuki, Yôko Fujiyama, Mitsukô Kasabue, Seizaburô Kawazu, Akira Takarada, Takashi Shimura, Yû Fujiki, Shigeki Ishida, Daisuke Inoue, Ikio Sawamura, Toki Shiozawa.

Long Way to Okinawa (March 7, 1962)

Credits: Director: Hideo Suzuki; Producers: Reiji Miwa, Sadao Sugihara; Screenplay: Toshirô Ide; Cinematographer: Yuzuru Aizawa; Format/Aspect Ratio: Color and Tohoscope [2.35:1]; Musical Score: Sei Ikeno; Production Designer: Yasuhide Kato; Production Company and Distributor: Toho Company; U.S. Release Date: April 26, 1963.
Cast: Akira Takarada, Yuriko Hoshi, Mie Hama, Nobuko Otowa, Yû Fujiki, Takashi Shimura, Keiko Awaji.

Kurenai no sora (March 21, 1962)

Credits: Director: Senkichi Taniguchi; Producer: Tomoyuki Tanaka; Screenplay: Shin'ichi Sekizawa; Cinematographer: Masaharu Utsumi; Format: Color and Tohoscope [2.35:1]; Editor: Yoshitami Kuriowa; Musical Score: Masaru Satô; Chief Assistant Director: Susumu Takebayashi; Aerial Photographer: Takao Saitô; Special Effects Director: Eiji Tsuburaya; Special Effects Art Director: Akira Watanabe; Director of Special Effects Photography: Sadamasa Arikawa; Special Effects Lighting: Kuichirô Kishida; Special Effects Cameraman: Sokei Tomioka; Production Company and Distributor: Toho Company; English Titles: *Blood in the Sky*, *Scarlet Sky*, *The Crimson Sky*; Running Time: 91 minutes.
Cast: Yûzô Kayama, Makoto Satô, Yôsuke Natsuki, Kumi Mizuno, Yôko Fujiyama, Akiko Wakabayashi, Takashi Shimura, Tadao Nakamaru, Kunie Tanaka, Tatsuo Matsumura, Yoshio Tsuchiya, Ikio Sawamura, Hideyo Amamoto, Masanobu Oki, Yutaka Nakayama, Yutaka Sada, Fuyuki Murakami, Yoshifumi Tajima, Kôji Iwamoto [Hironobu Wakamoto], Hiroshi Takagi, Hideo Shibuya [Shinpei Mitsui].

Yôsei Gorasu [Gorath, the Monstrous Star] (March 21, 1962)

Credits: Director: Ishirô Honda; Producer: Tomoyuki Tanaka; Screenplay: Takeshi Kimura, (1964 U.S. Version) John Meredyth Lucas; Story: Jojiro Okami;

Cinematographer: Hajime Koizumi; Format/Aspect Ratio: Eastmancolor and Tohoscope [2.35:1]; Processing: Tokyo Laboratory, Ltd.; Editor: Reiko Kaneko; Musical Score: Kan Ishii; Production Designers: Teruaki Abe, Takeo Kita; Sound Recording Engineer: Toshiya Ban [Perspecta Stereo]; Sound Effects: Hisashi Shimonaga; Assistant Directors: Katsume Ishida, Kôji Kajita, Shôji Kuroda, Masashi Matsumoto; Lighting Technician: Toshio Takashima; Special Effects Director: Eiji Tsuburaya; Assistant Director of Special Effects: Teruyoshi Nakano; Special Effects Production Manager: Kan Narita; Special Effects: Sokei Tomioka; Special Effects Art Director: Akira Watanabe; Assistant Optical Technician: Kôichi Kawakita; Director of Special Effects Photography: Sadamasa Arikawa; Special Effects Lighting: Kuichirô Kishida; Optical Effects: Yukio Manoda, Taka Yuki; Matte Work: Hiroshi Mukoyama; Stunt Choreographer: Haruo Nakajima; Stills Photographer: Tessei Tanaka; Production Manager: Yasuaki Sakamoto; Production Company and Distributor: Toho Company; U.S. Distributor: Brenco Pictures Corporation; U.S. Release Date: May 15, 1964; Running Time: 88 minutes; U.S. Release Running Time: 83 minutes.

Cast: Ryô Ikebe (Dr. Tazawa, Astrophysicist), Yumi Shirakawa (Tomoko Sonoda), Akira Kubo (Tatsuma Kanai, Cadet Astronaut), Kumi Mizuno (Takiko Nomura), Hiroshi Tachikawa, Yukihiko Gondô (Wakabayashi, Pilots of Ôtori), Akihiko Hirata (Endô, Captain of Ôtori), Kenji Sahara (Saiki, Vice Captain of Ôtori), Jun Tazaki (Raizô Sonoda, Tomoko's Father), Ken Uehara (Dr. Kôno, Astrophysicist), Takashi Shimura (Kensuke Sonoda, Paleontologist), Seizaburô Kawazu (Tada, Minister of Finance), Kô Mishima (Sanada, Engineer), Sachio Sakai (Physician), Takamaru Sasaki (Prime Minister Seki), Kô Nishimura (Murata, Secretary of Space), Eitarô Ozawa (Kinami, Minister of Justice), Masaya Nihei (Ito, Astronaut of Ôtori), Kôzô Nomura, Toshiko Furuta, Masayoshi Kawabe (Observers of Ôtori), Keiko Sata (Prime Minister's Secretary), Hideyo Amamoto (Man in Bar), George Furness [Jôji Fânesu] (Hooverman), Ross Benette [Rosu Benetto] (Gibson), Jun'ichirô Mukai (Space Base Security Guard), Nadao Kirino (Manabe, Takiko's Lover), Fumio Sakashita (Hayao Sonoda, Tomoko's Brother), Ikio Sawamura (Taxi Driver), Yoshiyuki Uemura, Tadashi Okabe (Mathematicians of Ôtori), Rinsaku Ogata, Ken'ichirô Maruyama (Engineers of Ôtori), Yasushi Matsubara, Yasuhiko Saijô, Katsumi Tezuka (Radio Operators of Ôtori), Kôji Uno, Bin Furuya, Saburô Kadowshi, Hideo Shibuya [Shinpei Mitsui], Yoshio Katsube, Haruya Sakamoto, Haruo Suzuki, Hideo Ôtsuka (Reporters), Akira Yamada, Hiroshi Takagi (Engineers of Hayabusa), Toshitsugu [Kôji] Suzuki, Kôji Ishikawa (Pilots of Hayabusa), Wataru Ômae, Takuya Yuki (Mathematicians of Hayabusa), Ichirô Shôji, Yasuo Araki (Observers of Hayabusa), Kazuo Imai (Radio Operator of Hayabusa), Yûsuke Suzuki (Fuel Checkout of Hayabusa), Takuzô [Jirô] Kumagai, Hiroshi Akitsu, Ryûtarô Amami, Ichirô Chiba, Shinjirô Hirota, Keiichirô Katsumoto, Akira Kitchôji, Akio Kusama, Someshô Matsumoto, Takashi Narita, Keiji Sakakida, Junnosuke Suda, Kamayuki Tsubono, Keisuke Yamada, Shin Yoshida, Yasumasa Ônishi (Government Personnel), Kenzo Echigo (Astronaut of Otori/Observer of Space Station), Tsurue Ichimanji (Maid of Sonods Family), Toku Ihara, Kuniyoshi Kashima, Shigeo Katô, Masahide Matsushita, Jirô Mitsuaki, Yutaka Oka, Osman Yusuf (Workers in South Pole Base), Saburo Iketani (News Anchor), Minoru Itô, Ikuo Kawamura (Astronauts of Ôtori), Edo Kin

(Representative of U.S.S.O.), Haruo Nakajima (Maguma, Walrus-like Reptilian Monster), Junpei Natsuki (Man at Funeral), Ryôji Shimizu (Base Designer), Kôichi Satô; English-dubbed Version: Enver Altenbay, Hank Brown, Ted Gunther, Ralph Jesser (Members in South Pole Base), Henrî Ban (Man in Convention Hall), Hans Horneff (Dr. König), William Eidelson, Paul Frees, Virginia Gregg, Vic Perrin, William Conrad (Voices)

Kujira gami [*Killer Whale,* aka *The Whale God*] (July 15, 1962)
Credits: Director: Tokuzô Tanaka; Producer: Masaichi Nagata; Screenplay: Kaneto Shindô; Cinematographer: Setsuo Kobayashi; Format/Aspect Ratio: Black-and-White and Daieiscope [2.35:1]; Musical Score: Akira Ifukube; Production Designer: Shigeo Mano; Special Effects Director: Chikara Komatsubara; Special Effects Photography: Hiroshi Ishida; Special Effects Art Director: Takesaburô Watanabe; Production Company and Distributor: Daiei; Running Time: 100 minutes.
Cast: Kyoko Enami (Toya), Kôjiro Hongô (Shaki), Takashi Shimura (Village Elder), Shiho Fujimura, Kôji Fujiyama, Shintaro Katsu, Bontarô Miake, Chieko Muruta, Michiko Takano, Kosuke Takemura, Kichijirô Ueda.

Chûshingura [*47 Samurai*] (November 3, 1962)
Credits: Director: Hiroshi Inagaki; Producers: Tomoyuki Tanaka, Hiroshi Inagaki, Sanezumi Fujimoto, (1963 U.S. Version) Edward Landberg; Screenplay: Toshio Yasumi; Based on the 1746 Kabuki Play Cycle *Kanadehon Chûshingura* by Izumo Takeda, Senru Namiki and Shoraku Miyoshi; Cinematographer: Kazuo Yamada; Format/Aspect Ratio: Eastmancolor and Tohoscope [2.20:1]; Processing: Tokyo Laboratory, Ltd.; Editor: Kôichi Iwashita; Musical Score: Akira Ifukube; Production Designer: Kisaku Itô; Assistant Art Director: Hiroshi Ueda; Sound: Yoshio Nishikawa; Sound Mixer: Hisashi Shimonaga; Chief Assistant Directors: Teruo Maru, Masahiro Takase; Lighting Technician: Shoshichi Kojima; Director of Special Effects: Eiji Tsuburaya; Choreographer: Ryû Kuze; Stills Photographer: Matsuo Yoshizaki; Production Manager: Shotaro Kawakami; Production Company and Distributor: Toho Company; U.S. Release Dates: October 3, 1963; 1966; Running Time: 207 minutes; U.S. Release Running Times: 108 minutes (1963); 204 minutes (1966).
Cast: Koshiro Matsumoto (Chamberlain Kuranosuke Oishi), Yûzô Kayama (Takuminokami Asano), Tatsuya Mihashi (Yasubei Horibe), Akira Takarada (Gunbei Takada), Yôsuke Natsuki (Kin'emon Okano), Makoto Satô (Kazuemon Fuwa), Tadao Takashima (Jûjirô Hazama), Seizaburô Kawazu (Chûzaemon Yoshida, Asano Official), Takashi Shimura (Hyôbu Chisaka), Daisuke Katô (Kichiemon Terasaka), Keiju Kobayashi (Awajinokami Wakisaka), Ryô Ikebe (Chikara Tsuchiya, Kira's Next-door Neighbor), Setsuko Hara (Riku Oishi, the Chamberlain's Wife), Yôko Tsukasa (Aguri Asano), Reiko Dan (Okaru, Kichiemon's Sister), Yuriko Hoshi (Otsuya, the Carpenter's Sister), Yumi Shirakawa (Ume), Kumi Mizuno (Saho, a Spy and Samurai Shiota's Sister), Mie Hama (Woman Refugee), Nami Tamura (Woman), Yôko Fujiyama (Miyuki, the Asano Maid), Junko Ikeuchi (Ofumi, of the Tea Shop), Keiko Awaji (Otoki, Hanbei's Wife),

Appendix A

Mitsukô Kusabue (Notsubone Toda), Michiyo Aratama (Ukigumo), Hisaya Morishige (Hanbei, Owner of the Secret Headquarters), Furanki Sakai (Heigorô, a Carpenter), Norihei Miki (Toshibei, the Male Geisha), Kingorô Yanagiya (Otokichi, of the Tatami Shop), Yoshitomi ["Keaton"] Masuda (Tachû Matsubara), Mutoshi Yanami (Tokuzô, of the Ueki Shop), Tôru Yuri (Nonta, Heigoro's Cousin), Toshiaki Minami (Denpachi, Heigoro's Cousin), Kyû Sazanka (Debashu Yanagisawa), Ichirô Arishima (Lord Denpachirô Tamura), Hiroshi Koizumi (Gengo Ôtaka), Yû Fujiki (Yushichi Takebayashi), Akira Kubo (Lord Sakyônosuke Date), Akihiko Hirata (Yajuemon Okajima), Kenji Sahara (Jûrôzaemon Isogai, Asano Samurai), Hiroshi Tachikawa (Aminori Uesugi), Tatsuyoshi Ehara (Daigaku Asano), Tadao Nakamaru (Heihachiro Kobayashi), Sachio Sakai (Shusui Kishima, a Spy), Yoshio Tsuchiya (Matanosho Shoita, Saho's Brother), Kamatari Fujiwara (Kyubei Kusuya, the Innkeeper), Jun Tazaki (Kiken Murakami), Susumu Fugita (Yosubei Kajikawa), Ken Uehara (Seikanji, of the Chunagons), Jun Funato (Sanjyuji Kai zuka), Kiyoshi Kodama (Hannojo Sugaya), Hisaya Itô (Sezaemon Oishi), Kôzô Nomura (Sandayu Muramatsu), Kô Mishima (Tozaemon Hayami), Kunio Ôtsuka (Hanpei Hirano), Ren Yamamoto (Yogoro Kanzaki, Asano Samurai), Hideyo Amamoto (Takano, of the Chunagons), Nadao Kirino (Kihachirô Okamoto), Heihachirô ["Henry"] Ôkawa (Katafu Kanse), Shigeki Ishida (Rishichi), Akira Tani (Hachiemon Hoshi), Yoshifumi Tajima (Shuzen Wakisaka), Ikio Sawamura (Yasuzô, Tatami Maker), Yoshio Kosugi (Yahei Hattori, Yasubei's Tough Father), Sonomi Nakajima (Otama, of the Drinking Place), Machiko Kitagawa (Okiyo, the Bathing Guard), Keiko Yanagawa (Shinano), Mieko Kurenai (Osen), Misako Asuka (Shioji), Yeako Izumo (Sasaya's Hairdresser), Tsuruko Mano (Mature Woman at Edo), Haruko Tôgô (Okyô, Sasaya's Wife), Atsuko Ichinomiya (Otomi, Kyubei's Wife), Chieko Nakakita (Ofude), Ryôsuke Kagawa (Souemon Hara), Sôji Kiyokawa (Matazaemon Fujii), Unpei Yokoyama (Matsuemon, Heigoro's Uncle), Haruya Katô (Kichichiyo), Yôji Misaki (Heihachirô Kondô), Gen Shimizu (Gensuke Koga), Jôtarô Togami (Ikkaku Shimizu), Sadako Sawamura (Tomiko, Konosuke's Wife), Kumeko Otowa (Haruno), Teruko Mita (Raku), Noriko Sakabe (Ruri), Naoko Sakabe (Kû), Senkichi Ômura (Concerned Citizen at Collapsed Bridge), Shin Ôtomo (Bungonokami Shinigawa), Yutaka Nakayama (Drunkard A), Mitsuo Tsuda (Masakichi), Keiichirô Katsumoto (Hisakazu Seki), Hiroshi Akitsu (Jûnai Onodera), Haruo Suzuki (Draper), Jun Kuroki (Gengarô Kobori), Kôji Iwamoto (Genzo Akagaki), Naoya Kusakawa (Gengoemon Suzuki), Akira Yamada (Juheiji Sugino), Junpei Natsuki (Hachisuke), Kôichi Satô (Jûrobei Saitô), Jirô Mitsuaki (Kihei Muramatsu), Ichirô Chiba (Yanagihara, of the Dainagons), Shôji Ikeda (Hikoemon Yasui), Gorô Sakurai (Drunkard B), Junichiro Mukai (Rihei Inoko), Hakuô Matsumoto [Somegorô Ichikawa] (Emoshichi Yatô), Kichiemon [Man'nosuke] Nakamura (Sanpei Kayano), Matagorô Nakamura (Tsunayoshi Tokugawa), Shikaku Nakamura (Kurobei Ono), Komazô Ichikawa (Kanroku Chikamatsu), Kichijûrô Nakamura (Shogen Okuyuki), Danshirô Ichikawa (Gengoemon Kataoka), Ennosuke Ichikawa [Danko Inchikawa] (Matsunojô Ôishi), Chûsha Ichikawa (Kozukenosuke Kira), Toshirô Mifune (Genba Tawaraboshi), Haruo Nakajima (minor role), Hiromi Mineoka, Kiyoko Tsuji, Kanzô Uni, Katsumi Tezuka, Akio Kusama, Kaneyuki

Tsubono, Kôji Uruki, Rinsaku Ogata, Hiroshi [Yû] Sekita, Hiroyoshi Yamaguchi, Masaki Shinohara, Yôichirô Kitagawa [Ryûichi Hosokawa], Saburô Kadowaki, Tadashi Okabe, Kenzô Echigo; 1963 U.S. Version: Michael Higgins (Narrator).

Taiheiyo no tsubasa [*Attack Squadron!*] (January 3, 1963)
Credits: Director: Shûe Matsubayashi; Producers: Tomoyuki Tanaka, Yasuyoshi Tajitsu; Screenplay: Shinobu Hashimoto. Shin'ichi Sekizawa, Katsuya Susaki; Tomoyuki Tanaka; Cinematographers: Takao Saitô, Takeshi Suzuki, Kazuo Yamada; Format/Aspect Ratio: Eastmancolor and Tohoscope [2.35:1]; Editors: Kôichi Iwashita, Yoshitami Kuroiwa; Production Designer: Takeo Kita; Art Director: Takeo Kimura; Musical Score: Ikuma Dan; Assistant Director: Kôji Kajita; Sound Recordist: Shin Watarai; Sound Effects: Hisashi Shimonaga; Sound Effects Editor: Minoru Kaneyama; Lighting Technician: Chushiro Ishii; Special Effects Director: Eiji Tsuburaya; Assistant Special Effects Director: Teruyoshi Nakano; Special Effects Art Director: Akira Watanabe; Special Effects Camera: Sadamasa Arikawa, Yukio Manoda, Sokei Tomioka; Special Effects Lighting: Kuichirô Kishida; Special Effects Opticals: Hiroshi Mukoyama; Production Company and Distributor: Toho Company; U.S. Release Date: February 1, 1975; Running Time: 101 minutes.
Cast: Toshirô Mifune (Lieutenant Colonel Senda), Yûzô Kayama (Captain Shiro Taki), Takashi Shimura (Admiral), Yôsuke Natsuki (Captain Nobuo Ataka), Makoto Satô (Teppei Yano), Susumu Fugita (Yamato Commander Ito), Jun Tazaki (Commander), Akihiko Hirata (Senda's Aide), Yoshifumi Tajima (Sailor), Yoshio Kosugi (Destroyer Captain), Senkichi Ômura (Transport Pilot), Seizaburô Kawazu (Kosaku Aruga), Haruo Nakajima (Crew of Destroyer/Officer at Air Base), Yuriko Hoshi, Ryô Ikebe, Kiyoshi Atsumi, Kô Nishimura, Mie Hama, Hideo Sunazuka, Ichirô Nakatani, Seiji Miyaguchi, Tadao Nakamaru, Masao Shimizu, Madao Kirino, Ren Yamamoto, Yutaka Nakayama, Kô Mishima, Katsumi Tezuka, Kôzô Nomura, Akira Wakamatsu, Shôichi Hirose, Wataru Ômae, William Schoolinger, Jack Davis, Toshihiko Furuta, Yukihiko Gondô, Shigeki Ishida, Hisaya Itô, Keiju Kobayashi, Hiroshi Koizumi, Tatsuya Mihashi, Fuyuki Murakami, Tetsu Nakamura, Yutaka Oka, Tadashi Okabe, Seiji Onaka, Yutaka Sada, Sachio Sakai, Yu Sekita, Hiroshi Tachikawa, Yoshio Tsuchiya, Yasuhisa Tsutsumi, Ken Uehara, Kôji Ono, Kôji Uruki, Shin Ôtomo.

Tengoku to jigoku [*High and Low*] (March 1, 1963)
Credits: Director and Associate Producer: Akira Kurosawa; Producers: Ryûzô Kikushima, Tomoyuki Tanaka; Screenplay: Hideo Oguni, Ryûzô Kikushima, Eijirô Hisaita, Akira Kurosawa; Based on the Novel *King's Ransom* by Evan Hunter [Edo Makubein/Ed McBain]; Cinematographers: Asakazu Nakai, Takao Saitô; Format/Aspect Ratio: Black-and-White with Eastmancolor insert and Tohoscope [Anamorphic 2.35:1]; Processing: Kinuta Laboratories, Tokyo; Editor: Akira Kurosawa; Assistant Editor: Reiko Kaneko; Musical Score: Masaru Satô; Production Designer: Yoshiro Muraki; Assistant Art Director: Jun Sakuma; Costume Designer: Miyuki Suuki; Hair Stylists: Yoshiko Matsumoto, Junjirô Yamada; Chief Assistant Director: Shiro Moritani; Assistant Directors:

Masanobu Deme, Yoichi Matsue, Kenjirô Ohmori; Sound: Fumio Yanoguchi; Sound Assistant: Jin Sashida; Sound Mixer: Hisashi Shimonaga; Sound Effects Editor: Ichirô Minawa; Assistant Camera: Kazutami Hara; Lighting Technicians: Ichirô Inohara, Hiromitsu Mori; Assistant Lighting Technician: Fukahirô Akike; Stills Photographer: Masao Fukuda; Transportation Coordinator: Ginzo Osumi; Production Supervisor: Hiroshi Nezu; Production Assistant: Shigeru Kishima; Script Supervisor: Teruyo Nogami; Acting Office: Yûichi Yoshitake; Locations: Enoshima, Kamakura, Kishigoe, Sakawa River and Yokohama, Kanagawa; Chiyoda-ku, Tokyo; Production Companies: Kurosawa Production Company, Toho Company; Distributors: Toho Company; U.S. Release Date: November 26, 1963 [Continental Distributing]; Running Time: 143 minutes.

Cast: Toshirô Mifune (Kingo Gondo), Tatsuya Nakadai (Chief Detective Tokura), Kyôko Kagawa (Reiko Gondo, Kingo's Wife), Tatsuya Mihashi (Kawanishi, Gondo's Secretary), Isao Kimura (Detective Arai), Kenjirô Ishiyama (Chief Detective "Bos'n" Taguchi), Takeshi Katô (Detective Nakao), Takashi Shimura (Chief of the Investigation Section), Jun Tazaki (Kamiya, National Shoes Publicity Director), Nobuo Nakamura (Ishimaru, National Shoes Design Department Director), Yûnosuke Itô (Baba, National Shoes Executive), Tsutomu Yamazaki (Ginjiro Takeuchi, Medical Intern and Kidnapper), Minoru Chiaki (First Reporter), Eijirô Tôno (National Shoes Factory Worker), Masao Shimizu (Prison Warden), Yutaka Sada (Aoki, the Chauffeur), Masahiko Shimazu (Shinichi Aoki, the Chauffeur's Son), Toshio Egi (Jun Gondo, Kingo's Son), Kôji Mitsui (Second Reporter), Kyû Sazanka (First Creditor), Susumu Fugita (Chief of the First Investigating Section), Kamatari Fujiwara (Cook at the Junkyard), Yoshio Tsuchiya (Detective Murata), Kazuo Kitamura (Third Reporter), Gen Shimizu (Chief Physician), Akira Nagoya (Detective Yamamoto), Jun Hamamura (Second Creditor), Masao Oda [Orita] (First Executor at the Tax Office), Kô Nishimura (Third Creditor), Yoshifumi Tajima (Chief Prison Officer), Kôji Kiyomura [Shimizu] (Fish Market Office Worker), Hiroshi Unanzan (Detective Shimizu), Yoshisuke Makino (Detective Takahashi), Jun Kondô (Identification Center Worker), Satoshi [Tomo] Suzuki (Detective Koike), Senkichi Ômura (Messenger Passing Note to Intern), Kazuo Katô (Identification Center Worker), Ikio Sawamura (Yokohama Station Trolley Man), Kin Sugai (Female Drug Addict), Keiko Tomita (Murder Victim), Isamu Onoda (Male Drug Addict), Seiichi Taguchi (Detective Nakamura), Takeo Matsushita (Second Executor at the Tax Office), Kiyoshi Yamamoto (Detective Ueno), Kenji Kodama (Detective Hara), Minoru Itô (Detective), Kazuo Suzuki (Detective Undercover as "Drug Addict"), Kôzô Nomura (Detective).

Hasshu yukyoden—otoko no sakazuki (June 30, 1963)

Credits: Director: Masahiro Makino; Screenplay: Kinya Naoi; Cinematographer: Minoru Miki; Musical Score: Taichiro Kosugi; Production Company: Toei Company; English Title: *Gambler Tales of Hasshu: A Man's Pledge*; Running Time: 83 minutes.

Cast: Chiezô Kataoka (Chuji Kunisada), Takashi Shimura (Chuji's Father), Shin'ichi [Sonny] Chiba, Junko Fuji.

Boryokudan (August 7, 1963)

Credits: Director: Shigehiro Ozawa; Producer: Shigeru Okada; Screenplay: Akira Murao; Cinematographer: Hanjirô Nakazawa; Musical Score: Taiichirô Kosugi; Production Company: Toei; English Title: *Violent Gang*; Running Time: 86 minutes.
Cast: Nobuo Yana (Hayakawa), Takashi [Kôji] Hio (Ryû), Kôji Tsuruta, Takashi Shimura, Tatsuo Umemiya, Jun Tatara, Hizuru Takachiko, Chiyoko Honma.

Taiyô wa yondeiru (September 29, 1963)

Credits: Director: Eizô Sugawa; Producers: Shin Morita, Tomoyuki Tanaka; Screenplay: Shirô Moritani, Eizô Sugawa; Based on the Novel by Yasushi Inoue; Cinematographer: Taiichi Kankura; Format/Aspect Ratio: Color and Tohoscope [2.35:1]; Processing: Kinuta Laboratories, Tokyo; Musical Score: Naozumi Yamamoto; Production Designer: Shinobu Muraki; Sound Recordist: Masanao Uehara; Lighting Technician: Ichirô Inohara; Production Company and Distributor: Toho Company.
Cast: Yûzô Kayama, Yuki Nakagawa, Yôko Fujiyama, Tsutomu Yamazaki, Takashi Shimura.

Dai tuzoku [*The Lost World of Sinbad*] (October 26, 1963)

Credits: Director: Senkichi Taniguchi; Producers: Tomoyuki Tanaka, Kenichiro Tsunoda, (U.S. Version) Samuel Z. Arkoff, James H. Nicholson; Screenplay: Takeshi Kimura, Shin'ichi Sekizawa; Story: Toshio Yasumi; Cinematographer: Takao Saitô; Format/Aspect Ratio: Eastmancolor and Tohoscope [2.35:1]; Processing: Tokyo Laboratory, Ltd.; Editor: Yoshitami Kuroiwa; Musical Score: Masaru Satô; Production Designer: Takeo Kita; Costume Designer: Shôtarô Maki; Production Manager: Hiroshi Nezu; Assistant Directors: Teruyoshi Nakano, Susumu Takebayashi; Sound Recordists: Shin Watarai, Shirô Yamamoto; Sound Effects: Hisashi Shimonaga; Art Director: Akira Watanabe; Lighting Technician: Kuichirô Kishida; Special Effects Director: Eiji Tsuburaya; Art Director of Special Effects: Kiichi Kukuda; Matte Process: Hiroshi Mukoyama; Directors of Special Effects Photography: Sadamasa Arikawa, Akira Watanabe; Optical Photography: Kuichirô Kishida, Yukio Manoda, Yôichi Manoda; Optical Photography: Taka Yuki; Special Effects Lighting: Sokei Tomioka; Production Company and Distributor: Toho Company; Alternate English Titles: *Samurai Pirate, The Great Thief*; U.S. Release Date: March 3, 1965 [American International Pictures]; Running Time: 96 minutes.
Cast: Toshirô Mifune (Sukezaemon Naya, alias "Luzon" ["Sinbad" in English Version]. Tadao Nakamaru (The Premier), Mie Hama (Princess Yaya), Kumi Mizuno (Miwa the Rebel Leader), Ichirô Arishima (Sennin the Wizard), Hideyo Amamoto (Granny the Witch), Mitsukô Kusabue (Sobei), Jun Tazaki (Itaka Tsuzuka of the Royal Guards), Akiko Wakabayashi (Yaya's Maid), Jun Funato (Ming, the Prince of Thailand), Makoto Satô (The Black Pirate), Jun'ichirô Mukai (Chief of Imperial Guards), Rokku Furukawa, Hideo Sumazuka, Masanari Nihei, Akira Shimada (Bandits), Takashi Shimura (King Raksha), Tetsu Nakamura (Chief Archer), "Little Man" Machan (Dwarf), Eishu

Kin (Giant), Yutaka Nakayama, Masashi [Shôji] Ôki, Hidezu Kane (Sailors), Nadao Kirino (Yuji, Member of Luzon's Crew), Nakajirô Tomita (Tenjiku), Haruo Suzuki (Poseidon), Yoshio Kosugi (Captain of Thai Ship), Yutaka Sada (Governor), Seiji Ikeda (Man with Whip), Senkichi Ômura (Peddlar), Hiroshi Hasegawa (Fighter in Street), Masako Shibaki (Girl in Village), Chiyoko Tanabe (Dancer), Yasuhisa Tsutsumi, Tadanori Kusagawa (Villagers), Tôru Ibuki (Pirate), Jun'ichirô Mukai, Kôzô Nomura, Akira Shimada, Rokumaru Furukawa, Shôji Ikeda.

Tsukiyo no wataridori (December 24, 1963)

Credits: Director: Hirokazu Ichimura; Screenplay: Shin Hasegawa, Eibi Motomochi, Yoshihisa Sakurai, Heigo Suzuki; Cinematographer: Tomomichi Kuramochi; Format: Color; Musical Score: Hirooki Ogawa; Production Company: Shochiku; Running Time: 93 minutes.

Cast: Yukio Hashi (Taro Tadashi), Chieko Baishô (O shino), Mieko Takamine (Ohama), Yoshiko Kayama (O to yo), Pichiku Haruno (Kanemachi no han tsugi), Takashi Shimura (Nagisa yo yuki jo), Yuko Takayama (Otami), Misae Enomoto, Mitsuo Nagata, Koji Nakada, Hiroshi Nawa, Yoshindo [Yoshito] Yamaji.

Chi to daiyamondo (July 1, 1964)

Credits: Director: Jun Fukuda; Producers: Reiji Miwa, Tomoyuki Tanaka; Screenplay: Moriyuki Mafuji, Ei Ogawa; Cinematographer: Shinsaku Uno; Format/ Aspect Ratio: Black-and-White and Tohoscope [2.35:1]; Editor: Shûichi Anbara; Production Designer: Kazuo Takenaka; Chief Assistant Director: Ken Sano; Production Company and Distributor: Toho Company; English Title: *Blood and Diamonds*; Running Time: 96 minutes.

Cast: Akira Takarada (Kuroki), Jun Tazaki (Utsuki), Hisaya Itô (Nonozawa), Asao Uchida (Sawada), Osman Yusuf (Paul), Chico Roland (Rufus), Tetsuo Ishidate (Jiro), Makoto Satô, Yôsuke Natsuki, Yû Fujiki, Kumi Mizuno, Takashi Shimura, Yuki Nakagawa, Chieko Nakakita, Tatsuo Endô.

Aku no monsho [*Brand of Evil*] (July 11, 1964)

Credits: Director: Hiromichi Horikawa; Producers: Sanezumi Fujimoto, Reiji Miwa; Screenplay: Sakae Hirosawa, Hiromichi Horikawa; Based on the Novel by Shinobu Hashimoto; Cinematographer: Yuzuru Aizawa; Format/Aspect Ratio: Black-and-White and Tohoscope [2.35:1]; Processing: Kinuta Laboratories, Tokyo; Musical Score: Toshirô Mayuzumi; Production Designer: Takashi Matsuyama; Sound Recordist: Kôichi Nakagawa; Production Company: Takarazuka Motion Picture Company, Ltd.; Distributor: Toho Company; U.S. Release Date: February 12, 1965; Running Time: 133 minutes.

Cast: Tsutomu Yamazaki (Detective Kikuchi, aka Inamura), Michiyo Aratama (Seksuko Asai), Kyôko Kishida (Mitsue Takazawa), Keiji Sada (Shigeharu Takazawa), Eijirô Yanagi (Hiroshi Ebihara), Shirô Ôsaka (Seitaro Matsuno), Akemi Kita (Emiko Ohara), Takashi Shimura (Tsukamoto, Manager), Kei Satô (Yasuhiro Egushi), Rokkô Toura (Kinichi Shibata), Tôru Abe (Teizo Yuasa).

Tensai sagishi monogatari: Tanuki no hanamachi (August 1, 1964)
Credits: Director: Kajirô Yamamoto; Producer: Hidehisa Suga; Screenplay: Tokuhei Wakao; Story: Koji Machida; Cinematographer: Fukuzô Koizumi; Format/Aspect Ratio: Color and Tohoscope [2.35:1]; Processing: Kinuta Laboratories, Tokyo; Editor: Eiji Ooi; Musical Score: Kenjiro Hirose; Production Designer: Kyoe Hamagami; Chief Assistant Director: Susumu Kodama; Sound Recordist: Norio Tone; Lighting Technician: Tsuruzô Nishikawa; Production Company and Distributor: Toho Company; Running Time: 96 minutes.
Cast: Keiju Kobayashi (Kiichi Senda), Norihei Miki (Gohei Kobotake), Hisaya Morishige (Monta Akai), Keiko Awaji (Teruko Senda), Noriko Sakabe (Tamae), Yôko Tsukasa (Toshiko Sudo), Hisaya Itô (Mamiya), Takashi Shimura (Komai), Noriko Takahashi (Miyo Koike), Keiko Sawai (Tomiko), Sadako Amemiya (Akiko), Machiko Naka (Akemi), Chieko Nakakita (Landlady), Yutaka Oka (Driver A), Hideo Shibuya (Driver B), Ikio Sawamura (Neighbor Man), Kamatari Fujiwara (Guard), Chishû Ryû (Komai), Kyû Sazanka (Shinsaku Kaibara), Machiko Kitagawa, Nadao Kirino, Tsuruko Mano.

San daikaijū: Chikyû saidai no kessen [*Three Giant Monsters: The Greatest Battle on Earth*], aka *Ghidorah: The Three-Headed Monster* (December 20, 1964)
Credits: Director: Ishirô Honda; Producer: Tomoyuki Tanaka; Screenplay: Shin'ichi Sekizawa; Cinematographer: Hajime Koizumi; Format/Aspect Ratio: Eastmancolor and Tohoscope [2.35:1]; Editor: Ryôhei Fujii; Musical Score: Akira Ifukube; Composer (Song "Call Happiness"): Hiroshi Miyagawa; Production Designer/Art Director: Takeo Kita; Chief Assistant Director: Ken Sano; Assistant Director: Koji Hashimoto; Sound Recordist: Fumio Yanoguchi; Sound Mixer: Osamu Chiku; Sound Effects Editor: Hisashi Shimonaga; Lighting Supervisor: Shoshichi Kojima; Special Effects Director: Eiji Tsuburaya; Chief Assistant Director Special Effects: Teruyoshi Nakano; Special Effects Art Director: Akira Watanabe; Special Effects Cameramen: Sadamasa Arikawa, Sokei Tomioka; Special Effects Assistant Production Manager: Tadashi Koibe; Matte Photography: Yukio Manoda; Matte Process: Taka Yuki; Special Effects Lighting: Kuichirô Kishida; Special Effects Opticals: Hiroshi Mukoyama; Production Manager: Shigeru Nakamura; Stunts: Haruo Nakajima; Dubbing Director (U.S. Version): Joseph Belluci; Production Company: Toho Company; Distributors: Toho Company; U.S. Release Date: September 13, 1965 [Continental Distributing]; Running Time: 93 minutes; U.S. Release Running Time: 85 minutes.
Cast: Yôsuke Natsuki (Detective Shindo), Yuriko Hoshi (Naoko Shindo), Hiroshi Koizumi (Professor Miura), Akiko Wakabayashi (Princess of Sergina), Emi Itô, Yumi Itô (Shobijin, Twin Fairies), Takashi Shimura (Dr. Tsukamoto), Akihiko Hirata (Chief Detective Okita), Hisaya Itô (Malmess, Chief Assassin), Minoru Takada (Prime Minister), Someshô Matsumoto (Alien Expert), Ikio Sawamura (Honest Fisherman), Kôzô Nomura (Geologist), Kenji Sahara (Editor in Chief Kanamaki), Susumu Kurobe (Mustachioed Assassin), Tôru Ibuki (Short-Tie Assassin), Kazuo Suzuki (Showoff Door-Opener Assassin), Haruya Katô, Hideo Shibuya (Journalists), Shin Ôtomo (Boss of Assassins), Senkichi

Ômura (Would-Be Hat Retriever), Yutaka Nakayama (Tourist with Lost Hat), Heihachirô Ôkawa (Astronomer), Yutaka Oka (Meteorite Scientist), Hideyo Amamoto (Princess Salno's Aide), Yoshio Kosugi (Chief of Infant Island), Yoshifumi Tajima (Heedless Ship Captain), Kôji Uno (Hotel Clerk), Shigeki Ishida (Guy in Crowd), Toshiko Furuta, Kôtarô Tomita (Villagers), Ichiya Aozora (Himself, Host of TV Show [Tall Man]), Senya Aozora (Himself, Host of TV Show [Short Man]), Yuriko Hanabusa (Shindo's Mother), Nakajirô Tomita (General Hyodo), Haruo Nakajima (Gojira), Shôichi Hirose (Kingugidora), Masaki Shinohara, Kôji Uruki (Radon), Katsumi Tezuka (Mothra), Seiji Ikeda (Man in Crowd), Kenzô Echigo, Bin Furuya, Yoshio Hattori, Toku Ihara, Kazuo Imai, Daisuke Inoue, Saburô Kadowaki, Keiichirô Katsumoto, Takuzô Kumagai, Jun Kuroki, Oshio Mukai, Jun'ichirô Mukai, Haruya Sakamoto, Kenji Tsubono, Mitsuo Tsuda, Tamani Urayama.

Kaidan [*Kwaidan*] (December 29, 1964)

Credits: Director: Masaki Kobayashi; Producer: Shigeru Wakatsuki; Associate Producer: Yoshishige Uchiyama; Assistant Producers: Takeshi Aikawa, Satoshi Kohinata, Minoru Tabata; Screenplay: Yôko Mizuki; Based on Stories by Yakumo Koizumi [Lafcadio Hearn]; Cinematographer: Yoshio Miyajima; Format/Aspect Ratio: Eastmancolor and Tohoscope [2.35:1]; Editor: Hisashi Sagara; Assistant Editor: Junichirô Ôsaka; Musical Score: Tôru Takemitsu; Musician (biwa): Kinji Tsuruda; Art Director: Shigemasa Toda; Assistant Art Director: Naotake Satsumoto; Set Decorator: Dai Arakawa; Set Designer: Kiyoharu Matsuno; Costume Design: Masahiro Katô; Costume Researcher: Yoshio Ueno; Makeup Artist: Shigeru Takagi; Hair Stylist: Ayako Sakurai; First Assistant Director: Gô Yishida; Background Artist: Makoto Nishida; Tannoura Battle Paintings: Masayoshi Nakamura; Sound Designers: Kuniharu Akiyama, Shigenosuke Okuyama, Akira Suzuki, Tôru Takemitsu; Sound Recordists: Masaharu Shioda, Kazutoshi Yagihashi; Sound: Hideo Nishizaki; Martial Arts: Tatsuo Hotta; Assistant Camera: Toshiyuki Isobe; Second Assistant Camera: Shôjirô Kamohara; Assistant Photographer: Susumu Ôishi; Gaffer: Akira Aomatsu; Stills Photographer: Yasuhiro Yoshioka; Color Consultant: Michio Midorikawa; Colorist: Shigeyuki Sekine; Continuity: Eiko Yoshida; Title Designer: Kiyoshi Awazu; Titles: Sofu Teshigahara; Researcher: Tadanosuke Sumida; Publicity Producer: Kazuya Uchida; Production Supervisors: Kazuo Kuwahara, Yôichi Ukita; Executive in Charge of Production: Michiyoshi Takashima; Production Companies: Bungei, Ninjin Club, Toho Company, Toyo Kogyo Kabushiki Kaisha; Distributors: Toho Company; U.S. Release Date: November 22, 1965 [Continental Distributing]; Running Time: 183 minutes; U.S. Release Running Time: 125 minutes.

Cast: ["Kurokami" Segment] Michiyo Aratama (First Wife), Misako Watanabe (Second Wife), Rentarô Mikuni (Husband), Kenjiro Ishiyama (Father), Ranko Akagi (Mother), Fumie Kitahara, Kappei Matsumoto, Yoshiko Ieda, Otome Tsukimiya, Kenzô Tanaka, Kiyoshi Nakano; ["Yuki-Onna" Segment] Tatsuya Nakadai (Mi nokichi), Keiko Kishi (Yuki the Snow Maiden), Yûko Mochizuki (Minokichi's Mother), Kin Sugai, Noriko Sengoku (Village Women), Akiko Nomura, Torahiko Hamada, Jun Hamamura; ["Miminashi Hôichi no hanashi" Segment] Katsuo Nakamura (Hoichi), Tatsurô Tanba (Warrior), Takashi

Shimura (Head Priest), Yoichi Hayahi (attendant), Eiko Muramatsu (Kenreiinmon), Kunie Tanaka (Yasaku), Kazuo Kitamura (Taira no Tomomori), Akira Tani (Huntsman #2), Ichirô Nakatani, Masanori Tomotake, Tokue Hanazawa, Shizue Natsukawa, Shin Tatsuoka, Makiko Kitashiro, Masakazu Kuwayama, Mutsuhiko Tsurumaru, Akira Tani, Yôsuke Kondô, Kiyoshi Yamamoto, Kinji Omino, Atsuo Nakamura, Ginzô Sekiguchi, Akio Miyabe, Gen'ya Nagai, Tôru Uchida, Hikaru Jinno, Toshio Fukuhara, Kirô Abe, Toshiro Yagi, Yuriko Abe, Yuri Satô, Kyochi Satô, Nobuo Aikawa, Taiji Kodama, Nobuaki Maeda, Teruhiko Shibata, Haruo Kaji, Michio Gina, Seiji Tabe, Mitsuko Narita, Noriko Mikura, Aiko Nagayama, Michiko Nakahata; ["Chawan no naka" Segment] Kan'emon Nakamura (Kannai, a Guard), Osamu Takizawa (Author/Narrator), Haruko Sugimura (Madame), Ganjirô Nakamura (Publisher), Noboru Nakaya (Shikibu Heinai), Seiji Miyaguchi (Old Man), Kei Satô (Ghost Samurai), Jun Tazaki (Kannai's Colleague #1), Shigeru Kôyama, Junkichi Orimoto, Akiji Kobayashi, Yoshirô Aoki, Isao Tamagawa, Hideyo Amamoto.

Jinsei gekijo: shin hisha kaku (1964)

Credits: Director: Tadashi Sawashima; Screenplay: Kazuo Kasahara; Cinematographer: Hanjirô Nakazawa; Format: Color; Musical Score: Masaru Satô; Production Company: Toei; English Title: *Theater of Life—New Hishaku Story*.
Cast: Kôji Tsuruta, Yoshiko Sakuma, Minoru Ôki, Jun Usami, Hiroyuki Nagato, Yoshi Katô, Takashi Shimura, Kei Satô, Rin'ichi Yamamoto, Masumi Harukawa.

Samurai [*Samurai Assassin*] (January 3, 1965)

Credits: Director: Kihachi Okamoto; Producers: Tomoyuki Tanaka, Reiji Miwa; Associate Producer: Toshirô Mifune; Line Producer: Masao Suzuki; Screenplay: Shinobu Hashimoto; Based on the Book *Samurai Nippon* [*Samurai Japan*] by Jiromasa Gunji; Cinematographer: Hiroshi Murai; Format/Aspect Ratio: Blackand-White and Tohoscope [2.35:1]; Processing: Kinuta Laboratories, Tokyo; Editor: Yoshitami Kuroiwa; Musical Score: Masaru Satô; Production Designer: Iwao Akune; Chief Assistant Director: Yuzuo [Michio] Yamamoto; Sound: Yoshio Nishikawa; Sound Mixer: Hisashi Shimonaga; Special Effects: Minoru Izumi; Fight Choreographer: Ryû Kuze; Lighting Technician: Tsuruzô Nishikawa; Production Company: Mifune Productions Company, Ltd., Toho Company; Distributor: Toho Company; U.S. Release Date: March 5, 1965; Running Time: 122 minutes.
Cast: Toshirô Mifune (Tsuruchiyo Niiro), Keiju Kobayashi (Einosuke Kurihara), Michiyo Aratama (Okiku/Kikuhime), Yûnosuke Itô (Kenmotsu Hoshino), Eijirô Tôno (Masagoro Kisoya), Tatsuyoshi Ehara (Ichigoro Hayama), Tadao Nakamaru (Shigezo Inada), Kaoru Yachigusa (Mitsu), Haruko Sugimura (Tsuru), Nami Tamura (Yae), Shirô Ôtsuji (Kaname Kojima), Yoshio Inaba (Keijiro Sumita), Akihiko Hirata (Sohei Masui), Hideyo Amamoto (Matazaburo Hagiwara), Ikio Sawamura (Tatsukichi Bisenya), Chôtarô Tôgin (Seiichi Morikawa), Yasuzô Ogawa, Masaya Nihei, Kôji Iwamoto, Fujio Tokita, Hiroshi Hasegawa (Ronin), Toshio Kurosawa (Katsunoshin Itamura), Yoshifumi Tajima, Nadao Kirino, Jun'ichirô Mukai (Samurai), Koraizô Ichikawa (Shuzen

Nakano), Naoya Kusakawa (Man with Sharp Eyes), Yasuhisa Tsutsumi (Manager of Sumoya), Mitsugu Terashima (Chuzaemon Nishikawa), Takashi Shimura (Narihisa Ichijô), Susumu Fujita (Tatewaki Todo), Shikaku Nakamura (Gengobei Nosaka), Chûsha Ichikawa (Sahyônosuke Matsudaira), Hakuô [Kôshirô] Matsumoto (Lord Naosuke Ii), Ren Yamamoto, Yurie Hidaka, Nagayo Kita, Kan Hôshô.

Akahige [*Red Beard*] (April 3, 1965)

Credits: Director and Associate Producer: Akira Kurosawa; Producers: Ryûzô Kikushima, Tomoyuki Tanaka; Screenplay: Masato Ide, Hideo Oguni, Ryûzô Kikushima, Akira Kurosawa; Based on the Short Story Collection *Akahige shinryô tan* ["Akahige Consultation Story"] by Shuguro Yamamoto; Cinematographers: Asakazu Nakai, Takao Saitô; Format/Aspect Ratio: Black-and-White and Tohoscope [Anamorphic 2.35:1]; Processing: Toho Developing Company; Editor: Akira Kurosawa; Assistant Editor: Reiko Kaneko; Musical Score: Masaru Satô; Production Designer: Yoshirô Muraki; Assistant Art Director: Nozomi Fukusako; Property Master: Akio Nojima; Costume Designer: Yoshiko Samejima [Kyoto Costume]; Hair Stylists: Yoshiko Matsumoto, Junjirô Yamada; Unit Production Manager: Hiroshi Nezu; First Assistant Directors: Shirô Moritani; Assistant Directors: Masanobu Deme, Yôichi Matsue, Kenjirô Ohmori; Sound Recordist: Shin Watari [4-Track Stereo]; Sound Assistant: Zen Sashida; Sound Mixer: Hisashi Shimonaga; Sound Effects Editor: Ichirô Minawa; Assistant Cameras: Kazutami Hara, Katsuhiro Kato; Lighting Technician: Hiromitsu Mori; Assistant Lighting Technician: Fumiyoshi Hara; Stills Photographer: Masao Fukuda; Transportation Coordinator: Yoshio Sekine; Production Assistant: Shigeru Kishima; Script Supervisor: Teruyo Nogami; Acting Office: Yûichi Yoshitake; Production Companies: Kurosawa Production Company, Toho Company; Distributor: Toho Company; U.S. Release Date: December 19, 1968; Running Time: 185 minutes.

Cast: Toshirô Mifune (Dr. Kyojô ["Akahige"] Niide), Yûzô Kayama (Dr. Noboru Yasumoto), Tsutomu Yamazaki (Sahachi), Reiko Dan (Osugi), Miyuki Kuwano (Onaka), Kyôko Kagawa (Madwoman), Tatsuyoshi Ehara (Genzô Tsugawa), Terumi Niki (Otoyo), Akemi Negishi (Okuni, the Mistress), Yoshitaka Zushi (Chôji), Yoshio Tsuchiya (Dr. Handayu Mori), Eijirô Tôno (Goheiji), Takashi Shimura (Tokubei Izumiya), Chishû Ryû (Mr. Yasumoto, Noboru's Father), Haruko Sugimura (Kin, the Madam), Kinuyo Tanaka (Madame Yasumoto, Noboru's Mother), Eijirô Yanagi (Madwoman's Father), Kôji Mitsui (Heikichi), Kô Nishimura (Chief Retainer), Nobuo Chiba (Matsudaira), Kamatari Fujiwara (Rokosuke, the Dying Man), Ken Mitsuda (Genpaku Amano, Masae's Father), Yôko Fujiyama (Chigusa, Masae's Sister), Yôko Naitô (Masae), Reiko Nanao (Otoku), Imari Tsuji (Okatsu), Akiko Nomura (Ofuku), Sue Mitobe (Otake), Yoshitaka Zushi (Choji), Kin Sugai (Chôji's Mother), Masanobu Ôkubo (Chôji's Father), Michiko Araki (Woman Owner of Brothel), Bokuzen Hidari (Patient A), Atsushi Watanabe (Patient B), Yasuzô Ogawa (Businessman), Yutaka Sada, Ikio Sawamura, Fumiko Homma (Residents), Miyoko Nakamura (Okoto), Shozo Kazami (Masae's Mother), Chisato Aoki, Kyoko Kurisu, Yukiko Yanagishita, Toshiko Fukai (Prostitutes), Keiko Tomita (Girl on Street), Shôji Ôki, Shôichi

["Solomon"] Hirose, Hiroyoshi Yamaguchi, Fujio Tokita, Yasuo Araki, Hiroshi Tanaka, Shin Ibuki, Kanzô [Kan] Uni, Hiroto Kimura, Shû Momoro, Ryû Kuze (Thugs).

Matatabi san ning yakuza (May 22, 1965)

Credits: Director: Tadashi Sawashima; Screenplay: Kazuo Kasahara, Sadao Nakajima, Tatsuo Nogami; Cinematographer: Osamu Furuya; Format/Aspect Ratio: Color and Toeiscope [2.35:1]; Musical Score: Katsu Sato; Art Director: Norimichi Igawa; Production Company: Toei Kyoto; English Title: *Wanderers: Three Yakuza*; Running Time: 120 minutes.
Cast: Kinnosuke Nakamura (Kaze-no-Kyutaro), Tatsuya Nakadai (Hatsukari-no-Sentaro), Hiroki Matsukata (Dani-no-Genta), Takashi Shimura (Kakegawa Bunzo), Hiroko Sakuramachi, Wakaba Irie, Junko Fuji.

Sugata Sanshiro [*Sanshiro Sugata*] (May 29, 1965)

Credits: Director: Seiichirô Uchikawa; Producers: Akira Kurosawa, Tomoyuki Tanaka; Screenplay: Akira Kurosawa; Based on the Novels *Sugata Sanshirô* by Tsuneo Tomita and the Screenplays *Sugata Sanshirô* [*Sanshiro Sugata*] (1943) and *Zoku Sugata Sanshirô* [*Sanshiro Sugata—Part Two*] (1945) by Akira Kurosawa; Cinematographer: Fukuzô Koizumi; Format/Aspect Ratio: Black-and-White and Tohoscope [2.35:1]; Musical Score: Masaru Satô; Art Director: Hiroshi Mizutani; Sound: Koji Onmi; Lighting Technician: Kazuo Shimimoura; Stills Photographer: Daizo Tai; Production Supervisor: Hiroshi Nezu; Production Companies: Kurosawa Production Company, Takarazuka Eiga Company, Ltd., Toho Company; Distributor: Toho Company; U.S. Release Date: August 27, 1965; Running Time: 159 minutes.
Cast: Yûzô Kayama (Sanshiro Sugata), Tsutomu Yamazaki (Genshiro), Eiji Okada (Gennosuke/Tesshin), Takashi Shimura (Mishima), Bokuzen Hidari (Priest), Daisuke Katô (Hansuke Murai), Yumiko Kokonoe (Sayo, Hansuke's Daughter), Tatsuhiko Namisato (Daisaburo Hidarimonji), Kinji Matsueda (Yoshimaro Dan), Hiroshi Aoyama (Toranosuke Shinkai), Yoshirô Aoki (Yujiro Toda), Kenji Kodama (Kohei Tsuzaki), Yoji Arisawa (Nemoto), Toshio Chiba (Torakichi), Chôko Iida (Old Lady), Takamaru Sasaki (Inuma), Toshirô Mifune (Shogoro Yano).

Taiheiyô kiseki no sakusen: Kisuka [*Kiska*] (July 4, 1965)

Credits: Director: Seiji Maruyama; Producers: Yasuyoshi Tami, Tomoyuki Tanaka; Screenplay: Katsuya Susaki, Walter Black (English-language sequences); Based on the Story *"Taiheiyo kaisen saidai no Kiseki"* ["The Most Miraculous Battle in the Pacific Ocean"] by Masataka Chihaya; Format/Aspect Ratio: Black-and-White and Tohoscope [2.35:1]; Editor: Ryôhei Fujii; Musical Score: Ikuma Dan; Production Designer: Takeo Kita; Chief Assistant Director: Yoshimitsu Banno; Sound Recordist: Yoshio Nishikawa; Sound Effects: Hisashi Shimonaga; Sound Effects Editor: Minoru Kaneyama; Lighting Technician: Tsuruzo Nishikawa; Director of Special Effects: Eiji Tsuburaya; Special Effects Assistant Director: Teruyoshi Nakano; Special Effects Photography: Sadamasa Arikawa; Special

Effects Art Director: Akira Watanabe; Matte Photography: Yukio Manoda; Matte Process: Hiroshi Mukoyama; Special Effects Lighting: Kuichirô Kishida; Stills Photographer: Matsuo Yoshizaki; Production Company and Distributor: Toho Company; Running Time: 105 minutes.

Cast: Toshirô Mifune (Omura), Sô Yamamura (Kawashima), Makoto Satô (Commander Amano), Tadao Nakamaru (Kunitomo), Susumu Fugita (Akitani), Jun Tazaki (Akune), Kô Nishimura (Staff Officer), Takashi Shimura (President of the Military Command), Akihiko Hirata (Dr. Kudo), Akira Kubo (Tawara), Yoshio Tsuchiya (Terai), Susumu Kurobe (Kato), Sachio Sakai (Kojima), Ren Yamamoto (Branch Chief), Yutaka Sada (Sano), Hisaya Itô (Captain Kiso), Yoshio Inaba (Tamai), Kiyoshi Kodama (Fukumoto), Shin Ôtomo (Staff Officer of the Five Squadron Institute), Akira Yamada, Nadao Kirino (Officers), Shôichi ["Solomon"] Hirose (Yamashita), Jun'ichirô Mukai (Staff Officer), Tadashi Okabe (Second Staff Officer), Yutaka Oka (Miyamoto), Hiroshi Hasegawa (Air Defense Chief), Yasuhisa Tsutsumi (Chief Accountant), Shigeki Ishida (Matsubara), Kunio Ôtsuka (Shigeki), Wataru Ômae (Communications Officer), Haruo Nakajima (Kiska's Soldier), Jun Funato, Masanari Nihei, Toshihiko Furuta, Tôru Ibuki, Chôtarô Tôgin, Yutaka Nakayama, Kazuo Suzuki, Katsumi Tezuka.

Furankenshutain tai chitei kaijū Baragon [*Frankenstein vs. Subterranean Monster Baragon*], aka *Frankenstein Conquers the World* (August 8, 1965)

Credits: Director: Ishirô Honda; Producer: Tomoyuki Tanaka; Executive Producers: Reuben Bercovitch, Henry G. Saperstein; (U.S. Version) James H. Nicholson, Samuel Z. Arkoff; Screenplay: Takeshi Kimura; Synopsis: Jerry Sohl; Story: Reuben Bercovitch; Cinematographer: Hajime Koizumi; Format/Aspect Ratio: Eastmancolor and Tohoscope [2.35:1]; Processing: Tokyo Laboratory (Japan), Pathé Laboratory (U.S.); Editor: Ryôhei Fujii; Musical Score: Akira Ifukube; Production Designer: Takeo Kita; Makeup Artist: Riki Konna; Chief Assistant Director: Kôji Kajita; Assistant Director: Koji Hashimoto; Sound Recordist: Wataru Konuma; Sound Effects: Hisashi Shimonaga; Sound Effects Editor: Sadamasa Nishimoto; Dialogue Re-recording Supervisor, English: Salvatore Billiteri; Director of Special Effects: Eiji Tsuburaya; Assistant Director of Special Effects: Teruyoshi Nakano; Art Director of Special Effects: Akira Watanabe; Special Effects Scene Manipulation: Fumio Nakadai; Directors of Special Effects Photography: Sadamasa Arikawa, Sokei Tomioka; Optical Photography: Sadao Iizuda, Yukio Manoda; Special Effects Lighting: Kuichirô Kishida; Stunt Choreographer: Naruo Nakajima; Casting Assistant: Ai Maeda; Color Consultant: Kiyashi Tsurusaki; Voice Dubbing (Dr. James Bowen): Gorô Naya; Presenters: James H. Nicholson, Samuel Z. Arkoff; Production Companies: Toho Company, Henry G. Saperstein Enterprises, Inc.; Distributors: Toho Company, American International Pictures (U.S. Release); U.S. Release Date: July 8, 1966; Running Time: 90 minutes; U.S. Release Running Time: 87 minutes.

Cast: Tadao Takashima (Dr. Yuzo Kawaji), Nick Adams [Nikku Adamusu] (Dr. James Bowen), Kumi Mizuno (Dr. Sueko Togami), Yoshio Tsuchiya (Mr. Kawai), Kôji Furuhata (Frankenstein), Jun Tazaki (Military Advisor), Susumu

Fugita (Osaka Police Chief), Takashi Shimura (Axis Scientist), Nobuo Nakamura (Skeptical Museum Chief), Kenji Sahara (Soldier), Yoshifumi Tajima (Submarine Commander), Kôzô [Terunobu] Nomura (Overzealous Reporter), Haruya Katô (TV Director), Ikio Sawamura (Man Walking Dog), Yoshio Kosugi (Mountain Soldier), Keiko Sawai (Kazuko, the Dying Girl), Noriko Takahashi (Girl in Lodge), Peter Mann (Dr. Riesendorf), Ren Yamamoto (Bystander), Yutaka Sada (Hospital Administrator), Hisaya Itô (Osaka Police Sergeant), Kenzô Tabu (Scornful News Editor), Shigeki Ishida (Chuckling Scientist), Nadao Kirino (Police Sergeant), Yutaka Nakayama (News Cameraman A), Senkichi Ômura (News Cameraman B), Tadashi Okabe (Sarcastic Reporter), Toshihiko Furuta (Bystander), Kenichiro Kawaji (Young Frankenstein), Hideaki Nitani (Hospital Official), Shin Ôtomo (Policeman), Shôichi Hirose (Tunnel Worker), Hideo Shibuya, Saburô Iketani (Reporters), Haruo Nakajima (Baragon/Self-Defense Force Personnel).

Buraikan jingi (December 4, 1965)

Credits: Director: Yûsuke Watanabe; Screenplay: Tatsuo Nogami, Kikuma Shimoiizaka; Cinematographer: Ichirô Hoshijima; Format: Black-and-White; Editor: Yoshiki Nagasawa; Musical Score: Chuji Kinoshita; Art Director: Mikio Mori; Production Company: Toei Tokyo; Distributor: Toei, Inc.; English Title: *Villain's Code*.

Cast: Kôji Tsuruta (Osamu Inamura), Shinichi [Sonny] Chiba (Soichi Jinnai), Junko Fuji (Nami Fukuhara), Hideo Takamatsu (Katsutoshi Maki), Akemi Negishi (Tokuko Kumagai), Hiroyuki Nagato (Gozo Nanba), Takashi Shimura (Genkichi Jinnai), Rin'ichi Yamamoto (Gozo Nanba), Isao Yamagata (Eitaro Oshika), Jôji Ai (Miyoshi), Hiroshi Yagyû (Wakabayashi), Masumi Harukawa (Sadako Fujiwara), Sen Hara (Kinu Jinnai), Fumitake Ômura (Gunji).

Kono koe naki sakebi (1965)

Credits: Director: Hirokazu Ichimura; English Title: *The Soundless Cry*; Running Time: 100 minutes.

Cast: Takashi Shimura, Yoshiko Kayama, Masakazu Tamura, Keisuke Sonoi, Chishû Ryû, Chieko Baishô, Kazuo Kitamura.

Kanto hamonjo (1965)

Credits: Director and Screenplay: Shigehiro Ozawa; Cinematographer: Sadatsugu Yoshida; Format: Color; Musical Score: Shunsuke Kikuchi; Production Company: Toei; English Title: *Expelled from the Kanto Mob*.

Cast: Kôji Tsuruta, Hideo Murata, Takahiro Tamura, Junko Fuji, Takashi Shimura, Minoru Ôki, Yuriko Mishima, Nobuo Kaneko, Kazuko Takamori.

Jigoku no hatobâ (1965)

Credits: Director and Screenplay: Masaharu Segawa; Cinematographer: Yoshikazu Yamazawa; Format: Black-and-White; Musical Score: Riichiro Manabe; Production Company: Toei; English Title: *Pier of Hell*.

Cast: Tatsuo Umemiya, Jirô Okazaki, Sanae Nakahara, Takashi Shimura, Reiko Ohara, Kyôsuke Machida.

Bâra kêtsu shobû (1965)

Credits: Director: Sadatsugu Matsuda; Screenplay: Yoshitake Hisa; Cinematographer: Shintaro Kawasaki; Musical Score: Toshiaki Tsushima; Format: Color; Production Company: Toei; English Title: *Hoodlum Match*.
Cast: Okawa Hashizo, Minoru Ôki, Takashi Shimura, Ryôhei Uchida, Hiroko Sakuramachi, Junko Fuji, Naoko Kubo, Shingo Yamashiro, Tatsuo Endô, Asao Uchida.

Bangkok no joru (June 17, 1966)

Credits: Director: Yasuki Chiba; Producer: Sanezumi Fujimoto; Screenplay: Ryôzô Kasahara; Cinematographer: Taiichi Kankura; Format/Aspect Ratio: Eastmancolor and Tohoscope [2.35:1]; Processing: Kinuta Laboratories, Tokyo; Musical Score: Naozumi Yamamoto; Production Designer: Shigekazu Ikuno; Sound Recordist: Toshiya Ban; Lighting Technician: Mitsuo Kaneko; Production Companies: Cathay Organisation, Taiwan Film Studio, Toho Company; Distributor: Toho Company; English Title: *Night in Bangkok*; Running Time: 105 minutes.
Cast: Yûzô Kayama (Shuichi Tsumura), Mei-Yao Chang [Meiyao Zhang] (Wang Meilan), Yuriko Hoshi (Masayo Harada), Fubuki Koshiji (Yoshiko Koshiyama), Praprapon Pureem (Prapra), Takashi Shimura (Dr. Yoshio), Haruko Tôgô (Kiyoko, Masayo's Mother), Ken Uehara (Bunnosuke, Masayo's Father), Jun Tazaki (Dr. Yamawaki), Hiroshi Koizumi (Kitajima), Dan Wang (Meilan's Mother), Yang Weixi (Meilan's Grandfather), Li Jia (Shi Yuan, Meilan's Uncle), Michiko Kawa (Haruko, Maid), Pohn Pailou (Duke Chennui), Zhuang Li, Jalee Nisakorn, Shôichi Hirose, Mitsuo Tsuda, Akira Kitchôji, Midori Uchiyama, Tanom Akalasane.

Kaerazeru hatoba (August 13, 1966)

Credits: Director: Mio Ezaki; Screenplay: Ryûzô Nakanishi, Nobuo Yamada; Cinematographer: Minoru Yokoyama; Format/Aspect Ratio: Color and Nikkatsuscope [2.35:1]; Musical Score: Harumi Ibe; Production Designer: Kazuhiko Chiba; Production Company and Distributor: Nikkatsu; English Title: *The Harbor of No Return*; Running Time: 89 minutes.
Cast: Ruriko Asaoka (Seako Mizusawa), Takashi Shimura (Detective Egusa), Eiji Gô (Otaki), Yûjirô Ishihara (Shiro Tsuda), Nobuo Kaneko (Sawada), Shôki Fukae (Nagae), Toshizô Kudô.

Zesshô (September 17, 1966)

Credits: Director: Katsumi Nishikawa; Planning Producer: Hideo Sasai; Screenplay: Katsumi Nishikawa, Toshio Yasumi; Story: Kenji Ooe [Ôe]; Cinematographer: Kuratarô Takamura; Format: Color; Editor: Akira Suzuki; Musical Score: Masayoshi Ikeda; Art Director: Akiyoshi Satani; Production Manager: Yasufusa Okada; Third Assistant Director: Akihiko Yamaki; Sound: Takinosuke Yagi; Lighting Technician: Aizô Kôno; Stills Photographer: Noboru Ogino;

Assistant to Planning Producer: Yûkichi Abe; Production Company: Nikkatsu; Running Length: 9 reels.
Cast: Ushio Akashi (Tamekichi), Michihiro Arimura (Comrade B), Kazuo Funaki (Junkichi Sonoda), Tokue Hanazawa (Shôzô, Koyuki's Father), Keiko Hara (Landlady), Kotoe Hatsui (Hama), Haruo Hayashi (Sasamoto), Takeshi Ida (Morimoto), Tatsuo Ishimori (Ôtani), Masako Izumi (Koyuki), Meiko Kaji [Masako Ôta] (Mihoko), Yasuhiro Kameyama (Tanaka), Dokô Kihara (Telegram Deliverer), Masahiro Kinoshita (Yoshiwara), Yasuko Kusama (Masa Kawada), Tomoko Naraoka (Sato, Koyuki's Mother), Takashi Shimura (Sôbei Sonoda), Hajime Sugiyama (Sano), Masuyo Suzumura (Yo-leave-ho Woman), Zenji Yamada (Gensuke), Masahiro Yatô (Comrade A), Keisuke Yukioka (Heikichirô Hashimoto).

Showa saidai no kaoyaku (1966)

Credits: Director: Kiyoshi Saeki; Screenplay: Akira Murao; Cinematographer: Ichirô Hoshijima; Format: Color; Musical Score: Chûji Kinoshita; English Title: *Greatest Boss of the Showa Era*; Running Time: 90 minutes.
Cast: Kôji Tsuruta, Tatsuo Umemiya, Tetsurô Tanba, Yûnosuke Itô, Takashi Shimura, Reiko Ohara, Hiroshi Nawa, Naoko Kubo, Asao Ushida, Jôji Ai, Tôru Abe.

Noren ichidai: jôkyô (1966)

Credits: Director: Tadashi Sawashima; Producer: Shigeru Okada; Screenplay: Tatsuo Nogami, Norifumi [Noribumi] Suzuki; Cinematographer: Sadatsugu [Sadaji] Yoshida; Format: Color; Production Designer: Inao Daimon; Production Company and Distributor: Toei Company; English Title: *Life of a Chivalrous Woman*; Running Time: 104 minutes.
Cast: Hibari Misora, Yoichi Hayashi, Takashi Shimura, Kayo Matsuo, Tatsuo Endô, Seizaburô Kawazu, Yoshiko Nakamura, Haruo Tanaka, Takehiko Kayama, Kayako Sono.

Sarutobe Sazuke [*Ninja Spy*] (1966)

Credits: Director: Shigeyuki Yamane; Producer: Kiyoshi Shimazu; Screenplay: Hidemitsu, Shigeyuki Yamane; Cinematographer: Hiroshi Takemura; Format: Color; Editor: Riichi Tomio; Musical Score: Shin'ichi Tanabe; Production Designer: Shigemori Shigeta; Sound: Tokio Hiramatsu; Production Company: Shochiku Company; U.S. Release Date: May 6, 1977; Running Time: 87 minutes.
Cast: Daijirô Harada (Kirikakure Saizo), Kyôsuke Machida (Rokuzaemon Senda), Keiko Matsuzaka (Kaeda), Takashi Shimura (Hakuunsai Tozawa), Gô Wakabayashi (Sanada Yukimura), Ichirô Zaitsu (Sarutobi Sasuke).

Satogashi ga kowareru toki [*When the Cookie Crumbles*] (June 10, 1967)

Credits: Director: Tadashi Imai; Executive Producer: Masaichi Nagata; Planning Producer: Hiroaki Fujii; Screenplay: Sugako Hashida; Based on the Novel by Ayako Sono; Cinematographer: Yoshihisa Nakagawa; Format: Color and

Daieiscope [2.35:1]; Editor: Toyo Suzuki; Musical Score: Takeo Watanabe; Art Director: Tomoo Shimogawara; Production Company and Distributor: Daiei Studios; Running Time: 96 minutes.
Cast: Jun Fujimaki (Tsuchiki), Eiji Funakoshi (Professor Amagi), Chisako Hara (Harue Sakai), Jun Negami (Azuma), Takashi Shimura (Kudo), Takahiro Tamura (Katsumi Gorai), Masahiko Tsugawa (Yutaka Okamura), Hisano Yamaoka (Mrs. Gorai). Ayako Wakao, Rieko Sumi, Mitsuko Tanaka, Masahiko Naruse, Takashi Nakamura, Kenji Oyama, Kôichi Itô.

Nihon no ichiban nagai hi [*Japan's Longest Day*] (August 3, 1967)

Credits: Director: Kihachi Okamoto; Producers: Sanezumi Fujimoto, Tomoyuki Tanaka; Screenplay: Shinobu Hashimoto; Based on the Book *Nihon no ichiban nagai hi* by Soichi Oya; Cinematographer: Hiroshi Murai; Format/Aspect Ratio: Black-and-White and Tohoscope [Anamorphic 2.35:1]; Editor: Yoshitami Kuroiwa; Musical Score: Masaru Satô; Production Designer: Iwao Akune; Sound: Shin Watarai; Lighting Technician: Tsuruzô Nishikawa; Production Company and Distributor: Toho Company; U.S. Release Date: March 26, 1968; Running Time: 157 minutes.
Cast: Seiji Miyaguchi (Foreign Minister Shigenori Togo), Matsuhiro [Rokkô] Toura (Shunichi Matsumoto, Vice-Minister of Foreign Affairs), Chishû Ryû (Prime Minister Baron Kantaro Suzuki), Sô Yamamura (Admiral Mitsumasa Yonai, Minister of the Navy), Toshirô Mifune (General Korechika Anami, Minister of the Army), Yoshio Kosugi (Keisuke Okada, Minister of Public Welfare), Takashi Shimura (Hiroshi Shimomura, Minister of the Board of Information), Etsushi Takahashi (Lt. Colonel Masutaka Ida, Military Affairs Section), Takao Inoue (Lt. Colonel Masahiko Takeshita, Military Affairs Section), Tadao Nakamaru (Lt. Colonel Jiro Shiizaki, Military Affairs Section), Toshio Kurosawa (Major Kenji Hatanaka, Military Affairs Section), Akira Kitchoji (General Yoshijiro Umezu, Chief of the Army General Staff), Haruo Yamada (Admiral Soemu Toyoda, Chief of the Naval General Staff), Ryôsuke Kagawa (Tadaatsu Ishiguro, Minister of Agriculture and Forestry), Ushio Akashi (President of the Privy Council Baron Kiichiro Hiranuma), Isao Tamagawa (Colonel Okitsugu Arao, Chief of Military Affairs Section), Hiroshi Nihon'yanagi (Admiral Takijiro Onishi, Vice-Chief of the Naval General Staff), Tôru Takeuchi (Naval Surgeon Kobayashi), Takeshi Katô (Cabinet Chief Secretary Hisatsune Sakomizu), Kyûzô Kawabe (Michio Kihara, Assistant to Sakomizu), Tatsuyoshi Ehara (Nobumasa Kawamoto, Private Secretary to Shimomura), Kôji Mitsui (Old Journalist on Political Affairs), Yoshio Tsuchiya (Lt. Colonel Hiroshi Fuha, Eastern District Army Staff Officer), Shôgo Shimada (Lt. General Takeshi Mori, Commander 1st Imperial Guards Division), Gorô Morino (Hachiro Ohashi, NHK Chairman), Minoru Takada (Vice-Admiral Zenshiro Hoshina, Director of the Naval Affairs Bureau), Daisuke Katô (Kenjiro Yabe, NHK Domestic Bureau Director), Shigeki Ishida (Daitaro Arakawa, NHK Technical Bureau Director), Jun Tazaki (Captain Yasuna Kozono, Commander 302nd Air Group), Akihiko Hirata (Commander Suguhara, 302nd Air Group), Sachio Sakai (Atsugi Air Base Crew Chief), Nobuo Nakamura (Minister Kidouchi, Lord Keeper of the Privy Seal Marquis), Shin [Susumu] Tatsuoka (Imperial Household Minister Sotaro Ishiwata), Ryûji Kita (General Shigeru

Hasunuma, Chief Military Aide to the Emperor), Akiji Nomura (Major Nakamura), Yû Fujiki (Major Seike, Military Aide to the Emperor), Kazuo Kitamura (Tomoo Sato, Cabinet General Affairs Section Chief), Fuyuki Murakami (Hiromasa Matsuzaka, Minister of Justice), Hyô Kitagawa (Hosaku Hirose, Minister of Finance), Masao Imafuku (Marshal Shunroku Hata), Hideyo Amamoto (Captain Takeo Sasaki), Shigeru Koyama (Susumu Kato, Imperial Household General Affairs Section), Jun Hamamura (Motohike Kakei, Imperial Household General Affairs Section Chief), Kaku Oze (Lt. General Tadakazu Wakamatsu, Vice-Minister for War), Makoto Satô (Major Midemasa Koga, 1st Imperial Guards Division), Akira Kubo (Major Sadakichi Ishihara, 1st Imperial Guards Division), Naoya Kusakawa (Shunichi Nagatmo, NHK Engineer), Kenjirô Ishiyama (General Shizuichi Tanaka, Commander in Chief of Eastern District Army), Keichi Taki (Colonel Tsukamoto, Tanaka's Adjutant), Susumu Fujita (Colonel Toyojiro Haga, Commander Imperial Guards 2nd Infantry Regiment), Hiroshi Tanaka (Major Kobayashi), Yutaka Sada (Keisaku Sano), Tadayoshi Ueda (Komonta Sano), Hiroyuki Katsube (Lt. Colonel Michinori Shiraishi, General Mori's Brother-in-Law), Yûnosuke Itô (Major General Toshio Nonaka, Commander 27th Air Brigade), Hirayoshi Aono (Grand Chamberlain Hisanori Fujita), Kiyoshi Kodama (Chamberlain Yasuhide Toda), Torahiko Hamada (Chamberlain Yasuya Mitsui), Tadashi Fukuro (Chamberlain Sukemasa Irie), Keiju Kobayashi (Chamberlain Yoshihiro Tokugawa), Ichirô Nakatani (First Lieutenant Kuroda), Tadasaburo Wakayama (Colonel Kazuo Mizutani, Chief of Staff to General Mori), Ren Yamamoto (Corporal), Kanta Mori (Major General Tatsuhiko Takashima, Chief of Staff Eastern District Army), Tôru Ibuki (Lt. Colonel Toru Itagaki, Eastern District Army Staff Officer), Seishirô Kuno (Battalion Commander), Yasuzô Ogawa (Policeman), Yoshifumi Tajima (Colonel Watanabe, Commander Imperial Guards 1st Infantry Regiment), Yûzô Kayama (Morio Tateno, NHK Broadcaster), Michiyo Aratama (Yuriko Hara), Akio Miyabe (Colonel Katsuhiko Inadome, Eastern District Army Staff Officer), Ginzô Sekiguchi (Chamberlain Okabe), Yû Sekita (Staff Kamino), Hisashi Igawa (Kempeitai Lieutenant), Hiroshi Koizumi (Nobukata Wada, NHK Broadcaster), Hakuô [Kôshirô] Matsumoto (Emperor Hirohito), Tatsuya Nakadai (Narrator), So Iwatani (Marshal Hajime Suguyama), Junnosuke Suda (Takeji Takahashi), Kazuko Iida, Shiro Kida, Shiyuki Tanaka, Keisuke Yamada, Yasuhisa Tsutsumi, Masao Akitsuki, Seiichirô Nomura, Hiroo Kirino, Yasuo Araki, Hiroshi Hasegawa, Yutaka Nakayama.

Gyangu no teiô (August 26, 1967)

Credits: Director: Yasuo Furuhata; Screenplay: Yoshihiro Ishimatsu; Format: Black-and-White and Toeiscope [2.35:1]; Production Company: Toei Company; Alternate Title: *Gyanju II*.
Cast: Noboru Andô, Shin'ichi [Sonny] Chiba, Masumi Tachibana, Shingo Yamashiro, Eijirô Yanagi, Takashi Shimura, Tetsurô Tanba.

Kyokotsu ichidai [*The Chivalrous Life*] (1967)

Credits: Director: Masahiro Makino; Screenplay: Isao Matsumoto, Akira Murao, Hideaki Yamamoto; Story: Ario Tomisawa; Cinematographer: Ichirô Hoshijima; Format: Color and Toeiscope [2.35:1]; Musical Score: Masao Yagi; Production Company: Toei; Running Time: 94 minutes.

Cast: Ken Takakura, Junko Fuji, Minoru Ôki, Kenjirô Ishiyama, Junko Miyazono, Takashi Shimura, Rin'ichi Yamamoto, Kenji Imai, Tatsuo Endô, Kôji Nanbara, Yôichi Numata, Gôzô Soma, Hiroshi Date, Kôsaku Okano, Ryô Suga.

Naniwa kyokaku: dokyo shichinin giri (1967)

Credits: Director: Shigehiro Ozawa; Screenplay: Norifumi Suzuki, Motohiro Torii; Cinematographer: Jûhei Suzuki; Format: Color; Musical Score: Ichirô Saitô; Production Company: Toei; English Title: *Killer of Seven Men*; Running Time: 88 minutes.

Cast: Kôji Tsuruta, Kayo Matsuo, Sanae Kitabayashi, Bin Amatsu, Takashi Shimura, Auto Yokoyama, Nobuo Kaneko, Masumi Tachibana, Asao Uchida, Toshi Amatsu, Tomoo Uchida, Masko Araki, Kôji Sekiyama, Yoshiko Nakamura, Yoshiko Sawa.

Ârappoi no ha gômen dazê (1967)

Credits: Director: Masaharu Segawa; Screenplay: Masaharu Ide, Tatsuo Nogami; Cinematographer: Ichirô Hoshijima; Format: Color; Musical Score: Chûji Kinoshita; Production Company: Toei; English Title: *Pardon My Violent Ways*; Running Time: 91 minutes.

Cast: Kôji Tsuruta, Naoko Kubo, Takashi Shimura, Hiroyuki Nagato, Kazuko Takamori, Asao Uchida, Bin Amatsu, Yuriko Mishima, Kyôsuke Machida, Minoru Ôki, Yoshitaka Toshi, Toshi Amatsu, Akemi Negishi.

Kurobe no taiyo [*The Sands of Kurobe*] (March 1, 1968)

Credits: Director: Kei Kumai; Producers: Yûjirô Ishihara, Toshirô Mifune, Akira Nakai; Screenplay: Masato Ide, Kei Kumai; Story: Sôjirô Motoki; Cinematographer: Mitsuji Kanau; Format/Aspect Ratio: Eastmancolor and Cinemascope [2.35:1]; Editor: Mutsuo Tanji; Musical Score: Toshirô Mayuzumi; Art Directors: Masayoshi Kobayashi, Hiroshi Yamashita, Masao Yamazaki; Costume Designer: Makoto Ikeda; Production Manager: Hideo Tomohisa; Assistant Directors: Toshi Aoki, Mizuho Doi, Hideo Miyau; Sound Recordist: Tetsuo Yasuda; Production Companies: Ishihara Productions Company, Ltd., Mifune Productions Company, Ltd., STAR Productions; Distributors: Nikkatsu, Toho Company; U.S. Release Date: October 2, 1968; Running Time: 196 minutes.

Cast: Toshirô Mifune (Kitagawa), Yûjirô Ishihara (Iwaoka), Osamu Takizawa (Otagaki), Takashi Shimura (Ashimura), Shûji Sano (Hirata), Jûkichi Uno (Mori), Ryutaro Tatsumi (Genzo), Isao Tamagawa (Sayama), Takeshi Katô (Kunikida), Sumio Takatsu (Ono), Eijirô Yanagi (Fujimura), Akira Yamauchi (Tsukamoto), Akira Terao (Kenichi), Eimei Nitani (Odagiri), Masahiko Naruse (Kumada), Fumie Kashiyama [Katayama] (Yuki), Mieko Takamine (Kayo), Tanie Kitabayashi [Kitamura] (Kiku), Kinzô Shin (Takemoto), Shinsuke Ashida (Kurosaki), Eiji Okada (Yoshino), Nagatake Shoji (Ohashi), Keisuke Yukioka (Seyama), Toshinosuke Nagao (Kurasawa), Jôji Hidehara (Yamaguchi), Mizuho Suzuki (Senda), Sayuri Kishido (Hazumi), Takashi Koshiba (Shibata), Gisuke

Makino (Takahashi), Hideji Ôtaki (Dojo), Norio Mineda, Sônosuke Niki, Kenji Shimamura, Tsuneo Arakawa, Jushiro Hirata, Yûzô Harumi, Yû Izumi, Hyôe Enoki, Hiroshi Chiyoda, Shôsei Mutô (Miners), Taketoshi Naitô (Doctor), Tappei Shimokawa (Abe), Yuichi Sato (Takagi), Takashi Nomura (Takeyama), Jun Miyazaki (Tokuda), Keiji Ishizaki, Yoshinobu Ogawa, Masao Uchikura, Katsumasa Yamayoshi, Daisuke Ômi (Workers), Masayoshi Miyasaka (Kihara), Aiko Mimasu (Restaurant Madame), Masao Shimizu (Geology Professor), Tomoe Hiiro, Aki Kawaguchi.

Botan-dôrô [Peony Lantern] (June 15, 1968)

Credits: Director: Satsuo Yamamoto; Producers: Tokuko Miyako, Masaichi Nagata; Screenplay: Yoshitaka Yoda; Based on the Novel by Encho San'yûtei; Cinematographer: Chikashi [Chishi] Makiura; Format/Aspect Ratio: Fujicolor and Daieiscope [2.35:1]; Musical Score: Sei Ikeno; Production Designer: Yoshinobu Nishioka; Sound Recordist: Tsuchitaro Hayashi; Gaffer: Reijirô Yamashita; Production Company and Distributor: Daei Studios; Alternate English Title: *Haunted Lantern*; Running Time: 89 minutes.
Cast: Miyoko Akaza (Otsuya), Kôjirô Hongô (Hagiwara Shinzaburou), Kô Nishimura (Banzou), Mayumi Ogawa (Omine), Takashi Shimura (Fortune Teller), Atsumi Uda (Kiku), Michiko Ôtsuka (Oyone), Hajime Koshikawa.

Zatôichi hatashi-jô [Zatoichi and the Fugitives] (August 10, 1968)

Credits: Director: Kimiyoshi Yasuda; Executive Producer: Masaichi Nagata; Producer: Ikuo Kubodera; Screenplay: Kinya Naoi, Kan Shimozawa; Cinematographer: Kazuo Miyagawa; Format/Aspect Ratio: Eastmancolor and Daieiscope [2.35:1]; Editors: Kanji Suganuma, Iwao Ôtani; Art Director: Shigeru Katô; Sound Recordist: Iwao Ôtani; Production Company: Daei Motion Picture Company; Distributor: Daei Studios, Daei International Films (U.S. Release); Running Time: 82 minutes.
Cast: Shintarô Katsu (Zatoichi), Kayo Mikimoto (Oshizu), Kyôsuke Machida (Ogano Genpachiro), Takashi Shimura (Dr. Junan), Shôbun Inoue (Kumeji), Jôtarô Senba [Sennami] (Minokichi), Jutarô Kitashiro [Hisatoro Hojo] (Genta), Hôsei Komatsu (Matsugoro), Kôichi Mizuhara (Sennosuke), Kazuo Yamamoto (Isuke), Ryuji Funabashi (Ushimatsu), Shôzô Nanbu (Tokuzaemon), Yukio Horikita (Inokichi), Seishirô Hara (Sakata), Rieko Oda (Osei), Yukari Mizamuchi (Yoshida-ya's Maid), Teruko Oumi (Osato), Yumiko Nogawa (Oaki), Hiroshi Hijikata (Yakuza).

Gion matsuri (February 12, 1968)

Credits: Directors: Daisuke Itô, Tetsuya Yamanouchi [Yamauchi]; Planning Producer: Daisuke Itô; Screenplay: Kunio Shimizu, Hisayuki Suzuki; Based on the Story by Katsumi Nishiguchi; Cinematographer: Shintarô Kawasaki; Format/Aspect Ratio: Eastmancolor and Shochiku Grandscope [2.35:1]; Editor: Katsumi Kawai; Musical Score: Masaru Satô; Production Companies: Nippon Eiga Fukko Kyokai, Shochiku Company; Distributors: Shochiku Eiga; English Titles: *Festival of Gion*, *Gion Festival*, *The Day the Sun Rose*; U.S. Release Date:

February 12, 1969 [Shochiku Films of America]; Running Time: 168 minutes; 1973 U.S. Re-release Running Time: 123 minutes.
Cast: Kinnosuke Nakamura (Shinkichi), Toshirô Mifune (Kumaza), Shima Iwashita (Ayame), Yûnosuke Itô (Akamatsu), Takahiro Tamura (Sukematsu), Takashi Shimura (Tsuneemon), Eitarô Ozawa (Kadokura), Kunie Tanaka (Gonji), Tomo'o Nagai (Matashiro Kawahara), Orie Satô (Otsuru), Hisako Takihana (Ichi), Kamatari Fujiwara (Genzo), Masami Shimojô (Jumbei Yamashina), Ryôsuke Kagawa (Bunsuke), Junkô Tôda [Toshiko Sawa] (Oyoshi), Osamu Takizawa (Narrator), Shinsuke Mikimoto, Tsutomu Shimomoto, Kiyoshi Atsumi, Ken Takakura, Katsuo Nakamura, Eitarô Matsuyama, Shirô Ôtsuji, Kin'ya Kitaôji, Hibari Misora.

Sangyo sapai (May 21, 1968)

Credits: Director: Eiichi Kudô; Producer: Shigeru Okada; Screenplay: Tatsuo Nogami; Cinematographer: Osamu [Shin] Furuya; Format: Fujicolor and Toeiscope [2.35:1]; Musical Score: Masao Yagi; Production Designer: Jirô Tomita; Production Company and Distributor: Toei Company; English Title: *Industrial Spy*; Running Time: 90 minutes.
Cast: Tatsuo Umemiya, Reiko Ônobuta, Kyôsuke Machida, Kenjirô Ishiyama, Takashi Shimura, Mistue Shimizu, Kikko Matsuoka, Meichô Soganoya, Fumio Watanabe, Akio Hasegawa, Akemi Hagishiyama, Hiroshi Nawa, Kiyoshi Hitomi, Ichiro Chagawa, Takamaru Sasaki.

Onno tobakushi amadera kaichô (July 27, 1968)

Credits: Director: Shigeo Tanaka; Format: Fujicolor; Production Company and Distributor: Daiei Studios; English Title: *The Woman Gambler and the Nun*; Running Time: 83 minutes.
Cast: Kyôko Enami, Yûsuke Kawazu, Mako Sanjô, Takashi Shimura.

Gendai yakuza: yotomono no okite (1968)

Credits: Director: Yasuo Furuhata; Screenplay: Akira Murao; Cinematographer: Ichirô Hoshijima; Format: Color; Musical Score: Shunsuke Kikuchi; Production Designer: Hiroshi Kitagawa; Production Company: Toei Tokyo; Distributor: Toei Company; Running Time: 92 minutes.
Cast: Bunta Sugawara, Kyôsuke Machida, Takashi Shimura, Tomisaburô Wakayama, Junko Fuji.

Ah kaiten tokubetsu kogetikai (1968)

Credits: Director: Shigehiro Ozawa; Screenplay: Gorô Tanada; Format/Aspect Ratio: Black-and-White and Toeiscope [2.35:1]; Production Company and Distributor: Toei Company; English Title: *Human Torpedoes*; Running Time: 104 minutes.
Cast: Bin Amatsu, Shin'ichi [Sonny] Chiba, Tatsuo Endô, Junko Fuji, Ryô Ikebe, Jûzô Itami, Nobuo Kaneko, Asao Koike, Jûshirô Konoe, Kyôsuke Machida, Hiroki Matsukata, Aiko Mimasu, Tomoko Ogawa, Yoshiko Sakuma, Hiroko

Sakuramachi, Kôtarô Satomi, Takashi Shimura, Kôji Tsuruta, Tatsuo Umemiya, Minoru Ôki.

Shin Abashiri Bangaichi (December 28, 1968)

Credits: Director: Masahiro Makino; Producers: Kôji Shundô, Wataru Yabe; Screenplay: Akira Murao; Story: Hajime Itô; Cinematographer: Makoto Tsudoi [Tsuboi]; Format/Aspect Ratio: Fujicolor and Toeiscope [2.35:1]; Editor: Osamu Tanaka; Musical Score: Masao Yagi; Art Director: Baku [Hiroshi] Fujita; Sound: Kenzo Inoue; Production Company: Toei Tokyo; Distributor: Toei; English Title: *The Man from Abashiri Jail Strikes Again*; Running Time: 94 minutes.
Cast: Ken Takakura (Katsuji Suematsu), Tatsuya Mihashi (Isamu Gunji), Hiroyuki Nagato (Tatô Komatsu), Rin'ichi Yamamoto (Genkichi Komatsu), Kayo Matsuo (Hidekoma), Kanji Imai (Yô Tai kô), Michitarô Mizushima (Tôru Ishizu), Takashi Shimura (Tetsutarô Fujigami), Ai Sasaki (Akiko Suehiro), Jerry Itô (Jimmy Nakata), Kôji Fujioka (Ryûzo Tsuruoka), Shigeyoshi Fujiyama (Detective Sakurada), Akikane Sawa (Yoshii), Nobuo Kaneko (Ryû), Kôji Sekiyama (Sai), Yukiko Anjô (Nanae).

Fûrin kazan [*Samurai Banners*] (February 1, 1969)

Credits: Director: Hiroshi Inagaki; Producers: Hiroshi Inagaki, Toshirô Mifune, Yoshio Nishikawa, Tomoyuki Tanaka; Screenplay: Shinobu Hashimoto, Takeo Kunihiro; Based on the Novel by Yasushi Inoue; Cinematographer: Kazuo Yamada; Format/Aspect Ratio: Eastmancolor and Tohoscope [2.35:1]; Processing: Tokyo Laboratory, Ltd.; Editor: Yoshihiro Araki; Musical Score: Masaru Satô; Production Designer: Hiroshi Ueda; Makeup: Ya Yamada; Chief Assistant Director: Teruo Maru; Assistant Director: Yoshikazu Tanaka; Sound: Shoichi Fujinawa; Sound Mixer: Hisashi Shimonaga; Special Effects: Cho Chiku; Optical Effects: Saburo Doi; Lighting Technician: Sachiro Sato; Coordinator: Shizuo Kanze; Swordplay Coordinators: Ryû Kuze, Yokai Nana; Archery: Greater Japan Mountain Archery Society; Executive in Charge of Production: Shoichi Koga; Production Companies: Mifune Productions Company, Ltd., Toho Company; Distributor: Toho Company; U.S. Release Date: June 24, 1969; Running Time: 165 minutes.
Cast: Toshirô Mifune (Kansuke Yamamoto), Yoshiko Sakuma (Princess Yufu), Kinnosuke Nakamura (Shingen Takeda), Yûjirô Ishihara (Kenshin Uesugi), Katsuo Nakamura (Nobusato Itagaki), Kanzaburô [Kankurô] Nakamura (Katsuyori Takeda), Gan'emon Nakamura (Nobukato Itagaki), Masakazu Tamura (Nobushige Takeda), Mayumi Ozora (Princess Okoto), Kôji Nanbara (Ronin), Umenosuke Nakamura, Ken Ogata, Takashi Shimura, Masami Harukawa, Haruko Tôgô, Keiko Sawai, Yoshiko Kuga, Akihiko Hirata, Yoshio Tsuchiya, Akira Kubo, Ichirô Nakaya, Sachio Sakai, Nakajirô Tomita, Tetsurô Sagawa, Kichijiro Murata, Jun'ichirô Mukai, Ryôsuke Kagawa, Masao Shimizu, Ryûnosuke Yamazaki, Jotaro Togami, Kôji Nambura, Ryûnosuke Tsukigata, Naraimon Nakamura.

Shôwa zankyô-den: Karajishi jingi (March 6, 1969)

Credits: Director: Masahiro Makino; Screenplay: Isao Matsumoto, Hideaki Yamamoto; Cinematographer: Makoto Tsudoi [Tsuboi]; Format/Aspect Ratio:

Color and Toeiscope [2.35:1]; Editor: Osamu Tanaka; Musical Score: Shunsuke Kikuchi; Composer (Theme Music): Ichirô Mizuki; Production Designers: Kôji Shundô, Tatsu Yoshida; Art Director: Baku Fujita; Set Decorators: Shôji Takei, Kiyoshi Yoshida; Production Manager: Genrô Itô; Assistant Director: Makoto Naitô; Sound: Tadayuki Komatsu; Gaffer: Yasunojô Kawasaki; Choreographer: Takashi Hio; Continuity: Kinuko Miyamoto; Production Company: Toei Tokyo; Distributor: Toei Company; English Titles: *Brutal Tales of Chivalry*, *The Man with the Dragon Tattoo*; Running Time: 90 minutes.

Cast: Ken Takakura, Ryô Ikebe, Junko Fuji, Kyôsuke Machida, Takashi Shimura, Seizaburô Kawazu, Iwao Dan, Hiroshi Date, Kôji Fujiyama, Bokuzen Hidari, Seiichiro Kameishi, Hiroshi Kawai, Keiichi Kitagawa, Koichi Kitami, Chie Kobayashi, Nenji Kobayashi, Akira Kuji, Shinsuke Mikimoto, Yôko Minakaze, Naoharu Miyatsuchi, Tamani Natsu, Kenichi Sakuragi, Seiya Satô, Shôken Sawa, Sakae Shima, Harumi Sone, Shinji Takano, Junnosuke Takasu, Kôji Takashima, Toshiyuki Tsuchiyama, Terutaka Ueda, Akira Yamada, Kôichi Yamada, Rin'ichi Yamamoto.

Kanto onna akumyo [*Unknown Woman of Kanto*] (May 1, 1969)

Credits: Director: Kazuo Mori; Screenplay: Koji Takada; Cinematographer: Fujio Morita; Musical Score: Hajime Kaburagi; Production Company: Daiei; Alternate English Title: *Kanto Woman's Bad Reputation*; Running Time: 83 minutes.

Cast: Michiyo Yasuda, Shintarô Katsu, Kô Nishimura, Yaeko [Yoshie] Mizutani, Takashi Shimura, Kayo Mikimoto, Shigeru Tsuyuguchi, Ryutaro Gomi, Fujio Suga.

Shin Abashiri Bangaichi: Runin-masaki no ketto (August 13, 1969)

Credits: Director: Yasuo Furuhata; Cinematographer: Shichirô Hayashi; Format: Color; Musical Score: Masao Yagi; Production Company: Toei Tokyo; English Title: *New Abashiri Prison Story—Harbor Duel*; Running Time: 109 minutes.

Cast: Ken Takakura (Shinichi Tsukibana), Takashi Shimura, Kaneko Iwasaki, Minoru Ôki, Sanae Tsuchida, Kenji Sugawara, Shingo Yamashiro.

Otoko wa tsurai yo [*It's Tough Being a Man*] (August 27, 1969)

Credits: Director: Yôji Yamada; Producer: Tsutomu Kamimura; Planning Producers: Shun'ichi Kobayashi, Yukio Takashima; Screenplay: Yôji Yamada, Azuma Morisaki; Cinematographer: Tetsuo Takaha; Format/Aspect Ratio: Eastmancolor and Shochiku Grandscope [2.35:1]; Editor: Iwao Ishii; Musical Score: Naozumi Yamamoto; Art Director: Chiyoo Umeda; Production Company: Shôchiku Eiga; Distributor: Shochiku Company; U.S. Release Title: *Am I Trying*; U.S. Release Date: July 18, 1974; U.S. Reissue Title: *Tora-san Our Lovable Tramp*; Running Time: 91 minutes.

Cast: Kiyoshi Atsumi (Torajirô Kuruma), Chieko Baishô (Sakura), Sachiko Mitsumoto (Fuyuko), Chishû Ryû (Gozensama), Takashi Shimura (Hyôichiro Suwa), Shin Morikawa (Ryûzô), Gin Maeda (Hiroshi Suwa), Taisaku Akino [Masaaki Tsusaka] (Noboru Kawamata), Gajirô Satô (Genkichi), Keiroku Seki (Shikaisha), Chieko Misaki (Tsune Kuruma), Hisao Dazai (Umetarô Katsura), Shunsuke Ômi

(Bucho), Taichirô Hirokawa (Michio), Fusatarô Ishijima (Michio's Father), Matsuko Shiga (Michio's Mother), Kiyoko Tsuji (Ikuko), Kiyo Murakami (Kawajij no Hosutesu), Ken'ichi Ishii (Kôin A), Tatsumi Ichiyama (Kôin C), Ryûsuke Kita, Terumitsu Kawashima (Yashi), Ryôko Mizuki (Umetarô's Wife), Kôsaku Mizuno, Nobuo Takagi, Toshio Ohkubo, Yoshiko Yonemoto, Kimiyo Ôtsuka, Yoshino Tani, Yasuko Gotô, Haruko Chichibu, Kazuko Satô.

Nihon boryoku-dan: kumicho to shikaku (November 20, 1969)
Credits: Director: Junya Sato; Screenplay: Fumio Kônami, Jun'ya Satô; Cinematographer: Hanjirô Nakazawa; Format: Color; Musical Score: Masanobu Higure; Production Company: Toei Tokyo; Distributor: Toei Company; English Title: *Japan's Violent Gangs—The Boss and the Killers*; Running Time: 92 minutes.
Cast: Kôji Tsuruta, Takashi Shimura, Ryôhei Uchida, Tetsurô Tanba, Hitomi Nozoe, Tadao Nakamaru, Asao Uchida, Fumio Watanabe, Ichirô Sugai, Michitarô Mizushima, Sanae Kitabayashi.

Shin Abashiri Bangaichi: Saihate no Nagare-mono [*The Vagrant Comes to a Port Town*] (December 27, 1969)
Credits: Director: Kiyoshi Saeki; Screenplay: Akira Murao; Cinematographer: Masahiko Iimura; Format/Aspect Ratio: Color and Toeiscope [2.35:1]; Musical Score: Masao Yagi; Production Company: Toei; Alternate English Title: *New Abashiri Prison Story: Vagrant Comes to a Port Town*; Running Time: 99 minutes.
Cast: Ken Takakura (Shinichi Tsukibana), Takashi Shimura, Kaneko Iwaskura, Minoru Ôki, Sanae Tsuchida, Kenji Sugawara, Shingo Yamashiro, Yuriko Hoshi, Michitarô Mizushima, Hayato Tani, Rin'ichi Yamamoto, Kenji Imai, Hiroyuki Shimozawa, Toshiaki Minami, Fujio Suga, Hideo Sunazuka.

Gekido no showashi "Gunbatsu" [*The Militarists*] (August 11, 1970)
Credits: Director: Hiromichi Horikawa; Producers: Sanezumi Fujimoto, Hiroshi Haryu; Screenplay: Ryôzô Kasahara; Cinematographer: Kazuo Yamada; Format/Aspect Ratio: Eastmancolor and Super Panavision 70 [2.35:1]; Processing: Kinuta Laboratories, Tokyo; Editor: Yoshitami Kuriowa; Musical Score: Riichirô Manabe; Production Designers: Iwao Akune, Shigekazu Ikuno; Executive in Charge of Production: Boku Morimoto; Chief Assistant Director: Masashi Matsumoto; Sound: Shin Watarai [Hyper 3D Three-Channel Stereo]; Lighting Technician: Chôshirô Ishii; Special Effects Director: Eiji Tsuburaya [archival footage]; Stills Photographer: Matsuo Yoshizaki; Production Company and Distributor: Toho Company: U.S. Release Date: March 10, 1971; Running Time: 134 minutes.
Cast: Keiju Kobayashi (Premier Hideki Tojo), Yûzô Kayama (Goro Arai), Toshirô Mifune (Admiral Isoroku Yamamoto), Sô Yamamura (Mitsumasa Yonai), Tatsuya Mihashi (Takijiro Onishi), Toshio Kurosawa (Kamikaze Pilot), Gorô Tarumi (Takei), Tôru Abe (Chuichi), Hideyo Amamoto (Professor Fuyuki), Tasuyoshi Ehara (Mikuni), Susumu Fugita (Nagano), Ryuichi Fujiyama (Hirota), Akihiko Hirata (Tomita), Shôichi Hirose (Hama), Ryûji Kita (Koshiro), Kazuo Kitamura (Yamanaka), Seiji Miyaguchi (Togo), Kanta Mori (Koyama), Gôro

Mutsumi (Ishida), Nobuo Nakamura (Koichi), Ichirô Nakatani (Sano), Tadashi Okabe (Noboyuki Abe), Kenji Sahara (Okamoto), Sachio Sakai (Kitamura), Gen Shimizu (Yoshizawa), Takashi Shimura (Editor), Yoshifumi Tajima (Ito), Isao Tamagawa (Sukamoto), Kôtarô Tomita (Miyamoto), Yoshio Tsuchiya (Okabe), Kenjirô Ishiyama, Sumio Takatsu, Kôji Iwamoto, Yoshio Katsube, Shin Kishida, Akira Kubo, Matagorô Nakamura, Yutaka Sada, Takamaru sasaki, Masao Shimizu, Kazuo Suzuki, Chôtarô Togin, Takeshi Yamamoto, Wataru Ômae.

Otoko wa tsurai yo: Torajirô renka [*Tora-san's Shattered Romance*] (January 15, 1971)

Credits: Director: Yôji Yamada; Screenplay: Yôji Yamada, Akira Miyazaki; Cinematographer: Tetsuo Takaba; Format: Color [2.35:1]; Editor: Iwao Ishii; Production Company: Toei; Distributor: Shochiku; English Title: Running Time: 90 minutes.

Cast: Kiyoshi Atsumi (Torajirô Kuruma), Chieko Baishô (Sakura), Ayako Wakao (Yûko Akashi), Shin Morikawa (Kuruma Tatsuzô), Chieko Misaki (Tsune Kuruma), Gin Maeda (Hiroshi Suwa), Chishû Ryû (Gozen-sama), Hisao Dazai (Tarô Ume), Gajirô Satô (Genkô), Hisaya Morishige (Senzô), Nobuko Miyamoto (Kinuyo), Tatsuo Matsumura (Doctor Yamashita), Gorô Tarumi (Yûko's Husband), Takashi Shimura.

Yomigaeru daichi (February 26, 1971)

Credits: Director: Noboru Nakamura; Producers: Takachika Daikuhara, Yûjirô Ishihara, Masahiko Kobayashi; Screenplay: Kengo Inomata; Based on the Novel by Shôji Kimoto; Cinematographer: Mitsuji Kanau; Format: Color; Editor: Shirô Watanabe; Musical Score: Tôru Takemitsu; Art Director: Takeharu Sakaguchi; First Assistant Director: Hiroshi Nagai; Second Assistant Director: Ryûzô Horiuchi; Sound: Yasuhiro Sato; Gaffer: Noboru Shiiba; Stills Photographer: Tetsuo Kubo; Production Company: Ishihara Productions Company, Ltd.; Distributor: Shochiku Company; Running Time: 119 minutes.

Cast: Yûjirô Ishihara (Kazuya Uematsu), Yôko Tsukasa (Minako Soejima), Rentarô Mikuni (Eisuke Noda), Mitsuo Hamada (Sakaguchi), Tamio Kawaji [Kawachi] (Yokoyama), Akira Terao (Tsuchiya), Tappei Shimokawa (Tatsuyoshi), Kanta Mori (Yusaku Tsuchiya), Dai Kanai (Kubo), Sumio Takatsu (Tajima), Katsumi Shiina (Azuma), Isao Tamagawa (Katsuzo), Yûji Odaka (Orihara), Toshio Takahara (Takii), Taketoshi Naitô (Assistant Professor), Kinzô Shin (Gensaku Tsuchiya), Tanie Kitabayashi (Toyo), Tomoko Naraoka (Yoshiko), Michie Terada (Kazuko), Chiyoko Toda (Kiyoe), Yuki Shirono (Sachiko), Eiji Okada (Mitsuo Iwashita), Takashi Shimura (Gondo), Osamu Takizawa (Corporate Chairman), Tetsuya Watari (Hironosuke Nakadate).

Gorotsuki mushuku (June 25, 1971)

Credits: Director: Yasuo Furuhata; Producers: Kôji Shundô, Hisashi Yabe; Screenplay: Toshiya Itô, Shin'ichirô Sawai; Cinematographer: Shichirô Hayashi; Format: Color; Editor: Osamu Tanaka; Musical Score: Takeo Watanabe; Art Director: Hiroshi Kitagawa; Assistant Director: Hiroshi Kodaira; Sound Recordist: Masuhiro Hirogami; Lighting Technician: Hideo Motomochi; Stills

Photographer: Tsutomu Endô; Production Company: Toei; English Title: *Rogue Wanderer*; Running Time: 100 minutes.
Cast: Ken Takakura (Isamu Tekada), Takashi Shimura, Rin'ichi Yamamoto, Yoshi Katô, Tanie Kitabayashi, Etsuko Nami, Toshiaki Minami, Yoko Hayama, Hiroshi Kondô, Fumio Watanabe, Mayumi Kajiwara, Kazuko Kamei, Kyoko Kamimura, Mayumi Matsushita, Takashi Takano, Chiaki Tsukioka, Tôkô Ueda, Norihiko Umeji.

Otoko wa tsurai yo: Torajiro koiuta [*Tora-san's Love Call*] (December 29, 1971)

Credits: Director: Yôji Yamada; Screenplay: Yoshitaka Asama, Yôji Yamada; Cinematographer: Tetsuo Takaha; Format/Aspect Ratio: Color and Shochiku Grandscope [2.35:1]; Musical Score: Naozumi Yamamoto; Production Company and Distributor: Shôchiku Eiga; U.S. Release Date: April 14, 1973; Running Time: 113 minutes.
Cast: Kiyoshi Atsumi (Torajiro Kuruma), Chieko Baishô (Sakura Suwa, Torajiro's Sister), Junko Ikeuchi (Takako), Hyôichiro Suwa, Hiroshi's Father), Gin Maeda (Hiroshi, Sakura's Husband), Shin Morikawa (Tatsuzo, Torajiro's Uncle), Chieko Misaki (Tsune, Torajiro's Aunt), Hisao Dazi (Umetaro, Hiroshi's Boss), Chishû Ryû (Priest), Masahiko Tanimura (Laborer), Takashi Shimura, Mari Okamoto, Yoshio Yoshida, Kanjirô Ôsugi.

Gokuaku bozu—nomu utsu kau (1971)

Credits: Director: Buichi Saitô; Screenplay: Akira Murao, Kôji Takada; Cinematographer: Nagaki Yamagishi; Format: Color; Musical Score: Toshiaki Tsushima; Production Company: Toei; English Title: *The Bloody Priest*; Running Time: 89 minutes.
Cast: Tomisaburô Wakayama, Bunta Sugawara, Takashi Shimura, Tôru Abe, Kyôsuke Machida, Sanae Kitabayashi, Fumio Watanabe, Yuriko Mishima, Takuzô Kawatani.

Gokudo makari touru (July 3, 1972)

Credits: Director: Shigehiro Ozawa; Screenplay: Koji Takada; Cinematographer: Sadatsugu [Sadaji] Yoshida; Format: Color; Musical Score: Michiaki Watanabe; Production Designer: Takatoshi Suzuki; Production Company and Distributor: Toei Company; English Title: *Gokudo's Notorious Reputation*; Running Time: 94 minutes.
Cast: Tomisaburô Wakayama (Shimamura Seikichi), Bunta Sugawara (Ishido Tsuneo), Masahiko Tanimura (Miyoshi), Takashi Shimura, Hiroshi Hasegawa.

Shin Zatôichi monogatari: Kasama no chimatsuri [*Zatoichi's Conspiracy*] (April 21, 1973)

Credits: Director: Kimiyoshi Yasuda; Producers: Shintarô Katsu, Ikuo Kubodera, Hiroyoshi Nishioka; Screenplay: Yoshi Hattori; Story: Kan Shimozawa; Cinematographer: Chikashi [Chishi] Makiura; Format/Aspect Ratio: Eastmancolor and Tohoscope [2.35:1]; Editor: Yoshiharu Hayashi; Musical Score: Akira Ifukube; Production Designer: Seiichi Ôta; Assistant Director: Masao Kobayashi; Sound: Masao Ôsumi; Lighting Technician: Shôzô Saito; Stills Photographer: Eiichi Oootani; Production Companies: Katsu Production, Toho Company; Distributors: Toho Company; U.S. Release Date: April 15, 1974 [Rising Sun Productions]; Running Time: 88 minutes.

Cast: Shintarô Katsu (Zatôichi/Blind Man Ichi), Yukiyo Toake (Miyo), Eiji Okada (Shinbei of Hitachiya), Kei Satô (Magistrate), Yoshio Tsuchiya (Superintendent Shobei), Shirô Kishibe (Ruffian), Rie Yokoyama (Yuri/Lily), Tatsuo Endô (Boss Iwagoro), Takashi Shimura (Sakubei), Kuniko Ishii (Virgin Farmgirl), Osamu Sakai (Gen), Yûsaku Terashima (Yahei), Naoyuki Asahina, Tamotsu Fujiharu, Takaji Fukui, Takamori Gen, Yûji Hamada, Hiroshi Kanda, Masayoshi Kikuno, Goro Kumon, Nobue Matsuoka, Yuzo Miyashita, Tokio Oki, Yuko Ota, Shoroku Shimada, Teiko Takeda, Saburô Ukita, Mitsuo Watanabe, Takeshi Yabuuchi, Satoko Yamamura.

Karei-yaru ichizoku [*The Family*] (January 26, 1974)

Credits: Director: Satsuo Yamamoto; Producers: Kiichi Ichikawa; Michio Morioka; Screenplay: Nobuo Yamada; Based on the Novel by Toyoko Yamasaki; Cinematographer: Kôzô Okazaki; Format: Color; Editor: Jun Nabeshima; Musical Score: Masaru Satô; Production Designer: Takeshi Ômura; Art Director: Yoshinaga Yoko'o; Assistant Director: Toshio Gotô; Production Company: Geiensha Company; Distributor: Toho Company; U.S. Release Date: August 10, 1982; Running Time: 211 minutes.

Cast: Shin Saburi (Daisuke Manpyo), Yumeji Tsukioka (Yasuko Manpyo), Tatsuya Nakadai (Teppei Manpyo), Yôko Yamamoto (Sanae Manpyo), Yûki Meguro (Ginpei Manpyo), Mari Nakayama (Makiko Manpyo), Wakako Sakai (Tsugiko Manpyo), Jirô Tamiya (Ataru Mima), Kyôko Kagawa (Ichiko Mima), Machiko Kyô (Aiko Takasu), Kôji Kawamura (Ichiro Okawa), Hideaki (Nitani (Shoichi Migumo), Mayumi Ohzora (Shiho Migumo), Kô Nishimura (Sentaro Watanuki), Michiko Araki (Mrs. Koizumi), Torahiko Hamada (Ohkame), Akihiko Hirata (Haruta), Toshio Hosokawa (Matsuo), Yoshio Inaba (Ichinose Factory Owner), Ryûnosuke Kaneda (Ryuhichi Arao), Yoshi Katô (Zentitaka), Seizaburô Kawazu (Tabuchi, Chief Secretary), Tanie Kitabayashi (Shuko Sahashi, First Lady), Kin'ya Kitaôji (Yoshihiko Ichinose), Shigeru Kôyama (Wajima), Nobuo Nakamura (Matsudaira), Tetsu Nakamura (Shirakawa), Eitarô Ozawa (Nagata, Ministry of Finance), Zenpei Saga (Yamamoto), Fukuko Sayo (Mrs. Itoh), Takashi Shimura (Yasuda, Makiko's Father), Akio Suzuki (Kawabata), Mizuho Suzuki (Lawyer Kuraishi/Narrator), Toshio Takahara (Tsunoda), Osamu Takizawa (Miyamoto), Yasukiyo Umeno (Isahaya), Hideji Otaki (Masayoshi Nakane), Kyosuke Aihara, Tomio Aoki, Kuniyasu Atsumi, Tokue Hanazawa, Takuzo Kumagai, Takeo Namai, Takamaru Sasaki, Tappei Shimokawa, Kenzô Tabu.

Ranru no hata (May 1, 1974)

Credits: Director: Kôzaburô Yoshimura; Screenplay: Ken Miyamoto; Cinematographer: Yoshio Miyajima; Format: Color; English Title: *The Tattered Banner*; Running Time: 115 minutes.

Cast: Rentarô Mikuni (Seizo Tanaka), Michiko Araki (Katsu, Seizo's Wife), Ikkô Furuya (18-Year-Old Boy), Jun Hamamura (Soroku), Sen Hara (Yone, Jihei's Mother), Akiko Kana [Yuko Ozeki] (Taki, Sohachi's Sister), Daigo Kusano (Sanji), Atsuo Nakamura (Kotoku), Toshiyuki Nishida (Jihei), Takashi Shimura (Shihei Furukawa), Kinzô Shin (Policeman), Tadahiko Sugano (Kinoshita), Ryô Tamura (Wasaburo), Kazunaga Tsuji (Sohachi).

Nosutoradamasu no daiyogen (August 3, 1974)
Credits: Director: Toshio Masuda; Producers: Osamu Tanaka, Tomoyuki Tanaka; Screenplay: Toshio Yasumi, Yoshimitsu Banno; Story: Ben Gotô; Based on the Book by Michel de Nostredame [Notredame]; Cinematographer: Rokurô Nishigaki; Format/Aspect Ratio: Eastmancolor and Tohoscope [2.35:1]; Processing: Kinuta Laboratories, Tokyo; Editor: Nobuo Ogawa; Musical Score/Arranger/Conductor/Synthesizer: Isao Tomita; Production Designer: Yoshirô Muraki; Chief Assistant Directors: Yoshimitsu Banno, Fumisuke [Fumisake] Okada; Second Assistant Director: Tsunesaburo Nishikawa; Third Assistant Director: Shindo Yasuda; Fourth Assistant Directors: Tadashi Masamori, Takao Okawara; First Assistant Director, Second Unit: Koji Hashimoto; Sound Recordist: Kanae Masua; Assistant Cameras: Kenichi Eguchi, Yoshinori Sekiguchi; Lighting Technician: Shinji Kojima; Director of Special Effects: Teruyoshi Nakano; Chief Assistant Director of Special Effects: Kôichi Kawakita; Art Director of Special Effects: Yasuyuki Inoue; Director of Special Effects Photography: Sokei Tomioka; Optical Photography: Takeshi Miyanishi; Special Effects Lighting: Masakuni Morimoto; Matte Processing: Kazunobu Sanpei; Script Supervisor: Akane Shiratori; Production Companies: Toho Company; United Productions of America (UPA); Distributor: Toho Company; English Titles: *The Last Days of Planet Earth*, *The Prophecies of Nostradamus*; U.S. Release Date: July 13, 1979; Running Time: 114 minutes; 1979 U.S. Release Running Time: 88 minutes.

Cast: Tetsurô Tanba (Dr. Nishiyama), Toshio Kurosawa (Akira Nakagawa), Kaoru Yumi (Mariko Nishiyama), Yôko Tsukasa (Nobuo Nishiyama), Katsuhiko Sasaki (Yoshihama, Assistant to Nishiya), Akihiko Hirata (Environmental Scientist 1), Hiroshi Koizumi (Environmental Scientist 2), Takashi Shimura (Pediatrician), Sô Yamamura (Prime Minister Kuroki), Tappei Shimokawa (Captain of Defense Forces), Mizuho Suzuki (Director General of Environment), Kazuo Katô (The Scholar), Taketoshi Naitô (Chief Cabinet Secretary), Jun Hamamura (Kida), Kyôko Kishida, Jack Ryland (Narrators), Tatsu Makamura (Katsuko Nakagawa, Akira's Mother), Franz Gruber (Dr. Wilson), Kuniyasu Atsumi (The Scholar), Ralph Jesser (Party Member 2), Shunsuke Kariya (Leader in Crowd), Toshizô Kudô (The Man Who Asks a Question), Chico Roland (Nigerian Ambassador), Masahiko Tanimura (Tayama), Yasuko Agawa [Tomoe Mari] (Kida's Daughter), Mikizo Hirata (Sanji Nakagawa, Akira's father), Kazuko Inano (Hamako Tayama, Tayama's Wife), Sayoko Katô (Bus Girl in Shikoku), Shôsei Mutô (Ihara), Gorô Naya (TV News Caster), Yusi Osugi (Akira's Brother), Kumeko Otowa (Kida's Wife), Kaori Taniguchi (Orin), Toshiko Yabuki (Housewife Who Asks a Question), Mayako Yoshida (Wife of Akira's Brother), Barry Haigh (Akira Nakagawa [voice]), Matthew Oram (Professor Nishiyama [voice]), Toshio Masuda (voice), Katsu Ryûzaki, Osman Yusuf.

Karajishi keisatsu (1974)

Credits: Director: Sadao Nakajima; Screenplay: Tatsuo Nogami; Story: Kaiji Kawaguchi; Cinematographer: Shigeru Akatsuka; Format: Color; Musical Score: Kenjiro Hirose; Production Designer: Takatoshi Suzuki; Production Company and Distributor: Toei Company; English Title: *Lion Enforcer*; Running Time: 90 minutes.

Cast: Akira Kobayashi, Noboru Andô, Tsunehiko Watase, Fumio Watanabe, Takashi Shimura, Yukie Kagawa, Hiroko Fuji, Shoji Arikawa, Takuzô Kawatani, Seizaburô Kawazu, Ryô Nishida.

Shinkansen daibakuha (July 5, 1975)

Credits: Director: Jun'ya Satô; Producers: Kanji Amao, Sunao Sakagami; Screenplay: Ryûnosuke Ono, Jun'ya Satô; Story: Sunao Sakagami [Arei Katô]; Cinematographer: Masahiko Iimura; Format/Aspect Ratio: Color and Toeiscope [2.35:1]; Editor: Osamu Tanaka; Musical Score: Hachirô Aoyama; Production Designer: Shuichiro Nakamura; Assistant Director: Akihisa Okamoto; Sound Recordist: Kenzo Inoue; Gaffer: Yasunojô Kawasaki; Production Company: Toei Company; Distributors: Toei Company; International Classics (1976 U.S. Release); English Title: *Bullet Train*; U.S. Release Date: January 1, 1976; Running Time: 152 minutes; 1976 U.S. Release Running Time: 115 minutes.

Cast: Ken Takakura (Tetsuo Okita), Shin'ichi [Sonny] Chiba (Aoki), Kei Yamamoto (Masaru Koga), Eiji Gô (Shinji Fujio), Akira Oda (Hiroshi Ôshiro), Raita Ryû (Kikuchi), Masayo Utsunomiya (Yasuko), Yumiko Fujita (Akiyama), Yumi Takigawa (SAS Staff), Etsuko Shiomi [Shihomi] (Telephone Operator), Fumio Watanabe (Miyashita), Toyota Fukuda (Tashiro), Hiroki Fuji (Female Teacher), Junko Matsudaira (Cashier), Koreharu Hisatomi (Hirota), Yoshirô Aoki (Senda), Jirô Yabuki [Chiba] (Construction Vehicle Officer), Kiyota Harada (Miyake), Akira Hamada (Nagata), Keisuke Nakai (Tetsu-chan), Kiyoshi Yamamoto (Takazawa), Sen Yano (Minami), Hiroshi Kondô (Matsubara), Hiroshi Tanaka (Tsutsumi), Hirohisa Nakata (Tokyo Working Office Clerk-in-Charge), Yutaka Hayashi (Naka-yan), Akio Yokoyama (Superintendent), Yoshitarô Asakawa (Passenger B), Shun Ueda (Shûichi Hirao), Ken'ichi Matsuno (Komiya), Yoshifumi Tajima (Sasaki), Miyako Tasaka (Kazuko Hirao), Hanako Tokachi (Female Passenger A), Yumiko Katayama (Bar Woman), Taeko Watanabe (Koga's Sister-in-Law), Rin Tsunami (Akanesô Okami), Mitsuru Mori (Yôko), Akiko Kazami (Yasuko's Mother), Hajime Shôji (Passenger A), Kakuya Saeki (Noguchi), Seigô Fukuoka (Sugimura), Kôichi Iwaki (Akira Togo), Nenji Kobayashi (Morimoto), Gorô Kataoka (Sawara), Rikinaga Nakano (Osaka Businessman), Takashi [Koji] Hio (Riot policeman), Saburô Date (Businessman's Man), Koji Fujiyama (Hiro-oka), So Takizawa (Kawamura), Seiya Satô (Passenger C), Shinji Kankhara (Kôan Ikka Chô), Yûsuke Mori (Hata), Kazuo Satô (Ono), Hachirô Okamoto (Yama-chan), Susumu Kurobe (Goto), Genji Kawai (Detective Superintendent), Toshiyuki Tsuchiyama (Iwagami), Keiko Aikawa (Waitress), Toshie Kokabu (Cleaning Woman), Norio Yamashita (Shimizu), Ryô Suga (Man), Midori Yamamoto (Female Customer), Akira Kuji (Fireman), Gôzô Sôma (Detective C), Kôichi Yamada (Passenger E), Osamu Kimura (Correspondent A), Chikara [Riki]

Gonoue (Detective A), Tadashi [Chû] Takatsuki (Hamamatsu Station Staff), Haruki Jô (Cook B), Teruo Shimizu (Substation Staff), tatsuya Kameyama (Policeman), Sakae Yamaura (Cook A), Shinzô Tanabe (Claustrophobic Man), Takuji Aoki (Passenger D), Fumiaki Nakajo (Passenger F), Yasuto Sugawara (Ken-ishi), Yoshitaka Nagaoka (Young Man), Hisakazu Uchikoshi (Stationmaster Shimura), Takashi Shimura (JNR President), Akira Yamauchi (Cabinet Chief Secretary), Tomo'o Nagai (Bullet train Overseas HQ chief), Mizuho Suzuki (Hanamura), Ken Utsui (Kuramochi), Tetsurô Tanba (Sunaga), Tamio Kawaji [Kawachi] (Satô), Kunie Tanaka (Koga's Brother), Osamu Saka, Hajime Akutsu, Shôji Yamamoto, Isamu Matsuzawa, Takeshige Hatanaka, Isamu Hamada, Jirô Sagawa, Yukiteru Akiyama, Masayuki Kawaguchi, Hisako Oka, Keiko Itô, Ryôzô Mihara, Kengo Miyaji, Shin'ichi Iwai, Yoshifumi Watanabe, Naoko Iumi, Fumio Niikura, Michiko Maeda, Yutaka Shino, Akemi Fujiki, Masataka Kikuchi, Kimitaka Ôizumi, Shigeru Yokoyama, Sanetoshi Takatori, Shizuyo Uno, Hideyuki Fujii, Kin'ya Kitaôji.

Zoku ningen kakumei (June 19, 1976)

Credits: Director: Toshio Masuda; Producer: Tomoyuki Tanaka; Screenplay: Shinobu Hashimoto; Story: Daisaku Ikeda; Cinematographer: Rokurô Nishigaki; Format: Color; Musical Score: Harumi Ibe; Production Designer: Yoshirô Muraki; Production Managers: Yoshio Nishikawa, Masao Suzuki; Chief Assistant Director: Koji Hashimoto; Sound Recordist: Kanae Masua; Lighting Technician: Chôshirô Ishii; Special Effects Director: Teruyoshi Nakano; Assistant Director Special Effects: Kôichi Kawakita; Special Effects Art Director: Yasuyuki Inoue; Special Effects Cameraman: Sokei Tomioka; Special Effects Lighting: Masakuni Morimoto; Production Companies: Scenario Kaisha, Toho Company; Distributor: Toho Company; English Title: *Human Revolution II*; Running Time: 159 minutes.
Cast: Tatsurô Tanba, Teruhiko Aoi, Michiyo Aratama, Junko Natsu, Shinobu Ôtake, Masumi Harukawa, Ichirô Nakatani, Hiroshi Koizumi, Akio Hasegawa, Susumu Kurobe, Akira Hamada, Takeshi Hashimoto, Shin Kishida, Yoshifumi Tajima, Torahiko Hamada, Kazuo Katô, Harumi Yamada, Eisaburo Komatsu, Shigeo Katô, Kazuo Suzuki, Tsutomu Harada, Shinsuke Ashida, Takashi Shimura, Tetsuya Watari, Tatsuya Nakadai, Shunsuke Kariya, Toshizô Kudô, Kôji Uruki.

Cozzilla [*Godzilla il re dei monstri*] (1977)

Credits: Directors: Luigi Cozzi, Ishirô Honda, Terry O. Morse; Producers: Luigi Cozzi, Tomoyuki Tanaka, Renato Barbieri; Screenplay: Takeo Murata, Ishirô Honda, Al C. Ward; Story: Shigeru Kayama; Cinematographers: Guy Roe, Masao Tamai; Format/Aspect Ratio: Color and Spectrorama 70 [1.33:1]; Editor: Alberto Moro; Musical Score: Akira Ifukube, Franco Bixio, Fabio Frizzi, Vince Tempera; Art Directors: Satoru Chûko, Takeo Kita; Special Colorization Effects: Armando Valcauda; Production Companies: Embassy [AVCO Embassy] Pictures, BBC di Renato Barbieri, Cozzilla, Toho Company; Distributor: Documento Film; Running Time: 106 minutes.
Cast: Raymond Burr (Steve Martin), Akihiko Hirata (Dr. Serizawa), Momoko Kôchi (Emiko), Takashi Shimura (Dr. Yamane), Akira Takarada (Ogata).

Appendix A

Ogin-sama [*Love and Faith*] (June 24, 1978)

Credits: Director: Kei Kumai; Producers: Tsuneyasu Matsumoto, Kyoko Oshima, Muneo Shimojo; Screenplay: Yoshitaka Yoda; Story: Tôkô Kon; Cinematographer: Kôzô Okazaki; Format: Color [1.37:1]; Editor: Tatsuji Nakashizu; Musical Score: Akira Ifukube; Art Director: Takeo Kimura; First Assistant Director: Takayoshi Miyagawa; Tea Ceremony Supervisor: Urasenke; Production Companies: Takarazuka Eiga Company, Ltd., Toho Company; Distributor: Toho Company; U.S. Release Dates: March 1979; July 6, 1982; Running Time: 154 minutes.

Cast: Ryôko Nakano (Lady Ogin), Kichiemon Nakamura (Ukon Takayama), Takashi Shimura (Sen Rikyu), Toshirô Mifune (Taiko Hideyoshi), Atsuo Nakamura (Soji Yamaguchi), Daijirô Harada (Mozuya), Eiji Okada (Ankokuji), Kô Nishimura (Sojin Kamiya), Kinnosuke Nakamura.

Otoko wa tsurai yo: Uwasa no Torajirô [*Talk of the Town Torasan*] (December 27, 1978)

Credits: Director: Yôji Yamada; Producers: Kiyoshi Shimazu; Planning Producers: Shun'ichi Kobayashi, Yukio Takashima; Screenplay: Yôji Yamada, Yoshitaka Asama; Cinematographer: Tetsuo Takaha; Format/Aspect Ratio: Fujicolor and Shochiku Grandscope [2.35:1]; Processing: Tokyo Laboratory, Ltd.; Editor: Iwao Ishii; Musical Score: Naozumi Yamamoto; Art Director: Mitsuo Degawa; Stills Photographer: Sôhei [Munehira] Hasegawa; Production Company and Distributor: Shôchiku Eiga; U.S. Release Date: September 28, 1979; Running Time: 104 minutes.

Cast: Kiyoshi Atsumi (Torajiro Kuruma), Chieko Baishô (Sakura), Masami Shimojô (Ryuzo), Chieko Misaki (Tsune), Gin Maeda (Hiroshi), Hisao Dazai (Shacho), Gajirô Satô (Gen-ko), Hayato Nakamura (Mitsuo), Yoshio Yoshida (Saku's Father), Pinko Izumi (Hitomi), Hideo Murota (Soeda), Hideji Ôtaki (Unsui), Chishû Ryû (Gozensama), Takashi Shimura (Hiroshi's Father), Reiko Ôhara (Sanae), Ushio Akashi, Masane Tsukayama, Ryûnosuke Kuze, Masato Endo, Masahiro Kumakura, Masaru Ikeda, Chieko Soda, Manami Taki, Eiko Hikari, Maki Izumi, Hidetoshi Hasegawa, Kenji Kimura, Akihiko Hanyû, Kazuhiko Kasai.

Dôran (January 15, 1980)

Credits: Director: Shirô Moritani; Producers: Kimio Ikeda, Yûsuke Okada; Screenplay: Nobuo Yamada; Cinematographer: Hanjirô Nakazawa; Format/Aspect Ratio: Color [1.85:1]; Editor: Takeo Toda; Musical Score: Hidenori Taga; Production Designer: Shuichiro Nakamura; Chief Assistant Director: Shin'ichirô Sawai; Gaffer: Yasunojô Kawasaki; Production Companies: Shinano Kaisha, Toei Company; Distributor: Toei Company; Running Time: 150 minutes.

Cast: Ken Takakura (Keisuke Miyagi), Sayuri Yoshinaga (Kaoru Mizoguchi), Masakane Yonekura (Shima), Junko Sakurada (Yoko Takami), Takahiro Tamura (Kanzaki), Takashi Shimura (Kosuke Miyagi), Kei Satô (Kozu), Kunie Tanaka (Komatsu), Shin Kishida (Kobayashi), Asao Koike (Misumi), Toshiyuki Nagashima (Hideo Mizoguchi), Akira Nishikino (Nogami), Akira Kume

(Kinzo Mizoguchi), Gorô Naya (Anaunsâ), Ryûnosuke Kaneda, Tonpei Hidari, Yûsuke Kawazu, Rokkô Toura, Kai Atô, Iwao Dan, Tatsumi Ishihara, Nenji Kobayashi, Susumu Kurobe, Hiroshi Nawa, Teruo Shimizu, Kazunaga Tsuji.

Tempyo no iraka (January 26, 1980)

Credits: Director: Kei Kumai; Screenplay: Yoshikata Yoda; Cinematographer: Shinsaku [Masahisa] Himeda; Format: Color; Musical Score: Tôru Takemitsu; Art Director: Takeo Kimura; Production Companies: Tempyo No Iraka; Tokyo Broadcasting System (TBS); Distributor: Toho Company; Network: Tokyo Broadcasting System (TBS); English Title: *Ocean to Cross*; U.S. Release Date: September 19, 1980; Running Time: 120 minutes.
Cast: Katsuo Nakamura (Fusho), Masaaki Daimon (Yoei), Mitsuo Hamada (Genro), Daigo Kusano (Kaiyu), Mieko Takamine (Yoroshime), Mariko Fuji, Hisashi Igawa, Yoichi Numata, Takashi Shimura, Akira Shioji, Hideo Sunazuka, Kôji Takahashi, Takahiro Tamura, Fujio Tokita, Shinobu Tsuruta, Hideko Yoshida.

Kagemusha (April 26, 1980)

Credits: Director: Akira Kurosawa; Executive Producers: Akira Kurosawa, Tomoyuki Tanaka, Francis Ford Coppola, George Lucas; Assistant Producer: Audie Bock; Screenplay: Masato Ide, Akira Kurosawa; Cinematographers: Takao Saitô, Shôji Ueda; Format/Aspect Ratio: Eastmancolor [Spherical 1.85:1]; Processing: Toyo Genzojo (Japan), DeLuxe (U.S.); Editor: Akira Kurosawa; Assistant Editor: Yoshihiro Iwatani; Negative Cutter: Tome Minami; Musical Score: Shinichirô Ikebe; Conductor: Kotaro Saito; Art Director: Yoshirô Muraki; Assistant Art Director: Aki Saburagi; Costume Designer: Seiichiro Hagakusawa; Hair Stylists: Yoshiko Matsumoto, Shigeo Tamura, Junjiro Yamada; Production Manager: Toshiaki Hashimoto; Unit Production Manager: Akira Fujita; Chief Assistant Director: Fumiryo Okada; Assistant Directors: Hideyuki Inoue, Takashi Koizumi, Takao Okawara; Second Unit Director/Directorial Advisor/Production Coordinator/Creative Consultant: Ishirô Honda; Property Master: Hatsumi Yamamoto; Sound Recordist: Fumio Yanoguchi [4-Track Stereo]; Assistant Sound Recordist: Mamoru Yamada; Sound Effects Editor: Ichirô Minami; Assistant Camera: Tamio Matsuo; Photography Consultants: Kazuo Miyagawa, Asakazu Nakai; Lighting Technician: Takeji Sano; Assistant Lighting Technician: Satoshi Kurikawa; Stills Photographer: Naomi Hashiyama; Transportation: Isamu Miwano; Scene Shifter: Masa Furugawara; Horseback Riding Instructors: Toshi Hasegawa, Tamihei Shirai; Production Advisors: Shinobu Hashimoto, Takao Saitô; Acting Office: Hiroaki Honda; Instructor, Samurai Etiquette: Ryû Kuze; Assistant to Producer/Script Supervisor: Teruyo Nogami; Assistant to Director: Michael Rich; Subtitle Supervisor/Subtitler: Donald Richie; Presenters: Francis Ford Coppola, George Lucas; Production Companies: Kurosawa Production Company, Toho Company, 20th Century–Fox; Distributors: Toho Company, 20th Century–Fox; U.S. Release Date: October 10, 1980; Running Time: 180 minutes; U.S. Release Running Time: 162 minutes.
Cast: Tatsuya Nakadai (Shingen Takeda/Kagemusha), Tsutomu Yamazaki (Nobukado Takeda), Ken'ichi Hagiwara (Katsuyori Takeda), Jinpachi Nezu

(Sohachiro Tsuchiya), Hideji Ôtaki (Masakage Yamagata), Daisuke Ryû (Nobunaga Oda), Masayuki Yui (Ieyasu Tokugawa), Kaori Momoi (Otsuyanokata), Mitsuko Baishô (Oyunokata), Hideo Murota (Nobufusa Baba), Takayuki Shiho (Masatoyo Naito), Kôji Shimizu (Katsusuke Atobe), Noboru Shimizu (Masatane Hara), Sen Yamamoto (Nobushige Oyamada), Shuhei Sugimori (Masanobu Kosaka), Kota Yui (Takemaru), Ysuhito Yamanaka (Ranmaru Mori), Kumeko Otowa (Takemaru's Nurse), Tetsuo Yamashita (Nagahide Niwa), Kai Atô (Zenjiro Amemiya), Takashi Ebata (Monk), Hiroshi Shimada (Jingoro Hara), Toshiaki Tanabe (Kugutsushi), Yoshimitsu Yamaguchi (Salt Vendor), Elichi Kanakubo (Kenshin Uesugi), Akihiko Sugizaki (Noda Castle Soldier), Norio Matsui (Tadatsugu Sakai), Yasushi Doshida (Kazumasa Ishikawa), Nobaru (Nori) Sone (Heihachiro Honda), Takashi Shimura (Gyobu Taguchi), Francis Selleck (Priest), Gorô Yamada (Foot Soldier), Yû Shimaka, Yugo Miyazaki, Masatsuga Kuriyama, Jirô Yabuki, Eihachi Ito, Senkichi Ômura, Shû Nakajima.

Nihon Philharmonic Orchestra: Honoo no dai gogakusho (September 19, 1981)

Credits: Director and Screenplay: Seijirô Kôyama; Producer: Yoshihiro Yûki; Cinematographer: Masaru Mori; Format: Color; Editor: Mitsuo Kondô; Musical Score: Hikaru Hayashi; Art Director: Katsumi Nakazawa; Sound Recordist: Fumio Hashimoto; Gaffer: Motohiro Noguchi; Production Company: NR Kikau; Distributor: Nikkatsu; Running Time: 115 minutes.

Cast: Morio Kazama (Noburo Kabasawa), Yûko Tanaka (Nobuko Mogi), Mitsuo Hamada, Naomi Hase. Tomoe Hiiro, Hisashi Igawa, Takao Ito, Kaneko Iwasaki, Asao Koike, Gin Maeda, Kyôzô Nagatsuka, Taketoshi Naitô, Seiya Nakano, Orie Satô, Tsutomu Shimomoto, Takashi Shimura, Tadahiko Sugano, Hiromitsu Suzuki, Taiji Tonoyama, Tsugiaki Yoshida.

Appendix B
Takashi Shimura Television Episodes

Following is the most complete listing of *verified* television episodes featuring Takashi Shimura ever published in either printed or electronic form. Multiple sources have been used in a meticulous research effort, especially to corroborate information and insure as much accuracy as possible.

The date accompanying each title is when the production was first broadcast in Japan. If the program subsequently was aired in the United States, that date also is included in the listing.

Shurushuru (August 11, 1966) television movie
Credits: Based on the Novel by Shugôrô Yamamoto; Format/Aspect Ratio: Black-and-White [1.33:1].
Cast: Michiyo Aratama, Chikako Hosokawa, Wakabe Irie, Tatsuya Nakadai, Takashi Shimura.

Kaze (premiered October 4, 1967) television series
Credits: Production Companies: Shochiku Company, Tokyo Broadcasting System (TBS); Network: Tokyo Broadcasting System (TBS); Series Length: 41 episodes (1967–1968); Episode Running Time: 56 minutes.
Cast: Ryô Ikebe, Akiji Kobayashi, Asahi Kurizuka, Takashi Shimura, Sanae Tsuchida.

Otoko janaika (premiered April 6, 1969) television series
Credits: Format/Aspect Ratio: Color [1.33:1]; Series Length: 6 episodes (1969–1971).
Cast: Yumiko Fugita, Shin'ichirô Mikami, Hideaki Nitani, Hiroshi Sekiguchi, Takashi Shimura, Jun Tatara.

Dokkoi daisaku (premiered January 8, 1973) television series
Credits: Musical Score: Michiaki Watanabe; Format/Aspect Ratio: Color [1.33:1]; Production Companies: Toei Company, TV Asahi; Network: TV Asahi; Series Length: one season (1973–1974).

Cast: Yoshinobu Kaneko (Daisaku), Michio Hazama (Narrator), Toshie Kobayashi (Tatsuko), Junko Natsu (Saeko), Chishû Ryû (School Master), Takashi Shimura (Jinpei), Toshiko Tsuyama (Sanae), Tôru Yuri (Magiochi), Tako Hachirô, Shigeko Kimura, Noriko Kitazawa, Hôsei Komatsu, Teizô Muta, Akira Nagoya, Ryûsei Nakao, Masaya Oki, Kôen Okumura, Mikio Ozawa, Junko Sakurada, Takeshi Sasaki, Kaho Shimada, Casey [Kêshi] Takemine, Yoshio Yoshida, Caroline Yôko, Akira Ôizumi.

Tasukenin hashiru: *"Adauchi dai satsujin"* (October 20, 1973) television series

Credits: Director: Koki Matsuno; Teleplay: Takeo Kunihiro; Format/Aspect Ratio: Color [1.33:1]; Musical Score: Masaaki Hirao; Production Companies: Shochiku Company, Asahi Broadcasting Corporation (ABC); Network: Tokyo Broadcasting System (TBS); Series Length: 2 episodes (1973-1974); Episode Running Time: 46 minutes.

Cast: Takahiro Tamura (Bunjuro Nakayama), Ichirô Nakatani (Heinai Tsuji), Atsuko Sano (Shino Nakayama), Takuya Kitano (Iizuka), Tsutomu Yamazaki (Narrator), Yumiko Nogawa (Okichi), Masahiro Sumiyoshi (Tamekichi), Kuniyasu Atsumi (Mondonosuke Tajima), Hiroshi Miyauchi (Ryu), Sôichirô Kitamura (Tadayasu Bigonokami Miyake), Kenji Imai (Shinshichi Isoya), Toshio Chiba (Gensai), Takurô Nakayoshi (Senpachi), Takeo Tabata (Matsuda), Chisa Kamata (Omitsu), Kiyoshi Kajimoto (Miyake), Taisaku Akino (Yushi no Rikichi), Toshio Nogi (Rô shujin), Yonehachi Shima (Muakami), Hideko Yoshida (Osayo), Yûnosuke Itô (Otowa no Manzô), Ryô Nishida (Matashichi), Tokuko Miura (Oman), Makoto Nishi (Yoichirô Inaba), Mitsuhiro Sugiyama (Yojirô Inaba), Ryûji Miyagama (Yosikawa), Minoru Sanada (Sejima), Shôhachirô Miki (Kawano), Kenji Kamei (Yasui), Yoshihiro Maruo (Morimura), Noriaki Katô (Sato), Shôgen Yamashita (Kikuchi), Kazuhiko Hirota (Akimoto), Yasushi Hirai (Nakazawa), Kikuichi Ôgida (Hirabayashi), Hachirô Yamauchi (Asakichi), Ippei Hara (Yokichi), Takashi Shimura (Tatewaki Otawara), Sô Yamamura (Seibe).

Hissatsu shiokiya kagyô: *"Ippitsu keijô meimu ga mieta"* (July 4, 1975) television series

Credits: Director: Kuniya Ôkuma; Teleplay: Yoshiki Hori; Format/Aspect Ratio: Color [1.33:1]; Musical Score: Masaaki Hirao; Production Companies: Shochiku Company; Asahi Broadcasting Corporation (ABC); Network: TV Asahi; Series Length: 4 episodes (1975-1976); Episode Running Time: 46 minutes.

Cast: Masaya Oki (Ichimatsu), Katsutoshi Tarashi (Ingen), Atsushi Watanabe (Sutezô), Mari Shiraki (Ritsu), Kin Sugai (Sen), Makoto Fujita (Mondo Nakamura), Mitsukô Kusabue (Narrator), Tamao Nakamura (Okô), Hatsune Ishihara (Ohatsu), Katsumi Munakata (Yoriki Murano), Masao Komatsu (Kamekichi), Kazuko Inano (Osode), Renji Ishibashi (Miyokichi), Akiko Kana (Orin), Zenji Yamada (Jinbe Yokomizo), Takashi Kanda (Izumiya), Keizô Kanie (Asakichi), Rie Yokoyama (Onaka), Kyôchi Satô (Sakon Toda), Hiroshi Hasegawa (Kisaburô), Kondô (Higure), Hisao Hata (Geki Iwata), Ryûtarô Gomi (Katsunoshin Oyama), Ryôei Itô (Isha), Katsumasa Uchida (Kansuke), Midori Hiro (Otoki), Takeo Tabata (Tanomo Hosokawa),Shin'ya Irie (Tashiro), Kyôko Katsuki (Jochû), Tatsuo Nagano (Echigoya), Shingo Ibuki (Takejiro), Gorô Aki (Todo), Yûjirô Ishihama (Akitaya), Kazutarô Kuni (Hamadaya), Kichijirô Jidai (Yasuke), Rumi Kagawa (Rumi), Masako Shimamura (Osen), Kayoko Matsui (Akane), Toshio Chiba (Higuchi), Nozomi Hishino (Nozomi), Kôtarô Mayuzumi (Karoku), Atsuo Omote (Senkichi), Yoshio Inaba (Sôemon Miharaya), Shigeru Mizota (Mizunuma), Seiichi Yoshida (Kinji), Ryôta Minowada (Kôshûya), Keiko Mikasa (Oyone), Toshiyo Shimomoto (Kojika), Shintarô Mibu (Tsumesho yakunin), Yoneko Machida (Okami), Hideki Hanaoka (Tsumesho yakunin), Yoshihiro Maruo (Yopparai), Akihiko Shibata (Shimano), Keiko Takeshita (Miwa), Shintarô Akatsuki (Kasi), Kazuhiko Hirota (Yopparai), Chikako Hon'ami (Osato), Kin Tôyama (Kisanji), Izumi Kobayashi (Mizunuma no tsuma), Minoru Kôno (Shita yakunin), Naoto Gotô, Takayoshi Kawabata (Detchi), Takashi Shimura (Bugyô Torii), Kyô Hanaki (Senri).

A un: *"Komainu"* (March 9, 1980); *"Chou chou"* (March 16, 1980); *"Ao ringo"* (March 23, 1980); *"Yajirobee"* (March 30, 1980) television series

Credits: Directors: Yukio Fukamachi, Jôta Watanabe; Producer: Takeshi Kobayashi; Teleplays: Kuniko Mukôda; Format/Aspect Ratio: Color [1.33:1]; Production Company and Network: NHK; Series Length: 4 episodes; Episode Running Time: 45 minutes.
Cast: Furanki Sakai (Senkichi Mizuta), Naoki Sugihara (Shuzo Kadokura), Jitsuko Yoshimura (Tami Mizuta), Kyôko Kishida (Kimiko Kadokura), Kayoko Kishimoto (satoko Mizuta), Shino Ikenami (Reiko Mitamura), Takashi Shimura (Hatsutaro Mizuta), Kenzô Tabu (Itachi), Taiji Tonoyama (Kinba), Kisho Ichiyama (Kenichiro Tsujimoto), Fumio Kirihara (Uokatsu), Nobuyoshi Matsukuma (Train Conductor), Gentaro Nakajima (Doctor), Tadayoshi Ueda (Kinji Ootomo, Shuzo's Help), Hiroko Isayama (Umeko), Kaoru Kurosu (Midori), Eri Kayama, Yasuo Fujita, Kikuko Hanaoka, Saburô Satoki.

Chapter Notes

Introduction

1. Donald Richie, *A Hundred Years of Japanese Film* (Tokyo: Kodansha International, 2001), pp. 10–11.
2. Richie, p. 11.

Chapter 1

1. Richie, p. 9.
2. Stuart Galbraith IV, *The Emperor and the Wolf: The Lives and Films of Akira Kurosawa and Toshirô Mifune* (New York: Faber and Faber, 2001), p. 43.
3. Galbraith, p. 44.
4. Galbraith, p. 43.
5. Galbraith, p. 48.
6. Donald Richie, *The Films of Akira Kurosawa* (Berkeley: University of California Press, 1996), p. 29.

Chapter 2

1. Akira Kurosawa, translated by Audie E. Bock, *Something Like an Autobiography* (New York: Vintage Books, 1983), p. 144.
2. Kurosawa, p. 140.
3. Kurosawa, p. 142.
4. Kurosawa, p. 142.
5. Richie, *The Films of Akira Kurosawa*, p. 31.
6. Kurosawa, pp. 142–143.
7. Stephen Prince, *The Men Who Tread on the Tiger's Tail* (Criterion Collection-Janus Films DVD, 2009).
8. Kurosawa, p. 144.
9. Galbraith, p. 59.
10. Kurosawa, pp. 148–149.
11. Kurosawa, p. 151.
12. Kurosawa, p. 150.
13. Kurosawa, p. 151.
14. Galbraith, p. 83.

Chapter 3

1. Kurosawa, p. 159.
2. Ian Burumu, "The Spoils of War," Akira Kurosawa's *Drunken Angel* (Criterion-Janus Films DVD, 2007), p. 6.
3. Kurosawa, p. 157.
4. Kurosawa, p. 157.
5. Kurosawa, p. 158.
6. Kurosawa, p. 158.
7. Burumu, pp. 4–5.
8. Burumu, pp. 6–7.
9. Burumu, p. 9.
10. Kurosawa, p. 159.
11. Imata Michihiro, Susunu Kinihiro and Akira Kurosawa, *Akira Kurosawa's Footsteps of Dreams* (Tokyo: Kyodo Tunshin-Sha, 1999), p. 107.
12. Kurosawa, p. 162.
13. Stephen Prince, *The Warrior's Camera: The Cinema of Akira Kurosawa, Revised and Expanded Edition* (Princeton: Princeton University Press, 1999), p. 88.
14. Prince, *The Warrior's Camera*, p. 88.
15. *Akira Kurosawa: It Is Wonderful to Create, Drunken Angel* (Toho Masterworks, Criterion Collection DVD, 2007).
16. Burumu, p. 5.
17. *Akira Kurosawa: It Is Wonderful to Create, Drunken Angel*.
18. Kurosawa, pp. 168–69.
19. Galbraith, p. 104.
20. Vincent Canby, "Film: 'The Quiet Duel' by Akira Kurosawa," *The New York Times*, 25 November 1983.

Chapter 4

1. Richie, *The Films of Akira Kurosawa*, p. 62.
2. Kurosawa, p. 176.
3. Kurosawa, pp. 175–176.
4. Michihiro, Kinihiro and Kurosawa, p. 122.

5. Prince, *The Warrior's Camera*, p. 95.
6. Prince, *The Warrior's Camera*, p. 96.
7. *BoxOffice*, 9 July 1963, p. 10.
8. Galbraith, p. 117.
9. Kurosawa, p. 177.
10. Kurosawa, p. 177.
11. Kurosawa, p. 178.
12. Kurosawa, p. 178.
13. Galbraith, p. 121.
14. *Akira Kurosawa: It Is Wonderful to Create, Ikiru* (Toho Masterworks, Criterion Collection Blu-Ray, 2015).
15. Kevin Thomas, "Two Great Directors Contrasted at Kabuki," *Los Angeles Times*, 23 June 1964.
16. Alex Cox, "Shimura Takashi: The Last Samurai," *BFI Film Forever*, 10 February 2012.

Chapter 5

1. Kurosawa, p. 180.
2. Kurosawa, p. 180.
3. Kurosawa, p. 181.
4. Kurosawa, p. 182.
5. Kurosawa, p. 184.
6. Kurosawa, p. 184.
7. *The World of Kazuo Miyagawa, Rashômon* (Criterion Collection Blu-Ray, 2012).
8. *The World of Kazuo Miyagawa*.
9. Richie, *The Films of Akira Kurosawa*, p. 75.
10. Takashi Shimura, interview with Gideon Bachmann and Donald Richie, Kapinski Hotel, Berlin, Germany, 1961.
11. Shimura interview.
12. Galbraith, p. 143.
13. Richie, *The Films of Akira Kurosawa*, p. 85.
14. Michihiro, Kinihiro and Kurosawa, p. 140.
15. Galbraith, p. 145.
16. Richie, *The Films of Akira Kurosawa*, p. 82.
17. Funichisya, ed., *Toshirô Mifune—The Last Samurai* (Tokyo: Mainichi-Shinbun-sha, 1998), p. 42.

Chapter 6

1. Prince, *The Warrior's Camera: The Cinema of Akira Kurosawa*, p. 113.
2. Richie, *The Films of Akira Kurosawa*, p. 96.
3. Richie, *The Films of Akira Kurosawa*, p. 95.
4. Richie, *The Films of Akira Kurosawa*, p. 86.
5. Shinobu Hashimoto, interview with Stuart Galbraith IV, 15 December 1999.
6. Shinobu Hashimoto, *Compound Cinematics: Kurosawa Akira and I* (New York: Vertical, Inc., 2015).
7. Miki Odagiri, Miki, "My Treasured Ikiru," *Ikiru* Japanese laserdisc, 25 July 1993.
8. *Akira Kurosawa: It Is Wonderful to Create, Ikiru*.

9. Michihiro, Kinihiro and Kurosawa, pp. 158–160.
10. *Akira Kurosawa: It Is Wonderful to Create, Ikiru*.
11. *Akira Kurosawa: It Is Wonderful to Create, Ikiru*.
12. *Akira Kurosawa: It Is Wonderful to Create, Ikiru*.
13. *Akira Kurosawa: It Is Wonderful to Create, Ikiru*.
14. Galbraith, pp. 159–160.
15. Galbraith, p. 162.
16. Richie, *A Hundred Years of Japanese Film*, pp. 169–170.
17. Richie, *The Films of Akira Kurosawa*, p. 92.
18. Richie, *The Films of Akira Kurosawa*, p. 93.
19. Galbraith, p. 165.
20. Bosley Crowther, "Screen Drama Imported from Japan: 'Ikiru' Has Premiere at the Little Carnegie. Shimura Stars as Petty Government Aide," *The New York Times*, 30 January 1960.
21. Arthur Knight, "Season in the Sun," *The Saturday Review*, 13 February 1960.
22. "'Ikiru' ('To Live') with Takashi Shimura and Miki Odagiri," *Harrison's Reports*, 27 February 1960, p. 35.
23. *Time*, 21 September 1962.
24. Raymond Benson, *Cinema Retro*, 2 December 2015.
25. Jeremy Carr, "New on Video: 'Ikiru,'" *Popoptiq*, 9 December 2015.
26. Alex Cox, British Film Institute, 2012.
27. Richie, *The Films of Akira Kurosawa*, p. 95.

Chapter 7

1. Joan Mellen, *Seven Samurai* (London: The British Film Institute-Palgrave Macmillan, 2002), p. 7.
2. Richie, *The Films of Akira Kurosawa*, p. 97.
3. Prince, *The Warrior's Camera: The Cinema of Akira Kurosawa*, p. 207.
4. Kenneth Turan, "The Hours and Times," *Seven Samurai: Eight Takes* (Criterion Collection Blu-Ray Special Edition, 2010), p. 9.
5. Turan, pp. 9–10.
6. *Akira Kurosawa: It Is Wonderful to Create, Seven Samurai* (Toho Masterworks, Criterion Collection Blu-Ray, 2010).
7. Toshirô Mifune, interview with Teruyo Nogami, Mifune Productions, Tokyo, Japan, 25 August 1993.
8. *Akira Kurosawa: It Is Wonderful to Create, Seven Samurai*.
9. Mellen, p. 6.
10. Mellen, p. 31.
11. Masaaki Tsuduki, *Kurosawa Akira to Shinichin no Samurai—Eiga no naka no eiga tanjo dokyu-mento* (Tokyo: Asahi Sonotama, 1999), p. 60.

12. Peter Grilli, "Civil Samurai," *Film Comment*, July 1984, p. 66.
13. Mellen, p. 31.
14. Prince, *The Warrior's Camera: The Cinema of Akira Kurosawa*, p. 210.
15. Mellen, p. 8.
16. Philip Kemp, "A Time of Honor," *Seven Samurai: Eight Takes* (Criterion Collection Blu-Ray Special Edition, 2010), p. 19.
17. Prince, *The Warrior's Camera: The Cinema of Akira Kurosawa*, p. 210.
18. Mellen, pp. 20–21.
19. Mellen, p. 30.
20. Dianna Waggoner, "In Homage to the Master, George Lucas and Francis Coppola Unleash Their Clout for Kurosawa," *People*, 1980.
21. Prince, *The Warrior's Camera: The Cinema of Akira Kurosawa*, p. 204.
22. Mellen, p. 9.
23. Galbraith, pp. 174–175.
24. *Akira Kurosawa: It Is Wonderful to Create, Seven Samurai.*

Chapter 8

1. Steve Ryfle, "Godzilla's Footprint," *Gojira: The Original Japanese Masterpiece*, p. 4.
2. Ryfle, p. 4.
3. Ryfle, p. 5.
4. Ryfle. p. 5.
5. Ryfle, p. 9.
6. Ryfle, p. 10.
7. Ryfle, p. 14.

Chapter 9

1. Richie, *The Films of Akira Kurosawa*, p. 113.
2. Richie, *The Films of Akira Kurosawa*, p. 113.
3. Galbraith, p. 220.
4. Donald Richie, "Kurosawa on Kurosawa," *Sight and Sound* 33, Summer 1964, p. 108.
5. Richie, *The Films of Akira Kurosawa*, p. 111.
6. Prince, *The Warrior's Camera: The Cinema of Akira Kurosawa*, p. 162.
7. Prince, *The Warrior's Camera: The Cinema of Akira Kurosawa*, p. 164.
8. Judith Crist, New York *World Journal Tribune*, 12 January 1967.
9. Richie, *The Films of Akira Kurosawa*, p. 114.
10. Bruce Eder, "Samurai III," *Samurai III: Duel at Ganryu Island* (Criterion Collection DVD, 1998).
11. Galbraith, p. 229.
12. *Motion Picture Herald*, 22 September 1956, p. 43.
13. Stephen Prince, "Shakespeare Transposed," *Akira Kurosawa's Throne of Blood* (Criterion Collection Blu-Ray Special Edition, 2014), p. 5.
14. Prince, "Shakespeare Transposed," p. 6.
15. Richie, *The Films of Akira Kurosawa*, p. 120.
16. Galbraith, p. 223.
17. Prince, "Shakespeare Transposed," pp. 10–11.

Chapter 10

1. Shimaji Takamaro, ed., *Kurosawa Akira Dokyumento* (Tokyo: *Kinema Jumpo* Special Edition, May 1974), p. 110.
2. "I Made a 100% Amusement Film," *Der Verbogene Festung*, European program for *The Hidden Fortress*, 1958.
3. "I Made a 100% Amusement Film."
4. Michael Joshua Brown, *The Hidden Fortress* (Criterion-Janus Films DVD, 2009).
5. Brown.
6. Richie, *The Films of Akira Kurosawa*, p. 135.
7. Galbraith, p. 269.
8. Galbraith, p. 269.
9. S. A. Desick, "The Vagabonds Shows Japan Master with Color," *Los Angeles Examiner*, 26 November 1960.

Chapter 11

1. Chuck Stephens, "The Higher Depths," *The Bad Sleep Well*. Criterion Collection DVD, 2003), p. 6.
2. Takamaro.
3. Richie, *The Films of Akira Kurosawa*, p. 140.
4. Bosley Crowther, "Four New Films Are Imitations," *The New York Times*, 6 February 1963.
5. Stanley Kauffmann, "From Bad to Worse,'" *The New Republic*, 26 January 1963.
6. Galbraith, p. 301.
7. *Akira Kurosawa: It Is Wonderful to Create, Yojimbo* (Toho Masterworks. Criterion Collection Blu-Ray, 2015).
8. Richie, *The Films of Akira Kurosawa*, p. 147.
9. Galbraith, p. 302.
10. Michihiro, Kinihiro and Kurosawa, p. 234.
11. Richie, *The Films of Akira Kurosawa*, p. 159.
12. Richie, *The Films of Akira Kurosawa*, p. 157.
13. Richie, *The Films of Akira Kurosawa*, p. 162.

14. Richie, *The Films of Akira Kurosawa*, p. 162.
15. Galbraith, p. 335.

Chapter 12

1. Cox.
2. Geoffrey O'Brien, "Between Heaven and Hell," *High and Low* (Criterion Collection Blu-Ray Special Edition, 2011), pp. 18–19.
3. Donald Richie, "On the Set of *High and Low*," *High and Low* (Criterion Collection Blu-Ray Special Edition, 2011), p. 30.
4. Galbraith, pp. 346–347.
5. Galbraith, pp. 369, 371.
6. Vincent Canby, "Presley Shares Billing," *The New York Times*, 16 December 1965.
7. Geoffrey O'Brien, "No Way Out," *Kwaidan* (Criterion Collection Blu-Ray Special Edition, 2015) p. 2.
8. O'Brien, "No Way Out," p. 2.
9. O'Brien, "No Way Out," p. 3.
10. Richie, *The Films of Akira Kurosawa*, p. 171.
11. Galbraith, p. 387.

Chapter 13

1. *Zatoichi and the Fugitives* (Criterion Collection DVD, 2004).
2. Galbraith, pp. 532–533.
3. Audie Bock, "Japan's Kurosawa is Staging His Comeback in Epic Style," *The New York Times*, 27 April 1980.
4. Akira Kurosawa, interview with Tony Rayns, "Talking with the Director," *Kagemusha* (Criterion Collection Blu-ray, 2009), p. 19.
5. Michael Rich, "Letters—Crossing Swords Over *Kagemusha*," *UCLA Daily Bruin*, 27 October 1980, p. 1.

Bibliography

Interviews

Hashimoto, Shinobu. Interview with Stuart Galbraith IV. 15 December 1999.
Kurosawa, Akira. Interview with Tony Rayns. "Talking with the Director," *Kagemusha*. Criterion Collection Blu-ray, 2009.
Mifune, Toshirô. Interview with Teruyo Nogami. Mifune Productions, Tokyo, Japan, 25 August 1993.
Sanjo, Miki. *The Quiet Duel*. BCI Eclipse Company DVD, 2003.
Shimura, Takashi. Interview with Gideon Bachmann and Donald Richie. Kapinski Hotel, Berlin, Germany, 1961.

Memoirs

Kurosawa, Akira. Translated by Audie E. Bock. *Something Like an Autobiography*. New York: Vintage Books, 1983.

Essays

Benson, Raymond. "Japan's Unsung Acting Genius," *Cinema Retro*, 2 December 2015.
Brown, Michael Joshua. *The Hidden Fortress*. Criterion-Janus Films DVD, 2009.
Burumu, Ian. "The Spoils of War," Akira Kurosawa's *Drunken Angel*. Criterion-Janus Films DVD, 2007.
Carr, Jeremy. "New on Video: 'Ikiru,'" *Popoptiq*, 9 December 2015.
Chiao, Peggy. "Kurosawa's Early Influences," *Seven Samurai: Eight Takes*. Criterion Collection Blu-Ray Special Edition, 2010.
Cox, Alex. "Shimura Takashi: The Last Samurai," *BFI Film Forever*, 10 February 2012.
Eder, Bruce. "Samurai III," *Samurai III: Duel at Ganryu Island*. Criterion Collection DVD, 1998.
Kemp, Philip. "A Time of Honor," *Seven Samurai: Eight Takes*. Criterion Collection Blu-Ray Special Edition, 2010.
O'Brien, Geoffrey. "Between Heaven and Hell," *High and Low*. Criterion Collection Blu-Ray Special Edition, 2011.
O'Brien, Geoffrey. "No Way Out," *Kwaidan*. Criterion Collection Blu-Ray Special Edition, 2015.
Odagiri, Miki. "My Treasured *Ikiru*," *Ikiru*. Japanese laserdisc, 25 July 1993.
Prince, Stephen. *The Men Who Tread on the Tiger's Tail*. Criterion Collection-Janus Films DVD, 2009.

Prince, Stephen. "Shakespeare Transposed," *Akira Kurosawa's Throne of Blood.* Criterion Collection Blu-Ray Special Edition, 2014.
"Recovery Effort," *No Regrets for Our Youth.* Criterion Collection-Janus Films DVD, 2007.
Richie, Donald. "On the Set of *High and Low*," *High and Low.* Criterion Collection Blu-Ray Special Edition, 2011.
Ryfle, Steve. "Godzilla's Footprint," *Gojira*: The Original Japanese Masterpiece. Classic Media DVD, 2006.
Sallitt, Dan. *A Mikio Naruse Companion: Notes on the Extant Films, 1931–1967.* https://mikionaruse.wordpress.com.
Silver, Alain. "The Rains Came," *Seven Samurai: Eight Takes.* Criterion Collection Blu-Ray Special Edition, 2010.
Stephens, Chuck. "The Higher Depths," *The Bad Sleep Well.* Criterion Collection DVD, 2003.
Turan, Kenneth. "The Hours and Times," *Seven Samurai: Eight Takes.* Criterion Collection Blu-Ray Special Edition, 2010.
Zatoichi and the Fugitives. Criterion Collection DVD, 2004.

Periodical Articles

"The Ashes of Death," *Time*, 29 March 1954.
Bock, Audie. "Japan's Kurosawa is Staging His Comeback in Epic Style," *The New York Times*, 27 April 1980.
BoxOffice, January 1961; March–June 1962; January–May 1963.
Canby, Vincent. "Film: 'The Quiet Duel' by Akira Kurosawa," *The New York Times*, 25 November 1983.
Canby, Vincent. "Presley Shares Billing," *The New York Times*, 16 December 1965.
Crist, Judith. New York *World Journal Tribune*, 12 January 1967.
Crowther, Bosley. "Four New Films Are Imitations," *The New York Times*, 6 February 1963.
Crowther, Bosley. "Screen Drama Imported from Japan: 'Ikiru' Has Premiere at the Little Carnegie. Shimura Stars as Petty Government Aide," *The New York Times*, 30 January 1960.
Desick, S. A. "The Vagabonds Shows Japan Master with Color," *Los Angeles Examiner*, 26 November 1960.
Film Bulletin, December 1956; January–May 1957.
"Foreign Language Feature Reviews: *Stray Dog*," *BoxOffice*, 30 September 1963.
Grilli, Peter. "Civil Samurai," *Film Comment*, July 1984.
"'Ikiru' ('To Live') with Takashi Shimura and Miki Odagiri," *Harrison's Reports*, 27 February 1960.
"A Japanese Apocalypse," *Time*, 21 September 1962.
Kauffmann, Stanley, "From Bad to Worse,'" *The New Republic*, 26 January 1963.
Knight, Arthur. "Season in the Sun," *The Saturday Review*, 13 February 1960.
Motion Picture Herald, 4 August 1956; 22 September 1956.
Rich, Michael. "Letters—Crossing Swords Over *Kagemusha*," *UCLA Daily Bruin*, 27 October 1980.
Richie, Donald. "Kurosawa on Kurosawa," *Sight and Sound* 33, Summer 1964.
Shimaji, Takamaro, ed. *Kurosawa Akira Dokyumento.* Tokyo: *Kinema Junpô* Special Edition, May 1974.
Thomas, Kevin. "Two Great Directors Contrasted at Kabuki," *Los Angeles Times*, 23 June 1964.
Waggoner, Dianna. "In Homage to the Master, George Lucas and Francis Coppola Unleash Their Clout for Kurosawa," *People*, 1980.

Original Film Programs

"I Made a 100% Amusement Film," *Der Verbogene Festung*. European program for *The Hidden Fortress*, 1958.

Books

Encyclopædia Britannica. New York: Merriam-Webster, Inc., 2017.
Funichisya, ed. *Toshirô Mifune—The Last Samurai*. Tokyo: Mainichi-Shinbun-sha, 1998.
Galbraith, Stuart IV. *The Emperor and the Wolf: The Lives and Films of Akira Kurosawa and Toshirô Mifune*. New York: Faber & Faber, 2001.
Galbraith, Stuart IV: *The Toho Studios Story, A History and Complete Filmography*. Lanham, Maryland: Scarecrow Press, 2008.
Hashimoto, Shinobu. *Compound Cinematics: Akira Kurosawa and I*. New York: Vertical, Inc., 2015.
Mellen, Joan. *Seven Samurai*. London: The British Film Institute-Palgrave Macmillan, 2002.
Michihiro, Imata, Susunu Kinihiro and Akira Kurosawa. *Akira Kurosawa's Footsteps of Dreams*. Tokyo: Kyodo Tunshin-Sha, 1999.
Nakao, Seigo. *Japanese-English, English-Japanese Dictionary*. New York: Random House, 1995.
Nollen, Scott Allen. *Three Bad Men: John Ford, John Wayne, Ward Bond*. Jefferson, North Carolina: McFarland, 2013.
Prince, Stephen. *The Warrior's Camera: The Cinema of Akira Kurosawa, Revised and Expanded Edition*. Princeton: Princeton University Press, 1999.
Ragone, August. *Eiji Tsuburaya: Master of Monsters*. San Francisco: Chronicle Books, 2007.
Richie, Donald. *The Films of Akira Kurosawa*. Berkeley: University of California Press, 1996.
Richie, Donald. *A Hundred Years of Japanese Film*. Tokyo: Kodansha International, 2001.
Richie, Donald. *Japanese Cinema: Film Style and National Character*. Garden City, New York: Doubleday, 1971.
Sawachi, Hisae. *Otoko arite: Shimura Takashi no sekai*. Japan: Bungei Shunju, 1994.
Tsuduki, Masaaki. *Kurosawa Akira to Shinichin no Samurai—Eiga no naka no eiga tanjo dokyu-mento*. Tokyo: Asahi Sonotama, 1999.

Documentary Films

Drunken Angel. Akira Kurosawa: It Is Wonderful to Create. Toho Masterworks. Criterion Collection DVD, 2007.
Drunken Angel: Kurosawa and the Censors. Criterion Collection DVD, 2007.
"Godzilla Story Development" Featurette. Classic Media DVD, 2006.
Ikiru. Akira Kurosawa: It Is Wonderful to Create. Toho Masterworks. Criterion Collection Blu-Ray, 2015.
"Making of the Godzilla Suit" Featurette. Classic Media DVD, 2006.
Rashômon: Testimony as an Image. Criterion Collection Blu-Ray, 2012.
Rashômon: The World of Kazuo Miyagawa. Criterion Collection Blu-Ray, 2012.
Seven Samurai. Akira Kurosawa: It Is Wonderful to Create. Toho Masterworks. Criterion Collection Blu-Ray, 2010.
"Seven Samurai": Origins and Influences. Criterion Collection Blu-Ray, 2010.
Yojimbo. Akira Kurosawa: It Is Wonderful to Create. Toho Masterworks. Criterion Collection Blu-Ray, 2015.

Websites

"The Jidai-Geki Knights," Lard Biscuit Enterprises, 2016, http://www.lardbiscuit.com/ji
"Takashi Shimura," Alchetron.com, https://alchetron.com/Takashi-Shimura daigeki/.
www.bafta.org
www.famousbirthdays.com
www.momat.go.jp
www.tohokingdom.com
www.yahoo.co.jp

Index

Numbers in **_bold italics_** indicate pages with illustrations

A un (1980 television series) 160, 263
Academy Awards (U.S.) 19, 69, 78, 93, 139, 148, 156, 161
Academy of Motion Picture Arts and Sciences (AMPAS) 148
Adams, Nick 144–145, 240
Ah kaiten tokubetsu kogetikai [*Human Torpedoes*] (1968 film) 150, 248
Ai to chikai [*Love and Pledge*] (1945 film) 21, 176
Ai to honobo to [*Challenge to Live*] (1961 film) 121, 224
Ai to nikushimi no kanata e [*Beyond Love and Hate*] (1951 film) 55, 186
Aika [*Elegy*] (1951 film) 55, 186
Ainu (ethnic group) 109–110
Aizawa, Yuzuru 115, 117, 180, 195, 218, 225, 227, 234
Akagaki Genzô (1936 short film) 17, 167
Akagaki Genzô (1938 film) 169
Akahige [*Red Beard*] (1965 film) 33, 139–143, 156, 161, 238
Akahige shinryôtan (short story collection) 140, 238
Akanishi Kakita [*The Capricious Young Man*] (1936 film) 15, 167
Aku no monshô [*Brand of Evil*] (1964 film) 136, 234
Akutagawa, Ryûnosuke 50, 62, 185, 189
Amamoto, Hideyo ["Eisei"] 135, 211, 215, 218, 221, 223, 228, 230, 233, 236–237, 245, 251
Anatomy of a Murder (1959 film) 69
Ánimas Trujano (El hombre importante) [*The Important Man*] (1961 film) 117
Ankokugai [*The Underworld*] (1956 film) 95, 202
Aoi sanmyaku Shinko no maki (1957 film) 100, 206
Aoi Shinju [*The Blue Pearl*] (1951 film) 58, 187
Aoki, Toshi 148, 246

Aoyagi, Nobuo 81, 89, 95, 186, 195–196, 198, 203
Arai, Ryohei 18, 171
Araki Mataemon: Kettô kagiya no tsuji [*Vendetta of Samurai*] (1952 film) 59, 188
Arakure [*Untamed Woman*] (1957 film) 94, 99–100, 205
Ârappoi no ha gômen dazê [*Pardon My Violent Ways*] (1967 film) 146, 246
Aratama, Michiyo 121, 123, 136, 138–139, 145–146, 196, 220, 222–223, 225, 230, 234, 236–237, 245, 257, 261
Arima, Yorichika 99, 205
Aru yo no tonosama [*Lord for a Night*] (1946 film) 28, 94, 178–179
Asada, Kenzô 20, 174, 178–180
Asahi Cultural Prize 141
Asakusa no yoru (1954 film) 80, 194
Asama, Yoshitaka 158, 253, 258
Asano, Takuminkami 128
Ashes and Diamonds (1958 film) 89
Asu o tsukuru hitobito [*Those Who Make Tomorrow*] (1946 film) 26, 94, 177
Ataka (Noh play) 23
Atsumi, Kiyoshi 152, 154–**_155_**, **_158_**, 231, 248, 250, 252–253, 258
"Auld Lang Syne" (song) 47, 110
Awashima, Chikage 123, 185, 206, 209, 226
Ayres, Lew 142

"Bagatelle for piano in A minor" ["Für Elise"] (Beethoven) 110
Baishô, Chieko 151, 154–**_155_**, 234, 241, 250, 252–253
Bake jizou [*Jizo the Spook*] (1898 short film) 13
Bakurô ichidai [*The Life of a Horse-Trader*] (1951 film) 58–59, **_60_**, **_61_**, 188
Bangkok no joru [*Night in Bangkok*] (1966 film) 145, 242

273

274 Index

Banshô, Yoshiaki 111, 216
Banshun [*Late Spring*] (1949 film) 27
Bâra kêtsu shobû [*Hoodlum Match*] (1965 film) 145, 242
Barbieri, Renato 157, 257
Barrymore, Lionel 47, 142
Bazoku geisha (1954 film) 87, 196
The Beast from 20,000 Fathoms (1953 film) 83, 86
Beethoven, Ludwig van 110
benshi (silent-film theater performers) 13, 14
Beran me-e geisha [*The Prickly-mouthed Geisha*] (1959 film) *111*-112, 216
Bergman, Ingmar 68
Berlin Film Festival 53, 92
Bijo to touzoku [*Beauty and the Thieves*] (1952 film) 62, 189
Bixio, Franco 157, 257
Black, Walter 143, 239
Blue Ribbon Awards (Japan) 78, 88, 108
Bôkyaku no hanabira (1957 film) 95, 203
Bond, Ward 4
Boryokudan [*Violent Gang*] (1963 film) 134, 233
Botan-dôrô [*Peony Lantern*] (1968 film) 148, 247
Bradbury, Ray 83
British Film and Television Awards (BAFTA) 69
Bronenosets Potemkin [*Battleship Potemkin*] (1925 film) 74
Brown, Clarence 47
"Brutal Tales of Chivalry" (film series) 151, 250
Brynner, Yul 79
Buraikan jingi [*Villain's Code*] (1965 film) 145, 241
Burns, Robert 47, 110
Burr, Raymond 85-86, 202, 257

Cagney, James 148-149
Cannes Film Festival 78, 92, 139, 161
Capra, Frank 47
Chi to daiyamondo [*Blood and Diamonds*] (1964 film) 135, 234
Chiaki, Minoru 4, **52**, **54**-55, 57-59, 62, 64, 68, 74, 76, 87, 90, 93, 95, 99, 105, 107, 110, 131, 179, 183, 185, 187-188, 190, 193, 197, 200, 203-205, 211-212, 214, 232
Chiba, Sinichi [Sonny] 134, 146, 150, 156, 162, 232, 241, 245, 248, 256
Chiba, Yasuki 55, 70, 123, 140, 185, 190, 225, 242
Chihaya, Masataka 143, 239
Chikagai nijuyojikan [*24 Hours of a Secret Life*] (1947 film) 28, 179
Chikamatsu monogatari [*Crucified Lovers*] (1954 film) 33
Chikemuri Takadanobaba (1937 film) 17, 168
Chikyû Bôeigun [*The Mysterians*] (1957 film) 101-103, 207
Chisaka, Hyôbu 128
Chóe, In-kyu 21, 176

Chûretsu nikudan sanyûshi (1936 film) 15, 166
Chûshingura [*The Loyal 47 Ronin*] (1958 film) *102*-104, 208-209
Chûshingura [*The Loyal 47 Samurai*] (1962 film) 128-129, 229-231
Civil Censorship Detachment (CCD) 37
"The Colour Out of Space" (short story) 145
Coppola, Francis Ford 160, 259
Cozzi, Luigi 157, 257
Crime and Punishment (1935 film) 58
Curtis, Tony 69
Curtiz, Michael 127
Cybulski, Zbigniew 69

Dai tuzoku [*The Lost World of Sinbad*] (1963 film) 134-135, 233
Daiei Company and Studios 38-39, 43-44, 50, 58-60, 62, 80, 87, 95, 103-105, 112, 117-118, 121, 127, 145, 148, 150-151, 156, 181, 183-189, 194, 196, 201, 208-210, 212-213, 215-216, 220-221, 223, 229, 244, 247-248, 250
Daikatsu Company 15
Daini no jinsei (1948 film) 31, 180
Dan, Ikuma 93, 189, 197, 200, 202, 214, 217, 223, 231, 239
Dan, Reiko 117-118, 125-126, 219, 220, 222, 226, 229, 238
Darwell, Jane 30
Dassin, Jules 131
Datsugoku [*Escape from Prison*] (1950 film) 55, 186
The Death of Ivan Ilyich (novella) 63
December 7th (1943 film) 19
Delannoy, Jean 69
Del Ruth, Roy 149
Desailly, Jean 69
De Sica, Vittorio 68
Dickens, Charles 119
Dr. Ehrlich's Magic Bullet (1940 film) 39
"Dr. Kildare" (film series) 141-142
Dr. Strangelove (1964 film) 84
Dodes'ka-den (1970 film) 153-154
Doi, Mizuho 148, 246
Dokkoi daisaku (1973-1974 television series) 154-155, 261
Donzoko [*The Lower Depths*] (1958 film) 106
Dôran (1980 film) 160, 258
Dostoevsky, Fyodor 32, 55-58, 186
Dotanba (1957 film) 101, 206-207
Dovzhenko, Alexander 21
Downs, Cathy 30

Ebara, Shinjirô 112, 207, 216
Eddoko matsuri (1958 film) 103, 208
Edo no akutarô (1939 film) 17, 170
Edo saigo no hi (1941 film) 18, 172-173
Egi, Toshio 131, 232
Eiga geijutsu kyokai [Film Art Association] 37, 41, 181-182, 186
"*Eiko-no Kagi-ni*" ["In the Shadow of Glory"] (proposed 1954 film) 82

Eisenstein, Sergei 74–75
The Empire Strikes Back (1980 film) 108
Enami, Kyôko 127, 229, 248
Endô, Seiichi 87, 95, 196, 198, 202–203, 213
Endo, Shigeru 77, 193, 204, 212
Enomoto, Ken'ichi ["Enoken"] 176–177, 179, 199
Eri, Chiemi 121, 223
Ezaki, Mio 145, 242

Fellini, Federico 68
Fisher, Carrie 108
Fonda, Henry 4, 30, 113
Ford, John 4, 19, 24, 26, 30, 33, 58, 61, 78, 90–91, 94, 98–**99**, 106
Foster, Stephen 30, 110
Frankenstein (1931 film) 2, 58, 112, 141
A Free Soul (1931 film) 47
Frees, Paul 113, 197, 203, 208, 217, 229
Freund, Karl 64
Frizzi, Fabio 157, 257
Fugita, Susumu 19–22, 24, 26, 28, 40, 102, 107, 113, 117, 121, 129, 131, 143, 145–146, 173–179, 182, 186, 207, 212, 217, 219, 221–222, 224, 230–232, 240, 245, 251
Fugita, Yôko 61–62, 189
Fugita, Yumiko 151, 261
Fujii, Shizuka 106, 207, 211
Fujiki, Yû 88, 198–199, 204–205, 212, 215, 220–221, 225, 227, 230, 234, 245, 257
Fujimoto, Sanezumi 128, 145, 181, 188, 190, 204, 206, 212, 214–215, 217, 219, 221, 224–225, 227, 229, 234, 242, 244, 251
Fujiwara, Kamatari 71, 78, 116, 118, 149, 180, 184–185, 187, 189–193, 195–196, 198, 200, 203–204, 206, 212–213, 219, 221, 225–226, 230, 232, 235, 238, 248
Fujiwara, Shinya 58, 187
Fujiyama, Yôko 134, 225, 227, 229, 233, 238
Fukunaga, Takehiko 121, 224
Fukuryu Maru [*Fortunate Dragon*] (boat) 83, 90
Fundoshi Isha [*Life of a Country Doctor*] (1961 film) 121, 223
Furankenshutain tai chitei kaijû Baragon [*Frankenstein Conquers the World*] (1965 film) 144–145, 240
Fûrin kazan [*Samurai Banners*] (1969 film) 150, 249
Furuhata, Kôji 144, 240
Furuhata, Yasuo 146, 150–151, 154, 245, 248, 250, 252
Furuya, Osamu 239, 248
Futari no musuko [*Different Sons*] (1961 film) 123, 225
Fuun senryobune (1952 film) 70, 191

Gabin, Jean 69
Gambare! Bangaku [*Master Fencer Sees the World*] (1960 film) 117, 219
Geisha Konatsu: Hitori neru yo no Konatsu [*The Tears of Geisha Konatsu*] (1955) 89, 198–199
Geisha no teodori (1899 film) 13
Gekido no showashi "Gunbatsu" [*The Militarists*] (1970 film) 152–153, 251–252
Genbauku no ko [*Children of Hiroshima*] (1952 film) 90
Gendai yakuza: yotomono no okite (1968 film) 150, 248
Genroku Chûshingura [*The 47 Ronin*] (1941 film) 104
Gideon's Day [*Gideon of Scotland Yard*] (1959 film) 98–99
Ginrei no hate [*Snow Trail*] (1947 film) 29–30, 43, 55, 158, 179–180
Ginza Sanshiro [*A Ginza Veteran*] (1950 film) 55, 186
Gion Festival 149
Gion matsuri [*Festival of Gion*] (1968 film) 149, 247–248
Godzilla [*Cozzilla*] (1977 film) 157, 257–258
Godzilla: King of the Monsters! (1956 film) 85–86, 95, 157, 202–203
Gojira [*Godzilla*] (1954 film) 2, 19–21, 82–87, 90, 95, 118, 157, 195–196
Gojira no gyakushû [*Godzilla Raids Again*] (1955 film) 87–88, 196–197
Gokuaku bozu—nomu utsu kau [*The Bloody Priest*] (1971 film) 154, 253
Gokudo makari touru [*Gokudo's Notorious Reputation*] (1972 film) 154, 253
"Gondola Song" (song) 65
Gorky, Maxim 106
Gorotsuki mushuku [*Rogue Wanderer*] (1971 film) 154, 252–253
The Grapes of Wrath (1940 film) 30
Grimaldi, Hugo 88, 113, 196–197, 217
Guinness, Alec 108
Gunji, Jiromasa 140, 237
Gyangu no teio [*Gyungu II*] (1967 film) 146, 245

Haha (1958 film) 105, 210
Haha no hatsukoi [*Mother's First Love*] (1954 film) 81, 194–195
Haha no kinembi (1943 film) 20, 174
Hahakogusa (1942 film) 173
Hakuchi [*The Idiot*] (1951 film) 30, 55–58, **56**, **57**, 115, 186–187
Hakuô, Matsumoto 128, 230, 238, 245
Hamamura, Kôichi 98, 193, 203, 212, 219, 222, 232
Hamlet (play) 25, 115
Hara, Kenichiro 104
Hara, Setsuko 5, 19, 27–28, 55–58, **56**, 111, 121, 128, 176–178, 187, 215, 223, 229
Hara, Yasumi 48–49, 174, 184
Hara Kiri (1962 film) 137
Harekosode [*Clear Weather*] (1961 film) 118, 221
Harryhausen, Ray 83

Index

Haru no mezame [*Spring Awakens*] (1947 film) 30
Harum Scarum (1965 film) 137
Hasegawa, Kazuo 103–104, 108, 174–175, 179, 191, 201, 208–209, 213, 222
Hasegawa, Kôen 21, 175
Hasegawa, Shin 121, 223, 234
Hashida, Sugako 145, 243
Hashimoto, Shinobu 50, 63–64, 71–73, 79, 89, 91, 96, 107, 109, 113, 115, 139, 145–146, 150, 156, 185, 190, 192, 199, 203, 206, 212–213, 217–218, 231, 234, 237, 240, 244, 249, 257, 259
Hasshu yukyoden—otoko no sakazuki [*Gambler Tales of Hasshu: A Man's Pledge*] (1963 film) 134, 232
Hawai Maree oki kaisen [*The War at Sea from Hawaii to Malaya*] (1942 film) 19
Hawai Middowee daikaikûsen: Teiheiyô no arashi [*Storm Over the Pacific*] (1960 film) 113, 217
Hayasaka, Fumio 33, 41, 43, 65, 74, 90, 107, 179, 181–182, 184–185, 187–188, 190, 193–194, 199
Hearn, Lafcadio 137–138, 236
Heston, Charlton 113
Hibi Heian (novel) 124, 226
Hidaka, Shigeaki 89, 196, 199
Hidari, Bokuzen 5, **47**, 59, 64, 90, 100, 109, 143, 151, 184, 187–188, 190–191, 193, 197, 200, 205, 214–215, 238–239, 250
Himetaru kakugo (1943 film) 20, 173–174
Hino, Shôhei 87, 196
Hirata, Akihiko 85, 110, 117, 124, 143, 155, 191, 196, 198, 200, 202, 207, 213–214, 215, 218, 221, 225–226, 228, 230–231, 235, 237, 240, 244, 249, 251, 254–255, 257
Hirohito (Japanese emperor) 32–33, 71, 130
Hiroshima (1952 film) 90
Hiryû (ship) 113
Hisa, Yoshitake 18, 104, 168, 170–172, 210, 242
Hisaita, Eijirô 27, 55, 115, 131, 178, 186, 218, 231
Hisamatsu, Seiji 81, 194
Hissatsu shiokiya kagyô (1975–1976 television series) 156, 262–263
Hitori musuko [*The Only Son*] (1936 film) 15
Honda, Ishirô 21, 41, 58, 61, 70–71, 83–86, 95, 98–99, 103, 109, 122–123, 126–127, 136, 144–145, 161–162, 174, 182–183, 186–188, 191–192, 195–196, 201–202, 204, 207, 213, 225, 228, 235, 240, 257, 259
Hong, James 86, 202
Honma, Noriko 54–55, 185, 190, 201, 205, 223
Honnô-ji gassen (1908 short film) 13
Hopu-san: sarariman no maki (1951 film) 58, 188
Hori, Yoshiki 156, 262
Horikawa, Hiromichi 124, 136, 152–153, 175, 178, 190, 193, 203, 234, 251
Hoshi, Yuriko 126, 213, 218, 221, 227, 229, 231, 235, 242, 251
Hoshijima, Ichirô 145, 147, 241, 243, 246, 248
The House at the End of the World [*Die, Monster, Die!*] (1965 film) 145
Hoyo [*The Last Embrace*] (1953 film) 70, 191–192

Ichiban utsukushiku [*The Most Beautiful*] (1944 film) 21, 175
Ichikawa, Chûsha 128, 230, 238
Ichikawa, Kon 55, 59, 94, 162, 186, 188
Ichikawa, Raizô 121, 209, 213, 215, 223
Ichikawa, Utaemon 104, 210
Ichimura, Hirokazu 135, 145, 234, 241
Ide, Toshirô 58, 70, 113, 181, 188, 190, 206, 217, 227
The Idiot (novel) 55–58, 186
Ieyusu, Tokugawa 9, 93, 117
Ifukube, Akira 85, 110, 118, 128, 179–181, 183, 185–186, 188, 195, 202, 207, 215, 221, 225, 229, 235, 240, 254, 257–258
Ihonbashi, Kazuko 42, 183
Iimura, Masahiko 156, 251, 256
Ikari no machi [*The Angry Street*] (1950 film) 48–49, 185–185
Ikebe, Ryô 44, 70–71, 81, 114, 123, 128, 151, 179, 184, 186–187, 191–192, 194, 198, 203, 206, 211, 217–218, 220, 225, 228–229, 231, 248, 250, 261
Ikebe, Shin'ichirô 161, 259
Ikeda, Tomiyasu 15, 17, 167, 169
Ikehiru, Kazuo 121, 223
Ikimono no Kiroku [*Record of a Living Being*] (1955 film) 89–92, 199–200
Ikiru (1952 film) 1–2, 5, 55, 63–70, 72, 74–75, 79, 84, 164, 190
Imai, Tadashi 21, 26, 28, 94, 145, 176–177, 179, 243
Imperial Japanese Naval Academy (IJNA) 129
Inaba, Yoshio 76, 193, 204, 223, 237, 240, 254, 263
Inagaki, Hiroshi 17–18, 44, 62, 70, 93–94, 111, 117–118, 121, 128, 150, 162, 168–173, 183, 189, 191, 200, 215, 220, 223, 229, 249
Inomata, Kengo 154, 252
Inoue, Masao 14
Inoue, Mike 91, 115, 218
Inoue, Yasushi 62, 150, 189, 233, 249
International Film Critics Prize 108
Inuzuka, Minoru 111, 215
Irie, Takako 125, 175, 226
Ishida, Tamizo 21, 94, 175
Ishihara, Shintarô 121, 206, 224
Ishihara, Yûjirô 148, 150, 242, 246, 249, 252
Ishihara Productions Company 147, 154, 246, 252
Ishimori, Nubuo 109, 213
Ishin no kagarabi [*Restoration Fire*] (1961 film) **123**–124, 226
Ishiyama, Kenjirô 132–133, 232, 236, 245–246, 248, 252

Ishizaka, Yojirô 70, 190
Itami, Mansaku 15, 166–167, 183
Itô, Daisuke 73, 149, 247
Itô, Emi 122, 136, 224, 235
Itô, Hisaya 136, 206–207, 211, 215, 217, 230–231, 234–235, 240–241
Itô, Jerî 122, 224
Itô, Kisaku 128, 200
Itô, Seiichi (Japanese Admiral) 129
Itô, Toshiya 154, 252
Itô, Yumi 122, 136, 224, 235
Itô, Yûnosuke 125, 131, 146, 183, 186, 190, 232, 237, 243, 245, 248, 262
It's a Wonderful Life (1946 film) 47
"It's Now or Never" (song) 133
Iwai, Hanshirô 24, 177, 213, 221
Iwao, Mori 25
Izu, Hajimi 61, 189

Jigoku no hatobâ [*Pier of Hell*] (1965 film) 145, 241–242
Jigoku no kifukin (1949 film) 40, 182
Jigokumon [*Gate of Hell*] (1953 film) 78
Jinsei genkijô—Seishun hen [*Theater of Life*] (1958 film) 106, 211
Jinsei Gekijo: shin hisha kaku [*Theater of Life—New Hishakaku Story*] (1964 film) 135, 237
Jiraiya (1937 film) 17, 168
Jirochô sangokushi kaitô-ichi no abarenbo (1954 film) 79, 194
Juichinin no jogakusei (1946 film) 27, 178

kabuki (theater) 13–14, 23, 33, 72, 104, 121, 229
Kaerazeru hatoba [*The Harbor of No Return*] (1966 film) 145, 242
Kaeriyama, Norimasa 14
Kagawa, Kyôko 5, 81, 116–117, 123, 131, 155, 195, 215, 219, 221, 224, 232, 238, 254
Kagemusha (1980 film) 23, 160–161, 259–260
Kagero ezu [*Stop the Old Fox*] (1959 film) 111, 214–215
Kaidan [*Kwaidan*] (1964 film) 137–139, 145, 236–237
Kaigun (1943 film) 20, 174
Kakushi-toride no san-akunin [*The Hidden Fortress*] (1958 film) 106–108, 118, 212
Kamei, Fumio 37, 181
Kaneko, Ienori 77, 193, 212
Kaneko, Nobuo 67, 190, 242, 246, 249
Kaneko, Yoshinobu 155, 262
Kanjincho [*The Subscription List*] (kabuki play) 4
Kanto hamonjo [*Expelled from the Kanto Mob*] (1965 film) 145, 241
Kanto onna akumyo [*Unknown Woman of Kanto*] (1969 film) 151, 250
Kanze, Nobumitsu 50
Karajishi keisatsu [*Lion Enforcer*] (1974 film) 156, 256

Karakkaze yarô [*Afraid to Die*] (1960 film) *112*, 216–217
Karei-yaru ichizoku [*The Family*] (1974 film) 155, 254
Karloff, Boris 2, 58, 64, 112, 145
Kasagi, Shizuko 34, 181
Kasahara, Ryôzô 152, 210, 216, 219–221, 227, 242, 251
Katagiri, Katsumoto 118
Katamori, Matsudaira 123
Kataoka, Chiezô *18*, 123, 134, 167–168, 170–173, 183, 226, 232
Katô, Daisuke 5, 59, 78, 99, 118–119, 128, 143, 146, 183, 185, 187–188, 190–191, 193, 198, 200, 206, 215, 217, 220, 222, 227, 229, 239, 244
Katô, Takeshi 116, 131, 194, 204, 212, 219, 222, 232, 244, 246
Katô, Tateo (Japanese Imperial Army Air Force Colonel) 20
Katô hayabusa sento-tai [*Colonel Katô's Falcon Squadron*] (1944 film) 20–21, 174–175
Katsu, Shintarô 103, 148–*149*, 151, 155, 160–161, 209, 213, 229, 247, 250, 253–254
Katsudô shashinkai (magazine) 14
Katsukake Tokijirô [*The Gambler's Code*] (1961 film) 121, 223–224
Katsuragi, Yôko 46, 184
Kawaguchi, Matsutarô 80, 118, 169, 194, 201, 221
Kawanakajima (battle) 150
Kawasaki, Keizô *102*, 104
Kawasaki, Shintarô 105
Kawasaki, Tamotsu 37, 179, 181, 184
Kawashima, Taizô 105, 113, 179
Kawashima, Yûzô 94, 217
Kawazu, Seizaburô 110, 118–119, 128, 151, 155, 194, 206, 214, 217, 221–222, 224, 227, 229, 231, 243, 250, 254, 256
Kawazu, Yusuke 150, 248, 259
Kayama, Yoshiko 135, 145, 234, 241
Kayama, Yûzô 125, 128–129, 134, 140, 143, 145–146, 154, 162, 218, 225–227, 229, 231, 233, 238–239, 242, 245, 251
Kaze (1967–1968 television series) 146, 261
K'damonô no torû michi [*Beast's Passage*] (1959 film) 109, 216
Kedamono no yado [*The Den of Beasts*] (1951 film) 58, 187
Ken wa shitte ita (1958 film) 109, 213
Kiken na eiyu [*A Dangerous Hero*] (1957 film) 100, 205–206
Kikushima, Ryûzô 41, 46, 71, 88, 96, 111, 115, 121, 124, 131, 140, 182, 184, 192, 197, 202–203, 212–213, 215–216, 218, 222–223, 226, 231, 238
Kikuta, Kazuo 95, 181, 203
Kimi shinitamo koto nakare (1954 film) 80–81, 194
Kimura, Isao [Ko] 78, 183, 185–186, 190, 193, 202, 204, 216, 234
Kimura, Keigo 58–62, 187–189
Kimura, Takeshi 101, 126, 203, 207, 227, 233, 240

Kinema Junpô (journal) 67, 78, 92, 126, 139, 141, 146, 152
Kinema Record (journal) 14
King Kong (1933 film) 82–83, 122
King Lear (play) 92
King's Ransom (novel) 131, 231
Kingu Kongu tai Gojira [*King Kong vs. Godzilla*] (1962 film) 126, 137
Kinoshita, Chûji 106, 110, 211, 216, 241, 243, 246
Kinoshita, Keisuke 21, 78, 110, 137, 140
Kinugasa, Teinosuke 14, 28, 78, 84, 94–95, 111, 178–179, 201, 214–215
Kinugasa, Toshizo 17, 169
Kishi, Keiko 81, 138, 185, 187, 195, 206, 236
Kishi, Matsuo 117, 173
Kita no san-nin [*Three People of the North*] (1945 film) 22, 94, 176–177
Kitabayashi, Tanie 46, 184, 187, 190, 246, 252–253
Kitazawa, Noriko 123, 226, 262
Kobayashi, Keiju 117, 215, 220, 222, 226, 229, 235, 237, 245, 251
Kobayashi, Masaki 137–139, 146, 162, 236
Kobori, Akio 81, 87, 194–196, 198
Kôchi, Momoko 85, 195, 198, 202, 207, 257
Kôda Ryoko [Yoshiko] 109, 214, 218
Kôdô, Kokuten 4, 28–29, 73, 100, 107, 173, 178, 180, 183–185, 187, 189, 193–195, 199–202, 204–205, 207, 212
Kogure, Michiyo 70, 179, 181–182, 190, 200, 209, 215
Koi no fuunjî [*Misfortunes of Love*] (1945 film) 22, 177
Koishi, Eiichi 111, 216
Koizumi, Fukuzô 121, 124–125
Koizumi, Hajime 123
Koizumi, Hiroshi 80, 87, 95, 122, 136, 191–192, 194–197, 199, 203–205, 217, 219, 224–225, 230–231, 235, 242, 245, 255, 257
Koizumi, Isanomukami 73
Komatsu, Hôsei 148, 247, 262
Komatsubara, Chikara 127, 229
Kon, Tôkô 157, 258
Kônami, Fumio 152, 251
Kôno, Akitake 29, 173, 176–180, 182, 184, 211, 226
Kono futari ni sache ari [*Be Happy, These Two Lovers*] (1957 film) 98–99, 204–205
Kono koe naki sakebi [*The Soundless Cry*] (1965 film) 145, 241
Kosugi, Yoshio 25, 29, 76, 146, 173, 177, 180, 186, 188–189, 192–193, 203, 207, 211–212, 214–215, 217, 221, 223–224, 230–231, 234, 236, 241, 244
Kotan no kuchibue [*A Whistle in My Heart*] (1959 film) 109–110, 213–214
Kramer, Stanley 84
Kubo, Akira 96, 146, 197, 199, 203–204, 206, 214–215, 217, 224, 226, 228, 230, 240, 245, 249, 252
Kubo [Yamauchi], Ken 109, 199, 214

Kubrick, Stanley 84
Kudô, Eiichi 150, 248
Kuga, Yoshiko 5, 30, 35, 48, 55–58, 117, 179–181, 184, 187, 221, 249
Kujira gami [*Killer Whale*, aka *The Whale God*] (1962 film) *127*–128, 229
Kumai, Kei 147, 157, 160, 246, 258–259
Kumonosu-jô [*Throne of Blood*] (1957 film) 95–99, 106–107, 115, 117, 161, 203–204
Kunihiro, Takeo 113, 150, 217, 249, 262
Kurama Tengu (1938 film) 17, 168–169
Kurenai no sora [*Scarlet Sky*] (1962 film) 126, 227
Kurihara, Kisaburô ["Thomas"] 14
Kurobe no taiyo [*The Sands of Kurobe*] (1968 film) 147–148, 246–247
Kuroi gashû dainibu: Kanryû [*Structure of Hate*] (1961 film) 123, 225
Kurosawa, Akira 1–5, 7, 17, 19–21, 23–48, 50–59, 61–68, 71–81, 83–84, 88–100, *99*, 102, 106–108, 110, 114–120, 124–126, 131–135, 139–144, 147, 149, *153*–154, 156, 160–162, 173, 175, 177–190, 192–194, 199–200, 203–204, 212, 214, 218–219, 222–223, 226, 231–232, 238–239, 259–260
Kurosawa, Yôko 44, 98–*99*
Kurosawa Production Company 116, 204, 219, 222, 226, 232, 238–239, 259
Kurutta ippêji [*A Page of Madness*] (1926 film) 14
Kusuda, Kiyoshi 28, 179
Kwaidan: Stories and Studies of Strange Things (novel) 137–139
Kyatsu o nigasuna [*I Saw the Killer*] (1956 film) 95, 202
Kyô, Machiko 33, 51, 55, 58–*60*, 62, 80, 84, 87, 95, 103, 105, 155, 162, 185, 187–189, 194, 196, 201, 209–210, 254
Kyokatsu ichidai [*The Chivalrous Life*] (1967 film) 146–*147*, 245–246

Ladd, Alan, Jr. 160
Lang, Fritz 58, 97, 115–116, 133
Lemmon, Jack 69
Leone, Sergio 119
Leyte Gulf (World War II battle) 129
Loew's, Inc. 103
Long Way to Okinawa (1962 film) 126, 227
Lorre, Peter 58
The Lost Patrol (1934 film) 78
The Lost World (1925 film) 83
Lovecraft. H.P. 145
Lucas, George 108, 160, 259
Lucas, John Meredyth 127, 227
The Luminous Fairies and Mothra (novel) 121–122, 224

M (1930 film) 133
Ma no ogon (1950 film) 44, 183
MacArthur, Douglas 20, 25
Macbeth (1948 film) 96

Macbeth (play) 96, 203
Machida, Kyôsuke 148, 243, 246–248, 250, 253
Maeda, Gin 151, 250, 252–253, 258, 260
The Magnificent Seven (1960 film) 78–79
Maigret Sets a Trap (1958 film) 69
Mainichi Film Concurs [Awards] 43, 67, 78, 141, 152, 154
Makino, Masahiro 17–*18*, 70, 79–80, 87, 134, 146–147, 150–151, 162, 166–170, 172, 191, 194, 196, 232, 249–250
Makino, Shôzô 13–14
Makiura, Chikashi 155, 247, 253
Manjôme, Tadashi 105, 174, 211
Mann, Anthony 131
Mann, Peter 144, 241
Mannix (1967–1975 television series) 127
Marune, Santarô 18, 171
Maruyama, Seiji 81, 88, 98, 194, 197, 199, 204, 239
Masuda, Toshio 156, 255, 257
Masumura, Yasuzô 112, 216–217
Matatabi san ning yakusa [*Wanderers: Three Yakuza*] (1965 film) 142–*143*, 239
Matsubayashi, Shûe 100, 117, 126, 129, 206, 217, 219, 227, 231
Matsuda, Sadatsugu 17–18, 103–104, 123, 168, 172, 208, 210, 226, 242
Matsukata, Hiroki 142, 239, 248
Matsumoto, Isao 146, 151, 245, 249
Matsumoto, Seichô 106, 111, 211, 215, 225
Matsumura, Masaharu 121, 208, 223
Matsumura, Shoji 104–105, 211
Matsuno, Kôki 155, 262
Matsuura, Takeo [Kenrô] 81, 183, 195–196, 198
Matsuyama, Takashi [Shu] 43, 50, 174, 176–177, 179, 181–182, 185–190, 192–193, 234
Matsuyama, Zenzô 113, 204, 217, 225
Matsuzaki, Keiji 27, 173, 178–179
Mayama Chûshingura (play) 104
McBain, Ed 131, 231
McLaglen, Victor 4, 78
McQueen, Steve 79
Mekura neko (1955 film) 87, 196
Melville, Herman 127
Meshi [*Repast*] (1951 film) 27
Mesu Inu [*Bitch*] (1951 film) 58, 187
Midway (1976 film) 113
Midway (World War II battle) 113, 129, 143
Mifune, Shirô 43
Mifune, Toshirô 3–5, 7, 19, 29–*39*, 41–46, *45*, 48, 51, 53, 55–62, *56*, *60*, 68–72, 74, 76–78, 88, 90–98, 100, 106–108, 110–111, 113–120, 124–126, 128–135, 139–143, 146–154, 156–158, 161, 164, 180–182, 184–189, 191–193, 198, 200–204, 206, 211–212, 214–215, 217–223, 226, 230–233, 237–240, 244, 246, 248–249, 251, 258
Mifune Productions Company, Ltd. 139, 147, 150, 237, 246, 249

Mihashi, Tatsuya 114, 121, 128, 150, 217–220, 222, 224, 229, 231–232, 249, 251
Mikami, Shin'ichirô 151, 261
Mikimoto, Kayo 148, 247, 250
Mikuni, Rentarô 62, 93, 138, 189, 192, 236, 252, 255
Mimura, Shintarô 21, 70, 172, 175, 191
Minami, Hiroshi 105, 211
Minato e kita otoko [*The Man Who Came to Port*] (1952 film) 70, 191
Mine, Dick 18, 170–171
Minshu no teki [*An Enemy of the People*] (1946 film) 26, 177
Misaki, Chieko 151, 250, 252–253, 258
Misora, Hibari *111*–112, 216, 243, 248
Mr. Smith Goes to Washington (1939 film) 47
Misumi, Kenji 117, 220
Mitchell, Thomas 33
Mitokomon kaikokuki (1937 film) 15, 167
Mitsubishi Mining Company 11
Miyabe, Kimiko 48, 185
Miyagawa, Kazuo 51–53, 119, 121, 148, 168–171, 185, 222–223, 247, 259
Miyaguchi, Seiji 78, 100, 146, 190, 192–193, 202, 204–206, 219, 225, 231, 237, 244, 251
Miyajima, Yoshio 137, 181, 236, 254
Miyake, Kuniko 81, 105, 195, 211
Miyama no otome [*Maid of the Deep Mountains*] (1919 film) 14
Miyamoto Musashi [*Samurai I: Musashi Miyamoto*] (1954 film) 93, 200
Miyamoto Musashi: Dai-san-bu - Kenshin ichiro (1940 film) 18, 171–172
Miyamoto Musashi kanketsuhen: kettô Ganrûjima [*Samurai III: Duel at Ganryu Island*] (1955 film) 93–94, 200–201
Miyau, Hideo 148, 246
Miyauchi, Shôhei 121, 223
Miyoshi, Eiko 58, 109, 178, 182, 186–190, 197, 200, 204, 212, 214
Miyoshi, Jûrô 110, 214
Mizoguchi, Kenji 5, 14–18, 34, 53, 57, 62, 73, 79, 104, 162, 166, 189
Mizuki, Yôko 137, 139, 181, 190, 205, 236
Mizuno, Kumi 109, 128, 214–215, 224, 227–229, 233–234, 240
Moby Dick (novel) 127
Mokushô, Mayuri [Kumiko] 48, 180–181, 185, 197
Momijigari (1899 short film) 13
Momijigari (kabuki play) 13
Monroe, Marilyn 69
Mori, Kazuo 59, 151, 188, 250
Mori, Masayuki 5, 25, 27, 33, 53, 55–58, *56*, 62, 99–100, 109, 116, 121, 177, 184–185, 187–189, 205, 214, 219, 224
Mori no Ishimatsu [*Ishimatsu of the Forest*] (1949 film) 40, 182
Morikawa, Shin [Nobu] 151, 205, 250, 252–253

Index

Morita, Nobuyoshi 19
Moro, Alberto 157, 257
Morricone, Ennio 93, 119
Morse, Terry 85, 202, 257
Mosura [*Mothra*] (1961 film) 121–123, 224–225
Mosura tai Gojira [*Mothra vs. Godzilla*, aka *Godzilla vs. the Thing*] (1964 film) 136
Motoki, Sojirô 37, 72, 147, 177, 179–188, 190, 192, 194, 199, 202–203, 246
Mugibue [*Love Never Fails*] (1955 film) 88, 197
The Mummy (1932 film) 65
Murakami, Genzo 87, 194, 220
Muraki, Yoshirô 96, 140, 181–182, 190, 193, 199, 203, 212, 218, 220–222, 226, 231, 238, 255, 257, 259
Murao, Akira 146, 150, 152, 154, 233, 243, 245, 248–249, 251, 253
Muteki [*Foghorn*] (1952 film) 62, 189
Muttsuri Umon torimonocho (1955 film) 89, 198
My Darling Clementine (1946 film) 30
"My Old Kentucky Home" (song) 30

Naganori, Asano 102–104
Nakadai, Tatsuya 5, 75, 99–100, 119, 124–126, 131–132, 134, 138–139, 142, 145–146, 155, 160, 194, 205–206, 222, 226, 232, 236, 239, 245, 254, 257, 259, 261
Nakai, Asakazu 28, 41, 43, 78, 97, 131, 140, 156, 176, 178–179, 182, 186–188, 190, 192, 199, 203, 205, 231, 238, 259
Nakajima, Haruo 84, 103, 137, 144, 162, 183, 189, 192–193, 195–197, 200, 202–203, 207, 212, 214, 217–218, 221, 225, 229–231, 235–236, 240–241
Nakajima, Sadao 156, 239, 256
Nakakita, Chieko 29, 34, 39, 175–176, 178, 181–182, 191, 197, 199, 205–206, 213–215, 221, 223, 230, 235
Nakamura, Katsuo 138, 160, 216, 236, 248–249, 259
Nakamura, Kinnosuke 142, 149–150, 213, 239, 248–249, 258
Nakamura, Nobuo 131, 190, 204, 219, 232, 241, 244, 252, 254
Nakamura, Shin'ichiro 81, 121, 194, 224
Nakamaru, Tadao 135, 197, 207, 212, 214, 217–218, 221, 227, 230–231, 233, 237, 240, 244, 251
Nakao, Ryûsei 155, 262
Nakayama, Mari 155, 254
Nakayama, Masao 59, 188
The Naked City (1948 film) 131
Namiki, Kyotaro 59, 188
Nangoku no hada [*The Skin of the South*] (1952 film) 62, 188–189
Naniwa, Chieko 96, 204, 206, 211, 213
Naniwa Ereji [*Osaka Elegy*] (1936 film) 15–*16*, 166

Naniwa kyokaku: dokyo shichinin giri [*Killer of Seven Men*] (1967 film) 146, 246
Narayama bushikô [*The Ballad of Narayama*] (1958 film) 137
Narazu-mono [*Blackguard*] (1956 film) 95, 203
Narusawa, Masashige 58, 187–188, 191, 201
Naruse, Masahiko 105, 148, 211, 244, 246
Naruse, Mikio 21, 27, 30, 37, 48–49, 85, 94, 99, 109–110, 113, 162, 173, 175, 179–180, 184, 205, 213, 217
National Film Archive of Japan 6, 144, 162
Natsuki, Yôsuke 113, 121, 128–129, 135–136, 162, 217, 220–223, 227, 229, 231, 234–235
Naya, Goro 144, 240, 255, 259
Nichijô no tatakai (1944 film) 21, 176
Nichiren ["Rencho"] (monk) 108
Nichiren to moko daishurai [*Nichiren and the Great Mongol Invasion*] (1958 film) 108–*109*, 212–213
Nihon boryoku-dan: kumicho to shikaku [*Japan's Violent Gangs—The Boss and the Killers*] (1969 film) 152, 251
Nihon no ichiban nagai hi [*Japan's Longest Day*] (1967 film) 145–146, 244–245
Nihon Philharmonic Orchestra: *Honoo no dai gogakusho* (1981 film) 161, 260
Nijûshi no hitomi [*Twenty-Four Eyes*] (1954 film) 21, 78, 110
Nikkatsu Corporation 13–15, 17, 118, 145, 147, 161, 167–173, 243, 246, 260
Ningen no jôken [*The Human Condition*] (1959–61 film series) 21, 110, 137
Nippon Kogaku Company 21
Nippon tanjô [*Age of the Gods*] (1959 film) 111, 215–216
Nishigaki, Rokurô 113, 204, 218, 227, 255, 257
Nishikawa, Katsumi 145, 242
Nishiki, Motosada 48, 71, 182, 184, 191
Nobunaga, Odu 72, 157, 161
Nogami, Teruyo 65, 185, 190, 193, 204, 212, 219, 222, 226, 232, 238, 259
Noh (theater) 23, 50, 96–97, 107
Nora inu [*Stray Dog*] (1949 film) 41–43, 131, 182–183
Noren ichidai: jôkyô [*Life of a Chivalrous Woman*] (1966 film) 146, 243
Nosutoradamasu no daiyogen [*The Last Days of Planet Earth*] (1974 film) 156, 255
Numasaki, Isao 29, 174, 179, 184
Nusumareta koi [*Stolen Love*] (1951 film) 59, 188

"'O Sole Mio" (song) 133
O'Brien, George 4
O'Brien, Willis 83
Oda, Motoyoshi 27, 87, 178, 196
Oda Nobunaga (1940 film) 18, 172
Odagiri, Miki 64–65, 68–69, 190
Ôe, Kenji 145, 242
Ôedo shichininshû [*Seven from Edo*] (1958 film) *103*–105, 210

Index

Office of War Information [OWI] (U.S.) 19
Ogin-sama [*Love and Faith*] (1978 film) 157–158, 258
Oguni, Hideo 17–18, 21, 28, 55, 63, 72, 89, 91, 96, 103, 106–107, 115, 124, 131, 140, 169, 172, 176, 179, 186, 190, 192, 199, 203, 208, 212, 218, 226, 231, 238
O'Hara, Maureen 4
Oikawa, Kojirô (Japanese admiral) 129–130
Oka wa hanazakari (1952 film) 70, 190–191
Okada, Eiji 155, 157, 207, 226, 239, 246, 252, 254, 258
Okada, Mariko 71, 81, 88, 192, 195–196, 198–200, 203
Okami, Jôjirô 126, 207, 228
Okamoto, Kihachi 43, 139, 145, 179, 187, 237, 244
Okawa, Nobuaki 87, 194
Ôki, Minoru 151, 237, 241–242, 246, 251
Ôkôchi, Denjirô 19, 24, 28, 71, 143, 173, 175, 177–179, 192, 201
Ôkuma, Kuniya 156, 242
The Old Curiosity Shop (novel) 48
On the Beach (1959 film) 84
Onna no issho (1949 film) 38, 181
Onno tobakushi amadera kaichô [*The Woman Gambler and the Nun*] (1968 film) 150, 248
Onoe, Kurôemon 93, 201
Onoe, Matsonosuke 14
Ore wa jojinbo [*I'm the Bodyguard*] (1950 film) 44, 183
Osaka Castle 10, 87, 117–118, 124
Ôsaka-jô monogatari [*The Story of Osaka Castle*] (1961 film) 117–118, 220–221
Osaragi, Jirô 62, 189
Oshidori tagassen [*Singing Lovebirds*] (1939 film) 17–**18**, 170–171
Oshima, Nagisa 92
Osone, Tatsuo [Tatsuyasu] 59, 187
Otoko arite [*No Time for Tears*] (1955 film) 88, 197–198
Otoko tai otoko [*Man Against Man*] (1960 film) 114, 218
Otoko wa tsurai yo [*It's Tough Being a Man*] (1969 film) 151–**152**, 250–251
Otoko wa tsurai yo: Torajiro koiuta [*Tora-san's Love Call*] (1971 film) 154–**155**, 253
Otoko wa tsurai yo: Torajiro renka [*Tora San's Shattered Romance*] (1971 film) 154, 252
Otoko wa tsurai yo: Torajirô Wagamichi o Yuku [*Stage Struck Tora-san*] (1978 film) 160
Otoko wa tsurai yo: Uwasa no Torajirô [*Talk of the Town Tora-san*] (1978 film) **158**, 258
Ôtomo, Ryûtarô 105, 208, 210–211
Otomo, Shin 136, 192–193, 197, 204, 207, 212, 214–215, 217–218, 220–221, 223, 226, 230–231, 235, 240–241
Otori-jo hanayome [*Samurai Bride Hunter*] (1958 film) 103, 208
Ozaki, Hotsumi 27
Ozaki, Shiro 106, 211

Ozawa, Eitarô 40, 46, 173–174, 182, 184, 186, 206, 209, 224, 228, 248, 254
Ozawa, Shigehiro 134, 146, 150, 154, 233, 241, 246, 248, 253
Ozu, Yasujirô 3, 5, 15, 20, 27, 30, 35, 40, 48, 140

Parker, Tom 137
Pearl Harbor (1941 Japanese attack) 19–20, 71, 104, 113, 129
Pen itsuwarazu boryoku no machi [*Streets of Violence: The Pen Never Lies*] (1950 film) **43**–44, 183–184
Per un pugno di Dollari [*A Fistful of Dollars*] (1964 film) 119
Perry Mason (television series) 85
Philippine Sea (World War II battle) 129
Preminger, Otto 69
Presley, Elvis 137
Production Code Administration [PCA] (U.S.) 39

Rains, Claude 47
Ran (1985 film) 63
Ranru no hata [*The Tattered Banner*] (1974 film) 156, 254–255
Rashômon (1950 film) 50–55, **52**, **54**, 58–63, 79, 108, 118–119, 185
Rashômon, Namigoro [Tsunogorô] 120, 222
Ray, Satyajit 68
"Red River Valley" (song) 30
Reifenstahl, Leni 21
Ren'ai-gai itchôme [*Number One, Love Street*] (1934 film) 14–15, 165
Rikyû, Sen no 157–158
RKO Radio Pictures 103, 185
Robinson, Edward G. 39
Rozsa, Miklos 93
Ryû, Chishû 40, 48, 117, 140, 146, 152, 155, 162, 174, 182, 219, 235, 238, 241, 244, 250, 252–253, 258, 262
Ryû, Daisuke 161, 260
Ryûzaki, Ichirô 40, 174, 182, 184–185, 209

Sabarashiki nichiyôbi [*One Wonderful Sunday*] (1947 film) 29
Sada, Yutaka 131, 174, 200, 202, 204, 206–207, 212–215, 217–219, 223, 226–227, 231–232, 234, 238, 240–241, 245, 252
Saikaku ichidai onna [*The Life of Oharu*] (1952 film) 62, 189
Saitô, Buichi 154, 253
Saitô, Takao 119, 124, 131, 140, 190, 192, 199, 203, 212, 218, 222, 226–227, 231–233, 238, 259–260
Saitô, Torajirô 21, 176
Sakai, Furanki 122, 160, 162, 224, 230, 263
Sakai, Sachio 34, 181, 185–186, 190–193, 195, 200, 202, 204–206, 211, 213–214, 217–218, 221–222, 226, 228, 230–231, 240, 244, 249, 252
Samukawa, Kotaro 55, 186

Index

Samurai [Samurai Assassin] (1965 film) 139, 237
San Daikaijū: Chikyū Saidai no Kessen [Three Giant Monsters: The Greatest Battle on Earth, aka Ghidorah: The Three-Headed Monster] (1964 film) 136–137, 235–236
San-jaku sagohei (1944 film) 21, 94, 175–176
Sangyo sapai [Industrial Spy] (1968 film) 150, 248
Sanjô, Miki 39, 181, 184
Sanjûrokunin no jôkyaku (1957 film) 99, 205
Sanjusan go sha otonashi [No Response from Car 33] (1955 film) 89, 198
Sano, Shûji 148, 201
Sanshiro Sugata, Zoku Sugata Sanshirô [Sanshiro Sugata—Part Two] (1945 film) 23
Sanshô dayû [Sansho the Bailiff] (1954 film) 33, 53, 57
San'yûtei, Enchô 148, 247
Sararîman Chûshingura [Salary Man Chushingura] (1960 film) 118, 219–220
Sarutobe Sazuke [Ninja Spy] (1966 film) 145, 243
Sasaki, Takamaru 71, 96, 174, 192, 196, 200, 204–205, 228, 239, 248, 252, 254
Sasaki, Takemi 95, 203
Sasaki, Yasushi 20, 174
Satô, Jun'ya 152, 156, 251, 256
Satô, Kei 139, 155, 234, 237, 254, 258
Satô, Makoto 129, 135, 205, 212, 217, 227, 229, 231, 233–234, 240, 245
Satô, Masaru 91, 93, 98, 107, 113, 119, 122, 133, 143, 146, 150, 161, 193, 196, 198–199, 203, 212, 218, 222, 224, 226–227, 232–233, 237–239, 244, 247, 249, 254
Satogashi ga kowareru toki [When the Cookie Crumbles] (1967 film) 145, 243–244
Sawai, Shin'ichirô 154, 252, 258
Sawamura, Ikio 119, 200, 202–204, 206, 211–212, 215, 219–223, 226–228, 230, 232, 235, 237–238, 241
Sawashima, Tadashi 135, 142–143, 237, 239, 243
Sazanka, Kyû 109, 118, 214, 219–220, 222, 230, 232, 235
The Searchers (1956 film) 106
Segawa, Junichi 29, 179
Segawa, Masaharu 146, 205, 214, 241, 246
Seimaru, Hiroshi 17, 168
Seishun gonin otoko: Kôhen (1937 film) 15, 17, 168
Seishun gonin otoko: Zempen (1937 film) 15, 16, 17, 167–168
Sekigahara (battle) 93
Sekigawa, Hideo 26, 28, 30, 90, 109, 177, 179–180, 216
Sekiguchi, Hiroshi 151, 261
Sekizawa, Shin'íchi 121, 136, 214, 224, 227, 231, 233, 235
Sen-hime goten [Princess Sen in Edo] (1960 film) 117, 220

Sengoku, Noriko 38–39, 45–46, 181–184, 187, 189, 193, 200, 205–206, 236
Sengoku burai [Sword for Hire] (1952 film) 62, 189
Sengoku gunto-den [The Saga of the Vagabonds] (1959 film) 111, 214
Shakespeare, William 12, 24, 92, 96–97, 115, 203
Shamisen yakuza (1938 film) 17, 169
Shane (1953 film) 121
Shibaidô (1944 film) 21, 175
Shibuya, Minoru 44, 185
Shichigatsu-za ("July Theater") 12
Shiina, Ryuji 106, 211
Shima, Kôji 80, 87, 103, 111, 194, 196, 208, 216
Shimazaki, Masako (wife of Takashi Shimura) 12, 17–18, 43–44, 64, 66, 120, 161
Shimazaki, Takao (brother of Takashi Shimura) 11, 21
Shimazu, Masahiko 131, 232
Shimazu, Yasujirô 21, 176
Shimomura, Hiroshi 146
Shimozawa, Kan 148, 247, 253
Shimura, Takashi (Shoji Shimazaki): on Akira Kurosawa 53–54, 66; acting awards and nominations 43, 69; ancestry 9–11; athletic activities 11, 155–156; birth 9; childhood 10, 11, 12; death 161; early employment 12; early film roles 14–15, 16–18; education 11–12; on Ikiru 65–66; illnesses 11, 64–65, 156–157, 160–161; kaijû film roles 2, 82–88, 95, 101–103, 121–123, 126–128, 127, 136–137, 144–145; Kurosawa film roles 1–4, 19–21, 24–43, 39, 44–48, 45, 47, 50–59, 52, 54, 57, 62–70, 72–80, 89–92, 95–99, 106–108, 114–120, 124–126, 131–134, 139–142, 160–162, 164; legal problems 18, 28; leisure activities 155–156; marriage 12, 17–18, 43–44, 64, 66, 120, 161; political associations 18, 28; relationship with Akira Kurosawa 115, 160; relationship with Toshirô Mifune 29, 43–44, 53, 74; theatrical experience 12, 37; vocal abilities 18
"Shin Abishiri Bangaichi" (film series) 150–152
Shin Abashiri Bangaichi: Runin-masaki no ketto [New Abashiri Prison Story—Harbor Duel] (1969 film) 151, 250
Shin Abashiri Bangaichi: Saihate no Nagaremono [The Vagrant Comes to a Port Town] (1969 film) 152, 251
Shin Abashiri Bangaichi [The Man from Abashiri Jail Strikes Again] (1968) 150, 249
Shin baka jidai [These Foolish Times] (1947 film) 31
Shin, Heike monogatari: Yoshinaka o meguru sannin no onna [Three Women Around Yoshinaka] (1956 film) 95, 201
Shin kurama tengu daisanbu (1955 film) 89, 198
Shin kurama tengu daiichi wa: Tengu shutsugen (1954 film) 81, 195

Shin kurama yengu daini wa: Azuma-dera no ketto (1954 film) 87, 196
Shin Zatôichi monogatari: Kasama no chimatsuri [*Zatoichi's Conspiracy*] (1973 film) 155, 253–254
Shindô, Kaneto 90, 117, 121, 182, 219, 224, 229
Shinichin no Samurai [*Seven Samurai*] (1954 film) 1, 4, 59, 72–81, 84, 90, 95, 97, 100, 108, 111, 118, 140, 147, 164, 192–194
Shinin no sosei [*Resurrection of a Corpse*] (1898 short film) 13
Shinkansen daibakuha [*Bullet Train*] (1975 film) 156, 156–157
Shinko Kinema 14, 165–166
Shintoho Studios 27, 41, 59, 182, 186, 188
Shiragiku monogatari [*The Tale of the White Chrysanthemum*] (1920 film) 14
Shirikawa, Yumi 101
Shizukanaru kettô [*The Quiet Duel*] (1949 film) 37–40, **39**, 181–182
Shobushi to sono musume (1959 film) 111, 216
Shôchiku Company and Studios 15, 45–46, 55–57, 110–111, 135, 137, 145–146, 149, 151–152, 155, 158, 173–174, 182, 184, 187, 214, 216, 234, 243, 247–248, 250, 252–253, 258, 261–262
Showa saidai no kaoyaku [*Greatest Boss of the Showa Era*] (1966 film) 145, 243
Shôwa zankyô-den: Karajishi jingi [*Brutal Tales of Chivalry 5*] (1969 film) 151, 249–250
Shûbun, aka *Skandaru* [*Scandal*] (1950 film) 44–48, **45, 47**, 184
Shunjû ittôryû (1939 film) 18, 171
Shura hakkô: Dai-san-pen (1936 film) 15, 166–167
Shurushuru (1966 television film) 145, 261
Shusse taikoki, Mazô, Jigoku no mushi (1938 film) 17, 170
"Silent Night" (song) 47
Simenon, Georges 41
Some Like It Hot (1959 film) 69
Sora kakeru hanayome [*The High-Flying Bride*] (1959 film) 111, 216
Sora no daijkaijû Radon [*Radon, Giant Monster in the Sky*, aka *Rodan*] (1956 film) 103, 121
Stagecoach (1939 film) 33
Star Trek (television series) 127
Star Wars (1977 film) 108, 160
Steiner, Max 93
Stevens, George 121
Stewart, James 69
Sturges, John 78
Sugai, Ichirô 21, 48, 71, 173–179, 183, 185, 188, 190, 192, 251
Sugata naki fukushû (1941 film) 18, 172
Sugata naki mokugekisha (1955 film) 89, 199
Sugata Sanshirô [*Sanshiro Sugata*] (1943 film) 19–20, 23, 173
Sugata Sanshiro [*Sanshiro Sugata*] (1965 film) 143, 239

Sugawa, Eizô 121, 134, 205, 224, 233
Sugi, Yôko 70, 81, 181, 191, 194
Sugie, Toshio 89, 95, 99, 101, 106, 110, 117–118, 162, 173–174, 198, 203, 205, 211, 214, 219, 221
Sugimura, Haruko 28, 179–180, 199, 215, 223, 237–238
Susaki, Katsuya 143, 239
Suzuki, Akira 110, 214, 236, 242
Suzuki, Hideo 95, 100, 123, 126, 201, 205, 225, 227
"Swanee River" (song) 110

T-Men (1947 film) 131
Taiheiyo kaisen saidai no Kiseki (story) 240
Taiheiyô kiseki no sakusen: Kisuka [*Kiska*] (1965 film) 143, 239–240
Taiheiyo no tsubasa [*Wing of the Pacific*, aka *Attack Squadron!*] (1963 film) 129, 231
Taiheiyo no washi [*Eagle of the Pacific*] (1953 film) 71, 192
Taii no musume [*The Captain's Daughter*] (1917 film) 14
Taira, Kazuji 87, 123, 196–197, 224
Taiyô ni somuku mono (1959 film) 110, 214
Taiyô wa yondeiru (1963 film) 134, 233
Takada, Kôji 151, 154, 250, 253
Takagi, Tokuko 14
Takakura, Ken 109, 146, 150–152, 154, 156, 160, 162, 216, 246, 248–251, 253, 256, 258
Takamine, Hideko 21, 28, **94**–95, 99, 162, 176, 178–179, 201, 205
Takamine, Mieko 55, 105, 135, 148, 160, 162, 186, 211, 234, 246, 259
Takamori, Saigô 11
Takarada, Akira 85, 126, 128, 135, 162, 195, 198, 202, 204, 206, 215, 217–218, 220, 222, 225, 227, 229, 234, 257
Takarazuka Motion Picture Company 117, 136, 157, 206, 219, 234, 239, 258
Takashi Shimura Memorial Hall 162, **164**
Takashi Shimura Museum **163**
Takigawa, Yukitoki 27
Takimura, Kazuo 87, 194, 196
Takizawa, Eisuke 20, 173
Takizawa, Osamu 139, 184, 194, 209, 215, 220, 237, 246, 248, 252, 255
Tamai, Masao 49, 85, 110, 184, 186, 189, 194–195, 197, 199, 202, 205, 213, 225, 257
Tamura, Takahiro 155, 160, 241, 244, 248, 258–259, 262
Tanaka, Eizo 14, 181, 183–184
Tanaka, Kunie 160, 219, 226–227, 237, 248, 257–258
Tanaka, Shigeo 105, 150, 210, 248
Tanaka, Tinoyu 62
Tanaka, Tokuzô 127, 185, 229
Tanaka, Tomoyuki 72, 82, 103, 121, 126, 128, 135, 143, 145, 177–179, 182–184, 189, 191, 194–199, 202–203, 205, 207, 213, 215, 217–218, 220, 222–224, 226–227, 229, 231, 233–235, 237–240, 244, 249, 255, 257, 259

Index

Tanba, Tetsurô 138, 221, 225, 237, 243, 245, 251, 255, 257
Taniguchi, Senkichi 29, 37, 43–44, 55, 62, 71, 89, 114, 126, 134–135, 162, 179, 181–183, 186, 189, 192, 198, 218, 227, 233
Tanji, Mutsuo 147, 246
Tasaka, Tomotaka 20, 173–174
Tasukenin hashiru (1973 television series) 155, 262
Tatara, Jun 151, 184, 193, 205–206, 233, 261
Taxi! (1932 film) 148–149
Tazaki, Jun 87, 185, 194, 209, 215, 217–218, 221, 228, 230–234, 237, 240, 242, 244
Teenagers from Outer Space (1959 film) 88
Tempura, Vince 157, 258
Tempyo no iraka [*Ocean to Cross*] (1980 film) 160, 259
Ten to sen [*Point and Line*] (1958 film) **105**–106, 211
Tengoku to jigoku [*High and Low*] (1963 film) 131–134, 141, 231–232
Tensai sagishi monogatari: Tanuki no hanamachi (1964 film) 136, 235
Tenya Wanya [*Crazy Uproar*] (1950 film) 44, 185–186
Tetsuwan tôshu Inao monogatari [*Inao: Story of an Iron Arm*] (1959 film) 109, 213
Tezuka, Katsumi 84, 192, 196–197, 201–203, 207, 213, 215, 221, 225, 228, 230–231, 236, 240
Thanhouser Company 14
Three Bad Men (1926 film) 106
Toba-Fushimi (1868 battle) 10, 124
Todoroki, Yukiko 19, 169
Toei Company 100, 103–105, 109, 111, 118, 123, 134, 142, 145–147, 150, 152, 154, 182, 207–208, 210–211, 213, 216, 226, 232–233, 237, 239, 241–243, 245–246, 248–253, 256, 258, 261
Toho Company and Studios 15, 19–31, 37–38, 41, 43–44, 50, 55, 58–59, 62, 71, 74, 80–88, 90, 93, 95, 98, 100, 103, 106, 109–111, 113–115, 117–118, 121, 123–129, 132, 134–137, 139–140, 143–147, 150–152, 155–157, 160–161, 173–182, 184–207, 211–215, 217–229, 231–240, 242, 244, 246, 249, 251, 254–255, 257–259
Tokkan ekichô [*The Brash Stationmaster*] (1945 film) 21, 176
Tokyo Broadcasting System (TBS) 146, 160, 259, 261–262
Tokyo monogatari [*Tokyo Story*] (1953 film) 27
Toland, Gregg 19
Tolstoy, Leo 63
Tomita, Tsuneo 19, 173, 186, 239
Tôno, Eijirô 5, 58, 119, 131, 139, 174, 183, 188, 190, 191, 193, 200, 205, 207, 211, 215, 220, 222, 224, 227, 232, 237–239
"Tora-san" (film series) 151–152, 154–155, 158, 160
Toro no o fumu otoko-tachi [*The Men Who Tread on the Tiger's Tail*] (1945 film) 23–26, 98–99, 177
Toura, Rokkô 146, 234, 244, 259
Toyoda, Shirô 88, 100, 179, 197, 206
Tsubaki Sanjûrô [*Sanjuro*] (1962 film) 124–126, 134, 141, 226
Tsubanari ronin (1939 film) 18, 171
Tsuburaya, Eiji 19–20, 70–71, 83–85, 103, 113, 123, 126, 129, 136–137, 143–144, 174, 189, 191–192, 195, 197, 202–203, 207, 215, 217, 221, 224, 227–229, 231, 233, 235, 239–240, 251
Tsuchiya, Yoshio 59, 119, 131, 143, 146, 193–194, 197–198, 200, 202, 204, 207, 212, 214, 217–219, 222, 226–227, 230–232, 238, 240, 244, 249, 252, 254
Tsudoi, Makoto 150–151, 211, 249–250
Tsukigata, Ryûnosuke 18, 166, 170, 172–173, 183, 213, 249
Tsukiyo no wataridori (1963 film) 135, 234
Tsunoda, Kenichirô 135, 204, 233
Tsuruta, Kôji 93, 95, 110, 145, 162, 185, 187, 194, 200, 202, 209, 210, 214–215, 233, 237, 241, 243, 246, 249, 251
Tsushima, Keiko 78, 193, 202, 204
20th Century-Fox Studios 160, 259

Uchida, Tomu 100, 206
Uchide, Kokichi 109, 213
Uchikawa, Seiichirô 143, 239
Ueda, Hiroshi 128, 200, 208, 215, 221, 229, 249
Ueda, Kichijiro **52**, **54**, 171–172, 183–186, 189, 193–194, 198, 200, 204, 212, 215, 221, 229
Uehara, Ken 55, 70, 81, 99, 122, 162, 186, 191, 195, 205, 217, 224, 228, 230–231, 242
Uehara, Misa 107, 110, 113, 212, 214–215, 217
Uekusa, Keinosuke 31–33, 181
Uemura, Kenjurô **39**, 181, 184
Ugetsu monogatari [*Ugetsu*] (1953 film) 33, 53
Uguisu-jô no hanayome [*The Bride in Uguisu Castle*] (1958 film) **104**–105, 211
Umeda, Haruo 71, 191, 198
Umi wo wataru sairei (1941 film) 18, 172
Umon torimonochô: Harebare gojûsantsugi—Ranma hen (1935 film) 15, 165–166
Umon torimonochô: Harebare gojûsantsugi—Saiketsu hen (1936 film) 166
Uno, Masao 121, 223

Valcauda, Armando 157, 257
Venice Film Festival 51, 62–63, 98
Von Sternberg, Joseph 58

Wadja, Andrzej 69
Waga seishun ni kuinashi [*No Regrets for Our Youth*] (1946 film) 27–28, 55, 178
Wakabayashi, Akiko 136, 227–228, 233, 235
Wakai ki [*Young Tree*] (1956 film) 95, 201
Wakao, Ayako 112, 145, 194, 206, 209–210, 216, 244, 252

Wakayama, Setsuko 29, 162, 179–180, 184, 194, 197, 205
Walsh, Raoul 149
Warner Bros. Studios 85, 148
Warui yatsu hodo yoku nemuru [*The Bad Sleep Well*] (1960 film) 115–117, 218–219
Watanabe, Atsushi 119, 175–176, 190, 193, 200, 222, 238, 262
Watanabe, Kunio 74, 102–103, 108–109, 208, 212
Watanabe, Misako 138, 236
Watanabe, Takashi 104, 208, 212
Watanabe, Yûsuke 145, 241
Wayne, John 4, 98
Welles, Orson 96
Whale, James 58, 112, 141
White Heat (1949 film) 149
Wilder, Billy 69
William, Warren 85
World War II 3, 19–20, 23, 38, 47, 57, 89, 102, 113–114, 116, 129–130, 143, 150, 154, 160

Yabu no naka ["In a Grove"] (story) 50
Yachigusa, Kaoru 93, 200, 237
Yaguchi, Yôko 21, 175
Yahiro, Fuji 117, 208, 220
Yama no oto [*Sound of the Mountain*] (1954 film) 27
Yama to kawa no aru machi [*A Path Through Mountains and Rivers*] (1957 film) 98, 204
Yamada, Isuzu 5, 15–**16**, 21, 28, 96, 113, 117, 119, 166, 174–175, 179, 204, 218, 220–222
Yamada, Kazuo 71, 93, 118, 128, 150, 152, 182, 192, 198, 200, 215, 217, 221, 223, 229, 231, 249, 251
Yamagata, Isao 104–105, 162, 193, 210–211, 241
Yamagata, Yûsaku 22, 173, 176–177, 179, 183
Yamaguchi, Isamu 39, 182, 184
Yamaguchi, Tamon (Japanese Admiral) 113
Yamaguchi, Yoshiko [Shirley] **45**–46, 62–63, 70–71, 184, 189, 191
Yamamato, Fujiko 103, 201, 209–210, 215, 220
Yamamoto, Hideaki 146, 151, 245, 249
Yamamoto, Isoroku (Japanese Admiral) 71, 113, 153–154
Yamamoto, Kajirô 19–20, 22, 26, 31, 37, 44, 55, 58, 89, 95, 136, 140, 174, 177, 179, 182, 186, 188, 198, 202, 235
Yamamoto, Reizaburô 34, 43, 169, 181, 183–185, 187, 217
Yamamoto, Ren 143, 146, 162, 191–193, 195, 197, 201–202, 206, 214, 217–218, 221, 224, 230–231, 238, 240–241, 245
Yamamoto, Rin'ichi 154, 216, 237, 241, 246, 249–251, 253
Yamamoto, Satsuo 43–44, 148, 155, 183, 247, 254
Yamamoto, Shugôrô 124, 140, 226, 261
Yamamura, Sô 30, 70, 121, 143, 146, 179–180, 191, 223, 240, 244, 251, 255, 262

Yamanaka, Sadao 73, 110, 117, 214, 219
Yamanouchi, Tetsuya 149, 247
Yamashita, Hiroshi 147, 246
Yamato (ship) 129
Yamazaki, Masao 148, 246
Yamazaki, Tsutomu 131, 136, 141, 232–234, 238–239, 259, 262
Yami no kageboshi [*Shadows of Darkness*] (1938 film) 17, 169
Yasuda, Kimiyoshi 118, 148–149, 155, 221, 247, 253
Yasuda, Michiyo 151, 250
Yasumi, Toshio 62, 71, 95, 106, 111, 128, 175, 177–181, 189, 191, 203, 206, 211, 215, 229, 233, 241, 255
Yasumoto, Jun 93, 186, 191, 206, 217
Yata, Noriyuki 81, 186, 194
Yoda, Yoshikata 104, 108, 118, 148, 157, 166, 221, 259
Yoidore tenshi [*Drunken Angel*] (1948 film) 26, 30–37, 57, 63, 131, 181
Yoidore tenshi [*Drunken Angel*] (play) 37
Yôjinbô [*Yojimbo*] (1961 film) 111, 118–120, 124–126, 134, 141, 222–223
Yokoyama, Minoru 145, 188, 242
Yokumo, Koizumi *see* Hearn, Lafcadio
Yomigaeru daichi (1971 film) 154, 252
Yoru no awari (1953 film) 71, 192
Yoru no hibotan (1950 film) 55, 185
Yoru no nagara [*Evening Stream*] (1960 film) 113–114, 217–218
Yôsei Gorasu [*Gorath, the Monstrous Star*] (1962 film) 126–127, 227–229
Yoshikawa, Eiji 93, 95, 171, 173, 200–201
Yoshimura, Kôzaburô 40, 156, 182, 254
Yoshinaka, Kira Kôzuke-no-suke 103
Yoshio, Ôishi Kuranosuke 104
Yuunagi (1957 film) 100

Za Pinattsu [*The Peanuts*] (vocal duo) 122
Zatiôchi hatashi-jô [*Zatoichi and the Fugitives*] (1968 film) 148–**149**, 247
Zesshô (1966 film) 145, 242–243
Zoku aoi sanmyaku Yukiko no maki (1957 film) 100, 206
Zoku mazô—Ibara Ukon (1939 film) 17, 170
Zoku Miyamoto Musashi: Ichijôji no kettô [*Samurai II: Duel at Ichijoji Temple*] (1955 film) 93, 200
Zoku ningen kakumei [*Human Revolution II*] (1976 film) 156, 257
Zoku sarariman Chûshingura [*Salary Man Chushingura Sequel*] (1961 film) 118, 221–222
Zoku sarariman shimizu minato (1962 film) 126, 227
Zoku Shimizu minato (1940 film) 18, 172
Zoku Sugata Sanshirô [*Sanshiro Sugata—Part Two*] (1945 film) 23, 239

www.ingramcontent.com/pod-product-compliance
Ingram Content Group UK Ltd.
Pitfield, Milton Keynes, MK11 3LW, UK
UKHW041928140426
5217IPUK00014B/369